HARDPRESS.NET
HOME OF HARD-TO-FIND BOOKS

The Teachings of the Ages ...
by H. K. W. Clark

Address:
HardPress
8345 NW 66TH ST #2561
MIAMI FL 33166-2626
USA
Email: info@hardpress.net

TEACHINGS OF THE AGES.

SNOW

Zion
Traveler

16773

200

THE

Teachings of the Ages:

IN TWO PARTS.

BY A. C. TRAVELER. *pseudonym*
for Mrs. "C. K. W. Clarke
" H. R.

"Thou, O Spirit, that dost prefer
Before all temples, the upright heart and pure,
Instruct me, for Thou knowest, Thou from the first
Wast present, and with mighty wings outspread,
Dovelike sat'st brooding on the vast abyss,
And madest it pregnant:—What in me is dark
Illumine; what is low raise and support:
That to the height of this great argument
I may assert Eternal Providence,
And justify the ways of God to Man."

SAN FRANCISCO:

A. L. BANCROFT & CO., PUBLISHERS.

1874.

SAN FRANCISCO:
PRINTED AT THE WOMEN'S CO-OPERATIVE PRINTING UNION
424 MONTGOMERY STREET.

DEDICATION.

———

With reverent love I dedicate "THE TEACHINGS OF THE AGES" to Humanity, whose great, suffering heart and ever questioning mind challenged me to write its pages.

A. C. TRAVELER.

CONTENTS.

PREFACE.

It has been the object of the Author to render the present work suggestive, rather than argumentative; and to trace, in " The Teachings of the Ages," the Logic of Events, in their sequential order of unfolding, and to show from them the universal principles of God's government, and the ever-present and protecting care of Heaven. When Moses desired to look upon the Almighty One that inhabiteth Eternity, he was called to the mountain heights of Sinai and concealed in the cleft of a rock, and was permitted to look only upon the back part of the glorious form tha trepresented the omnipotent Jehovah;—even so we of to-day are also permitted, like the ancient Prophet of Israel, to look upon the Divine Ruler of the Universe after He has passed by in his marvellous providences, and they can be recognized as parts of a grand, harmonious system of Moral Government, adapted to the whole nature of Man.

CHAPTER I.

INTRODUCTORY.

Who hath believed our report ?   And to whom is the arm of the Lord revealed ?

The mind of the day is active and expectant.   It is highly charged and electrical.   Sparks flash from the point of every thought-conductor.   The brain of the century is stimulated in one direction, and books on kindred subjects are multiplied. Fellow traveler of earth, the crisis of ages is approaching.

Note the peculiar direction of thought, and mark the signs of the times.   Observe the shadows of coming events that loom above the moral horizon of the age, projected from the world of cause upon the world of effects.   They are the heralds that are sent before, to announce *His* coming to the nations.

Whichsoever way we turn our mental eye, we recognize the index-hand of the Divine Ruler of the Universe, pointing toward the second advent of the Messiah.   And the most enlightened minds of the day are occupied with the subject, and attracting to the important event the attention of the Christian world. Glance at the religious record of the day—it demonstrates the proposition.   Books on the Second Advent, and on the character of Christ and his teaching, have been and are being multiplied to that extent that it would appear, at a partial view, that these subjects could present no new aspects of importance to the human mind.   But as principles involving infinite truths and relations are inexhaustible, they must continue to exhibit new points of interest to the earnest inquirer, from which may be drawn fuller and clearer deductions.

Ideas are the slow products of centuries, although they often culminate in some grand result during the short period of one generation. And like unto the fruits and flowers of earth they exhale their own peculiar aroma in unfolding, which forms an intellectual and moral atmosphere by continual accretion. The atmosphere of mind thus formed lies in stratifications, if you please, like the soil of the natural world, and possesses, like the latter, a richer fructifying power as it rises to higher levels, and receives the rays of light emanating from Divine Intelligence, or the Moral Sun of the universe. Hence persons occupied in searching for truth in the same intellectual stratifications, observe and grasp the same principles ; and thus simultaneous discoveries in science are often made in remote parts of the earth. In like manner, also, those who are engaged in seeking for moral and spiritual truths will arrive at kindred results. The unusual excitement at the present period of time in regard to the Second Advent of the Master, in accordance with Biblical prophecy, is because the hour of fulfillment is drawing nigh, and many minds have ascended to higher spiritual eminences than ever before, and received a fuller influx of light in reference to this important event. And every mind strongly acted upon by the permeating atmosphere of intelligence, conceives new ideas, and seeks to clothe them in language, or form, each one in accordance with his highest conceptions. And in this manner, widely different phases of the same truth have been, and will continue to be, presented to the expectant age. For even the world itself could not contain the books that might be written.

And Art, baptized in the quickening spirit of the century, joins the great cloud of witnesses, and contributes her testimony to the weight of evidence in an immortal creation. The Man of Nazareth has recently received from her plastic hand a new and higher interpretation. An American artist has sculptured a head of Christ in marble, in which he has succeeded in blending with the look of tender, pitying love, attributed to him by the Old Masters, the expression of a commanding intellect, and the glorious majesty of a God. And when we remember that, in him dwelt *all the fullness of the Godhead,* we naturally expect, in a representation of the Messiah, a subtle union of divine tenderness and strength, of all-directing power and all-regardful love; in verity, a representation of both the Divine Father and Mother God.

No intelligent Christian of the present day can be fully satisfied with the paintings of Christ by the old masters that are extant, for they do not approach the higher ideal creation of each individual mind. And yet those portraitures were miracles of art and beauty to his admiring worshippers of past centuries. The reason of the change we note is obvious. As the Christian world becomes more enlightened, and grows more and more into the likeness of Christ, the people gain a clearer understanding of his profound intellect and wonderful teachings, and form a juster and fuller estimate of his nature, and, consequently, demand of Art a higher interpretation of his character.

The early artists were intuitional men, and they caught the spirit of the Christian Dispensation of Love and Free-will, addressed more particularly to the *affections, or heart* of the youthful age of the world, in Christ's first mission to earth; and, imbued with its spirit and power, they sought to represent in Christ the tender pitying love, such as the Divine Mother of Humanity might be supposed to feel for her erring and sorrowing children of time. The one idea filled their hearts and minds, and they could present but the one phase of the Redeemer's character to the world.

And the true artists of the present are likewise intuitional; and they, too, catch the spirit of Christ's second mission to earth, addressed more particularly to the *understanding or mind* of the reasoning age, and new Christian era; and their representations of him must also conform to their fuller and grander conceptions of his nature. And we may look confidently forward for yet truer and higher delineations of the Messiah's form and character, as the world advances in wisdom and in the knowledge of God.

The work of Art to which we allude is only the begininng of a new series of productions which will more perfectly represent the Master. It is a prophecy of the higher appreciation that he will yet receive from a still more enlightened age. We recognize, in this new and higher interpretation of the man of Nazareth, one of the remarkable signs of the times.

A journal of the day, that publishes a notice of this marvelous work of Art, inquires : "Is this Western world to have the honor of conveying to the eye a more truthful conception of the person of Christ than the highest genius has succeeded in representing ?" We respond, ay, certes ; because the government of our country is founded in the principles of the Christian religion, and is a Christian Democracy ; and, consequently, American artists, nurtured under such humanitary influences, are highly imbued with the spirit of Christian Democracy ; and, hence, are more capable than artists educated under any form of monarchy of understanding, and portraying Christ Jesus the great Democratic Philosopher of the world.

It is a remarkable fact in the history of our time, that Biblical scholars, leading minds among the various denominations of the Christian church, have announced the belief, drawn from sacred prophecy, that the Second Advent of our Savior may be looked for during the latter part of the nineteenth century.

Observe the Israelites of to-day, in connection with this subject. Large numbers of that branch of the Church of God, influenced by the spirit of the hour, have recently acknowledged Christ as the true Messiah, the Holy One of Israel. The prophecies connected with the Second Advent are thus being accomplished, and the Jews are now coming in to the fullness of the Gentiles, at the appointed time and in the prescribed order of Heaven.

During the movements that have been already recorded, parties have been sent abroad to visit Palestine, for the purpose of searching for *sacred relics* in localities recorded in the New Testament connected particularly with the history of Christ and His disciples, and none the less dear and holy to the hearts of believers, although buried beneath the dust of eighteen centuries. Many valuable discoveries have already been made ; and new companies, at each return of Spring, gravitate eastward, for the purpose of more thorough and accurate examinations. Are they not, in verity, rolling back the stone from the door of His sepulchre, and preparing the way for a risen Savior ?

In the renewing and growth of physical nature, there is everywhere a periodical return of past influences, to stimulate the forces of the earth ; and, in addition to such influences, there is an aggregated sum of power, gained through successive advancing seasons of spring-time and harvest, which ever tends, in an increased ratio, (commensurate with the accumulated and accumulating force) toward still higher and more perfect reproductions ; and the same proposition is analagously true in the moral world.   Every new cycle of human progress has been rebaptised with the early quickening spirit of the old, which has returned with the accumulated strength and power of the intervening ages, and swept over the earth, like a great tidal wave, from the agitated ocean of truth.

Thus the moral world, like the material, moves ever on, completing its eternal circles, while regenerating itself with old truths which receive new and higher interpretations at each successive revolution.   Ay, truly, the hour is at hand when the Son of Man shall be revealed.   A returning wave of the past is even now breaking upon the shores of the present, and we feel in our souls its baptismal benediction.   The waters of Jordan, that lose themselves in the sands of the Orient, rise again in the fonts of the Occident, to rebaptise the Church of the new Christian Era. And, lo ! the cedars of Lebanon wait at our altars.   Are not these events gentle and touching reminders of His presence ? Do they not say to the heart and mind of the Christian, in a language more thrilling than words, the Master is near, even at the door ?

Turn your attention also to the controversies, bearing upon this event, that are now agitating the Christian Church, both at home and abroad.   The prelates of the old world and the dignitaries of the new are discussing, with profoundest interest, a broader Christian faith and practice.   Extremes have met. The early idea of the conservative Roman Catholic body of a *Universal Christian Church* on earth, has been taken up and advocated by the Unitarian denomination, the most liberal sect

of all called by the Christian name.   The Rev. Dr. Bellows, of
New York, made an attempt to inaugurate the idea in the broad
church movement which attracted much attention a few years
ago.   And about the same period of time, Rev. Thomas Starr
King, of San Francisco, one of the brightest lights of the age,
attached the symbol of the Cross to the noble edifice that he
reared on the shores of the Pacific, and dedicated it to God and
Humanity.   He desired thereby to weaken sectarian prejudices,
and show forth the *oneness* of the Church of God of every name.
Again, we repeat, extremes have met, and the circle of the first
Christian Era has been completed. .

Fellow traveler of earth, do you reply that yon see no promise in all these signs of the times of the Second Advent of the
Messiah ?

Let us pursue the subject farther, and view it in the light of
philosophy, remembering that the laws of the moral world are
as uniform and certain in their operations as the laws of the
material universe.   It is an accredited truth, that like causes
conditions being equal, produce like effects throughout the wide
range of animate and inanimate nature.   Occult principles and
imponderable forces are everywhere influenced by fixed laws,
analagous to those that govern the demonstrable and the pon-
derable.   In the physical world, rising clouds are a prophecy of
descending rain ; and in the world of intelligence, an unusual
disturbance of the moral elements tends to attract together multitudes of men from divers points, and in the meeting of conflicting passions, human blood is poured out like water upon
the earth.   And all physical and moral restraints, not in harmony with the laws of matter and of mind, presuppose a reaction proportionate with the restraining forces.   If the source be
high, the fountain will well strongly upward; and, if the popular
mind be excited from any operating cause, it will seek the level
of the truth that moves it to action.   Men do not expect to
gather grapes of thorns or figs of thistles in the material world;
they look everywhere for the natural products of plants of each
class and variety, and are never disappointed.   And in the moral
as in the physical world, any tree, of either good or evil, must

bear its own peculiar fruit; for mind, like matter, must every-where manifest itself in accordance with uniform and immutable laws; similar qualities of mind, under similar circumstances, will be moved to like action and produce like results. And if cultivated men and women are able to divest themselves of the prejudices of education, and to look calmly and philosophically at operating principles in the moral world, they will comprehend the laws of intelligent as well as of material nature, and will be equally rewarded in the result of their labors.

If any important event in the moral world has been preceded by, and attended with, any peculiar and striking phenomena, it is logical to conclude that, if like phenomena again appear, after an interval of time, we may look confidently for the recurrence of an event similar to that which they preceded and attended in the past. And now, we are prepared to state, that there are, at present, wide-spread spiritual phenomena on our earth, the peculiar phases of which are the same as those that attended the First Advent of our Savior. The phenomena appear in modern times, as one would rationally expect, with an accession of power and influence, gained by the increased spiritual growth and preparation of eighteen centuries of the Christian religion, which has mightily prevailed over the earth. And they are among the most remarkable signs of the times, and point unmistakably to the Second and more spiritual Advent of the Master.

We are not prepared to state, in this connection, in what manner the Master will again appear on earth; whether incarnate, as in the first Era, and crowned by Heaven with the insignia of power and authority to rule the Nations as the King of kings— as many Christian denominations believe and teach—or whether he will come in invisible glory to the hearts and minds of the faithful, and in newness of spirit, instead of the oldness of the letter, to rule with a subtle and higher power the empire of mind, forming a more perfect alliance of the Church militant and the Church triumphant. Yet we are assured, from the advanced condition of intelligence in the world, that in the Second Advent, He will gain the ascent of *Reason* to the truth of Revelation, as well as the deeper devotion of the heart to His Gospel of Love; and that the Church will become more consistently Christian.   For, in addition to her enlarged religious experiences and renewed aspirations, she will be blessed with the accumulated knowledge of the ages to broaden her vista of truth, and the light of a quickened reason to lead her along the true path of progress.

> RELIGION to one point attracts the sight,
> The source divine of Uncreated Light;
> KNOWLEDGE to many, e'er divergent draws,
> Thro' all His works to learn of the First Cause.
> Religion ever toward the *inner* turns,
> Where the concentred fire of being burns,
> And worships blindly what it may not know,
> Warmed by the heat and dazzled by the glow :
> KNOWLEDGE outreaches through the vast of space
> The infinite of truth to seek, embrace ;
> Then to the altar of the heart it brings
> The treasured lore of all material things,
> And, in RELIGION'S warmth and kindling glow,
> *Knows* how divine a good it is to KNOW !
> Becomes productive, consecrated, too,
> While ever broad'ning pure Religion's view,
> Showing through matter all and teeming sod
> The ever-present care and thought of God.
> And Reason, quicken'd, sees the Heavenly plan,
> Nor Knowledge, nor Religion makes the man,
> But both in action, in the human kind,
> Perfect the nature, form the God-like mind.

But, although we are unprepared to state, in this connection, in what way the Son of Man shall be revealed again to the world; yet it is rational to infer, from the history of the First Advent, that there will be grand preparations in heaven and on earth for his coming; and that a new Christian Era will be inaugurated to receive the Master by some exalted and inspired Teacher and Seer of Christendom.   How beautiful upon the mountain of Zion appears the Prophet of the Lord, sent before to prepare the way for his coming, to inaugurate the promised Era of Humanity in the maturity of the Church and World, to establish the truth of Revelation in the light of reason and philosophy, and to point out to the expectant Nations the glorious *renewed Church* of the World's Reasoning Age, which is the New Jerusalem of prophecy, that was seen, in extatic vision, descending from God out of heaven, adorned as a bride for her husband.

And now, fellow traveller, having stated the proposition that the Second Advent of the Messiah is at hand, and having shown that the signs of the time are indices of this event, which event includes a new Christian Era and a Prophet to inaugurate the New Era ; we are prepared to enter more fully into our labor, and render cogent reasons for the faith that is in us. Let us then turn to the Law and the Testimony, to both Revelation and Philosophy, and learn in what manner the Master will again appear on earth, and what will be the character of the New Era, that is being prepared to receive Him when it shall culminate in meridian glory. And let us open our minds and hearts to the Teachings of the Ages.

We will first turn over the leaves of Sacred History, and mark the peculiar unfolding of the character of the Church of God on earth from its earliest age ; for the reason that each religious -Age, or Era, is but the natural outgrowth, or logical sequence, of its predecessor. And we must observe, farther, in connection with the Church, the general development of Society and its requirements. For He who wisely governs the Universe of matter and of mind, adapts means to ends, through the wide range of Intelligent as well as of Material Nature and conditions, everywhere, to the needs of Humanity.

2

CHAPTER II.

The morning stars sang together, and all the sons of God shouted for joy.

In the beginning God created the heaven and the earth. And the earth was without form, and void ; and darkness was upon the deep, and the Spirit of God moved upon the face of the waters. And God said, Let there be Light.

Nature heard and obeyed the mandate. Morning dawned upon a new creation. The exulting earth made haste to cover herself with verdure. She arrayed her valleys and plains in living green, gemmed with many-colored flowers of perfumed breath, and dotted with fruit-bearing shrubs and trees, in munificent adornment. And she spread her primal forests far and wide, crowning her hills and mountain heights with evergreens, whose lofty spires uplifted themselves into the blue of heaven. And her rejoicing waters flashed back the brightness of the glorious sun, while their grand organ tones mingled with the wind-harps of the groves, the song of birds, and the hum of insects, until the vibrant air itself seemed music. Manifold orders of animal life walked forth in beauty and freedom from her forest aisles, discoursing eloquently, in the expressive language of form and motion, of the divine Gospel of Liberty and Love, written all over the wide universe of God.

But there was no joyous response from human intelligences, kindred with the Divine, and the heart of Deity yearned for appreciative sons and daughters. And God said to his coequal and beloved companion of eternity, Let us make man in *our* image, after *our* likeness. So God created man in his own image, in the image of God created he him ; *male and female* created he them. And God blessed them, and said unto them, Be fruitful, and multiply, and replenish the earth, and subdue it : and have dominion over the fish of the sea, and over the fowl of the air, and over every living thing that moveth upon the earth. And God formed man of the dust of the ground; and breathed into his nostrils the breath of life ; and man became a living soul. And God saw everything that he had made, and, behold, it was very *good*. It was not yet *perfect;* for perfection is the grand *ultimatum* of creation. And the evening and the morning were the sixth day ; or the sixth period of earth's progressive unfolding.

· The crowning work of Almighty power and love was consummated in man. The morning stars sang together, and all the sons of God shouted for joy. Nature, animate and inanimate, united in a grand anthem of praise. And thus was the magnificent cathedral, earth, lighted in the vast of space, and dedicated to the worship of the Creator.

And, on the seventh day of the week of ages, God rested from all his work which he had made. And God blessed the seventh day and sanctified it. Periodical seasons of rest for material nature, on the plane of *external manifestations*, were thus established in the Divine economy of power ; in order that the *internal forces* of the earth might gather themselves together, and work out, in the grand laboratory of nature, those chemical principles which would prepare the earth for yet finer results in reproduction. And our stupendous globe, whose surface the All-Father had enriched and beautified with various orders of vegetable and animal life, was left to perfect itself through continuous series of annual and centennial periods of rest, attended by their successive seasons of improved growths, ever preparatory for yet higher manifestations of Almighty power. And earth continues still, " After the flight of untold centuries," to move in swift obedience to those immutable laws by which it was first suspended in the vast of space, to revolve in its eternal circles.

The earth had been elaborately prepared and magnificently

endowed by the Almighty Father long before the advent of Adam and Eve in the Garden of Eden, whose duty it was to populate it with a race of human beings, in the image or form and after the likeness or essential qualities of the Divine.   First in the order of Heaven, is the natural, after that which is spiritual.   And century had succeeded century, rounding the cycles of time, and the physical life of the earth had put forth improved forms of vegetable and animal existence under the inspiring influences of many returning seasons, preparatory for the important event.   For it was needful, in the wisdom of God, that the life of the material world should be quickened and energized, for many ages, by the light and heat of the natural sun, and do perfectly its preliminary work for the higher spiritual life and development that was ordained to succeed and to attend it in progressive unfolding.

And thus we learn, from Biblical history, that man came into being on the sixth day of creation, after an extended preparation of five days of the first week of ages ; and that he was made of the dust of the ground, informed by the Spirit of Creative Intelligence ; and was the crowning work of Almighty Power; the fullness of Creative Energy culminating in him, and the governing principles of the universe, in their beautiful order, being latent in his nature, awaiting only the hour of unfolding ; the hour of destiny, when the key-note of the soul should be touched by stirring passion, or lofty sentiment, and its mighty forces aroused to action.

And hence the logical sequence, that man is an epitome of all things of earth and heaven ; and, consequently, adapted, by his dual nature, composed of matter and of mind, to two spheres of existence, the material and the spiritual.   And, as man was introduced into the world as a child of the Great Spirit, being inspired with his own breath of life, and adapted by a two-fold nature to both the material and visible earth, and the immaterial and invisible heaven, he was, manifestly, intended by the All-Parent to become heir of both spheres, to inherit the overflowing natural riches of the one and the inexaustible treasures in knowledge and wisdom of the other.   And, being of the highest spiritual origin which involves a spiritual destiny, man was installed Lord of the natural world by the great Creator ; and was attended, guarded and instructed, orally, by spiritual existences, ministers of the Divine Being, through the period of early infancy ; even as loving earthly parents, by the ordination of Heaven, cherish and teach their helpless little ones.

And as man, male or female, is a child of the Creative Intelligence of the Universe, he is pre-eminently a religious being; and was born, simultaneously, into the world and into the Church or family of God.   Ay, man is himself the Church, and, as saith the Apostle Paul, the Temple of the Living God.   And God's Church on earth was established in the sacred family-Trinity—Father, Mother and Child—the Trinity of *monogamic marriage*, instituted by Heaven.

And man was created in a state of innocence and of ignorance; but with latent powers of mind and heart to be developed through the unfolding influences of education.   In his physical organism he was born to the prescribed statue of a man; in his spiritual, to the unknown measure of a God.   And, hence, the measure of the Church must needfully be the measure of a man whose progressive nature is—as we are taught by Revelation—both human and divine ; human in weakness, ignorance, and limitations through matter ; divine in strength, knowledge and sense of Liberty in Law, through Spirit, as a child of Deity.   And, consequently, the Church Militant was, and is, destined to grow in grace and in the knowledge of God, through the unfolding powers of man, male and female, from period to period of Time's weeks of ages.

And it appears to have been the plan of Heaven, from the dawn of man's creation, to aid him in the journey of life only in accordance with his needs, and with his ability to receive instruction and to reduce it to practice.   And it was so wisely designed, in order that man might grow by his own effort and become a self-poised and self-governing power, a grand type of the divine man.

And, as man constitutes the Church of God, his successive stages of unfolding, from the cradle to the grave, are indices of the order of development in the Church, and, also, in the Nation and in the World. And, hence, the Church, the Nation and the World, like the individual Man, must pass through the hour of helpless and ignorant Infancy—the season of unreflecting and reckless Childhood—the period of heroic and impassioned Youth—the day of noble, reasoning Manhood—and the Age of moral beauty and perfection, after a life of obedience to the Divine Law.

But, as large bodies move slowly through their prescribed orders of unfolding, the Church, the Nation and the World cannot pass through either stage of development in a single generation, or the life of an individual man. And in confirmation of this statement, we learn, from the history of the past, that human progress has ever been slow on earth. But we learn, also, that the advancement of society has always borne a true relation to its knowledge ; and, consequently, it is logical to infer, as well as encouraging to believe, that its future progress will bear an exact ratio to its advancing intelligence.

To man's impatient watching and limited vision, human progress not only appears slow, but it seems often to linger in the paths of the centuries, and to turn aside before the enemies of right ; yet, it is not so in view of the observing angels. The battle-cry of intelligent nature is, ever—Onward !

The sublime march of human progress may be compared to the great ocean's inflowing tide. Its waters recede again and again, but only to return with accessions of power, and uplift themselves to higher levels. Even thus the mighty tide of human progress—notwithstanding its seeming delay and apparent retrogression—is rising evermore, and bearing the family of man forward to the fulfillment of a glorious destiny as children of God.

CHAPTER III.

THE JEWISH DISPENSATION OF LAW AND AUTHORITY, OR SPECIAL
REVELATION OF THE DIVINE FATHER IN THE CHILDHOOD OF THE
CHURCH AND THE WORLD.

Darkness covered the earth, and gross darkness the people.

It was the evening of the first day of the second week of ages;
the evening that succeeded the first period of rest instituted by
heaven. Darkness covered the earth, and gross darkness the
people. There was apparent retrogression every where in society, because it was a season of transition from the early infancy to
the childhood of the human family. The moral forces, interiorly at work in preparation for new and advanced conditions, were
concealed from the undeveloped children of earth. Angel
attendants were now rarely visible, and there was little light of
knowledge to guide them aright on their journey.

Bnt the evening and the MORNING were the first day. Light
at length penetrated the pervading darkness. The Spirit of God
moved upon the face of the moral world, even as the informing
life had passed over the physical elements of nature at the beginning, causing order, light and beauty to succeed earth's dark
night of confusion.

And out of *social chaos* the Almighty Father called into existence his ORGANIZED CHURCH to become the great executive body
of the moral world, to carry into effect among the nations of
earth the principles of his moral government. The *Written Law*
now succeeded the *oral instruction* of the infant church of Eden;
and the leadership of inspired men took the place of angel
teachers and attendants, to control and regulate the great human

family on the material plane of development.   For the world had progressed to its season of childhood, and the beautiful angel ministrations, appropriate to its helpless infancy, were no longer adapted to its conditions.   There was intense and unremitting energy on the material plane, such as we observe everywhere in children.   The higher governing powers of mind were yet latent, and hence organization and leadership became necessary for discipline and concert of action, as well as for progressive unfolding in the knowledges of material things.   For it was (and still is) needful that the physical nature of man should be first developed on the physical plane, in order that he might become adapted to his material conditions and surroundings.

It was remarked in a preceding chapter that man was born simultaneously into the world and into the church, or family of God.   But to the Organized Church was committed a revelation of the *special arcana* of nature concerning the origin and destiny of the human family, the relations of its various members to the All-Parent as children, and, consequently, to each other as brethren, and the natural obligations attendant upon these relations; which principles involve the right and wrong of human actions.   We recognize this existing difference between the members of the organized church and the children of the Universal Church or family of God ; the former acknowledge their allegiance to the government of heaven and pledge themselves to obey its laws, and to strive to promote its interests among men ; while many of the latter *tacitly* accept the higher law as the rule of life, yet make no profession of so doing ; and still larger numbers, who are on the more material plane of thought and action, and do not perceive spiritual truths and their relations, disregard or ignore altogether the government of heaven.

The organized Church is the *affirmative or positive power* of the moral world, of which the outside family of God is the negative principle ; and there naturally exists, between the former and the latter, a strong and continuous philosophical action, which is less antagonistic than reciprocal.   The fearful religious contests of Christendom, that have deluged earth with human blood, have never arisen between the organized and unorganized church of God ; but between the *positive religionists*. Because all denominations of the Christian Church, that style themselves *the Church*, become positive to each other, and, hence, naturally repellant, and often violently antagonistic, as the past history of the world bears testimony. And, yet, from the seeming evil God educes good. Through the active animosity of rival sects, the stagnant pool of thought becomes agitated, and new principles of truth are evolved, by which the human soul enlarges, until it bursts its denominational trammels, and gains the true liberty of a child of God. Then man recognizes broadly the universal principles of God's government and their adaptation to the needs of the WHOLE human family, and becomes AT-ONE with the Divine, seeking to do His will on earth, even as it is done in heaven. And thus the wrath of man eventuates evermore in the glory of God.

The organized Church is as essential to the order, peace, progress and continuance of society as the organized civil government. Indeed, the government of a nation is simply an external manifestation of the interior character or quality of its church ; it is, certes, the very spirit of its religion exhibiting itself on the lower material plane of practical action. A live, intelligent and elevated Christian Church will produce a strong, vital and incorruptible Christian Democracy. And we may learn this instructive lesson from the pages of history, that, when a nation loses the earnest, vitalizing spirit of its religion, from whatever cause, and whatever may be the peculiar character of that religion, its government will fall, through the enervated and demoralized condition of the people. It is because the church or religion of a nation is the soul of its government, and when the soul is diseased and torpid, the body will become corrupt and lifeless. Ancient Egypt, Greece and Rome are striking illustrations of this melancholy truth. And yet, in the early physical ages of ignorance, the fall of nations through such causes was a necessity of advancing intelligence. For human progress is inevitable. A nation must, sooner or later, outgrow the special forms of its received religion. And if its *forms* of worship have been far more imposing, attractive and essential in promoting the zealous

3

devotion of the people, than the *spirit* of the truth which they represent, (which is the case with the undeveloped mind of every period of time,) then, when the shell of forms is broken and cast aside, there will be no spiritual life within, and no soundness, no vital recuperative moral power to quicken in the mind and heart of the people and produce newness of life ; and universal prostration and ruin will follow for ages. For the reaction from all diseased conditions of human beings, both physical and moral, is always in proportion to the vital or renewing power of the soul.

The Christian Church of to-day has outgrown the special forms in which her religious views were presented to the world, in her youthful or heroic and affectional age of the first Christian Era ; and if she do not awake in the dawn of the present reasoning day, and accept her advanced age of maturity and of *questioning faith*, and winnow her wheat from the chaff of her youthful creeds, and resow the living principle in the hearts and minds of the people, THEN the nations of Christendom will likewise become weak, demoralized, and, finally, fall to decay. God forbid that such should be their doom. But are there no signs of dissolution now? What means the startling cry of watchmen on the walls of Zion? "Protestantism is a failure ! !"—and the fearful rejoinder from the people—"Ay ! and the Christian religion is a failure ! ! !" Alas ! the soldiers of the cross are already surrendering the sword of the spirit, to the advancing army of materialistic Rationalism. But all the increasing *knowledge* of the world will not, yea, CANNOT, supply the place of VITAL RELIGION. Man has a heart as well as a head, and both unitedly active, supply light and heat to the human system, causing it to become vigorous and fruitful. But, if the heart have no warmth, the light of the intellect will be like the cold, unproductive glitter of the glacier.

And a combination of the temporal and spiritual powers, in a union of Church and State, tends, also, slowly and surely to the dissolution of society. For, know ye, O, Children of the Church of the most high God ! ye cannot serve two masters. In the union of the civil and religious powers of a nation, the Church loses her zeal for God and conforms to the standard of the outside world in manners and morals ; and society degenerates in exact proportion with the conformity of the Church to the world. A union of Church and State is fatal, because it undermines the foundation of morals upon which society rests. It necessitates unceasing compromise, in which the eternal principles of Righ, are continually made subservient to mere political expediencyt political strategy, and the fine moral sense of the millions becomes bewildered, at length, in endless sophistries by which politicians strive to make the wrong appear the better way ; and the nation will be lost, if its leaders have not statesmen-like foresight to perceive the impending danger, and sufficient moral sense, vitality and strength remaining to grapple with the imminent evil, to separate the Church and Civil Government, and to call upon the people to awake, and, with repentant prayers and tears, to return to their allegiance to Heaven. All Ecclesiastic forms of Government were adapted only to the childhood and early youth of the world, when the ignorant and helpless millions required leading strings. And the representatives of these ancient forms of Government, in the present enlightened age, will ere long be forced, by the Advance Guard of Intelligence and Morals, to yield the sceptre of temporal power to the Civil Executive Body of the nation.

Let us return to our subject. To the Organized Church was committed the Oracles of God, to hold in trust for the human family, until they should become of age to rightly understand and appropriate those rich treasures of wisdom ; and for this reason the Church became, necessarily, the moral Conservative Power of the Nation. And all the various members of the human family, outside of the Organized Church, constitute the Radical Power which acts as an invigorating stimulus upon the Conservative, impelling it to continual effort to indoctrinate and draw to itself the free element of mind ; while the former Power is influenced to resist the persuasions and arguments of the latter, with reasons drawn from its own independent stand-point. An increasing action and reaction is the result, which tend to promote a healthy moral condition in the community. And thus we learn from the teachings of Philosophy that a dual Power, analagous to that which holds the planets in their courses, is required in the moral, as well as in the material world, in order that there may be both equipoise and impulsion.

The Organized Church may, in verity, be termed the grand centripetal force of the moral world ; for its office is to draw the soul of man to the great soul-centre of Nature—God! While the outside family of man may be correctly named the centrifugal force; for its members tend, in their erratic course, to fly off in tangents into the vast unknown of Nature, and lose the God, even while engaged in observing and admiring His marvelous works.   But the two independent forces, acting and reacting, through a vigorous intellectual and moral restraint and constraint produce both motion and advancement in the elements of mind; one drawing the Radical Power toward the central point of light and heat ; the other attracting the Conservative Power outward toward the circumference of principles.

But the mind of man is progressive, and he must advance, step by step, up the ever-ascending heights of knowledge.   In his Childhood and Youth, while occupied in gathering the beautiful flowers which attract his eyes to earth, he is unable to look abroad and observe and comprehend the grand governing principles of material and Intelligent Nature.   And the particular phases of truth which he receives on authority, without the consent of Reason, during these periods of partial development, is, of necessity, partial and exceedingly limited.   And yet, as the undeveloped man does not perceive his own limitations, and that he is incapable of grasping the broad relations of principles, and as he cannot measure farther advanced minds that he recognizes as authority, he wills to believe that what the latter teach, and what he accepts as truth, is the acme of human intelligence. And this condition of the undeveloped individual man illustrates the state of the Church during the Childhood and early Youth of the world.

The leaders of the Church could gain but limited views of God's truth, presented to their minds for universal propagation, belief and practice ; and, consequently, could reveal but glimpses of Heavenly truth and light to the waiting millions. And, as the early leaders were men possessed of indomitable wills, such as the crude forms of civilization in the physical ages of the world required of those who would meet and overcome difficulties, and as they verily believed that they were especially favored of Heaven, and permitted to comprehend the whole plan of God's Government, they naturally manifested earnest zeal for His service; and there was fierce dogmatic assertion of *mere points* of doctrine, together with tenacious observance of the *special forms* of presentation, which has rendered it exceedingly difficult for the Church of every age to attain growth, and to progress sufficiently to meet the demand of outside enlightenment. And we learn, hence, the important service of a Radical Power in society, unconnected with the Conservative Church; a Power which is broadened by research in the *general arcana* of Nature, and that can reason independently of authority, and of received opinions and prejudices, from the altitude of Philosophy, which is the lofty plane of Deity.

And man may see the perfect wisdom of the Divine Government manifested as clearly and strikingly in the Radical as in the Conservative Body, if he can set aside his traditional religion, and observe the action of these two powers in the moral world. For, then, he will perceive that the Radical Power leads the Conservative out from the central point of truth—THE GOD—toward the circumference of truth—OF THE GOD—in ever-widening circles, impelling the moral world to revolve in the grand orbit of intelligence prescribed by the Creator, receiving the while from the Divine Sun of the Universe the warmth of Religion and the light of Knowledge, which infuses through it the true life of Heaven, and will cause it to flower, ere long, in celestial beauty, and to produce the perfect fruits of righteousness.

But the Almighty Parent himself demonstrates for his children of time the marvelous problem of human progress and destiny.

"God is his own interpreter,
And he will make it plain.

Deep in unfathomable mines
Of never-failing skill,
He treasures up his great designs,
And works his Sovereign will."

It is our part, as dutiful children and pupils, to observe and point out the lines and curves that he has already described upon the pages of human existence, which show the wonderful methods of solution, and the directions of His power, whereby man may be guided inductively, point by point, in his progress in the knowledge of God, and finally approximate to His conclusions. And by glancing at the dial of advancing intelligence, and noting the degrees of light already marked, and observing where the shadow still lingers, we may be able to estimate the intervening hours before it will be rational to look for the meridian day of humanity.

None must understand us to mean that man can fully comprehend God. Who can find out the Almighty unto perfection ? Not one. The finite cannot measure the Infinite Mind. And yet man, being a child of God, created in His image and likeness, may acquire a knowledge of the principles of His Government, when his observing and reasoning powers are no longer latent, but developed and active, and he is patiently, earnestly and lovingly engaged in seeking to know, in order that he may obey His laws with all his heart, and mind, and soul. And to seek to know the Lord is not only a privilege that man may enjoy, but it is a moral obligation, binding on every faculty of his being.

And when the mind of man attains a highly developed and receptive condition, he will not fail to perceive that the controlling principles of intelligent, as of material Nature, are Order, eternal Justice, Progress and Perfection, all actively tending evermore to produce Moral Harmony ; and that these governing powers are included in all-embracing Love, which is the Alpha and the Omega of Creation. Therefore, Love is the fulfilling of the Law. And all the shadows and the gloom of the moral world, and all the destructive phenomena of the physical, do not militate against the truth of the proposition. For we are assured by the teachings of Philosophy and Experience, as well as of Revelation, that, through the wide range of Nature, animate and inanimate, clouds and darkness are as essential to vigorous and healthy development as sunbeams. The darkness and the light are both alike to Him who regardeth not the seeming, but the real good of His creations. He doth not afflict willingly, nor grieve the children of men. Like as a father pitieth his children, so the Lord pitieth them that fear Him. For He knoweth our frame; He *remembereth* that we are dust. And, through all the gloom, in all the sorrows and disciplinary trials of life, we may ever be assured that :

Behind a frowning providence
He hides a smiling face.

And, inspired with this loving confidence in the only Unchangeable All-One, the same yesterday, to-day and forever, we wander back cheerfully and hopefully for man, through the deepening shadows of departed centuries, to linger for awhile in the gloom of the first day of the Second Week of Ages, among the undeveloped children of the world, in the time of gross ignorance and reckless daring ; of cruel passion and unpitying revenge ; when earth was filled with violence, because the animal nature of man was strongly in the ascendant, and reason and the moral sentiments were latent and inoperative. We wander back to the first Organized Church of God in the world, which is the starting point of moral progress in the history of man, in order to review the course of the human family, from age to age, in their progress through the wilderness-world forward to the Canaan of their immortal inheritance, and observe, through all their wanderings, the directions in which they were led by the guiding care of Heaven. We wander thoughtfully back through the solemn monuments of departed Nations, that are scattered along the highways of the ages, on whose ruins we may still trace for our instruction the brief inscriptions of their rise and fall.

Fellow traveler of earth, wilt thou turn back with us, and journey for awhile in the shadows of the past ? We shall return ere long, and leaping, the barriers of the present, dwell for a season in the unclouded light of the millennial day of perfected humanity.

The history of the Organized Church of God commences with the call of Abraham, which remarkable event occurred

nearly two thousand years before the advent of Christ.   We learn
from biblical records, that Abraham was a great spiritual medium, that he held direct communication with the Almighty
Parent and his angel ministers, and was directed in all the important events of his life by spiritual intelligences.   He was
Heaven's chosen founder of the Jewish Nation, and representative
of the patriarchal age of authority in the Childhood of the World.

And it came to pass in those days, that the Lord appeared to
Abraham and said unto him, I am the Almighty God ; walk before me and be thou perfect.   And I will make my covenant
between me and thee, and will multiply thee exceedingly.   And
I will establish my covenant between me and thee and thy seed
after thee in their generations, for an everlasting covenant, to be
a God unto thee and to thy seed after thee.   And I will give unto thee and to thy seed after thee the land wherein thou art a
stranger, all the land of Canaan, for an everlasting possession ;
and I will be their God.   And the covenant which God made
with Abraham, symbolic of denial or cutting off of gross, unhallowed passions, and of purification in regeneration, was sealed in
the living flesh of the covenanters, at the very fountain of life, in
order that it might be a continual reminder of the dedication of
the human body and its fruit to the Divine Author of existence.

And when Abraham was far advanced in age, and Sarah his
wife was also well stricken in years, and without hope of offspring, the Almighty Parent revealed to him the startling intelligence that Sarah should become A MOTHER OF NATIONS, and that
his seed should be as innumerable as the stars of heaven, and
that in them all the families of the earth should be blessed.
And he believed in the Lord, and He counted it to him for
righteousness.

And in her appointed hour, Sarah became the joyful mother of
the promised son,—of the Jewish nation,—and of the Organized
Church of the most high God, which has influenced the character and destiny of the world.   Ay, and that Church will continue
to broaden and increase in numbers, power and glory, until
thrones shall be cast down, and the Ancient of Days shall sit,
whose dominion is an everlasting dominion, and whose kingdom

is from generation to generation. For He who called Abraham to go forth from his kindred and from his father's house, and to drive out the heathen nations of Canaan, through his posterity, while he was yet a childless man, and to take possession of their strange country and establish there, in an age of anarchy, ignorance and idolatry, the worship of the true and living God, DID, THEN, set up a kingdom which shall never be destroyed ; but shall break in pieces and consume all kingdoms. and stand forever.

And we learn further from the sacred record, that the Organized Church of the Childhood of the World, like the Infant Church of Eden, was established in the Sacred Family Trinity—Father, Mother and Son. The promise unto Abraham was, In Isaac shall thy seed be called ; in him (the legitimate offspring of monogamic marriage, after the divine order,) shall all the families of the earth be blessed. And so Abraham was required, at the birth of Isaac, *to cast out the bondwoman and her son.* For it was all-important that the Organized Church of God on earth should be thoroughly radical, should be founded in the deepest and fullest truth of Nature—the Sacred Family Trinity.

It is recorded that the act of sending forth Hagar and the innocent Ishmael, to become wanderers of the wilderness, was *very grievous* in Abraham's sight. But his suffering was the natural result of the sin of violating the holy law of marriage. The brief mention of his sorrow is a grand commentary for all ages. It proclaims the great law of Retributive Justice. The act of wrongdoing involves, also, the penalty ; and man cannot escape from the consequences of his deeds ; sooner or later his sin will find him out, and harrow his soul with remorseful anguish. In verity, sin is only another name of suffering.

The promise of the Almighty Father to Abraham, " In Isaac shall thy seed be called ;" was fulfilled in the following manner : Long after the Patriarch had departed from earth, an Angel of the Lord met Jacob, the son of Isaac, the son of Abraham, in the way, as he journeyed forth from the house of Laban toward the land of his Fathers. And Jacob wrestled all night with the Angel, even until the break of day, saying, I will not let thee go

4

until thou bless me.   And the Angel answered, Thou shalt be
called no more Jacob, but Israel, for as a prince hast thou power
with God and with men, and hast prevailed.   And Israel became thereafter a representative of the Divine Father to the
Jewish nation, and Church of the first Dispensation.   And the
people were called the Children of Israel.   And they continue
still, after the lapse of centuries, to bear that ancient appellative;
because they have not yet learned, through the Messiah, their
claim to a higher title—Children of God.

And unto Israel were born twelve sons, who were led by the
providence of God down to Egypt, which country was, at that
period of the world's history, the most enlightened part of the
earth, in order that they might acquire a knowledge of the sciences, and the industrial arts of the Egyptians, and gain a starting point in civilization as a Nation.   And they were held in
bondage by the Pharaohs of the land for the space of four hundred years, *and obliged to labor;* otherwise, they would have returned to the land of their fathers as ignorant as when they departed therefrom.   But an hour of *freedom* was appointed by
Heaven, and a man for the hour, wise and learned in all the
knowledges of the Egyptians, and skilled in the principles of
governmental policy, to lead the Children of Israel forth out of
slavery, and forward to the long prayed for Canaan of promise.
And Moses became the great Lawgiver of the Jewish Church
and people.

We are taught by Revelation that the Holy Commandments
for the government of human conduct, of the first Dispensation
of Law and Authority in the Childhood of the World, was given
to Moses on the summit of Sinai.   The event was attended with
marvelous phenomena.   There were thunders and lightnings,
and a thick cloud upon the Mount, and the voice of the trumpet exceeding loud ; so that all the people that were in the
camp trembled.   And Mount Sinai was altogether on a smoke,
because the Lord descended upon it in fire; and the whole
mount quaked greatly.   And when the voice of the trumpet
sounded long, and waxed louder and louder, Moses spake, and
God answered him by a voice.

The spectacle was grandly imposing, and calculated to strongly impress the undeveloped people of the Childhood of the World, whose minds could alone be acted upon through the external senses. And in that perfect code of moral laws for the government of Intelligent Nature, periodical days of rest, analagous to the seasons of rest in the physical, were instituted in the natural world. And we are impelled to acknowledge the wisdom and provident care of Heaven in establishing the Sabbath day for man. For, throughout the universal system of nature, *external rest* implies *internal activity.* And the remission of labor, both physical and mental, on every seventh day of the week, breaks the old routine of habit, which is a serious check to progressive ideas, and induces a continuous periodic action of the more interior forces of the human mind, thereby promoting systematic development of its higher powers. And thus the entire change produced in the mind, by turning the current of thought into fresh channels, serves a double purpose in the economy of nature ; namely, to relieve over-tasked powers of body and mind, and to promote directly the growth of the soul. And, viewed in this light, the periods of rest become far more important to the true life of man than the seasons of practical action. And periodic days of rest tend also to promote health and longevity, by relieving the tension of both mind and body.

In our observations of material and intelligent nature, we cannot fail to notice the *dual* character of controlling powers, and are taught that the laws of the physical universe are everywhere repeated in the spiritual : nay, the converse is true ; the laws of the spiritual, being the governing principles of all things of earth and heaven, are everywhere ultimated or repeated in the material world. And we may be greatly aided in our search for the more interior spiritual laws, by acquiring a knowledge of those which govern material things, and seeking to comprehend their dual action.

And thus we learn from sacred history that the Organized Church of the Childhood of Man, like the Infant Church of Eden, was introduced into the world, by strong and decided manifestations of spirit, presence and power. And Spirit phenomena continued to attend the Children of Israel through all the vicissitudes of their eventful history, until near the close of the second Week of Ages, and the termination of the religious dispensation of law and authority, at the coming in of the farther advanced Youth of the World.

The Children of Israel were received and treated by the higher powers of earth and heaven as parents and teachers uniformly regard and treat unreflecting, ignorant children. Their lawgivers and prophets, under the direction of the Almighty Father, addressed them in tones of authority, and required of them unquestioning faith, and implicit obedience. And they were very particularly directed in all their *temporal* as well as spiritual affairs ; and held always in leading strings, like dependent, helpless children. How wonderfully and tenderly they were cared for by the Father in their early, adventurous journey out of Egypt, toward the promised land of Canaan ; protected by an overshadowing cloud by day, and guided by a pillar of fire by night. And through the period of forty years of nomadic life in the wilderness, food was provided for them in marvellous ways, and they were fed with manna from heaven.

And we observe that the religion of the Israelites was one of forms and ceremonies, addressed particularly to the external senses, and thereby adapted to the undeveloped mind, which can more easily perceive and appreciate spiritual truths when they are presented in symbolic forms.

And the laws of the Israelites for the regulation of social life (prohibiting vices and excesses in sensuality that appear, at the present age, so monstrous, that it seems incredible that human beings could ever have imagined, much less have indulged in such, even during the periods of grossest ignorance in the history of man,) denote distinctly the undeveloped condition of the people of the Childhood of the World. And the existence of the degrading institutions of slavery and polygamy among the Israelites, (of which evils they purified themselves in their progress toward maturity,) manifest clearly their low condition of intelligence and morals, during the darkness of the physical ages. Many persons unacquainted with the progressive character and the true spirit of God's government, blame the All-Father for not having prevented the introduction of those institutions in Israel ; while others, who are on a still lower plane of thought and action, and clouded with an unregenerate self-hood, assert that the Almighty sanctioned, because he did not directly prohibit them ; and find in their weak, sophistical arguments to maintain the illogical position, encouragement for indulging in kindred wrongs of slavery and license toward their fellow beings, male and female, in the increased light of the present reasoning age. We should not lose sight of the fact which is common in the experience of all mankind, that it is not the method of Heaven to *force* human beings into obedience to the Divine Law. The exercise of arbitrary power is human, and the result of impatient haste and limited vision. He who sees the end from the beginning, awaits the slow development of higher and yet higher principles, as the race of man advances through many successive generations. Man, in his generic and specific character, *must learn the nature of evil*, either through the teaching of history, observation, or painful experience, and comprehend the enormity of wrong-doing, behold how it dwarfs and deforms the whole being, before he can learn to abhor it as a foul moral excrescence, and will be able to eradicate it, voluntarily, from his thought and practice, and individualize himself in the truth of nature. And, so, Right and Wrong both bear rule on earth ; and they are both teachers and ministers of the Divine Love to the children of men. We may recognize the former by the light which breaks in upon the soul, while listening to her lessons of wisdom ; and know the latter by the darkness, humiliation and sorrow that attend obedience to his counsels. Man is left in liberty to follow either, while God calls pleadingly upon all his sons and daughters of time : Choose ye, this day, whom ye will serve. And the path of truth and virtue may be reached, alike, through joyful obedience to right ; or, painful experience in wrong, expiated with remorseful and repentant tears.

> But grant *me*, God, from every care,
>   And stain of passion free,
> Aloft, through *virtue's* purer air,
>   To hold my course to thee !

No sin to cloud, no lure to stay
My soul, as home she springs ;—
Thy sunshine on her joyful way,
Thy freedom in her wings !

The work of regeneration in the heart, mind and soul of man cannot be effected by compulsory measures. It is a well-observed fact that coercion has a direct tendency to stimulate antagonism which is unfavorable to the reception of spiritual truth. Be *still* and know that I am God. It is only in the quiet of the soul that the Divine can be felt and seen. Man is so constituted by the Creator that he needs to feel that he holds the liberty of choice, and is responsible to a higher power than himself for his actions, before his moral nature can become fully alive and sensitive to right and wrong, his aspirations kindled, and his whole being aglow with loving fervor for the truth. And there must be knowledge of principles, attended with conviction of the right so clear, forcible and convincing, that one could no more easily mistake and reject it, than deny the radiant glory of the noonday sun. And there must be *voluntary acquiescence* of the whole nature of man to the Divine Law, before he can be born again, born of the Spirit, and become at-one with God. The loving obedience of the heart must accompany the intelligent assent of the enlightened mind Therefore man, as an individual and as a race, can only become fully regenerate in the maturity of his powers.

But in the Childhood and Youth of the Church and World, when Reason was latent and inoperative in man, and there was little light of Knowledge to guide him aright, God accepted the *partial worship* of his undeveloped children, appealing to them, through his inspired prophets and teachers, in tones of infinite tenderness : Oh, that there were in my people the *heart* to obey my laws!

And the numerous wars of the ancient Israelites, as well as their peculiar modes of warfare, indicate, also, their primitive state, their undeveloped conditions and resources. Indeed, one cannot review their history and character without remarking in how true a sense they were Children; requiring line upon line, and precept upon precept, here a little and there a little. Like children, they cared more for the immediate gratification of their appetites than for the great principles of liberty and independence, and their condition as a people. During their journeyings through the wilderness toward the promised land of Canaan, they often lusted after the garlics and flesh-pots of Egypt, and would gladly have returned to slavery to obtain them. Esau sold his noble birth right, when he came back hungry from the field, in impatient longing for a mess of pottage.

Like children, the ancient people of God were refractory and rebellious without cause, and filled with unreasonable complaints and reproaches against their teachers and guides. Like children, they were easily disheartened by obstacles; and as readily encouraged and comforted again. Like children, it was difficult to keep their minds interested for many consecutive moments of time in a given direction ; they required constant surveillance, daily and hourly instruction and representation of the line and motive of action, or they would wander into forbidden paths. During the short space of time that Moses wan absent on Mount Sinai, receiving the Commandments from Heaven, they forgot the living God of their Fathers, and made themselves a golden calf to worship. They appear, in verity, to have been as much attracted to idols as children are to dolls and toys. And even in advanced epochs of their history, after they had passed the nomadic period of Patriarchal rule and attained position among the Nations, and notwithstanding all the sublime manifestation of Almighty Power and of protecting care, that had attended them for ages, they often turned aside from the worship of Jehovah, the God of Gods, and offered sacrifices to Idols, under every green tree, and on every mountain height, like the heathen peoples by whom they were surrounded. Even King Sólomon. the wisest prince of Israel and of the East, formed no exception to the universal tendency to idolatry in the Childhood of the World. And, whenever this tendency to the worship of idols manifested itself strongly, there was a corresponding decline of the spirit of their religion, which was attended by national decadence. Because, with the loss of vitalizing moral power, the Children of Israel lost also their physical prowess, and were easily conquered and led into captivity by their enemies.

And, like children, the Israelites were charmed with spectacular displays, they delighted in gigantic feats of strength, and in all the clamor and pageantry of war. Physical might was their highest conception of power and glory. And, consequently, the Almighty Father appeared to them in the aspect of a grand military Chieftain, a God of thunders and of battles ; a God of vengeance, of retributive Justice, who would humble the proud rebels against his government, and exalt the men of low degree, obedient to His Law.

And, as they were Children unstable in all their ways, (undeveloped individuals and nations are always children, however mature they may be in their physical organization,) the wise, Heavenly Parent governed them as such, adapted their religion to their condition and needs, and rendered it attractive to their senses. But they were taught to look through its symbols and rites for the higher spiritual ideas and truths that they were intended to embody and represent. And, in addition to this educational process, their spiritual natures were constantly stimulated by direct instructions from the Spirit World to their prophets and teachers, as well as through their required exercise of faith in the unseen and Eternal Father. Thus, slowly, as generation succeeded generation, the people attained spiritual growth, and, in fullness of time, the world was prepared for the higher Christian Dispensation of Love and Free-Will to man.

We have not attempted an elaborate narration of the History and Character of the Children of Israel. Our design is simply to show, by a running review of their record, that the Jewish Church was but the Childhood of the Christian. And it should not be forgotten in Christendom that the latter Church is indebted to the former for the spiritual growth and knowledge of Deity the that rendered her own existence possible. There can be no progressed conditions of the human race, in the principles of Religion and Civil Government, that have not been anteceded by much early effort in the right direction, by long continued and mighty struggles with Ignorance and its host of evils.

Numerous errors and gigantic wrongs attended of necessity the millions of the undeveloped physical ages. For then it was the Divine Right of Kings to oppress, as well as to bless humanity, when they chanced to be unregenerate, ignorant men, governed by selfish, unscrupulous ambition. And those were times of fearful experiences in evil; and of stern unmitigable discipline. While knowledge to lighten the rugged path could alone be acquired by slow, persevering effort; and it was carefully withheld from the "common people," lest they should become as Gods, knowing good from evil—should become thinking individualized men, independent of guides and rulers. And those were times of grossest superstition, as well as of ignorance and errors, when he was regarded as the most unfortunate of all his fellows, who could penetrate farthest into the deep mysteries of Nature.

> THEN, to be blind was safer than to see :
> For light was magic ; wisdom, sorcery.
> But, now, in knowledge all our safety lies.
> And all our danger in not being wise ;
> THEN, men of thought climb'd with a cautious tread
> The rugged steep of science, rarely fed
> With crumbs of knowledge from the Master's store,
> Their hunger to appease, their cry for more.
> And when at eve they gained the mountain height,
> Where they had hoped to stand serene in light,
> Like Moses, they were blest with only *vision*,
> Of promised riches—far-off fields elysian,
> Which man would sometime reach by effort strong,
> And well-directed, early, late and long ;
> Whilst they must be content to die alone
> Upon the summit—by the world unknown—
> Till other ages should their level reach,
> And other men their words of wisdom teach;
> Content to know proud banners *then* would wave,
> Posthumous honors fall upon their grave.

The Jews passed through all the severe trials of early, crude conditions for us ; and we are deeply indebted to them. They were the chosen people of God, to establish his Organized Church in the world, because they possessed the qualities that were needful to contend with obdurate circumstances, the firmness that is not easily moved, and the tenacity that is loath to let go. And they have retained for centuries their peculiar characteristics. They are to-day the same persistent and resist-

5

ing forces in the world as when they escaped from the bondage
of the Egyptians, and received the commandments of Heaven
from the summit of Sinai, and went forth on their pilgrimage,
armed with the counsels of Jehovah, and fortified with Almighty
Power, to conquer the heathen nations of Canaan, and possess
their land for an everlasting inheritance.   During their long absence from their native country, they have remained distinct as
a people, but little influenced by modern forms of civilization,
and have held intact the ancient worship of their fathers.   Their
peculiar and striking qualities of firmness and tenacity have cemented them strongly together, and consolidated them into a
religious pyramid of majestic proportions, that will loom up
sublimely above the ruins of the past, its mouldering altars and
its crumbling thrones, an enduring monument of Heaven's protecting and directing care.

But, in consequence of these very adhesive qualities, as well as
through their blindness and willful unbelief, they cut themselves
off from reaping the advantages of their own growth in the freer
and fuller Christian Dispensation.   And they have continued for
eighteen centuries to grope their way darkly through the dead
past of types and shadows that were ultimated in the coming of
the Messiah ; while the Gentile nations have gathered the fruit
of their early labors.   But a new Chaistian Era is already dawning on the earth, in which the Jews, in their turn, will share the
riches of the Gentiles, in accordance with the eternal law of com-
pensative justice.   St. Paul saw with illumined vision the sacred bond that would eventually unite the Jews and Gentiles in
a holy brotherhood of nations, when he made his grand argument to the Romans, showing the spiritual relations of both, in
the great progressive future of humanity.   And he declared to
the Gentiles : I would not, brethren, that ye should be ignorant
of this mystery, lest ye should be wise in your own conceits, that
blindness in part is happened to Israel, until the fullness of the
Gentiles be come in.   And so all Israel shall be saved, as it is
written, there shall come out of Zion the deliverer, and shall
turn away ungodliness from Jacob ; for this is my covenant unto
them when I shall take away their sins.   As concerning the gos-

pel, they are enemies for your sakes ; but as touching the election, they are beloved for the fathers' sakes. For the gifts and calling of God are without repentance. For as ye in times past have not believed God, yet have now obtained mercy through their unbelief; even so have these also now not believed, that through your mercy they also may obtain mercy.

The day is already breaking, and the shadows are retreating before the rising glory of the Sun of Righteousness. The Jews will ere long look upon their despised and rejected Messiah with sorrow and anguish of soul. And they will bring the freewill offerings of their hearts with deep contrition of spirit, instead of the blood of goats and of lambs, to lay upon their consecrated altars, and will dedicate them anew to God and humanity, in the name of the crucified Redeemer. We extend to them the open palm of Christian Fellowship and Love, and give them a joyful welcome to the banquet of our Lord. There is room for all nations and for all people. The holy tree of life, that was planted in Palestine by the chosen seed of Abraham, has grown and spread forth its branches, far and wide and high, until they overshadow earth, and uplift their boughs into the light and glory of Heaven.

The close of the Jewish Dispensation was also a period of transition from the Childhood to the Youth of the Church and World. And it was, consequently, an age of apparent retrogression in morals. For the spiritual forces that were strongly at work, interiorly, in preparation for the advent of the Messiah to the Youth of the world, to re-establish the kingdom of Heaven on earth, were impalpable and unseen by the ignorant and unreflecting millions. The Jews had become blind adherents of a traditional religion. and lost faith in direct spirit manifestation and power, and in the ever-present protecting love and directing care of Heaven. They believed, as do modern religionists, that the period of Spirit Intercourse with man closed with the written word of Revelation, transmitted to the fathers. And the vital, energizing spirit of their Religion was dead. The people were sordid and filled with the spirit of trade. Mammon was enthroned in the courts of their magnificent Temple, and the

House, once so sacred to the worship of the God of Heaven and of earth, was profaned by market stalls and money-changers' tables. The vital spirit of their religion being gone, there was no life nor soundness in their government; and the Children of Israel lost their position among the kingdoms of the world. They were conquered and led into captivity by their enemies, and scattered abroad over the face of all the earth, even as at this day.

When we remember their long exile of eighteen centuries and the terrible persecutions to which they have been subjected among foreign nations, far from Jerusalem, far from the venerated and beloved land of their Fathers; our sympathies and fraternal feelings are deeply awakened; and we pity more than we blame them for all the errors of the past, recollecting that they were ignorant, undeveloped children of the Childhood of the World. And we hold them closely to our hearts as brethren of a common origin and destiny. Who can read the touching lamentations of their poets over their captivity and not share the grief and loneliness of the exiled ones, and weep with them by the water-courses of strangers? By the rivers of Babylon, there we sat down, yea, we wept when we remembered Zion. We hanged our harps upon the willows in the midst thereof. For there they that carried us away captive required of us a song; and they that wasted us required of us mirth, saying, sing us one of the songs of Zion. How shall we sing the Lord's song in a strange land? If I forget thee, O Jerusalem, let my right hand forget her cunning. And let my tongue cleave to the roof of my mouth, if I do not remember thee, if I prefer not Jerusalem above my chief joy.

And, when we view their singular social isolation, scattered abroad and dwelling in many remote countries, yet not of the people; not mingling with the confluent waters of Humanity, saving in the currents of trade and commerce, where they are pre-eminently successful in achieving the favors of Fortune, we are forcibly reminded of the intended curse of the enemies of ancient Israel, that the Almighty Father converted into a blessing. It is written that at the call of Balak, Balaam took up his parable and said, Balak, the King of Moab hath brought me from Aram, out of the mountains of the East, saying, Come, curse me, Jacob, and come, defy Israel. How shall I curse whom God hath not cursed? or how shall I defy whom the Lord hath not defied? For from the top of the rocks I see Him, and from the hills I behold Him. Lo! the people shall dwell alone, and shall not be reckoned among the nations. Who can count the dust of Jacob, and the number of the fourth part of Israel? And again at the call of Balak, Balaam took up his parable and said, Rise up, Balak, and hear? hearken unto me, thou son of Zipor : God is not a man that he should lie ; neither the son of man that he should repent : hath he said, and shall he not do it? or hath he spoken and shall he not make it good? Behold, I have received commandment to bless: and he hath blessed ; and I cannot reverse it. Surely there is no enchantment against Jacob, neither is there any divination against Israel.

And again Balaam lifted up his eyes, and he saw Israel abiding in tents according to their tribes ; and the Spirit of God came upon him ; and he took up his parable and said, Balaam, the son of Beor, hath said, and the man whose eyes are open hath said : he hath said which heard the words of God, which saw the vision of the Almighty, falling into a trance, but having his eyes open ; how goodly are thy tents, O Jacob, and thy tabernacles, O Israel ! As the valleys are they spread forth, as the gardens by the river's side, as the trees of lignaloes, which the Lord hath planted, and as cedar trees beside the waters. He shall pour the water out of his buckets, and his seed shall be in many waters. Blessed is he that blesseth thee.

And in these modern days, O, Israel, while standing by the altars of the Western world, sacred to the God of Heaven and of earth, and looking forth from the tops of the rocks and from the mountains of His holiness, beholding thy seed dwelling by many waters, yet not reckoned among the nations ; we take up also our parable :

> And like the Midianite of old,
> Who stood on Zophine Heaven controlled.
>   *   *   *   *
> Still overawed by high behest,
> We bless thee, and thou shalt be blest !

CHAPTER IV.

THE FIRST CHRISTIAN ERA—THE RELIGIOUS DISPENSATION OF LOVE
AND FREE-WILL TO MAN, OR SPECIAL REVELATION OF THE DI-
VINE MOTHER. THE YOUTH OF THE CHURCH AND WORLD, THE
HEROIC AND AFFECTIONAL AGE.

*Glory to God in the highest, and on earth peace, good will toward
man.*

It was the evening of the first day of the THIRD WEEK
OF AGES. The mystic hours were pregnant with mighty
events. Angel ministers were abroad in active preparation for
the swiftly approaching dawn of the New Era in the history of
man, the Youth of the Church and world, in which a higher
Evangel would be opened for the progressive human family, and
the millions of earth, baptized into their true, generic name—
Children of God.

And they whispered in the ears of mortals the wonderful tale
of a mighty Spiritual Prince that would shortly appear in Israel,
to *re*-establish the Kingdom of Heaven on earth ; and of a great
prophet who would come of the order of the Priesthood, to be
born of Elizabeth of the daughters of Aaron, who would go before the infant Prince of Israel, in the Spirit and power of Elias,
to herald the coming of the greater than he ; and that he should
be called the Prophet of the Highest, to prepare the way of the
Lord.

And the virgin Mary, of the house and lineage of David, was
saluted by the angel Gabriel as the appointed Mother of the
Prince of Peace. Hail, thou that art highly favored ; the Lord
is with thee ; blessed art thou among women. For thou hast

found favor with God. And, behold, thou shalt conceive, and bring forth a son, and shalt call his name JESUS. He shall be great, and shall be called the Son of the Highest, and the Lord God shall give unto him the throne of his father David ; and he shall reign over the house of Jacob forever ; and of his kingdom there shall be no end. The Holy Ghost (or Divine Mother) shall come upon thee, and the power of the Highest (or Divine Father) shall overshadow thee ; therefore, also, that holy thing which shall be born of thee shall be called the Son of God.

And Mary said, Behold the handmaid of the Lord ; be it unto me according to thy word. My soul doth magnify the Lord, and my spirit hath rejoiced in God my Savior. For He hath regarded the low estate of His handmaiden ; for, behold, from henceforth all generations shall call me blessed. For he that is mighty hath done to me great things ; and holy is His name. And His mercy is on them that fear him, from generation to generation. He hath shewed strength with His arm ; He hath scattered the proud in the imagination of their hearts. He hath put down the mighty from their seats, and exalted them of low degree. He hath filled the hungry with good things ; and the rich He hath sent empty away. He hath holpen his servant Israel, in remembrance of His mercy ; as He spake to our fathers to Abraham, and to his seed forever.

And the prophet John, who was the chosen of Heaven to inaugurate the first Christian Era in the Youth of the Church and world, appeared in fulness of time, in accordance with the revelation of the angels and of the seers of Israel. And he preached in the wilderness of Judea, in conformity with the prophecy of Esaias, the doctrine of remission of sins through repentance toward God. to congregated multitudes, attracted from afar by the fervor of his inspired eloquence ; and baptized believers in the waters of Jordan, declaring the while : I, indeed, baptize you with water unto repentance : but he that cometh after me is mightier than I, whose shoes I am not worthy to bear : he shall baptize you with the Holy Ghost (or the sacred truth of Divine Maternity) and with fire (or the penetrative power of Divine

Love) to work in the heart and mind of man ; to convict of sin, to purify the affections, and to infuse into the soul the spiritual life, warmth, light and joy of Heaven.

And, lo, at the appointed hour, the advent of the long expected Messiah was announced, by the angel of the Lord, to the humble shepherds of Bethlehem : Behold, I bring you glad tidings of great joy, which shall be to ALL PEOPLE. For unto you is born this day in the city of David a Savior, which is Christ the Lord. And the early dawn of the nativity of the Prince of Peace was ushered in with hallelujahs by a multitude of the heavenly host praising God, and saying, glory to God in the highest, and on earth peace, good will toward man.

The offspring of the Highest, he was born in the humblest earthly position ; because his mission was neither to wealth nor station ; but broadly, to humanity. The wise men of the East, guided by the light of his risen star, went to pay homage to the infant Redeemer, and to present unto him gifts—gold, frankincense and myrrh.

In his prescient childhood he sat in the Temple with the learned Doctors of Law, amazing them with the wonderful intelligence of his questions and answers. As he advanced in years he grew in favor with God and man ; while responding everywhere to the innermost thoughts of those around him ; for he could read the secrets of the human heart. He knew what was in man.

In his early youth, he passed through the fiery ordeal of temptation peculiar to his remarkable position among his people, which temptation appears to have been a needful preparation for a full understanding of his important mission. He was aware that the Children of Israel were looking for the appearance of a mighty king, who would relieve them from the irksome bondage of the Roman yoke, and were prepared to robe in imperial purple and crown the man who should present himself in their midst with delegated power from above to accomplish this desirable object. And in the ardor of early youth, moved by the patriotic love of his own peculiar people, and sharing with them the sentiment of indignant justice toward the foreign oppressor, it was natural that he should experience, for a brief space of time, a strong desire to exercise authority and temporal power, in order that he might effectively redress their wrongs.

But during the forty days and nights of fasting and trial in the wilderness, far removed from the people with whom he deeply sympathized, and from all the influences that stimulate worldly ambition, he weighed the value of human greatness against the incorruptible worth of immortal principles. For there, in the deep solitude of nature, alone on the, mountain heights with the Father and Mother God, he saw the true and elevated relations of the human family to Deity, comprehended the Divine Unity of all intelligence, and was fully inspired with the greatness of the mission to establish the Kingdom of Heaven on earth, in the hearts and minds of the sons and daughters of time ; to impress the world of man with truths indestructible as the soul— eternal as the Infinite Jehovah.

And crowned with the diadem of Heaven, and armed with the two-edged sword of the Spirit, tempered in the fire of heavenly Love, he went forth on his divine mission to combat the prejudices, errors and sins of ignorance in the world ; and to reveal to the members of the human family their true relations to the All-Parent as children, and to each other as brethren, and point out the obligations imposed on them by their high relations to the Divine Father and Mother God, and to the divine humanity. In Christ Jesus dwelt ALL THE FULLNESS OF THE GODHEAD. And we find in his character a subtle union of divine tenderness and strength ; a comprehensive knowledge of the conditions and requirements of humanity, combined with marvellous wisdom, to adapt his teachings and labors to the heart and understanding of man.

And we read that, in the spirit of his elevated mission, He went about doing good, while teaching by familiar illustrations the universal principles of God's moral government. He preached to assembled thousands in the grand Cathedral of Nature, with the winds and waves for his choristers, that rose and fell at his bidding. He fed the congregated multitudes of "common people," who heard Him gladly, with a few small

6

loaves and fishes, and there was always an abundant supply.
And he took upon himself the infirmities, sorrows and sins of
the people, healed their sick in body and mind, and sent them
on their way rejoicing.

The Spirit manifestations and power that announced the Master's
coming and final advent in the world, continued to attend
Him through his brief and marvellous career.   On his baptismal
day, when He went forth to John, in the beautiful spirit of humility,
to be immersed by him in the waters of Jordan, the
Spirit of God descended like a dove and lighted upon Him.
And a voice of unutterable tenderness fell in music from the
bending heavens, thrilling the hearts of the assembled thousands:
This is my beloved Son, in whom I am well pleased.   On the
Mount of Transfiguration, His disciples saw the Shining Ones
with whom He held high converse, and so real was the presence
that Peter exclaimed : Lord, let us make here three tabernacles,
one for thee, and one for Moses, and one for Elias.   And at the
close of His divine ministrations to humanity the vail of the
Temple was rent in twain by the trembling earth, which yielded
up her long imprisoned children, while the sun was darkened
in His meridian splendor.

> Sun! didst thou fly thy Maker's pain, or start
> At that enormous load of human guilt
> Which bowed His blessed head, o'erwhelm'd His cross.
> Made groan the centre, burst Earth's marble womb
> With pangs, strange pangs ! delivered of her dead ?

And, finally, when the morning of His resurrection dawned,
radiant angels rolled back the stone from the door of His sepulchre
and announced to His mourning friends the sublime truth
that He had risen from the grave.   And after He had burst the
bands of death and led captivity captive, He manifested Himself
to His disciples in His glorified form, to reassure them of the
truth of immortality, and to point out more clearly to their mental
vision the various prophecies recorded in the Sacred Word,
concerning his life, death and final resurrection.

Such is a brief statement of the Bible narrative of the Master.
But it conveys to the mind no adequate idea of the peculiarity

and greatness of his character, nor of the extent and fullness of his mission. And we propose, in a farther advanced chapter of our work, to review more critically the character of Christ and His teachings, and to show the twofold nature of His mission contained therein. And this twofold mission, which is foreshadowed in the New Testament, yet which has been but faintly perceived in the past, and, in consequence, but imperfectly comprehended, has, nevertheless, intimated to the Christian Church of all ages, two distinct advents of the Master on earth. The first advent was ultimated in the Natural ; the second is to be perfected in the Spiritual ; in correspondence with the twofold nature of man, and with the natural and spiritual significance of the Sacred Word.

In view of the peculiar unfolding of the Church of God on earth, in its correspondence to the order of development in the individual and in the race of man, we have passed naturally from its season of Childhood to its further progressed Youth. And we have, therefore, denominated the first Era of the Christian Dispensation of Love and Free-will to man, the Heroic and Affectional Age of the Church ; and propose to show, subsequently, that its eventful history of eighteen centuries justifies the denomination.

But, before entering upon these interesting topics, let us glance once more at the introduction of the Spiritual Adam of the Youth of the Human Family, and compare it with the presentation of the Natural Adam of the Infancy of the race, in order to note that the most sublime and important truth of Nature— THAT MAN IS THE CHILD OF DEITY—was more fully and strikingly revealed to the world at the advent of the second, than at that of the first Adam. And, to note farther, that the DUALITY OF THE GODHEAD was enunciated more clearly and forcibly at the latter than at the former period.

In the beginning God said, (to the Universal Mother,) Let *us* make man in *our* image, after *our* likeness. So God created man in his own image, in the image of God created he him ; male and female created he them. And the Lord God breathed into his nostrils the breath of life, and man became a living soul.

And the Natural Adam, of the Infancy of the Human Family, became the representative man of the early, physical, or experimental ages.

In the beginning of the early Youth of the world, it was ordained, in the wisdom of the Divine Councils, that the Human Family should be more fully indoctrinated in the radical truths of Nature. And they were to be instructed in their aspiring Youth by no partial medium, seer, or prophet, as Israel, Moses, or Elias, of the Childhood of the Church; but by the grand typeman Christ Jesus, of the vast progressive future. One in whom dwelt *all the fulness of the Godhead*, in order that he might have power to reveal to man and woman the divine mysteries of being, and show clearly their high origin and destiny; and one who was able to illustrate in his own character the possibilities of human growth and perfection through the unfolding, from age to age, of the intuitional or inspirational powers of the soul.

And the Angel Gabriel was sent from above to announce the advent of the Spiritual Adam to the Youth of the Church and world; and he made, in advance of the event, a concise yet comprehensive statement of the sublime principles to be taught by the coming Messiah—namely: THE DUALITY OF THE GODHEAD AND THE SPIRITUAL FAMILY TRINITY, in which are involved the relations of man and woman to Deity. Mark well, and consider, in the deep silence of thy soul, fellow traveller of earth, the graphic statement of these marvellous truths by Gabriel to the virgin Mary, who was the favored child of Heaven to receive the profound, elementary principles of Nature, and the honored medium of the Divine to illustrate them to the Human Family through her own experience. The Holy Ghost (or Divine Mother) shall come upon thee, and the power of the Highest (or Divine Father) shall overshadow thee : therefore, also, that holy thing which shall be born of thee shall be called the Son of God. And in Heaven's own appointed time and order of events, the GRAND MAN appeared on earth. And the Spiritual Adam of the heavens became the great representative man of the intellectual and moral, or intuitional ages.

And the Natural and Spiritual Adam of the two distinct and

remote periods of the world, represent also the twofold nature of every human being, one of which is of the earth, earthy and perishable ; the other, of the heavens, heavenly and imperishable. And this view of the subject is in accordance with the teachings of the great apostle of the Gentiles. He asserts that, as we have borne the image of the earthly, after the order of the Natural man, and return to dust ; even so also shall we bear the image of the heavenly, after the order of the Spiritual man, and return to the eternal source of our existence. And St. Paul farther declares that, as man and woman sustain the relations of Children to Deity, they become, as a natural and logical sequence of such relations, heirs of God and joint heirs with Christ.

And, in pursuing the comparison between the permanent and fundamental teachings of the old and new revelations, we observe that the Christian Church of love and free-will of the Youth of the World, like the Israelitish Church of law and authority of its Childhood, was re-established in the profoundest truth of Nature—the Sacred Family Trinity. The TRINITY of the early dispensation, as already shown in a preceding chapter, was manifested more particularly on the natural, or Adamic plane ; while that of the latter, was revealed on the higher Spiritual or Christian. And the statement of the angel of the Lord to the medium Mary, concerning the conception of Christ, is a lucid exposition of the truth of the DUAL GODHEAD, and of the SPIRITUAL FAMILY TRINITY ; and clearly teaches the high origin, destiny, or divinity of the human family, as Children of God. And the Holy Ghost, or Divine Mother, that took possession of Mary when the Son of God and Son of Man was conceived in her womb, must, ere long, represent to the reasoning mind of the Christian world the Universal and Divine Maternity, and the power of the Highest, or Divine Father, that overshadowed her, the Universal and Divine Paternity. And the medium Mary became thenceforward a practical teacher to all ages, of the doctrine of the SPIRITUAL FAMILY TRINITY ; as well as an exemplar of the wonderful truth, that woman, in her sacred office of maternity, represents the Universal and Divine Mother of the human family.

And thus we are taught by revelation, that there is accorded to each individual member of the human family, at the starting point of existence, a twofold conception, one in the Natural, and the other in the Spiritual ; and that, whenever and wherever the holy laws of procreation are evoked by human parents, the Divine Father and Mother God, in whom we live and move and have our being, are also present to impart the enduring elements of spiritual life to the offspring which is to bear their image and likeness. And every son or daughter of earth, while forming a close and tender triune relation with human parents, forms also with the Divine—THE ETERNAL SPIRITUAL FAMILY TRINITY—Father, Mother and Child.

And, in the coming ages, when this sublime and beautiful truth shall be clearly seen and accepted by the world, there will be no knowledge equally as precious, sustaining and elevating to the human soul. Child of Deity! whoever and wherever thou art, whether a favored one of fortune, dwelling in palatial halls, where many generations of noble ancestors look down protectingly and lovingly upon thee from stately marble and glowing canvass; or whether a lonely uncared for offspring of unhallowed passion, abiding within the dingy, ungarnished walls of narrow, gloomy alleys, and the poor pariah's by-places in the purlieus of strange, unfriendly cities, debase not thy elevated nature, and despair not, whatever may be thy condition. Remember, always, that thou, art of royal lineage—thou art son or daughter of the King of Kings ! And thou hast regal estates apportioned thee in the vast and glorious universe of God, exclusively thine own inheritance. But thou must make good thy claim and heirship, by a life of obedience to the divine laws of thy being, a life of noble use and love, and prove thyself worthy of thy heavenly origin and exalted destiny.

But, although the DUAL GODHEAD AND SPIRITUAL FAMILY TRINITY, were clearly revealed in both Religious Dispensations to Man, yet these fundamental truths of nature were neither seen by the Church of the Childhood of the World, nor comprehended by that of its Youth, in consequence of the partially developed character of the Teachers of both periods of unquestioning faith in authority, and in the traditions of the Fathers ; as well as by reason of the inability of the ignorant millions to perceive and understand spiritual principles, and the consequent lack of demand for higher light and guidance. And so it was impossible that the grand *rationale* of those profound doctrines, deep in the heart and mind of Deity, should have been presented to mankind in the past in such a form as could insure universal acceptance in the future, or in the maturity and Reasoning Age of the Church and World.

And because the Dual Godhead and Spiritual Family Trinity have not been recognized by the Church of the past, and neither, also, the Divine and Universal Maternity and Paternity, which are kindred truths, the Church has never believed and taught that each HUMAN FAMILY, with its Dual Head, represents the Divine—Human—Universal—Family of the Father and Mother God.

And, farther, for the reason that the Spiritual Family Trinity of the heavens has not been perceived, the relative Natural Family Trinity of the earth, which is also holy, being a pattern of the Divine Trinity, is not held, and has not been held, inviolable by the Organized Church, which is the moral conservative power of society, and, consequently, NOT by the outside world. And so we find that legalized and unlegailzed prostitution, in the forms of polygamy and wandering lust, have desecrated the Family Altars of both Israelite and Christian. And man and woman, the temples of the living God, have therefore been profaned ; and the *image* of Deity, as a consequent of this prostitution, has been deformed in reproduction ; and the *likeness* of the eternal Intelligence and the Eternal Love blurred in the Human Offspring.

But the Organized Church, during unnumbered generations, has held the *letter*, containing the Oracles of God, patiently in trust for the sons and daughters of time, even while not perceiving in its Childhood, nor understanding in its Youth, the true *spirit* of the formula. For these divine truths could not be seen and appreciated when the human mind was on the material plane of thought and action. And they awaited, of necessity, and must continue to await, the riper age and finer spiritual per-

ception of the Church and world.   For they can not be generally received until the Human Family shall become more developed and intuitional, until they shall possess more of the
mind that was in Christ Jesus, the great exemplar of the children of earth, as the high and holy representative of the Heavens.

In view of all the wonders of Divine Wisdom and Love, we
also rejoice in spirit with the glorified Nazarene, and thank
thee, O Father, Lord of heaven and earth, because Thou hast hid
these things from the wise and prudent of earth in their pride
of opinion and unregenerate selfhood, and hast revealed them
unto babes, who humbly, earnestly and lovingly sought to learn
in order to obey Thy law : even so, Father, for so it seemed good
in Thy sight.

We have stated, in the caption of the third and fourth Chap-
ters of this work, that the Israelitish Dispensation of Law and
Authority was a more special Revelation of the Divine Father to
the sons and daughters of time ; while that of the Christian, of
Love and Free Will, was a more special Revelation of the Divine Mother God to Man.   And in confirmation of the truth of
the propositions, we learn that the Organized Church of one Era
was distinguished by a *specific* masculine name ; and that of the
other, by a specific feminine name—the former being termed
Israel; the latter, the Bride, the Lamb's wife—while the true
generic name of the members of both has ever been—Children
of God.   And there are many other confirmations of the above
statement which will be seen in the progress of our argument.

If any inquire : Why was not the Christian Dispensation of
Love and Free-Will represented by a woman, even as the Israelitish Dispensation of Law and Authority was represented by a
man, if it be true that it is a more special Revelation of the Divine Mother to the Human Family?   We reply to the querist:
At the time of the first advent of the Master, society was on the
material and practical plane of action.   The masculine idea was
everywhere dominant in the civil and religious creeds of the
day; and consequently woman would not have been listened to
as a Teacher, much less as a Reformer, and could have made

no mark on the age. And for this reason the Divine Mother, yielding to the prejudices of her partially developed Children of Time, chose to manifest herself to them through a son of her love, rather than a daughter, as their minds were more receptive of instruction through Man than through Woman. But the baptism of the Holy Ghost and of fire has, thus far, been only intimated to the human family. It is yet to come in its fullness and power, and it can come alone through woman. The beautiful and perfect Christ-man went before and ameliorated for her the rough conditions of the course ; and, walking in his footprints, along the narrow way of life, she will ever find her yoke of submission to the Divine Law easy, and her burden of duty light.

It is a striking fact in the history of Christendom, that Mediæval Art caught the spirit of the special revelation of the Divine Mother to the Youth of the Church and world, and, true to this great truth of Nature, always represented Christ with the face of a woman. But it did not, and could not, in a partially developed age, recognize and portray in the Master ALL THE FULLNESS OF THE GODHEAD. For it is a logical necessity that a complete recognition of the grand God-man, the type of the intellectual and moral ages, should await the maturity of the world, when the faculties of man would be more fully unfolded, and heart and mind act in concert, God-like reason being the great guiding and controlling power of regenerated humanity.

In pursuing the comparison between the Israelitish and Christian dispensations, we are taught that the Church of the Youth of the world, like that of its Childhood, was re-established in the truth of revelation, and was introduced by decided and striking manifestations of Spirit presence and power. And we farther observe that the peculiar phenomena that attended both dispensations were of a kindred character, such as we should naturally expect to find from the intimate relations of the two, the latter Church being but the advanced growth, or youth, of the former. The Master's own words sustain our view of the relative position of the old and new dispensations. He declared to the listening multitudes : Think not that I am come to destroy the law or

7

the prophets ; I am not come to destroy, but to fulfill ; not come
to found another Church of God on earth, but to re-organize
that already established, and to vitalize it with higher regenerating truths, adapted to a broader and richer civilization.

And as all the types and shadows of the Old Testament, the
propitiatory offerings and sacrifices, were ultimated in the Advent
of Christ, the Lamb slain before the foundation of the world,
for, and by, the sins of the world, it follows of necessity that
they lost their significance and energizing power at his appearance on earth, and became merely historical symbols, or milestones by the way, of past centuries, to show how the ancient
Church travelled out of darkness into light ; and out of bondage into the glorious liberty of the Children of God.

And so it occurred that the Children of Israel, continuing to
cling to dead forms after the advent of the Messiah, became decayed branches of their own living and quickened religious tree,
and were needfully cut off for a season, as shown by the subtle,
yet clear and powerful reasoning of St. Paul to the Romans, in
order that the Gentile nations might be graffed in, and the principles of Christianity prevail over the earth.   In verity, the
favored people cut themselves off from experiencing the benefits
of the Christ's vitalizing and regenerating truths, by their rejection of his mission, because of their preconceived and erroneous ideas of the manner of his appearing, and also because
of their pride of opinion, petrified conservatisms, and coldness
to the spiritual truth in which their religion was founded.   For,
at the time of the Christ's appearance, like our modern religionists whose love has grown cold, the Israelites talked learnedly
of *former* Revelations and Inspirations in the Church ; but declared that such manifestations had passed away forever with the
age of miracles of the ancient fathers.   The upheaval of the
foundation of their faith by mightier Spirit forces than those of
old, showing that past and then present Spirit phenomena were
kindred, startled and shocked the Chief Priests and rulers of the
people ; but did not impress their minds with the important
truth that these marvellous manifestations attended the inauguration of a New Era in the Church of God, on a higher plane of

development.   And thus the peculiar people continued to bear the specific masculine apellative. Israel, after the Christ, the representative of the fullness of the Godhead, had been commissioned by the Universal Father and Mother to baptize them into their true generic name——Children of God.

But, after the accumulated light of eighteen centuries shall have revealed to them their true relation to the modern Church of God through the Messiah, they will fly to the open arms and heart of the Christian Church, as clouds and as doves to their windows, and be graffed into their own religious tree on Gentile branches.   And then will they share, also, in their turn, in harmony with the perfect and eternal law of compensation, the fruit of the spiritual growth and knowledge of the Gentiles.   For God is able to graff them in again.   O, the depth of the riches, both of the wisdom and knowledge of God ! how unsearchable are his judgments, and his ways past finding out !

Let us now view the Church of the first Christian Era in her heroic aspect, when she was filled with the ardor of youthful enterprise, and had a zeal for God, but not according to knowledge. When she bore the standard of the Cross in one hand, and the unsheathed sword in the other, and, thus armed with the emblem of universal brotherhood and the instrument of death, went forth to establish the kingdom of Heaven in heathen lands, and to *enforce* its religion of peace and good-will toward man.   When Constantine, in the Old World, and Cortez, on the soil of the New, rallied their legions round the banners of the cross, to go forth to conquer and destroy their fellow-beings, for the purpose of enlarging her borders, and extending her influence.   And when she poured out human blood with reckless prodigality, in the long and frightful wars of the Crusades of the eleventh century for the same object, and hundreds of thousands were slain.. And when, as late as the sixteenth century, she consented to the fearful massacre of St. Bartholomew, which filled the earth with dread and lamentation, and dyed her threshold so deeply and darkly with the blood of her purest and best worshippers, that all the waters of Jordan could not wash away the damning stain. And when, in the twelvth century, she established the terrible Inquisition in Christendom, (at a period in her history when her adherents began to enlarge in mind, through a more general diffusion of knowledge, and to outgrow the special formulæ of faith,) in order that she might the more effectually suppress liberty of thought on religious questions, and punish apostates from her prescribed forms of doctrine; at which time, it is estimated by historians, that upwards of one and a half millions of men and women were destroyed by the most cruel tortures, in the name of the Divine Redeemer, whose mission on earth was only —LOVE.

For many centuries, alas! her record was full of horrors. And do not the long and bloody struggles of the Church to establish the Christian Religion in heathen countries, and to punish heretics in Christendom, protestants against the restrictions and corruptions of her leaders, exhibit in a singularly striking manner the reckless daring and heroism of unreflecting Youth? And do they not forcibly illustrate the unreasoning character of the Church of the first Christian Era, in the Youth of the World? She did not, and could not, in her early undeveloped condition, see the monstrous inconsistency of seeking to promulgate a Religion of Love with the destructive enginery of war. No! she verily believed that she was doing God service in her sacrilegious work of destroying His children; and thereby increasing, instead of diminishing, the frightful sum of human suffering, crime and death. The Church knew and understood that the Author and exponent of the Christian faith had declared that the whole sum of moral obligations was included, broadly, in Love to God and Love to Man. And she accepted the letter of the truth from authority, by an effort of the will, and was eager to prove her earnestness and devotion to the doctrines she received, at the point of the glittering steel. She would manifest her faith in spiritual and unseen principles, by some startling physical achievement. And this is in accordance with the habit of the youthful mind. It is not disposed, and neither is able, to grapple with subtle moral questions and to comprehend and assimilate them; and for this reason, holds those which it receives on authority, and from the traditions of the Fathers, forcefully in the will, instead of calmly and strongly in the understanding. And, when these appear to be endangered, the believer is ready to fight for them on the low material plane ; but not to practice them on the higher moral and spiritual. And as the Church was in the externals of religion, and striving to hold intact the Letter of the Word, she was incapable of comprehending the sublime and elevating principles of the Gospel of Christ, and, consequently, of practicing its broad humanitary Spirit. For she had not entered upon her age of Reason and Philosophy, which looks everywhere for adequate results in the operation of principles, and requires consistency in profession and practice.

Let us now glance at the early Christian Church in her affectional character, remembering that Youth is eminently the season of the affections. Viewed in this aspect, how significantly she has been termed by the volume of inspiration, The Bride, the Lamb's Wife. And, certes, never has any religion so moved the *heart* of the world. From the earliest period of her history, the Christian Church has embraced large numbers of devotees of both sexes; but, in every age the larger proportion of her worshippers has been women; and, for the reason that they live more in the affections and sentiments than men, and are, consequently, more sensitive to lofty and ideal attractions.

And never before was as grand an object presented to the human heart and mind for unqualified love and admiration, as in the person of Christ, the Second Adam, the Lord from Heaven; who is represented to have taken, voluntarily, upon himself the nature of man, and the limited conditions of this rudimental sphere, its attending hardships and sorrows, in order that he might more closely sympathize with the great suffering heart of Humanity in all its temptations, trials and needs, and thus become a more efficient Redeemer;—who was the first grand Democratic Philosopher and Teacher of the World; the first to recognize the Divine in humanity, and to teach the holy unity of all intelligence, and the sacred brotherhood of man;—who burst the barriers of class and the chains of degrading despotism, and placed the poor, oppressed and despised

millions on an equality with Kings, as children of the Universal
Parent, and equal sharers of a common origin and destiny;—
who stood on a lofty moral elevation no other man had ever
attained and uplifted the whole human family to his own high
level, praying them to become *at-one* with him, *even* as he was
one with God ; commanding them everywhere to love as brethren ;—who came to earth to Take of the Father and show it unto
the world, that the world through Him might be saved from the
consequences of its ignorance, errors and sins; by a knowledge
of the true and high relations between man and man, and between
man and Deity ; to reveal clearly to the sons and daughters of
Time that the Almighty One that inhabiteth Eternity is not a
God of wrath and vengeance, but a tender, pitying parent ; Willing not that any should perish, but that all should come to a
knowledge of the truth ;—who came to bring life and immortality to light ; to bridge, with the beautiful bow of hope, the dark
river of death, whose unreturning tide had hurried the human
family for ages, shuddering, on to rayless oblivion ;—and who
submitted, finally, to painful crucifixion, and illustrated by his
own death the sublime fortitude of a soul whose anchor is cast
within the vail ; and by his glorious resurrection, the truth of
the immortality that he taught.   And thus he stamped the sig-
net of a deathless love upon the forehead of Humanity ; and
his precepts and example can never be forgotten ; immortal in
time, they will bear fruit for eternity.

No marvel that the heart of the world was touched by such a
wonderful exhibition of divine compassion and love, and that
there should have risen so many devotees and martyrs to a religion whose Founder was so self-abnegating and heroic.   Human
beings naturally emulate that which they admire.   And it was
comparatively easy for those who lived exalted, self-abnegating
lives, walking in the footprints of their noble exemplar, to yield,
cheerfully, their mortal frames to the fires of the stake and the
tortures of the rack, which were of momentary duration, in the
sublime faith that a brighter morning than Earth's would break
upon the gloom of the grave, and that they would be reunited
to their Divine Redeemer and Friend in nearer and dearer com-
panionship forever.

How wise appears the prescribed order of unfolding in the Church and world where we examine it in the light of Reason. At the period of the development of the affectional nature of man, the grand God-man was presented to the Human Family, in his glorious consecrated manhood, as one to love with all the soul, and to imitate in every act of the life. The moral and spiritual faculties were therely stimulated more powerfully than ever before, which tended to elevate the passional nature to the plane of the sentiments, and encourage the race to seek for worth and nobleness in love.

> Passion took wing and soared in purer air
> With lofty sentiment, serene and fair.

Thenceforward it became possible for the heart to be attracted by a high ideal object of moral beauty and perfection. And so human love was purified, through the Christ-Man, from the dross of sensuality, and uplifted to the Divine.

Reason, or pure intellect alone, is cold and calculating. It observes the relations of objects, or of intangible principles, and demostrates the results which will be gained by such relations, without reference to moral qualities. And so it was needful that the moral nature, which acts as Judge in the Supreme Court of Conscience, should be developed in advance of the intellectual, in order that there might be a deeply rooted love of right in the heart when the age of Reason should arrive, which would enable it to exercise its noble functions on an elevated plane, and thus produce the grandest results both in the physical and moral world.

In the early Youth of the Organized Church, as in her Childhood, the powers of Reason were but partially developed in the Human Family, saving in a small class of prescient minds that were inspired of Heaven to be the lights of the ages; and the ignorant millions continued to require the word of command, and support of Authority. But, as the World advanced toward maturity, Reason became more operative, and the most progressive minds of the Church began to resist, more and more, the leading strings of Youth, and to strive to shake themselves free from trammeling creeds that were unadapted to their larger growth of intellect. And, in the natural spirit of early, self-reliant manhood, that seeks to assert itself and to demand recognition of others, many scoffed at authority, refusing to recognize the ancient way-marks, and ridiculed and satirized the superstitions and falsities that had sprung up, as virulent weeds, in the garden of the Lord, until they became, at length, infidel to the truth of Revelation and to the spiritual inspirations of the human soul.

And thus, at the commencement of the reactionary period of the Christian Church, when the reasoning mind of the world slowly awoke from its long slumber during the physical ages, and strove to divest itself of crippling forms of religious faith, there was a direct tendency among the most liberal thinkers of the time, to absolute negation of spiritual principles. And the Age of *Reason* was inaugurated on the materialistic plane of demonstration. Several causes contributed to produce this result ; among the most prominent of which were—first, the natural law of mental unfolding, (of which we propose to treat more fully in a subsequent chapter,) as observed in the order of individual development, and in that of the Church, as a collective body, and in the whole human family, which shows that the early manifestations of reason, both in the individual and in the race of man, have always been on the material plane of demonstration.

A second cause was the materialistic tendency of the Heathen Philosophy of Ethics, which was partial in its character, and undeserving of the name of Philosophy. For while it admitted a future state of existence for man, it excluded woman, the other half of the human family, from the enjoyment of its privileges. And when the reasoning mind of the world became capable of broader generalizations, it rejected that portion of the partial and irrational theory of the ancient Philosophers which constituted sex a barrier to immortal life and blessedness, and, as a logical necessity, debarred the whole family of man, from a future state of existence beyond the boundary of time. But the rationalism of the present may be regarded as the culmination of Heathen Philosophy, notwithstanding the rejection of this peculiar feature of its teachings, because the system of morals involved therein were addressed to the *reason* of man at an age of the world when this noble power of the *mature mind* was undeveloped in the race, and man was, consequently, incapable of responding intelligently to its appeal. And this undeveloped condition of the popular mind rendered it needful that principles then demanding the exercise of ratiocination, or the higher metaphysical reasoning faculties, should await a farther progressed period of the human family, and challenge the understanding of the world's reasoning age. For ideas are living things, and can never be annihilated. And they were not designed by Heaven to enrich one mind, or one class of minds, or one nation, only, but UNIVERSAL MAN. Hence those that were sent forth on their mission of enlightenment in the early history of mankind, and imperfectly seen, because of the partially developed character of the millions of the crude physical ages, must be brought to the light of the world's riper years, by a law of their own order and use, in the vast laboratory of human intelligence, and tested in the crucible of Reason, in order that the dross of ignorance that adhered to them in the past may be consumed, and the genuine ores of truth shine forth in their own peculiar beauty and incomputable value.

Another cause of the tendency to Materialistic Rationalism, may be attributed to the peculiar or partial presentation of the Gospel of Christ to the popular mind. The people were taught by their professional guides that it was a Religion of the heart alone, and not of the understanding. And, hence, it was not permissible, by the ruling Priests and Doctors of Divinity, for the laity to exercise intelligent thought on subjects of religion. They were required to receive all such on authority, by an effort of the will, and an act of faith that questioned not the Oracle. And thus the *reasoning elements* of the human mind, through the progress of many generations, were cultivated apart from the *spiritual*, ay, divorced therefrom, being regarded as wholly distinct in character and action, and confined to secular subjects alone. Had the *understanding* of the millions of Christendom been stimulated instead of stultified, in the direction of spiritual principles, the World's grand Age of Reason would have been ushered in gloriously on the loftier plane of SPIRITUALISTIC RA-

8

TIONALISM.   But the perfect unity of the various faculties of the human soul, and their adaptation to the highest truths, were not seen, and, consequently, the divineness of all the powers of heart and mind could not be comprehended.   And thus the mental vision of the strongest intellects of the age was weak in the direction of spiritual principles, and when the day of Reason dawned it was unable to view clearly the complicated relations of the natural and spiritual, and adjust itself quickly to its broader and higher conditions.   It was dazzled by the glory of the awakening light that stimulated, but did not fully direct its newly aroused activities ; and partially blinded by traditionary prejudices and peculiar forms of selfhood.   Its observations were, necessarily, limited and imperfect ; and its conclusions, *ex necessitate*, partial and illogical.   And so the savans of the dawning day of humanity reasoned concerning the mighty currents of the illimitable Ocean of Truth, from the little waves that broke upon their own material shore of being.   And in their impatient haste to overturn the old order of Faith without Reason, and to introduce the new order of Rationalism without Faith, they rejected the whole of Revealed Religion as fabulous, unprofitable and even deleterious to the highest interests of society.   And they would leave no window of the soul unsealed that could open upon the glorious prospect of immortality.

Another prominent cause of the materialistic tendency of the age, was the abominable corruptions in the Christian Church, which were regarded by the partially awakened reasoning minds of that day as normal products of the Religious Body, instead of moral excrescences, disfiguring her symmetrical proportions. And they manifested decided opposition and disgust toward her doctrines and influence, and sought to blot out her existence forever.   They verily believed that she had culminated in false and evil principles, and must eventually pass away before the clearer light of Reason and Knowledge, like other forms of error, superstition and despotism.

Ay, because the BRIDE had stooped to earth, and soiled her beautiful robe of purity, and lost her former prestige, they believed that she would die, like a base worm of the dust, and pass into nameless oblivion.   They did not comprehend her Protean power, and could not see that it was *transition* from one period of growth to another, and not *death*, that had wrought the change. They discovered not her spiritual wings of faith and love within the decaying chrysalis of creeds, which would, sometime, be sustained in their heavenward soaring by all-powerful Reason, and would uplift her regenerate soul, clothed in the glorious coloring of its immortal beauty, to higher regions of thought, and light, and life, to fold themselves only in the presence of Infinite Majesty —Infinite Truth and Infinite Love.   They could not penetrate deeply enough into the councils of Infinite Intelligence to learn her true origin, character and destiny.   They did not see that the Organized Church had been but an unreflecting, reckless CHILD in Judaism, requiring authority, discipline and guidance ; and a heroic, impassioned YOUTH in Christianity, dependent still upon authority and strong determined leadership, and that her worship of the Deity had corresponded with her partial development, and been a blind devotion of the heart, unillumined by the understanding, which manifested itself in zeal for God, but not according to knowledge ; and that, in her conditions of unreflecting ignorance, she had not always rightly interpreted the Sacred Word, and had, consequently, inwrought much of error into her formulæ of doctrine, which must be cast aside in her progress towards maturity, and a Religion of the Reason, as well as of the sentiments and affections; and that, in this radical change from youth to maturity, she must, of necessity, do violence to much that was held sacred in her less enlightened age, must become her own iconoclast, and break and cast aside the cherished gods of gold and silver and iron and clay, together with the many falsities that inhered to her early conditions ; and that, in this process of change, vastation and renewal, the evils which were concealed in her early, quiescent state, must come to the surface and be seen, in order that they might be discarded ; and that, in appearing on the surface, they must attract attention and become palpable evils to those who had not before observed them, and naturally surprise and shock their moral sentiments; and, that they would continue to produce the same effect on the minds of earnest seekers after truth and purity, until the transition should be complete, and the Church should rise again in the renewed strength of her maturer years, and recommence the worship of the God of Heaven and Earth, with all the awakened *fullness* of her powers, uniting with the devotion of the renewed heart the commanding force of the reasoning mind, and become grander in high endeavor, and stronger for noble action.

France, the most sensitive of all the enlightened nations of Christendom, was the first to feel the impression of the approaching Age of Reason in the Church and World. That terrible episode in her history of the eighteenth century, was as decidedly a religious as a political Revolution. The enthusiastic and eloquent writings of Descartes, Bayle, Rousseau, Voltaire, and other gifted minds, which were directed against all forms of Civil and Ecclesiastic Despotisms, stimulated the popular mind to independent thought and hastened the crisis of ages. These radical and earnest thinkers viewed with the deepest disgust and abhorrence the false and irrational theories predicated of the teachings of Christ and his Apostles, and the peurile dogmas of an ambitious and licentious Ecclesiastic Power, which strove to exercise entire control over the Reason and Conscience of the Laity, to regulate their daily conduct, and to direct and guard their business interests for selfish purposes ; thereby circumscribing their sphere of action, limiting their means of usefulness, and dwarfing, instead of enlarging, their intellect and moral nature. And, in their burning indignation and vehement protest against the monstrous wrong to the human heart, mind and soul, they cried out impassionedly—" THERE IS NO GOD !" If there were, he would not permit such fearful crimes against humanity to be perpetrated under the sanction of "authority from Heaven." These zealous advocates of Human Rights had not learned from the Teachings of the Ages that He causeth the evils of the World to prove its most effective instructors, and leadeth the human family, through the severe disciplinary fires of purification, upward to loftier heights of intelligence and virtue. And France closed the Tabernacles of the Most High where the nature of Man had been profaned in the name of Religion.

But an anarchy followed this striking event in the history of the Church, more fearfully demoralizing than the abuse of power and misrule of a corrupt Ecclesiastic Body. And the exercise of the same reasoning power that, in its early awakening, induced the Liberal Minds of France to expunge the Church, because of the unworthiness of its Officers, led them, upon farther reflection, to consider what must be the calamitous consequences to society when the restraints of Religion, and the moral obligations which it imposes, are removed from an *igno-rant, and, therefore, non-selfgoverning populace,* and undisciplined passions are let loose to sweep over a nation with a more withering power than the breath of the deadly Siroceo. And France threw open, once more, the doors of the Tabernacles of the Most High ! and voted back Religious Worship on a purely rational basis—"As a necessity of the nature of Man."

But although France was the first to be strongly impressed and shaken by the influence of the advancing Age of Reason in the Church and World, other nations of Christendom were powerfully awakened by the stirring appeals of their foremost men, who were also inspired with its quickening spirit. Witness the writings of Pope, Hume, Gibbon and Paine of the British Isles. Pope's Essay on Man is a masterly product of Reason and Philosophy, that will remain an imperishable record of the progress of the human mind so long as man shall continue a citizen of Time. Turn also to Germany, and review the profound works of the great magnates of Philosophy who adorned that epoch, Leibnitz and Kant, together with their numerous and brilliant Satellites, that shone upon the age in constellated glory. And farther North, behold the luminous mind of Emanuel Swedenborg! that like the sun imparted warmth, as well as light, causing the cold and barren land of his nativity to become genial and rich in thought forevermore, borrowing brightness and beauty from his munificent nature and sharing his own immortality.

Exalted Genius, that for ages slept,
Unfolded her bright wings, once more on earth awoke,
And held in check the Sceptre and the Rod ;
   While embryo Art and Science sprang to birth ;
And great Philosophy, serene like God,
   Familiar converse held with sons of earth.

The Reformation of the Sixteenth Century was the early prelude to the glorious Anthem of the Reasoning Age of the World. It startled and electrified the nations of Christendom who had become torpid under the lethargic influence of the long, monotonous and painful solos of the ages of despotic rule—ages of faith in the Divine Rights of Kings, and diviner Rights of ambitious Popes and Prelates, who ignored the individuality and inherent Rights of Man, using the faith of the millions in their authority to hold them in most degrading ignorance, while requiring of them abject submission to their dictum. And in that stirring prelude to the Anthem of the Reasoning Age, in which epoch is involved a higher interpretation of the Christian Religion and understanding of the Rights of Man, the grand harmonic chords of Human Nature were touched, and they vibrated through the deep of being, awaking the latent powers of the soul, and kindling immortal aspirations. The ears of the Human Family were then attuned to other strains than those of Despotism. For, then, the key-note of Christian Democracy was sounded, once more, as in the days of the Master, and its clarion tone awakened the ME of Man, the self-respecting and self-directing forces of his nature. It stirred the Divinity within, which reveals the Royal Lineage of the Children of men, showing them to be Heirs of God, and joint heirs with Christ. Ay, the Reformation was a reassertion of the great principles of Christian Democracy, which may be simply yet comprehensively stated thus : God is the Universal Parent ; and all Mankind are brethren. And, hence, Man is the peer of Man, from the Poles to the Equator. Intelligence and Moral Power are the ruling principles on earth, as in heaven; and will, ere long, be recognized as Chiefs among men. And they who possess these in the fullest measure, who comprehend and practice broader and diviner principles of Right and Justice, are the only legitimate Kings and Priests unto God, and hold divinest Rights from Deity to represent the All-One to their fellow beings, and indoctrinate them in the great principles of his Moral Government. We do not wish to be understood to mean that Civil and Religious Organizations are to be subverted in the progress of society, in anywise; but that, (in the more perfect understanding of Christian Democracy in the coming ages, through increasing knowledge and enlightenment,) the millions will learn to choose wisely, for their rulers and representatives, the most intelligent and worthy members of the community; instead of the most *available*, in political parlance, as at this present.

The Reformation was, also, a strong reassertion of the great truth taught by the Master in the following remarkable text: The Sabbath was made for Man ; and not Man for the Sabbath. It was a recognition of the fact in human existence and experience, that man is everywhere superior to the creeds, both civil and religious, which he frames for the regulation of his conduct. On this eternal truth rests the might of the Protest Power of the Reformation. It underlies, also, the great principles of Human Progress, which declare to the World that the creeds of a barbarous people shall not be binding upon an enlightened one ; and that, as the Human Family shall outgrow, from age to age, their peculiar formulæ of faith, they shall cast them aside and reconstruct others better adapted to the requirements of farther advanced conditions.

The Protest Power of the Christian Church is of higher authority than Protestantism. It is derived from God himself. For it is the result of the increased activity of the reasoning faculties of mind, with which Heaven has endowed the Human Offspring, but which were partially latent during the Childhood and early Youth of the World, awaiting their advanced hour and prescribed order of unfolding. And, through the increased activity of these faculties, man saw more clearly his relations to the Divine, and to the Divine Humanity, and recognized and claimed his individual Right of Search, through the vast arcana of intelligent nature, for the governing principles of Human actions, independently of transmitted opinions enforced by authority. And the Protest Power was the result of a fuller recognition of the broad principles of equal and eternal justice, upon which all Institutions must rest, in order to be permanent in the maturity of the Human Race. And it will prove the salvation of the Chris-

tian Church.   Were there no Protest Power, there could be no
Christian Church extant, in the advanced Reasoning Age of the
World. Because the required exercise of unquestioning faith in the
truths of the Gospel of Christ, as imperfectly seen and taught by the
Church of the partially developed Youth of the World, admits
of no media of Reason, no adjustive measures, to meet the demands of progressive enlightenment.   And the result would be
an entire renunciation of Christianity by the more radical members of the Church, and a still firmer grasp of the doctrines of
the past by the more conservative, who, closing their eyes to the
increased light of the present, would fall back, for a limited
season, into the darkness of the religionists of the Middle Ages,
to be shaken, in their turn, from their stronghold of faith by a
mightier force of advancing Reason and Intelligence.   The
Protest Power acts as a safe conductor, relieving the Christian
Body when it becomes too highly charged with the electric force
of new ideas, thereby protecting it from destructive ruptures
and disorgainzations.   In the beginning the Protest Power was
a result of awakening Reason ; it became, at length, her strong
ally for efficient action on the moral battle-field.   It became,
in verity, the Advanced Guard of Truth, for removing the
barriers of prejudice, superstition and all ancient errors of
ignorance, and preparing a broad highway before the Grand
Army of the KING of Kings.

The required exercise of unquestioning faith in the doctrines
of the Gospel, as taught by the Church of the past, had the
tendency, and still has, to prevent Believers from coming into
close, sympathetic relations with their own time, its peculiar conditions and needs.   It separates them from the actual, every-day
experiences of the Christian life.   And they are unable to perceive the growth of the Christ-power in the world around
them ; be cause they live either in the past or future, and cannot, therefore, exercise reason on the spiritual things of the
present, and perceive the broad relations of spiritual principles
of all ages.   And, consequently, while they profess to believe
in an ever present Deity, in whom we live and move and have
our being, they are startled and shocked at every manifestation

of His power. And, wrapped in their mantle of blind, unreasoning faith, they worship God in the abstract, unconnected with practical life and the dear Humanity—He loves. And, thus vailed from present manifestations of spiritual principles, they assume in their blindness that the days of Apostolic power have passed away forever. They deny, pointedly, nay, angrily, that there can be any manifestation of the Spirit in these later days ; and deny this truth, too, in presence of the Master's positive assertion to the contrary, in his parting exhortation to his disciples : Go ye into all the world, and preach the Gospel to every creature. And these signs shall follow them that believe. In my name shall they cast out devils ; they shall speak with new tongues ; they shall take up serpents ; and if they drink any deadly thing, it shall not hurt them ; they shall lay hands on the sick, and they shall recover. And, lo, I am with you alway, even unto the end of the world. And greater works than these which I have done, shall ye do, and because I go to the Father. Because, as the children of men shall advance in knowledge and wisdom, and the understanding of spiritual truths, they will be prepared for grander manifestations of Almighty Power.

The rational thinking man and woman demand, everywhere, a REASON for the exercise of faith, and cannot be satisfied without. And, because, they are so constituted by the Supreme Author of existence, the source of pure Spirit, and Reason. And reasoning minds must be assured, in their search after truth, in any direction of material and spiritual nature, that they perceive the relations of cause and effect, and recognize law; then they repose confidently in the present, and look forward with renewed faith from their firm stand-point, in immutable truth, for yet grander results in the future. And reasoning Christians are willing, from what they have already learned of God's Righteous Government, and its relations to universal man, to trust him for all ages and all conditions of the human race. They believed, from the exercise of reason, that the Christian religion is the purest and highest form of Democracy, that it is a simple statement of the primary truths of Intelligent Nature, in which are involved all moral obligations—the relations of man to man,

9

and of man to Deity.   They believe, from the exercise of reason, that it proceeds forth from Eternal Truth, even as the fountain springs from its mysterious source.   We know not where it conceals its crystal treasures, or to what secret reservoir of nature it bears its overflowing fullness ; but we perceive the beauty of the light shining through its pure falling spray, and experience in our souls the benediction of its healing waters. And the individual Christian, and the denomination of the Christian Church, whose faith is sustained by active Reason. rest on Infinite Intelligence, and cannot be shaken from their stronghold by the upheaval of any form of religion, or of government ; for their faith is immovable and indestructible, like the Eternal Truth on which it reposes.   The Church is beginning to feel strongly the influence of the Reasoning Age, and will be able, ere long, to render a reason for the faith that is in her, in accordance with the earnest recommendation of St. Paul—the profoundest reasoner of all the ages—and with the great underlying principles of human progress.

In view of all the blindness and inconsistency of the finest reasoning minds of the past, it must not be forgotten that reason is of slow growth, and also of late development in the individual human being, and, consequently, in the Organized Church and in the whole family of Man, which unfold in the same prescribed order.   And it should be remembered, also, that the knowledges which enlighten society and rectify its fearful evils are gained through the thorny experiences of many generations.   All love and honor are due to the noble heroes and martyrs of the truth in the Childhood and Youth of the Church and World.   They were men and women, born out of due time, with reasoning minds far in advance of the unreflecting millions around them. *They could die for principles* that were as clear to their mental and moral vision as the noonday sun is to the natural eye, *but they could not renounce them ! !*

And yet, it is saddening to reflect that this lovely earth has been converted into a fearful Golgotha at every advancing step of the millions towards Light and Liberty in Religions and Governments.   It is painful to know that the standard-bearers of

Heaven's own truth and love, have been cut off in the midst of their years by stringent adherents of crippling *forms* of Religious faith, and by stern conservators of every kind of Despotism. But the elevating truths of Christian Democracy that stimulate the love of Universal Liberty, and the Brotherhood of Man, were, and are, and ever will be, an ever-present —God with us ! ! Men die ; but principles live. And it is encouraging to learn from the history of the past that, although so many of the noblest of our race have fallen in the great cause of Human Progress, the principles for whtch they died perished not like their mortal part ; but rose with their ransomed spirits in living power and beauty from the tomb, because they were also immortal ;— and that these valuable truths, like healthy, vigorous plants, nurtured from period to period by the precious blood of our glorious Martyrs, took deeper and deeper root in the hearts and minds of the millions, growing stronger and grander with the ages ;— and that the Church and World have been made purer and better by the sacrificial offerings of those devoted sons and daughters of God that were laid voluntarily upon the crimson altar of Humanity.

At the termination of the first Christian Era, or of the Youthful period of the Church, its Heroic and Affectional Age, as at the close of its Seasons of Childhood and Infancy, a transitionary period was a natural and inevitable result of progress. And a season of transition, and, consequently, of apparent retrogression, will continue to mark each advancing age, or epoch, in the history of the human race. But the passage from Youth to Maturity is more strongly marked in the life of the individual Man than that of any previous change, because there is a stronger intellectual power awakened, and a clearer perception in the mind of human and Divine relations, and of the obligations which these impose ; and the responsibilities of practical life press more heavily on the soul, and a mightier effort is put forth to bear and to lighten life's burthens. Even so the transitionary period of the Church and world, forward from Youth to Maturity, or to the Reasoning Age, is more important and eventful than any preceding one in the history of the human race, because of the greater acquisition and diffusion of knowledge, the wider diversity of material interests, and the broader views of humanitary principles involved therein.   This transitionary state of Society towards a higher condition, while there is everywhere seeming retrogression, may be aptly illustrated by the experiences of the traveler of a day.   The more rapidly he advances towards a given point in his journey, the more swiftly every object in the distance appears to be moving in an opposite direction.   And, because of this transition and seeming retrogression, many superficial observers of the signs of the times have taken alarm.   They fear that the tendency of Society is backward and downward, towards endless perdition. They have lost confidence in God and Man.   And they are terrified to find themselves borne along the irresistible current of events—"While hell beneath is gaping wide"—and all the horrors of a traditionary future crowd about their fearful Tartarus. Let them look upward, instead of downward, and take courage, while striving to live in accordance wirh their highest ideas of Right ; for then they will behold angels, and not demons, and will feel assured that God is still over all, blessed forevermore ; and that he is the great Positive Good and Guiding Power of the Universe, and of His Kingdom there will be no end.

It has long appeared to the weak faith of doubting Christians that the Spiritual Life of the Church is passing entirely away, so faint have been its manifestations.   But, while they have been mourning over the retreating footsteps of the angels, beneficent Heaven, ever attentive to the conditions and needs of the children of Earth, has been marshalling a mightier army of witnesses to send forth on a grander mission to humanity, to herald the Second Advent of the Messiah to the Reasoning Age of the Church and World.

CHAPTER V.

*Who is this that cometh from Edom, with dyed garments from
Bozrah ? this that is glorious in his apparel, traveling in the greatness of his strength ?*

I that speak in righteousness, mighty to save.

It was the evening of the first day of the Fourth Week of Ages.
France had put out the lights within her dedicated fanes, and
barred the people from their consecrated altars. It was the
grand crisis of the centuries ! And there was a pause in Heaven
about the space of half an hour. Then the seal of a New Christian Era was broken, in accordance with the fiat of Divine Wisdom and Love, and the Second Mission and Advent of the Messiah announced to earth by the rejoicing angels. The Church
Militant responded to the call of the Church Triumphant.
France threw open once more the doors of her consecrated
temples, that no man can shut, and invited the waiting millions
to return to their allegiance to Heaven. And thus was the coming in of the New Christian Era as signally defined as the going out of the Old.

It is worthy of particular attention, as marking the order or
system of the Divine Government, that, at the introduction of
the New Era of Reason in the Church and world, the worship
of God was re-established on a purely rational basis, as a " NE-
CESSITY OF THE NATURE OF MAN." And it is also deserving of
note that France, " The Poet of the Nations," should have been
the chosen seat of the reaction from the *unquestioning faith in au-*

thority of the Childhood and early Youth of the Church, to the *questioning religion* of the future, of the maturer age of Rational Conviction.   For it would not have been possible to have produced so wonderful a change in thought in any other country of Christendom, at that period of time, as that which was effected in volatile, erratic, and yet, philosophic France, of whom Mrs. Browning writes, in her inimitable style :

> " I am strong to love this noble France,
> This poet of the Nations, who dreams on,
> And wails on, (while the household goes to wreck,)
> For ever, after some ideal good,—
> Some equal poise of sex, some unvowed love
> Inviolate, some spontaneous brotherhood,
> Some wealth, that leaves none poor and finds none tired,
> Some freedom of the many that respects
> The wisdom of the few."

In turning over the pages of History, we learn from the teachings of the Ages, that all significant events recorded there were strongly marked by subsequent preparation commensurate with their importance.   And we are instructed that all radical changes that have taken place in the moral and religious world were inaugurated by inspired persons, who themselves believed that they received their commission from above, and who possessed the unconquerable will to do, and courage to dare, and the kindling enthusiasm that awakened the electric spark of Divinity in other souls and drew them along their heroic course by an irresistible attraction.   And such persons have always proved equal to the great occasions which called their powers into action.

And it is interesting to observe that, a short time before the commencement of the reactionary period of the Church, Emanuel Swedenborg stood grandly forth in a northern land, remote fram France, the colossal John the Baptist of the New Era, empowered from on High to bestow on the Church the Baptism of Reason, and of Science that enlightens, in order to prepare the minds of her worshippers for the reception of new and higher interpretations of the Gospel, and also for the Second Coming, in all the power and glory of God-like Reason, of the Greater than he.

In view of the peculiar mission of Swedenborg, as the inaugurator of the Second Christian Era, it is a remarkable fact, that, previous to his birth, his parents were so strongly impressed to call him Emanuel (which, being interpreted, is God with us,) that they were unwilling to confer on him any other name. His biographers represent him as a man of fine physical proportions, with an intellectual and moral nature of the highest order. He ranked with the profoundest savans of his age ; and was an earnest and devout student of Nature. Indeed, no mind of that day could compare with his own in scope and fullness of power. His intellet combined the rare endowments of inductive and deductive reasoning qualities. which are alone the birthright of Genius. The minds of most persons are limited to either the former, or latter, process of argument ; his logical intellect took the lead in both methods, because he observed facts from two planes of existence, the natural and spiritual ; and could trace the complicated relations of these broad principles, whether ascending link by linkin the chain of sequence; or descending from the height of the great argument in sweeping generalities to the world of effects. He is farther represented as being a man of pure heart and simple life, and endowed with a strong love of use that stimulated him to persevering labor for the benefit of mankind.

Swedenborg wrote several valuable scientific works in the early part of life, and a variety, in his prime, on Medicine, Mathematics, Finance, and the principles of Government, throwing light from his illumined pen on every subject that he elaborated. At the advanced age of fifty-seven he began his religious writings, through which he has been widely known in the world, and completed seventy-five volumes before his departure. The Seer informs us that, while he remained an inhabitant of this rudimental Sphere, he was often permitted by the Lord to visit in spirit the higher planes of life in the heavens, for the purpose of learning the operations of principles there, as well as in the material world, in order that he might be able to unfold more clearly to man the conditions and requirements of the life beyond the grave, and aid him in advancing the preparation here for the great hereafter of the soul.

Many persons have objected to the teachings of Swedenborg on the plea that he attempted to disclose more concerning the Spiritual world than Christ himself. But it should be borne in mind by this class of objectors, that the first advent of the Master was in the Youth of the Church, and that he adapted his instruction to the understanding and requirements of that age. And it should not be forgotten that his special mission was, to bring life and immortality to light, and to show the true relations of the various members of the human family to the All-Parent as children, and to each other as brethren, and the consequent obligations of such relations, in order that he might establish on earth the Fraternal Society of the heavens. And he intended that these sublime truths, which reveal the unity and eternity of all intelligence, created and uncreated, should shine forth in the world with the defined clearness of the noonday sun, in order that the light of conviction might radiate through the human soul with a power and glory as inextinguishable as the splendor of its meridian beams. It was the marked policy of Christ to speak in generalities of the other state of existence. And we recognize in this, as in all his methodic teachings, the wisdom that cometh from above. Had he attempted to portray all of the peculiar features of the life beyond, it would have diverted the popular mind from the great essential truths which he taught, and thereby, of necessity, weakened their force. And the complexity of the subjects presented would have confused also the mind of that age, which required simple and direct teaching. And in addition to this view of the subject, there is yet a weightier reason for the reticence of the Master concerning the conditions of the hereafter ; the Church was not in a state of development adapted to the understanding of such Spiritual Knowledges ; and so they were reserved for her Reasoning Age, after she should have attained the spiritual growth of eighteen centuries of preparation, to enlarge her experiences and receptive powers.

Swedenborg was commissioned of Heaven, in anticipation of the Second Advent of Christ, to reveal *special truths* concerning the higher life, in order to prepare the way, not only for the coming of the Master on a more elevated plane of intelligence ; but, also, for the more wonderful spirit-phenomena that would attend that important event. And his writings are calculated to infuse a subtler spiritual perception into the mind of the age, to turn it in the direction of coming events, and to kindle in the soul of man an unquenchable thirst after knowledge.

Swedenborg's "True Christian Religion," and commentaries on the received doctrines of the Church, are clear, forcible and convincing, as well as energizing to the mind. He exhibits, in an earnest and masterly style, the miserable inconsistency of professing faith in Christ, and practicing at the same time the principles of Satan, declaring, with an inspired apostle of the first Christian Era, that faith without works is dead ; that a professed follower of the Master, who does not manifest his spirit, is none of his. And he teaches, also, that the ordinances of the Church do not of themselves, possess saving grace; that can come alone through loving obedience to the requirements of the Gospel, exhibited in corresponding works. The fruits of the Spirit are love, joy, peace, long suffering, gentleness, patience and charity.

And Swedenborg exhorts the Church to exercise Reason as well as Faith in her religion. He charges her members to acquire a knowledge of the Creator through his works, declaring that the truths of science are an ever-present God, upholding and directing all of matter and of spirit. He broadly states that a knowledge of science is indispensable to a proper understanding of spiritual and religious truths, and their full acceptance by intelligent human beings. Man must become acquainted with the laws of matter and mind, and his relations to these laws, before he can yield perfect obedience to the Divine requirements. And they are, in the truest and highest sense, the Children of God who *know*, and *obey;* who study the inspired Book of Nature in connection with that of Revelation.

We have classed Swedenborg with the order of Genius. But the general acceptation of that term does not fully express the rare and peculiar qualities of his nature. He was a Spiritual and Intuitional—Intellectual man, after the type of the Master. His Religion was a consecration of knowledge to high moral

10

uses, an enlightened union of the heart and brain. It was, in verity, a dedication of the whole being to the service of the Divine.   The elevated principles of Christianity culminated in his character.   And he stands before the world as the exemplar of its sublime truths, and the representative man of the highest knowledge and wisdom of the past, as well as the inspired prophet of the future.   His luminous mind shines out from the clouded mental and moral atmosphere of his day in beautiful and majestic proportions.   We can point to no other Son of earth as strikingly adapted as he to the great mission to which he was called——to Inaugurate the Christian Era of Reason.   And his fitness will appear the more remarkable when we shall review the character of Christ in the light of the Nineteenth Century.

A large class of intelligent persons in various parts of the United States of North America have been attracted to the writings of Swedenborg, and have formed themselves into New Church Societies, for the purpose of living more Spiritual and useful lives, and teaching and circulating his comprehensive views of the Christian Religion.   And these Societies are increasing in numbers yearly, and enlarging, as the people read and investigate the principles discussed in his religious works, which principles we propose to state more fully in a subsequent chapter.

In turning over the leaves of history, it is deeply interesting to learn that, a short time previous to the close of the first Christian Era, the New World was opened· in the wisdom of the Divine Councils for the introduction of the renewed Church of the Era of Reason.   It was a needful preparation for the great work of regenerating the Church.   Because the civilizations of the Old World, with their Hereditary Rights, Traditionary Religions, and deeply rooted Conventionalisms were altogether unfavorable to the reception of progressive ideas, and would not admit of a higher interpretation of the Master's Gospel of peace and good will to Man.   Reason was everywhere subservient to Authority. And the teachings based on authority, and received by the millions with unquestioning faith, controlled the popular mind with a power so absolute that the introduction of New Ideas implied Revolution, with all the attending horrors of its sanguinary wars.

It is one of the most remarkable features in the settlement of North America, viewed from this point of observation, that it was colonized by men and women of earnest religious character, who fled from persecution in Father-land, leaving the comforts of home, and the refinements of old forms of civilization, to come to a wilderness of uncultivated Nature, inhabited by rude, untutored races of man, and beasts of prey, for the sacred purpose of worshipping God in accordance with the dictates of conscience.

> Uplift the curtain Time hath dropp'd between
> The past and present. Lo ! a far-off scene,
> Where Winter reigns supreme in Northern skies,
> Alike some stately bird the Mayflower lies,
> With folded wings on Narraganset bay,
> While round her prow the crested billows play.
> The noble "Pilgrims" rise in view once more—
> A glorious group ! on dear New England's shore.
> Behold them stand on Plymouth's hallow'd ground,
> The great Republic of the World to found!
> Eventful morn, our country's natal hour !
> From whence she rose to numbers, wealth and power.
> Heroic Souls! WE treasure each proud name –
> But ye are FREEDOM'S!—all the World's in fame!—
> The princely few who fear no Tyrant's rod—
> For, ah! ye walk by faith sublime with God.

THEN the ancient Coventionalisms of aristocratic society were weakened, the strong bands of Traditionary Religion were loosed, and the iron rod of Despotism was broken. Verily, it was a grand preparation for the introduction of the noble Reasoning Age of the Church of God. Our "Pilgrim Fathers" were the representatives of the advanced political, as well as religious ideas of their time. And they stood forth in the New World on a broader and freer plane of thought and action, to attract to our Western Eden the most enlightened and liberty-loving minds of all Nations.

It appears to have been the intention of Heaven that the Church of the Reasoning Age should be thoroughly radical and strike deep root in virgin soil ; and that the country in which she should be established as the Executive Power of the Moral World, of God's Spiritual Kingdom on earth, should grow up from the first principles of development in National Life, and unfold and strengthen through severe struggles with a tyrannical government abroad ; and severer contests with savage foes, obdurate nature, and hard conditions at home ; while it should pass rapidly through the various stages of the social, civil, and religious life of the past, on to the culminating glory of civilization—a pure Democracy, leavened with the Spirit of Christianity ; which is the natural and logical product of a pure Christian Church.   And such is the true " levelling-up Democracy " that " makes *gentle*-men of all " classes of citizens.   The principles of Christian Democracy rest upon the bed-rock of human nature; they are innate in the soul of universal Man, and hence their adaptation to the comprehension and requirements of the millions of earth.   They embody the very essence of Divine Justice, of Liberty and Equality for all of God's children, male and female.   And hence Christianity has never thrived, and never can thrive, for a long period of time, under any form of Despotism, either Civil or Ecclesiastic.   When its informing, and reforming, Spirit has no longer power to model the government of a people through the subtle influences of a broad humanitary life and love, which acts from heart to brain, from the centre to the circumference of society, to enliven, purify and elevate ; THEN the Religious Body will grow cold and petrify in its external forms, and the ever-living Spirit will pass on to quicken another branch of the representative Church, in another country, or another age more propitious to the reception and exposition of its universal principles.   Such is the philosophical and, consequently, inevitable result ; because the *highest* is ever the controlling principle in the Divine order of progress, and must obtain on earth, even as it does in heaven. God's Government being over all, and tending everywhere, through the widest diversity of parts, towards the most perfect unity or harmony. The Spirit of Love and Spirit of Despotism are altogether antagonistic in character, and can never combine in action and direct, conjoinlty, either the individual being or Society.   One must give place to the other.

Christianity is radical in its tendency.   It strikes deep root in the heart of man and sends up vigorous branches through his intellectual and moral nature, which put forth evergreen leaves and fragrant blossoms, until the human plant is symbolized at length by the perfect tree that towers in symmetrical beauty towards heaven. And by its FRUIT ye may know of the Doctrine. Despotism is superficial in its nature and action, and is not homogeneous to man. It is a parasitic plant that fastens itself on the trunk and branches of either the political or religious body of Society, and puts forth, also, leaves and blossoms fair to view, in in the early stages of its growth, that conceal the many serpentine coils with which it slowly but surely binds and dwarfs the whole noble structure of society, from whose vital sources it draws its nourishment, until the nation becomes weakened, loses its power of resistance, and finally falls an easy prey to the unscrupulous despoiler. And, by its fearful wrongs against humanity, ye may know likewise of its principles.

And Christian Democracy is universal in its adaptive power, because it includes the whole scale of human progress, from the lowest note of the gamut to the highest of the ascending series, which reaches upward to infinite and divine perfection. And it may be regarded as the *ultimatum* of earthly governments, because its principles are of universal application, adapted to all times and all conditions of the various races of Man. Universal principles are permanent. And Christian Democracy is the grand resultant of all past religions and governments under heaven, from the Childhood of the Church and World forward to the reasoning maturity. And, being thus, it is essentiully all-including—as the whole contains the sum of all its parts. And because it is all-including it must necessarily present, in the early stages of its progress, many of the peculiar and striking features of old forms of civilization;—and for the reason, also, that the millions are yet but partially and unequally developed; and, hence, large numbers continue to be attracted to past restrictive forms of religion and government. And we find, consequently, many of the worst institutions of old systems of Despotism, both civil and religious, that existed in the Childhood and Youth of the Church and World, the ages of unreflecting ignorance and moral darkness, still sending up virulent shoots from their yet but partially decayed roots of evil. And this is the philosophic reason for the existence of Slavery* and Polygamy in our noble Republic. They are not component parts of either our religious or political creeds, but, as we have already stated, shoots from the yet but partially decayed roots of former civilizations. And they must flourish for a brief season, during the early part of the New Era, or its transitionary period ; for this is favorable to every kind of growth, to strong and decided manifestations of both good and evil.

It often appears to impatient, doubting Christians that, because judgment against an evil work is not speedily executed, therefore the hearts of the children of men are fully set in them to do evil, and that there is but little hope of the final triumph of Truth and Right over Error and Wrong. And, as they look abroad over the earth and observe the existing evils of Society, they declare that the world is growing worse, instead of better, with advancing intelligence. For the films of fear and unbelief cloud their vision. They do not pause to reflect that it is the ever-increasing light which reveals, and will eventually disperse the darkness. They are not careful to compare the present age with past cycles of time, extending back to the infancy of the human race, and to note the peculiar characteristics of each successive century, and its condition of morals, and when the full sums of evil and of human progress are stated, to strike the balance, which will tell immeasurably in favor of our own age. Were they willing to investigate the past and present conditions of Society carefully and patiently, THEN they would realize how deep and wide and high are the humanitary interests and moral tendencies of to-day over those of every other epoch in the history of Man. Indeed, the aggregated amount of all the good of all the previous ages will scarcely approximate the sum of the progressed nineteenth Century. For is it not written, The last shall be first, and the first last ? Each succeeding generation of Man inherits the experiences and knowledges of the millions which have preceded

---

* At the time that the " Teachings of the Ages " was written, Slavery was not abolished in the United States.

it in their prescribed order, and must, inevitably, take one step forward and upward toward the elevated goal of humanity. Ah! they forget the while WHO is the Supreme Ruler of the Universe—that He who created all things by the word of his power, still upholds all in wisdom and love. They do not consider that GOOD is a positive and controlling principle in His world; while EVIL is but the result of unreflecting ignorance, which will pass away before the meridian day of Knowledge, and the sway of enlightened Reason, in the full maturity of the Church and World. For enlightened Reason is the great ADJUSTIVE POWER on the material and on the moral planes of action.

He who spake and it was done, who commanded and it stood fast, could have created man at the beginning incapable of wrongdoing. But it was not consistent with his wise design. He did not intend to speak a race of human automatons into existence, for such would not have been in the Father's image, and after his likeness. But he purposely evoked a race of beings, endowed with intelligence, kindred with his own, differing only in degree, in order that they might be capable of understanding,' of obeying, and of loving his laws; of choosing the good and rejecting the evil; of individualizing themselves in truth, that truth might endow them with the freedom of the Universe. Ay, we are created to work out our own salvation from ignorance and its consequent sins, while the Divine Spirit worketh in us, and by us, to will and to do of His own good pleasure.

It was needful for the highest good of society that the worst evils which existed in the Childhood and Youth of the Church and World, and outlived those experimented ages, should again appear in the light of man's reasoning maturity and clearer moral perceptions, in order that their enormities might be more strongly marked and deeply felt, and awaken in the human soul a burning indignation that would not be appeased, until every form of Despotism should be swept from off the face of the whole earth. We have laid the axe at the root of the Upas tree of slavery:—Shall Polygamy likewise perish by the sword ? Its destruction is also inevitable.

These two forms of slavery that belong to the Adamic ages of ignorance and of physical rule, when might was the test of right, the slavery of labor, and the bondage of the affections, were essentially weakened by the coming of Christ, the spiritual Adam, in accordance with the words of prophecy.   For even in the darkness of those physical ages. (when man was condemned through the sin of ignorance to eat bread by the sweat of his brow, and woman to be subject to her husband through *blind affections*,) it was declared, in order to stimulate the hope of many generations, that, in the *fullness of time*, THE SEED OF THE WOMAN *should bruise the serpent's head;* that man should be redeemed from ignorant, servile toil, and woman from the degrading servitude of animal passions, through the new and quickening life and light that should be revealed to the world, by the grand type-man of the intellectual and moral ages.

This promise, which had but a partial fulfillment in the Youth of the Church, will be gloriously realized in its reasoning maturity.   Already there is an accelerated movement in society toward higher humanitary conditions.   The prevailing faith in Christendom that the Second Advent of the Master is near— that the glorified Nazarine is, even now, knocking at the door of the Century for admission to the Reasoning Mind, as well as loving heart, of his followers—awakens among believers a new interest in his Gospel of Peace and goodwill to Man ; and there is, consequently, a broader and clearer perception of its high principles.   Lo! another tidal wave is already surging from the deep ocean of Truth, gathering up its forces and drawing to itself the lighter billows of successive periods of progressive movement, while it is impelled onward by a mighty, yet unseen, Spiritual Power, missioned to sweep over the whole face of the habitable globe, and rebaptize the Nations.

The Christian Religion is stimulating to the Soul of Man, because it is adapted to the requirements of his progressive nature. It awakens hope, and kindles aspiration, which act as powerful incentives to both intellectual and moral culture.   It leads human beings away from their present surroundings into fresh paths of investigation and action.   Hence, we find that Christian Nations are in advance of others in noble, humanitary deeds ; and

in the broad fields of natural and of speculative philosophy, as
well as in the mechanical and fine arts, and the sciences. And
they are never weary in devising easier and more rapid methods
of performing labor, in order that the higher faculties may have
an opportunity for development, and the hunger of the soul be
appeased with knowledge. And so our day is rife with Invention, and man is being redeemed from the curse of interminable toil for a meagre subsistence. And the same benign agency
is also acting upon his affectional nature to check its tendency to
excess, and to elevate it to a higher plane, where it will be more
directly under the guidance of Reason. Ay, through the aspi-
rational influences of the Christian Religion.

Passion takes wing and soars in purer air
With lofty Sentiment, serene and fair.

And through the same means Woman is also being relieved
from the bondage of jealous and exacting passion on the part of
man, and from the trammels of her own undisciplined and blind
affections. For her aspirations are likewise kindled the while
her intellect is enlarged, and a noble career of usefulness opened
before her in the direction of her attractions and capabilities.

The Public Schools of the United States have forwarded the
great designs of Heaven by silently co-operating with the Christian Religion. Through their means intelligent labor has more
rapidly succeeded sterile, unreflecting toil; and the industrial
interests of our Nation have become more popular, productive
and remunerative. Lo, Prometheus is unbound! The Occident
answered the long, agonizing cry from the Orient, and liberated
the spiritual powers of the human soul forever. Physical conditions can no longer chain them to earth. For the material
forces of Nature have been converted into workmen that cannot
tire.

Behold, the human BRAIN—O, wondrous grace!—
Supplies with ease the weary MUSCLE's place;

the while rejoicing in its consciousness of larger freedom.

The Public Schools of America have had, indeed, an important part to perform in the preparation for the second coming

11

of the Messiah in the Reasoning Age of the Church and World, to plead with the maturer minds of the people for a higher interpretation of his Gospel of Love.   These Institutions of learning contribute grandly toward the general diffusion of knowledge.   They are a mighty power in our land—say, rather, in the world—for the children of all nations have been, and are being, freely educated in them, and prepared to go forth and sow the seeds of Knowledge, and of Christian Democracy, far and wide over the earth.

The preparation is going rapidly forward, by day and by night; and the night is even as the day.   The globe has completed its grand circle of civilization.   The ever restless tide of human life has swept across the entire Western Continent, and connected itself by steam navigation with the Eastern Hemisphere.   And the free electricity of heaven has become bearer of dispatches between the Occident and the Orient.   Under the ocean, and over the land, we transmit our words of cheer and of mutual interest to kindred, sympathetic humanity.   Our Commerce floats on distant seas, and returns with the voice of many waters, exchanging the various products of the Zones; as well as the subtle emanations of the human mind of every land, through which we recognize more fully the brotherhood of Man, and the Divine Unity of all intelligence.

But the early part of the New Era is of necessity a transitionary State, because it is an advance from one period of growth towards another, from the Youth to the Maturity of the Church and World.   And as in the human organism, the intervening years between youth and confirmed manhood are marked by important vital changes in the system, which often appear adverse to healthy action, and yet are tending rapidly toward that end; so, in the progress of the Organized Church and of the World, from the age of Youth and of unquestioning faith in authority, towards the grander period of maturity and of rational conviction and enlightened opinions, there must needfully exist a season of *seeming retrogression*, as at this present, which will continue until there shall be a thorough examination, in the clearer light of Reason and Knowledge, of traditionary religion, and of the so-

cial, civil and political creeds of Christendom; and a more perfect adjustment of principles involved in these to human conditions and requiremnets. And, thus, the transitionary period is consequently, chaotic. It is violently active and reactive, and productive of sanguinary revolutions. It is the fruitful season of
"free-thinkers,"—of "come-outers,"—of "falling from grace,"—
of rank infidelity to creeds—and of loss of faith, alass! in God
and man.

But the reactionary spirit of the times is most seriously felt
in the sacred Institution of Marriage, which underlies the whole
structure of society. No marvel that the Church is taking alarm.
For in these radical changes, the holiest human ties are reckless-
ly sundered, and undisciplined passions riot even in the Sanctuary of the Most High. Christian fathers, in the ripeness of their
years, venerable with silver hair and the deep lines of thought,
often become regardless of paternal obligations outside of their
own apparently happy homes. Their unfortunate children of
illegitimate connections are left to the cold charity of society,
whose members mock at unrecognized offspring, even while
they themselves indulge in the unrighteous abuse of passion.
Many of these lonely wretched ones fall before their prime, like
untimely fruit, worm-eaten at heart, cursing the authors of
their miserable and blighted existence. Have these Christian
fathers (?) no fear of Retributive Justice? Do they ever imagine,
for a moment, that these neglected little ones, whose angels do
always behold the face of the Father which is in Heaven, may
meet them in that other state of existence, and sting their souls
with shame and terrible remorse? And even mothers do sometimes forsake their tender babes, under the erratic and un-
balancing influences of the hour. And they desecrate the sanctity of their natures, by merely passional alliances, unfitting them
for their sacred prerogative of reproducing and perpetuating a
pure and noble race of men and women in the Divine image
and likeness.

And, in this transition of the world from its season of Despotic rule, and of unquestioning faith in authority, and of the
bondage of the affections, forward to Democratic Institutions,

and a freer and more elevated life on the plane of Reason and Philosophy, which is also that of the Higher Law, all classes of society are shaken. The people everywhere are being affected by the influences of larger social, civil and religious liberty. For the age is pregnant with the *new life* of the world. And the volatile passions of mankind feel the impetus of the quickening spirit, and fly off to seek "affinities" and "attractions," before the judgment of the Reason and Moral nature has time to operate and control their actions. And thus many persons have already fallen, and more will fall into fatal errors, before society will be able to reach the higher plane of true marriage on the broader bases of Reason, sentiment and affection. And so we find that FREE LOVE is abroad, revelling in change of objects, and finding arguments for his sensuality in the purely animal kingdom. Pointing to the brutes of the field he cries exultingly—Lo! Nature's teaching. And in his pitiable degradation he does not perceive that he has fallen, not only beneath the human level, but below the beasts that perish. Because he has ignored Reason on the passional plane, and through excess has created morbid conditions and activities, and is cursed with insatiable desire, while he is not endowed with the dumb animal's attending instinct, that acts as a wholesome check upon absusive indulgence. Alas! for man, when he looks beneath, instead of above himself for guidance. He does this only when he is conscious of violating his higher nature, and wishes to excuse himself for past sins, and to find reasons for farther indulgence in wrong-doing. But let him BEWARE. The crime against his soul will meet an avenger. Violated Laws are inexorable. And let no one be deceived by such specious arguments in favor of sensual indulgence. Excess and impurity leave their desecrating marks alike upon individuals, communities, and nations. He that runneth may see and read their fearful records.

The present transitionary period is pre-eminently the day of false teachers and false prophets. Because there is a universal protest, among the most intelligent members of the community, against the authority, and the crippling restrictions of the past;

and against the equally inconsistent and injurious infidelity and latitude of the present; and there is everywhere an imperative demand for Reconstructive Leadership on higher intellectual and moral planes. And strong, daring, and ambitious minds of every class in society, feeling the demand and the stimulus of the times, are attempting to lead off in the direction of their own peculiar opinions. And they are drawing large numbers of like constituted natures along their erratic course.

The timid are everywhere shaken with apprehension, and cling the more closely to past forms of unquestioning, traditionary religion. Meanwhile, the tide of the higher reasoning life of the world sets in so strongly from the illimitable ocean of God's truth, that many are wrenched, per force, from former standpoints and strongholds of opinion, and carried forward, whither, they know not, urged onward by the current. And it often happens that, before they are able to reach out and clasp new and higher supports, they are bruised and sorely wounded in the strife of conflicting opinions, while borne along the rapid waves of events. And they are painfully pelted with the floating capital of ideas, concretions of the ages, that are everywhere active in the moral atmosphere, waiting a favorable moment to shape themselves into civil, political and religious Institutions. It is needful that there should be a breaking away from all supports before new and higher aids can be grasped. The noble Bark must be loosed from her moorings ere she can launch forth into deep waters in majestic freedom.

It has been said that the transitionary period is favorable to strong manifestations of both good and evil. We find, indeed, that evil is everywhere rampant; and many are alarmed and disheartened. But while there is manifest cause for alarm and vigilance, there is none for discouragement. If the wicked energize themselves in sin, and crime increases, the good will become more active for the right; and the standard of virtue will be lifted higher. If Satan and his legions be loosed for a season from the bottomless pit, be sure that the Master will be near with thousands of his saints to vanquish them.

It appears to be needful in God's moral government that evils

of all descriptions should culminate in the world at certain transitionary periods, as at this present, and show their true character and influence on society, in aggravated forms of manifestation; in order that they may stimulate thought among the reflective members of the community, which will lead to effective
action, and will arouse a spirit of resistance sufficiently strong
to annihilate them. Movement of any kind, either in the physical or moral world, is more favorable to a return to healthy
conditions than unresisting torpidity.

There never was a time in the history of the Church and
World when earnest and true workers, loyal sons and daughters
of the Most High, were more needed than at the present crisis.
Who is ready to come up with clean hands and a pure heart to
the help of the Lord against the mighty Man of ignorance and
sin, and aid in establishing, in the Reasoning Age of His appointing, the Renewed Church on the higher and surer foundation of knowledge and understanding, that it may, indeed, become
the light of the World? Who is ready to come up to the work?
The moral atmosphere is full of change; and the Almighty
Father calls in thunder-tones from the disturbed and conflicting
elements—Who will come up to the work? The Divine Mother
speaks, also, in the still small voice of pleading love—Who will
prepare the way before my beloved?

Behold, he cometh with CLOUDS; and every eye shall see him,
and they also which pierced him; and all kindreds of the earth
shall wail because of him! Even so, Amen. The prophetic
hour is at hand, when the Jews and Gentiles will alike recognize
and accept the coming Messiah, who is to unite in one Church
the great denominational family of man. The clouds or judgments thus graphically announced, as attending the Second Advent of the Master, are for purification. The corrupted .Church,
like the diseased human system, must be thoroughly cleansed
before it can take on healthy action. Already, the clouds are
before, and around us. Men and women, of all classes and all
denominations, will feel obliged to define their position strongly,
and to rise on the side of truth and progress; or to fall back into the ranks of error and darkness. These are the times which

will try men's souls; the times in which every individual will be tested by the Divine Laws of use and love, and in which they who retain faith in God and Man, and who work for humanity, will appear with a new name written on their foreheads, as a mark of Reasoning Intelligence, and will stand each in his lot and place, firm and unmoved amid the general upheaval and reconstruction of society. But the fearful and unbelieving, the abominable, the whoremonger, the adulterers and all liars will be swept away as chaff from the summer threshing floor. Their sins will find them out, and they cannot escape. Say ye to the righteous, that it shall be well with them; for they shall eat the fruit of their doings. Woe unto the wicked! it shall be ill with them, for the reward of their hands shall be given them. War, pestilence, famine, plague, calamity, disease and death, these are the impending CLOUDS of purification over the Church and World. And they are also agents of mercy and love to man. For, in God's grand Democratic Government throughout the vast Universe of Worlds, individuals must fall for the well-being of milions; parts must suffer for the benefit of the whole.

Who is this that cometh from Edom, with dyed garments from Bozrah? this that is glorious in his apparel, travelling in the greatness of his strength?

I that speak in rightousness, mighty to save.

Zion, behold thy King! Lo! he is attended by thousands of his saints. He hasteneth to become incarnate in the Humanity that he loves. His great heart and comprehensive intellect radiate light and warmth, like the noon-day sun; and he bears the sceptre of universal dominion. Let the choral song of praise and blessing, by a multitude of the heavenly hosts that announced his early advent in Bethelem, rise from a united Brotherhood of Nations to meet him in his coming. Glory to God in the highest, and on earth peace. good will toward Man.

CHAPTER VI.

Come now, and let us reason together, saith the Lord: though your sins be as scarlet, they shall be as white as snow; though they be red like crimson, they shall be as wool.

Lo! the darkness is past, and the true light now shineth from zenith to nadir. For He who spake in the beginning to physical nature, and it obeyed the mandate, now speaks, once more, in grander significance to the soul of matter, to the mind of his Intelligent Creation—LET THERE BE LIGHT! The Sun of Reason ascends the moral heavens in glory, scattering before its resplendent beams the fogs of error and superstition, emanations from the dark physical ages of ignorance and despotism. Thank God. Under its stimulating influence the present chaotic confusion of ideas and principles will hasten to take form in higher organizations, Social, Civil, and Religious; and perfect order, Heaven's first law, prevail at length in the moral world, as it is everywhere dominant through the wide range of material nature. For the human mind will feel the inspirational light and heat of a Religion of Reason and Intelligence, and, like the quickened earth under the influence of the diurnal Sun, will put forth new and ever-renewing powers of beauty and excellence. And Man, enlightened by Reason and Knowledge, and redeemed by Love, will walk forth in the true freedom and majesty of the sons and daughters of the Most High, the Christ of God being formed in them, the beauty of intelligent goodness and the hope of eternal glory.

But before this progressed condition of the Church and World can arrive there must be much earnest work and patient waiting. For Man can only advance step by step, in Heaven's prescribed order of unfolding. And the transitionary period, of which we treated in the preceding Chapter, has not yet passed ; neither has it reached its height of revolution and change, preparatory to the rule of Reason, and the reconstruction of the Christian Religion on its enduring foundation. And, when that advanced period shall arrive, the Gospel of the Master will be the universal Religion, for the people everywhere will then be able to recognize its divine and humanitary character, and will be attracted to its consecrated altars. And in that luminous day it will be clearly seen that Man is a religious being, outside of the Church, as well as in her organizations ; and that the Christian Religion is the only system of ethics that has obtained in the world, that is adapted to his highest and fullest development. And, for the reason before stated, that it recognizes Man, broadly, as children of the Eternal Intelligence ; this High Power requiring of them simple obedience only to the great law of Love—Love to God, and Love to fellow Man—irrespective of class, color and condition ; for the fulfillment of which obligations it confers on them the highest happiness of which they are capable, and the Freedom of the Universe—the largest Liberty in Law. Let no one understand Liberty to signify, in the least degree, License. The former is a divine, the latter, an evil principle, the parent of excess, crime, and human degradation and ruin. License dwarfs and enslaves, while Liberty enlarges and elevates the soul of Man.

ENLIGHTENED REASON may be regarded as an active, an adjustive, and a creative faculty of the human mind. It enables man to adapt himself to circumstences and conditions, to take advantage of his resources, and to improve his surroundings. It is the power by which he comprehends the thought of God in Nature; and which elevates him above the lower orders of the animal kingdom, constituting him the Lord of Creation. It is rarely operative in childhood and youth—saving in an *exceptional class* of intuitional minds, of which the Master is the highest type—

12

because it is an element of advanced intellectual growth and culture, belonging to the ripeness of years.

And, hence, we find that in the Childhood of the Church and World, under the Judaical Dispensation, the laws for the regulation of human life were *objective* and *restrictive* in their character, being addressed to material disciplinary needs, rather than spiritual, in order that they might meet the necessities of the people, who were on the more material plane of thought and action, and required strong and determined Leadership. And in the farther advanced Youth of the Church and World, under the Christian Dispensation of Love and Free-will, although the base of moral operations was changed from the exterior to the interior plane of human life—in order to meet the higher spiritual needs of the farther advanced Human Family—the people were still blinded, through ignorance, were still impetuous and reckless of consequences, and continued still to be governed, to a very great extent, by objective and restrictive measures, and by authority, and to be influenced by prejudice; and so they still continued to look outward, rather than inward, for light and guidance; and thus failed to read the law of God written upon the *heart*, instead of upon *tables of stone;* and continued to be governed in the New Dispensation, as they had been in the Old, by the formulæ of the Letter, rather than by the power of the Spirit. Yet the latter dispensation was a marked advance on the former. The appeal of the Higher Law was more powerfully addressed to the conscience and to the affections of Man, in order to awaken more fully the Moral Sentiments, elevate the Passions, and stimulate the *motive power* of the heroic and ardent Youth of the World.

But in the Maturity of the Church and World, toward which we are rapidly tending, the grand appeal will be made, directly and strongly—and is even now being made—to the enlightened Reason of Man, which is the great adjustive force and self-governing power of the individual, and of the whole Human Family. Because this noble faculty of the mind, which was latent in the Childhood of the World, and but partially developed in its Youth, will become active and grandly operative in its

Maturity, under the stimulating influence of Knowledge widely diffused among the millions. And, in that day, the rulers of both Church and State will see and acknowledge that Man is a self-poised and self-governing being, when all the faculties of Mind and Heart are developed in accordance with the Revealed Word of God to Man, and the Revealed Will in Man ; and that he is lighted and guided, from within, by the inextinguishable flame of Deity.

The influence of Authority becomes neutralized and gradually passes away before the higher control of enlightened Reason. The power that it once exercised in the Childhood and Youth of the Church, is gone forever. An individual man could as easily go back to the undeveloped conditions of his childhood and youth, after he had progressed to maturity, as the Church could return to the conditions of her former periods of blind unquestioning faith in Authority. She must pass on with the world to her Maturity, to her noble Reasoning Age—there is no escape. And she must free herself of her youthful robes, of the *special forms* of her early faith, or she cannot stand erect in her prime. When one has attained his physical stature, he can no longer wear the garments of his boyhood without losing the free play of his limbs, or cramping painfully and dwarfing his physical proportions. Neither can the mind of Man cling to past interpretations of truth, adapted to ignorant childhood and unreflecting youth, without crippling his soul. Let the Church consider seriously this word of inspiration: The letter killeth; but the Spirit maketh alive. Let her seek to renew herself, day by day, in the divine life of intelligent Use and Love, and, standing firmly on these great and indestructible principles, reach forward and upward, to grasp stronger and higher aids, that she may grow in grace daily, and in the knowledge of God.

It has been stated that Reason is an adjustive and a creative faculty of the human mind which is not fully developed until the age of maturity, either in the individual being, or in the Church and World of Man, which are obedient to the same law and order of progressive unfolding. The truth of these propositions may be demonstrated by the life of each member of the Human

Family of the present, and by the History of the Church and World of all past ages.

This noble Reason of the mature mind, which appears to be latent in infancy and childhood, and but imperfectly active in youth, is quickened in early Manhood, at the period of existence when the physical, intellectual and moral forces are more fully unfolded, and more equally balanced. For then the human need is greater, because the duties and responsibilities of life make stronger appeals from without and from within. Formerly, the individual being was a passive *receiver* of the gifts of Heaven and of the benefits of home, of society and of country; but, NOW, he takes rank with men, and must go forth into untried paths of enterprise and action; and he must become a *dispenser* of both natural and acquired endowments, and give aid and place, in turn, with his father—to younger generations. In early Manhood, when Reason first displays increased activity, it manifests itself more particularly on the physical plane of action, its energy and power being engaged more fully with natural or material objects. But, as the individual being advances in years and in experience, knowledge and wisdom, Reason takes a higher and broader metaphysical range of observation and action, and seeks to evolve from new combinations of principles more perfect systems of ethics, and juster codes of civil and criminal laws, by which to remodel Institutions and Governments, and bring them into harmony with the Higher Law.

In the present Transitionary state of Society, which period corresponds to the early manhood of the individual being, the stirring influence of active Reason, on the *natural* plane, is everywhere noticeable. Under its stimulating power material objects meet in new relations, and new and valuable results are obtained in every department of Science, and in all the various methods of Labor.

> The forge is honored, for a God, once more,
> Stands at the anvil—as in days of yore—
> And strikes the glowing iron with his thought
> As well as hammer, as the work is wrought;
> While sparks flash out with every blow of might,
> The path to new discoveries to light.

The mechanic forces are set grandly in motion, to work out the wonderful problems of Reason. Old, cumbrous machines for performing labor give place to lighter, more graceful, ingenious, and effective instruments. The steam engine becomes a cultivator of the soil, as well as an agent for conveying its various products from one climate to another, far over the teeming land and the wide waste of water. Earth, sea and air pay tribute to this King of the Mental Realm, whose throne is established among the stars of Heaven, and whose ministers are fleet, firey messengers from Nation to Nation.

And this early, erratic Manoood—daring and adventurous, that speaks of possibilities with the assurance of certainty, and prepares some electrifying surprise in science for each revolution of the globe—this youthful Manhood of the World—is the glorious AGE OF INVENTION. It laughs at the deeds of the mythic giants of the olden time, and the puerile exaggerations of ancient fable, as it goes forward on its appointed mission, clothed with the power of God-like Reason, to obey the Deity's injunction to man, to subdue the earth and possess it. Inert matter is everywhere set in motion by the quickened soul of intelligent Nature, and hastens to do the bidding of its Lord.

The Age of Invention, or of Reason on the material plane of manifestation, is, even now, culminating, and the mature Metaphysical Age of the Human Family is pressing urgently forward. And the Moral World will be shaken in its turn by this great comprehensive Reason, this active, adjustive and creative mind, that grasps principles, observes relations, and prophecies results from the altitude of the immortals. Old things will pass away, and all will become new as it advances. Thrones will crumble and fall before the majesty of its presence. And there will remain no pillow on earth on which any form of despotism can repose securely. Social, Civil and Religious Institutions will be shaken to their foundations, and reorganized on the broader bases of Universal Justice and the Rights of Man.

Ay, henceforward, there will be no rest for Institutions and Governments that are not established on these great humanitary principles; but they will continue to overturn and overturn, until HE whose right it is to rule shall govern the nations;—until the Stone that was cut out of the mountain without hands, shall smite the false governments, he image of gold and silver of brass and iron and clay, and they shall become like the chaff of the summer threshing floors, and the Stone shall become a great mountain and fill the earth;—and until the Church of God shall thoroughly purify herself from all unnatural and unholy polygamic marriages, and all forms of legalized and unlegalized prostitution,—and shall throw off the crippling formulæ of faith that was adapted to her undeveloped Childhood and Youth,—and shall go forth in her noble Maturity, adorned as a Bride for her Husband, to establish the Christian Church Universal,—to proclaim Liberty and Love to all lands, and to all their inhabitants,— and to indoctrinate the whole Human Family in the profoundest truths of Intelligent Nature—THE DUAL GODHEAD, AND THE SPIRITUAL FAMILY TRINITY.

In the resplendent Day of the Church Universal, under the glorious rule of Reason, the gigantic evils that have so long afflicted society,—crouching, like the ancient Sphinx, by the highways of the nations, propounding their fearful riddles and destroying their ignorant victims,—will be clearly seen and fully interpreted by the great moral Alchemist, Reason, that is commissioned to solve all social enigmas, and vice and crime will retire abashed before its God-like power, and destroy themselves upon their own unholy altars.

And the Word of Prophecy responds to the teachings of Philosophy, and assures us of a Day for Humanity of universal light and knowledge ; when many shall run to and fro, and knowledge shall be increased, until a knowledge of God shall fill the earth.   The Christian scholar and philanthropist confidently anticipates this desirable result for the children of men.   For he understands the progressive nature of Man, and sees the perfect adaptation of Christion principles to all his moral requirements; and, consequently, believes in their universal acceptance in the world, as well as in their regenerating and elevating influence. In that long expected Day of Humanity, there will be a more perfect understanding of the laws of matter and of mind, by which all things are created and sustained in harmonious relations; which understanding will enlarge and renew the life of Man, and impel loving obedience to the Divine requirements.

In view of this advanced period of human development, the Creator no longer speaks to the Church, as aforetime in her ignorant Childhood and Youth, with the voice of Authority and in the awfulness of his Majesty—I AM that I AM. But the All-Father addresses the *understanding* of his more intelligent children of the maturity of the world, appealing to their minds in words of thoughtful tenderness: Come now, and let us REASON TOGETHER, saith the Lord: though your sins be as scarlet, they shall be as white as snow; though they be red like crimson, they shall be as wool.

A marvellous lesson is conveyed in this paternal and encouraging address to the sons and daughters of earth. It presupposes power in *enlightened reason*, to evolve good out of evil, and to overcome sin. And when we remember that it is the province of reason to take comprehensive views of principles—their relations, operation and results—we can readily understand how strangely and effectually she can admonish, instruct, and guide, by pointing out consequences, and revealing the ,true and righteous way.

In the unreasoning ages of the past, the individual, the Christian Church, and Christian Nation committed outrageous crimes against humanity, in the name of Religion and Right, and with avowedly good intentions. Could they have foreseen the *consequences* of their fatal errors, they themselves would have been shocked at the result, and rendered incapable of perpetuating such enormities. But their mental view was limited and partial, and they could neither see their terrible mistakes, nor rectify them. They did not comprehend the Divine Unity of the human race, and of all intelligence, nor the Divine adaptation of the Gospel of Christ to the conditions and needs of humanity, requiring mankind to love as brethren. But, now, that the Sun of Reason has risen in the moral Heavens, evil doers will remain without excuse. The sins of ignorance may be winked at; but wilful adherents of error will be beaten with many stripes.

The Eternal One, who spake in times past through the prophets, speaks again in these later days through the Son of His Love, whom he hath created heir of all things; saying, Come now, and let us REASON TOGETHER. How many of the different denominations of the Christian Church are ready to obey the call, to listen to the voice of Reason? He that hath an ear to hear, let him hear.

We have already shown the Christ of the Youth of the Church, as he appeared to the partially developed mind of that age. We approach, now, with profound reverence the Manhood of the Master, in its glorious fullness of beauty, strength and perfection. It is, in verity, the Word with us. In regarding his remarkable character analytically we observe that Christ was a Spiritual, Intuitional-Intellectual and Harmonial God-man; the representative of Deity to the Human Family; as well as the Type-man of the intellectual and moral ages of the Church and World. And, in view of Christ as the great standard-bearer of Heaven, and the exemplar of its light and truth to Mankind, we have termed the Second Christian Era,—or Reasoning Day of the Church and World in which his Gospel and mission will be more fully understood, and his life more perfectly imitated and represented by Humanity,—Man's Spiritual and Intuitional-Intellectual period of development. And we hope to justify our position in the mind of the Reasoning Age.

The advanced minds of the coming Day of Reason will not claim that Jesus himself was the Almighty One incarnate; but they will accept him as the Mediator, or special Medium of Deity, in whom dwelt ALL THE FULLNESS of the Godhead—Divine Father, Divine Mother God. They will regard him as a created being, in whom the physical, intellectual and moral qualities of our common humanity were so finely balanced that he was in perfectly harmonious relations in himself, and, consequently, in harmonious relations with universal Nature—of which Man is the product, or ultimate. And being thus organized in body, and constituted in mind, Christ Jesus was open to all Spiritual and Divine influences, and able to receive, and to transmit, the truth of Heaven, as perfectly as a crystal receives and emits the rays of light that fall upon its surface. And as he was a true Child of Nature, in the highest significance of the term, open to all the influences of the Creative mind,—one with God,—it follows, as a logical sequence, that he was receptive of the scientific truths of matter and of mind contained in, and emanating from, all material things and all created intelligences.

The first Adam was of the earth, earthy; the second Adam is the Lord from Heaven. The former was the representative of the ignorant physical ages in the infancy of the human race, and the Childhood of the Church and World; the latter is the grand Spiritual, Intuitional-Intellectual and Harmonial God-man of the advanced mental and moral ages. He is the Sun of Righteousness, to prepare and enlighten the way; the Sun of Truth, to unfold the arcana of Nature; the Sun of Love, to kindle the flame of devotion in the hearts and minds of the sons and daughters of earth, and attract them to the Divine, until they shall be transformed into his own perfect likeness. Ah! the Christian Church has scarcely begun to comprehend the deep significance of the prophecy of St. Paul. As we have borne the image of the earthly, (passing through the physical ages of unreflecting ignorance and consequent sin,) so shall we also bear the image of the Heavenly, when man shall become enlightened and redeemed from ignorance and sin, through the quickening and elevating power of the Gospel of Christ. Ay, we shall, indeed, be like him, when we shall see him as he is—the Son of Man and the Son of God; when our hearts and minds are open, like his, to receive the Divine Love, and to understand, to accept, and to practice the Master's broad humanitary principles; and when, from a lofty mental and moral intuitional plane of thought and feeling, we shall be able to comprehend the full significance of the sublime truths which inspired him, and to view the purity, grandeur and perfection of his character. For the reason that, being children of the Highest, "We needs must love the highest when we see it;" and needs must emulate that which we most admire.

The divine Teacher calls upon the sons and daughters of earth, of every age and nation, to be ONE with him, *even as he*

13

is one, or at-one with God, that they, like him, might become willing and perfect Mediums of the Divine Spirit.   Listen to the Master's remarkable words: Greater works than these (which I have done) shall ye do, and because I go to The Father. It is as if he had told them that, Because I go to the illimitable Source of Inspiration, of Eternal Truth, and Light, and Love, I will return and fill your souls with these immortal principles; and they shall be received into the hearts and minds of the millions, and shall prepare the way for yet greater manifestations of Divine Wisdom and Love.

But, alas, how feeble is our faith! How cold are our affections! The Church has even ceased to believe the dear Master's words of inspiration and encouragement.   She lifts up her voice against the prophecy.   She cries aloud in the ear of the listening World, that the days of Spirit manifestations and power have passed away forever; amazing the more intellectual and spiritual minds of the age with the blind assertion.   For they see the great miracle of Creation renewed with each revolution of the earth; and they believe in still greater miracles of power and love that will be alike adapted, physically, intellectually, and morally, to the progressed, and to the ever progressing, conditions of the Human Family.   It may be wise to say, in this connection, that we use the term miracle as it is understood by the intelligent mind; not as a manifestation contrary to law and independent of an established chain of cause and effect; but as a sequence resulting from an unknown cause.   An ignorant person may regard a peculiar phenomenon as a miracle, that a Scientist sees clearly to be the legitimate result of some operating cause.   That has often been regarded as a miracle in one age of the world which became a well-understood principle in another.

A large number of the class of liberal and intelligent minds in Christendom, to which we have alluded, are outside of Church organizations but are, nevertheless, the outgrowth of the Christian Church.   Many of them are men and women of the highest order of intellect, who are unable to accept the special interpretation of the Gospel embraced in the creeds of the various denominations of the Christian Church; but, yet, who truly believe in Christ and his teachings, and seek earnestly to live the life of the great exemplar. They have already received the baptism of the Holy Ghost and of fire, and have accepted the Gospel of the Master, with the *intellect*, as well as the affections. They are the valiant vanguard of the reasoning maturity of the Church of God. Ay, more! They are the chosen of Heaven, to stand as an impregnable bulwark between the timid, half-doubting Christian Church and the watchful, questioning World, to show to the Church that God can raise up for himself a people, with his laws written upon their hearts, who shall be as independent of creeds as the great Teacher himself, and who shall impart strength and courage to his weak and wavering children, and enable them to exercise Reason in the investigation of truth, and a profounder faith in the immutability of His Universal Government—a people of heroic souls, who will hang out the Christian Banner on the outer walls of Zion, with the stirring call of the New Christian Era of Reason traced on its folds in letters of light— Come now, and let us reason together, saith the Lord—a people who will stimulate the cold and torpid Church to awake! arise! —and rally her forces for the impending moral conflict in the name of the God of Reason—as well as of justice and of love;— a people, we repeat, chosen of Heaven, to stand as an impenetrable fortress between the waiting, watchful and questioning World, on one side, and time-serving Church on the other, to prevent his outside children from entering the fold of the Good Shepherd, while there are so many wolves in sheep's clothing, desecrating the sanctuary of the Most High, by converting its sacred altars into money changers' tables; while there are so many cold-hearted formalists ministering there, uttering the formulæ of the Oracles of God, while destitute of the Spirit that quickeneth and maketh alive. They are God's chosen and peculiar people of the Reasoning Age of His appointing; and they are no tonly commissioned to protect the family of man from the deleterious influences of the Church of the first Christian Era, when her light has become darkness; but are ordained of Heaven to form, at the same time, a broader and higher platform of religious faith, for the Church of the Second Christian Era of the Reasoning age of the World; a platform of faith that shall be supported by the comprehensive principles of Love to God and Love to Man, which principles include the *whole sum* of moral obligations; a platform by which earnest and enlightened inquirers after spiritual truth may ascend, by simple and rational gradations, to the sublime height of the great argument.

The Master, and his Gospel of Love, received but a partial recognition in the Youth of the Church and World.   Even the immediate disciples and followers of Christ did not fully comprehend his character, nor the marvellous import of the doctrines that he taught; because the mind of that age was but partially developed.   And it is, therefore, needful, for the full completion of his Mission, that he should be again " Revealed" in the Maturity of the Church and World, that the Human Family may see his mental as well as moral Status; and thus, that he might not only receive a fuller and juster measure of appreciation from all teachers and believers in his Gospel; but in order that the Spiritual Life of the Church and World might be renewed on the indestructible bases of Reason and Philosophy. For there can be no appeal from the convictions and verdict of an enlightened understanding.

And, in consequence of the two-fold Mission of Christ—addressed to the heart of Man in the Youth of the World, and to the mind of Man in its Maturity or Reasoning Age—and in consequence of the partial view of his nature and teachings by the Church of the first Christian Era, and the subsequent abeyance of Reason to traditionary Religion, Modern Teachers and Writers have, also, been partial in their delineations of his character, and equally so in their statements of his doctrines. None has ever fully portrayed the comprehensive INTELLECT of the Master, with its broad generalization of principles.   He viewed the relations of Intelligent Nature from the altitude of Philosophy, and observed and presented to the Human Family those elevated truths which are adapted to their progressive nature as children of God.

Many may reply: The profound reverence felt for the person

intelligence outside of his religious prejudices,) on the future state of existence, he said to us, with evident sincerity and earnestness: "We shall not carry our intellect to Heaven; human reason and knowledge will be of no account there, for we shall be purely spiritual beings." Such a proposition is monstrous to an unprejudiced, reasoning mind. The Eternal Creative Spirit is the infinite source of Reason and Knowledge. All things were made by them, and without them was not anything made that was made. And it is absurdly irrational to suppose that the great Creative Intelligence of the Universe could be better pleased with the worship of the spiritual nature of man, rather than of the intellectual, (could it be possible, indeed, to separate the one from the other,) or that he could be better pleased with the partial devotion of the blind affections of the Human Famliy, rather than with the intelligent worship of the higher reasoning faculties with which he endowed them, in order that they might understand his laws, and render willing obedience to them. The great exponent of Heaven's will concerning man, and of the obligations of Man in view of their relations as sons and daughters of Deity, declares that God requires the full and perfect service of all the *heart*, and *mind*, and *soul*, of Created Intelligence. And if this complete service of the whole human being is required on this rudimental sphere of life, with all its limitations and blindness, would it be morally possible that the All-Just, could demand *less*, when the capability would be *greater ?* Will God require partial worship of the children of men, after they shall have attained the fullness of their powers in that higher state of existence beyond the grave ?

Ah! the Church has not yet learned that the Affections, the Intellect, and the Sentiments of Man are all alike spiritual and immortal, because inherited from the only Source of Spirit, the Divine Father and Mother God. The Church has not yet learned that every faculty of the human Soul is formed for infinite unfolding. When God breathes into the material embryo the breath of life, the new-born babe becomes immortal; becomes inspired by His life, to inherit His own Eternity. Then commences the great progressive life of the human Soul, that is destined to approach nearer and nearer to the Divine Source of Infinite Intelligence through interminable ages.

Alas ! that human beings in their blindness forge restraints for the human intellect, unmindful that by so doing they oppose the God in Man that seeks expansion from the very force of its Divinity. The powers of the human mind, that are thus unnaturally checked and confined, become a consuming fire to prey upon the soul, producing morbid and restless conditions of both mind and body. A large proportion of the diseases of the human race result from mental causes ; from the eternal and ineffectual cry of the imprisoned spirit for more light, more knowledge, for a fuller understanding of its own nature, and a juster measure of appreciation and sympathy from its kind ; the while it bruises itself against its prison bars in its struggles for fuller development ; for larger freedom. And, sadder still, a great proportion of the vices and crimes of society originate from the same prolific source of evil, from the suppressed faculties of human beings. It is the law of the vegetable plant, when its germ is embedded in fertile soil, to grow and put forth roots and branches. If it have favorable conditions, adapted to the necessities of its life—space, sun and air—it will tower in symmetrical beauty toward heaven. And if obstacles are placed in its way, and it be partially deprived of these healthful influences, it will continue to struggle for growth, in obedience to the great law of its nature, which demands development, and it will stretch itself beneath its barriers, when it cannot rise above them into freedom ; but it will be diseased, root and branch, and pitiably deformed. And it is so, emphatically, with the human plant. All the religious restraint that may be imposed on youth, and all the moral instruction that may be imparted to them, will not obviate the necessity for the normal development of their intellectual faculties and tastes. Because the intellectual faculties look at the consequences of human conduct, as well as at the results of any operating cause ; and when these faculties are cultivated and, consequently, in an active condition, they impart a consciousness of power to execute, and move with an impelling force toward some given end, opening up avenues of useful and attract-

ive industry.   And ATTRACTIVE OCCUPATION is one of the great
secrets of human success, purity and happiness.

Ah! if Christian teachers would remember that the faculties
of the human soul are infinite in their capability and destiny,
and that their natural unfolding would have the tendency to
render men and women self-poised, and self-governing, and not
only healthier, wiser, and more useful members of society, but
happier in time, and better prepared for eternity; *then* they
would become, in verity, the agents of Heaven for ennobling
and enlarging the human intellect; instead of being, as now,
the means of circumscribing and dwarfing the minds of their
fellow beings.

Yes, every faculty of the human soul is infinite.   Number is
infinite.   Lo! its inverted pyramidal column rises grandly from
the unit earth to the throne of the Invisible, measuring the eternal ages.   Music is infinite.   It fills the human soul with immortal longings as it sweeps through the world in soft Æolian
strains of melody, or grander Organ tones of harmony, missioned to attract all discord and compel it, by the divine law of
its nature, to form a part of the universal Anthem.   Ideality is
infinite.   It rises from the survey of material forms of loveliness, until its wings sweep the boundaries of the unknown,
seeking for more perfect and imperishable forms of beauty.
Reason is infinite.   It stands firmly on the broad plane of God's
uniform and universal laws, and reaches forth with Titanic power
to grasp the end from the beginning, while predicting the possible future of unborn generations from the operating principles of the present.   The affections of Man are infinite.   They fly
impassionedly through the wide universe of God, in search of
the loved and lost, questioning eagerly of all things of earth and
heaven, in the agony of their immortal yearnings.   Ah! when
we remember that God is Infinite, let as not forget that He hath
endowed His Human Family, fashioned in his own image and
likeness, with His own Infinity.   And let us seek to develop in
our fellow beings the germs of their immortal existence, and
thus co-operate with the Deity in perfecting His beautiful creations.

14

There are exalted moments in the experience of every son or daughter of Deity, who seeks to live the life of Christ, to do justly, love mercy, and walk humbly before God, when the sense of his immortality enfolds him like a mantle, when he feels a tender, loving, and sublime approach to the Divinity, when he can exclaim with rapturous joy——"Yes, in my Spirit doth thy Spirit shine! As shines a sunbeam in a drop of dew;"——when he delights in believing that he shall revolve as a star forever and ever, around the great central Sun of Truth, Light and Love; to be filled with, and to radiate Heaven's glory.

The limited views of the various denominations of the Christian Church in regard to the education of human beings, and the development of every power of *mind*, as well as of heart, in order that all the faculties of man might be employed in the service of God, are the more remarkable, because they are in direct opposition to the Master's definite teaching; and they can be only satisfactorily explained by understanding the relation of the Church of to-day to the past of its early unreflecting Youth, and by its adherence, in the present Reasoning Age, to a traditionary religion. For the Church, in her ignorant Youth, did not recognize the impress of Divinity on every faculty of the human soul; but, on the contrary, she attributed as many qualities of the human mind to his Satanic Majesty as to the Supreme Creative Intelligence of the Universe, influenced in her views, to a great extent, by the teaching of the Pagan schools, concerning the gods of good and evil; which peculiar views Heathen Nations had inherited from the Childhood of the World. And under the influence of these erroneous opinions, she naturally exercised her own judgment in reference to what particular faculties it would be better to develop in man, and what to restrain. And the Church of the first Christian Era was also influenced, in a great degree, by the mental philosophy of the Childhood and Youth of the World, which taught—from a more external plane of thought and reason than that of the nineteenth century—that the qualities of the human mind were not innate, but were the result of educational culture. As late as the eighteenth century, one of the greatest poets of that day wrote, under the influence of the same philosophy, the often repeated quotation:

"Just as the twig is bent the tree 's inclined."

And the best poets of every time may be regarded as the exponents of the highest enlightenment of the period; for they dwell in glorious beauty on the apices of the intellectual and moral monuments of the age.

The history of Christ and his labors for humanity indicate plainly that Reason was grandly operative in his character. How wisely he adapted his teachings to the specific requirements of his own time, and how broadly, in far-sweeping generalities, to those of every other age. In addition to the dual significance of his Gospel, in the natural and spiritual sense of the word, it contains also a dual form of truth, which is addressed to the heart and to the mind of man, and is adapted to two distinct eras of development in the Church and World; to the season of affectional Youth, and to the period of reasoning maturity.

In regard to the Master's general plan of operation, as well as his method of conveying instruction, he displayed marvellous Knowledge of human conditions and requirements, and wonderful insight of the soul of Man, together with the retrospective and prophetic vision that views the end from the beginning. He commenced his labors among the poorer classes of society, in order that his great Humanitary Work might be radical, and that he might show to the world the pure Democracy of his Religion, which included the whole Human Family, and uplifted all on one broad platform as equal children of the Divine Father and Mother God; and equal inheritors of all things of earth and heaven, by the high law of equal ability, equal knowledge of truth, and equal obedience to its requirements. And yet another motive of wise policy induced him to open his mission among the common people, who heard him gladly; they were outside of the schools, and of religious organizations, and the conventional rules of society, and were less influenced by the peculiar prejudices of such, and, consequently, more open to listen to, and to receive instruction; having everything to gain, and nothing to lose, in future fields of thought and enter-

prise.   The Israelitish Church of that day was torpid within its
chrysalis of forms, and society, paralyzed by its time-honored
usages, and the ears of the religionists and scholars, were closed
against the New Doctrines of the Philosoper of Nazareth.

The Master spake to the congregated multitudes in parables,
in order that the truths that he taught might not startle and repel,
by their newness and power, before the people had time to fully
consider the meaning that they were intended to convey; and,
also, in order that he might help to form in their undeveloped
minds the habit of thought and careful reflection, and develop
in them the ability of understanding religious truths.

In his intercourse with the world the Master himself obeyed
the precept which he enforced on the minds of his disciples, to
unite the wisdom of the serpent with the harmless innocence of
the dove.   How wise and admirable was his answer to the
emissaries of the Scribes and Pharisees who wished to entangle
him in his talk, and thus involve him in a dangerous political
question of the day.   After artfully complimenting the Master
on his knowledge of truth, and independence in promulgating
it, they inquired: Is it lawful to give tribute unto Cæsar, or
not?   Jesus answered: Show me the tribute money.   And they
brought unto him a penny.   He immediately inquired, on seeing the vignette of the King: Whose is this image and super-
scription?   They reply, Cæsar's.   Then said he unto them,
Render unto Cæsar the things which are Cæsar's and unto God
the things that are God's.   His great reasoning mind could not
be entrapped by their childish subterfuges; for he saw the motives that actuated them.   They marvelled at his understanding, and went their way.

What profound knowledge of the operations of the human
mind he evinced when the poor woman was brought before
him who was taken in the act of breaking the seventh commandment; her accusers declaring that the law of Moses required that she should be stoned for the transgression—But
what sayest thou?   They hoped that the Master would commit
himself, knowing his charity for poor, ignorant and erring Humanity, and His independence of thought and action, and say

something contrary to the law of Moses, that they might accuse him before the Chief Priests and Rulers of the people. But Jesus stooped down and with his finger wrote on the ground, as though he heard them not. Calm and self-possessed in the presence of those excited and double-minded men and their unfortunate victim, the Master continued to write on the ground, in order to attract their attention to himself for a moment, and break the concentrated force of their thoughts upon the woman and her relation to the Mosaic law, and thereby to weaken, by diversion, their temporary excitement of feeling on the subject ; and, thus, by relieving their minds of preoccupying thoughts, prepare them to receive other ideas, and to feel the full force of his wise and searching response. And it may have been that he was also considering the most effective form of speech in which to address their hearts and understandings. While they continued to press the case upon his notice,—at the right moment for action,—he lifted himself up in the sublime purity and strength of his uncorrupted manhood, and said with startling emphasis— *He that is without sin among you, let HIM first cast a stone.*

These remarkable words of the Master, while they did not extenuate the fault of the woman, charged home upon the consciences of her accusers the greater sin of publicly exposing her to a fearful penalty for being caught in the commission of a crime, such as they themselves perpetrated in secret with impunity. No marvel that all forsook him and fled, convicted by the high tribunal of Conscience.

But while the Master exercised God-like charity toward the poor, degraded, and ignorant who, from the cradle to the grave, are placed in such unfavorable conditions that it is difficult for them to learn the first lesson in virtue, self-respect, he never failed to rebuke, with the stinging severity of indignant Justice, sinners in high places, who were the Rulers of the millions and the expounders of the Law, and in more propitious circumstances for understanding their duties to themselves, to their fellow beings and to their Creator.

All the teachings of the Master bear, in verity, the impress of a great generalizing mind. His Sermon on the Mount is full of lofty and comprehensive principles which are of universal application, and adapted to all times and to all conditions of the human race. When the Pharisees had heard that Jesus had put the Sudducees to silence by his superior wisdom and understanding of the Mosaic Law, they came to him, in their pride of opinion, and with their deeply-rooted prejudices against all innovators, and all innovations of their time-honored usages, and with their preconceived idea of the precedence of certain points of the Law, hoping that they should tempt Christ to say something contrary to the pronounced opinions of the expounders of the sacred text, by which they might entrap him. One of their number, addressing him said—Master, which is the GREAT COMMANDMENT in the law? Jesus replied—Thou shalt love the Lord thy God with all thy heart, and with all thy soul, and with all thy mind. This is the first and great commandment. And the second is like unto it, thou shalt love thy neighbor as thyself.

What broad generalizations of moral principles, and what clear and concise statements of human obligations are embodied in these remarkable sentences! When the Master uttered this profound Doctrine of Love, THEN was anuonnced the comprehensive Creed of the Church Universal. For every denomination of the Church of God, of every nation under Heaven, can unite on this broad platform of faith and practice. There is no opportunity for questioning the meaning of the doctrine; no open door for caviling. It is direct and forcible, and sublime in its simple comprehensiveness. And after thus graphically stating the whole sum of Christian duty, he liberates the timid mind from past formulæ of religious faith by declaring—On these two commandments hang all the law and the prophets. With what a masterly stroke he sweeps the ages, announcing the universal principles of God's government. The past and future are one to his far-extending vision. Love to God and love to man are the Alpha and Omega of his Church militant and triumphant— its great Forever. Yes, all the moral law of all the ages, and all the teachings of all the prophets, are only parts of the Divine plan of uniting the hearts and minds of the Human Family together in Love, until earth shall indeed become a Paradise of God, and his loving and obedient sons and daughters ONE with Him in truth and action.

These commandments require the consecration of MIND, as well as *heart*, to the service of the Deity in whom we live, and move and have our being.   The Master illustrated this required active service of the intellect, when he likened the Kingdom of Heaven to a household, the Lord of which purposed to travel into a far country.   Before departing, he called together his servants, and distributed talents among them, which he required that they should improve during his absence.   After his return, he called them together again, in order to learn what disposition they had made of the talents entrusted to their care.   The subsequent commendation of those who had improved their talents, and the severe reproof and punishment of the slothful servant who had buried his *one* talent in the earth, evince clearly that Heaven requires the cultivation and exercise of every faculty of mind bestowed on man, and that it is sinful to bury *one* in the unproductive earth of the physical nature, and not to improve each as the gift of Heaven.   Man cannot worship the great Creative Spirit of the Universe with undeveloped powers of mind, more effectively than an infant could sustain a part in one of Handel's grand Oratorios that shake the Heavens.   The required worship of the mind, implies intelligent devotion, demands the exercise of the understanding.

When the Mind of the Christian Church is fully awake and active, THEN she will not rest until she has Christianized the World.   And when she shall undertake this Mission in its true spirit, THEN she will adopt the simple and comprehensive Creed of Love, framed by the Master, for God's Church Universal. This sublime Creed of Love is the central truth of Intelligent Nature; and it will radiate light, warmth and joy, from the Christian Church of the Reasoning Age, to the uttermost bounds of earth, to the people who sit in darkness and the *shadow* of Death.

The Philosopher of Nazareth understood, perfectly, the character, tendency, and force of the Gospel that he revealed.

He knew that its principles were adapted broadly to all human conditions and needs, of all times, and to the whole nature of Man.   And he knew that when the Church of God should become more enlightened, she would also perceive and accept this sublime truth.   And he had this universal acceptance of the Gospel of Love in view, when he declared to his disciples—If I be lifted up I will draw all men unto me.   He saw, from his lofty intellectual and moral standpoint of observation, that the love that would first attract the hearts of the millions would prepare the way for the reception of the truths of Natural Religion in the Minds of the people,—and that the light of advancing Reason and Knowledge in the world would eventually render those principles of truth universal.

But a prominent reason why the comprehensive mind of the Master has *not* been more fully appreciated by his followers and biographers, is because of its rare and peculiar order.   His mind, as before stated, was Intuitional-Intellectual.   Men of talent, merely, cannot understand the Intuitional Mind, because its action is so unlike to that of their own.   In this intuitional peculiarity lies the distinction between talent and genius.   The man of talent acquires his knowledge through " drill."   His capability of inductive and deductive reason is the result of laborious study.   The man of genius appears to leap at conclusions, so rapid is the action of his reasoning powers, and so clear his view of the relations of principles, and the logical sequences of such relations.   And he reasons with equal facility and perspicuity, whether he rise by a continuous chain, link after link, of inductive argument to universal principles; or sweep down from the lofty height of Cause, in sublime strength of generalizing power, to the world of Effects.   He is able to accomplish this, because of the nice balance or harmony of his faculties, and their consequent receptivity of influx from higher spheres of intelligence.

Indeed, genius has never been definitely understood and portrayed, because there have been so limited a number of intuitional minds in the past among the scholars of the world.   In our peculiar habitude of thought we speak of natural genius, and of partial, and of universal genius. Yet all that is understood by these terms is an exalted condition of some one faculty, or many faculties of the human mind, which appear to have spontaneous action. One is said to possess genius for Mathematics, who can solve abstruse problems at the moment that they are presented to the mind, without subsequent preparation. Another is accredited with genius for Music, who is able to understand and compose harmony without a previous knowledge of its rules, and finds no difficulties where an average student meets with discouraging obstacles. We call the Poet a genius, who can bear us on the wings of imagination to ideal realms of beauty, where our souls are filled with joy and blessedness, and we forget awhile the stern realities of life in the unalloyed delight of spiritual existence. And we term the Orator a genius, whose marvellous power sways the popular mind, even as mysterious winds, sweeping forth from eternity of ether, bow the forests in passing, and uplift and impel onward the waves of Ocean. And the Inventor is also styled a genius, whose active brain elaborates spiritual machines in the sphere of thought, which he ultimates in material forms, and sends forth on their mission of use to Mankind.

Persons possessing this peculiar order of mind, which is of like character with the Master's intellect, and bears the stamp of genius, cannot be said to be purely spiritual, in the common acceptation of the term. For men and women of weak understandings are quite as often spiritual in their natures, as those who are endowed with the highest order of intellect. One of the most spiritual persons we have ever known fell far below the average ability. Spirituality is the manifestation of active religious sentiments, as marvellousness, ideality and veneration. Simple goodness is the manifestation of a large endowment of the Moral qualities of benevolence, conscientiousness and hope. Intellectuality is the result of full perceptive and reasoning powers. Offensive and defensive action have their origin in the faculties of destructiveness and combativeness, which Man shares in common with the lower orders of animals. It may be truthfully asserted that a large majority of Mankind, while possessing

15

all the variety of human faculties in an appreciable degree, find their peculiar individualities in a single order of the classes of faculties.   And hence it occurs that one person is noted for piety ; another, for goodness ; a third, for intellectuality ; and a fourth, for belligerent propensities. A full development of the various classes of the human faculties, in harmonious action, constitutes a universal genius ; a full-statured, Spiritual, Intuitional—Intellectual and harmonial God-Man ; and such an one was the great Democratic Philosopher of Nazareth.

We are tempted to pause in this connection, to treat more fully of the faculty of vèneration, its nature and service to man; for the reason that we have recently seen, in Buckle's History of Civilization and an inadequate and incorrect description of this important faculty of the mind.   Buckle tells us that, " The origin of veneration is *wonder* and *fear*.   *   *   *.   We *wonder* because we are ignorant, and we *fear* because we are weak."   Philosophy and Science teach that veneration is not a *composite*, but a *simple* faculty of the mind; and that, because of man's relation to the highest Creative Intelligence of the Universe, it turns . naturally and *involuntarily*, with a sentiment of devotion, toward the highest object of which the human being is capable of conceiving, as he progresses slowly through the circling ages, from the infant state of passive innocence and ignorance, forward to the mature state, in the fullness of all his powers, the state of positive innocence and knowledge, of completeness and harmony.

Veneration may, in verity, be termed the unbilical chord of the Spirit, which holds the human being bound to the Divine, the uncreated source of existence; although in the embryonic states of the soul—the periods of infancy, of childhood, and of youth;—man may only behold the awful majesty and power of Jehovah, and may not perceive the infinite wisdom, justice, and love of the ETERNAL FATHER.

In the Infancy of being, when man is on the physical plane of thought and action, and ignorant of the latent God-like attributes of his own high nature, veneration turns *outward*, toward some visible object of worship, and in his blindness, man makes obeisance to the hosts of Heaven, or bows in reverence to useful members of the animal kingdom, that fall below the human level. In the Childhood of being, when the forces of the soul move more powerfully the yet undeveloped intellect, and man feels still more strongly conscious of a spiritual controlling power in nature, *then* veneration takes a more spiritual direction, and man models symbolic forms of Gods, of good and evil, spirits of earth, and sea, and air, and bows reverently before these representative powers. In the Youth of being, when the perceptive intellect is developed, and the aspirations of the soul are kindled, and are manifested in oratory, poetry and art, and in manifold forms of beauty, and when the love of fame is awakened, and man feels the sublimity and power of his own nature, *then* veneration turns in the direction of noble and exalted human beings, and man becomes the worshipper of heroes. In the maturity of being, when the reasoning intellect is developed and the moral sentiments are active and in harmony, and the affectional nature is in abeyance to these high powers of the soul, Veneration turns *inward*, and man recognizes the God in whom we live, and move, and have our being; and, understanding human nature more perfectly from seeing its relation to the Deity, exhibited in the complete adaptation of powers to the truths of Intelligent Nature, man learns to claim with joyful elevation of heart and mind, the high relation of offspring to the Supreme source of being, the Cause of causes; and *then* Veneration takes the highest spiritual direction, and man becomes, in the fullness and perfection of his powers, an intelligent, devout and humble worshipper of the God of gods.

Wonder and Fear are aids to, but they do not compose the faculty of Veneration. Wonder has its origin in marvellousness. It stimulates the mind to search out the concealed and mysterious. Fear is the offspring of cautiousness. When this faculty is exalted to terror by impending evil, it stimulates the mind to turn toward some object for succor, and Veneration leads off in the direction of the highest Power of which the mind has yet conceived. Thus Wonder and Fear act only as motive-powers of Veneration. It would be as correct to assert that steam which impels a machine forward is itself the engine which is set in motion, as it is to assume that Wonder and Fear are constituent parts of Veneration. When this marvellous power (whose organ points the coronal region of the brain, thus denoting its position of honor among the other faculties of the mind) is enlightened by knowledgge and reason, then the human being turns *voluntarily*, or with active volition, toward the Supreme Source of existence, conscious that their is his only place of perfect REST. Hope has been termed the anchor of the soul. But hope is excitative, soaring, and speculative, rather than reposeful. Veneration is the anchor of the soul. It penetrates within the vail into the deep profound of the Eternal God. And the more tempest-tost the mariner is upon the sea of life, the more constantly he turns to his mooring in the Infinite and Unchangeable, in whom is no variableness, nor shadow in turning.

In the intuitional and harmonial mind, Veneration may be clearly recognized as the focal point of the soul, where the rays of the Spiritual Sun converge and kindle the holy and inextinguishable flame of devotion and love. And the human being who is endowed with this high order of nature possesses, in like proportion with the endowment, the same mind that was in Christ Jesus, and; like him, is AT-ONE with the Divine.

Our great Exemplar was in *rapport* with the whole Universe of Matter and of Spirit, and, consequently, open to the reception of all truths, scientific as well as moral, by the great laws of adaptation, unity, and harmony. All other orders of genius have been partial. He sprang full-statured from the brain of Jove. In him dwelt all the fullness of the GODHEAD; divine knowledge and power, divine wisdom and love. And he exexemplified in his marvellous life the commanding force of the Universal Father, blended with the persuasive tenderness of the Universal Mother. How remarkably the Divine Mother sentiment is expressed where he weeps over the prospective fall of his beloved city. O Jerusalem, Jerusalem, thou that killest the prophets, and stonest them which are sent into thee, how often would I have gathered thy children together, even as a hen gathereth her chickens under her wings, and ye would not!

Our hearts expand and our eyes overflow when we realize for a moment how Christ exalted our humanity by his elevated nature and by his glorious life of purity, use and love ; and, also, by his sublime death and resurrection, in that he triumphed over the terrors of the grave, and ascended to the Celestial City, leaving its gates of light ajar for us to follow and share with him the joys of immortality. And it is encouraging to remember, again and again, that he uplifted the whole Human Family to his own high level, by declaring them to be alike Children of God, and exhorting them to be one with him in truth and love, even as he was one with the Father. Ah, how holy, useful and joyful our lives would become, could we fully appreciate the present and prospective blessedness of the divine relation—Children of God ! For, says the word of inspiration, If children, then heirs, heirs *of* God, and joint-heirs *with* Christ.

It may be assumed by skeptics that, if Christ possessed inspirational knowledge of the laws of matter, as well as of mind, he would have taught the principles of science to his disciples. But this does not follow as a logical sequence. The capacity to receive limits the ability to impart knowledge. But if all the *fullness* of the Godhead dwelt in Christ, it follows, of necessity, that the scientific truths of Nature were open to his perceptive intellect, and that he saw the relations of material things and the laws governing those relations, as clearly as his higher metaphysical intellect observed moral and religious truths and their adaptation to the human heart and mind. It must be remembered that the disciples were merely children, compared with the great Philosopher of Nazareth, and that his object was to impart moral and spiritual truths to them, and through them to Mankind, and thus to prepare the way for the right use of Knowledge when the reasoning age of the Church and World should arrive. Had the Master taught his disciples scientific principles, it would have diverted their minds from the great essential moral lessons which he wished to enforce on their hearts and understandings, that he might arm them with power to meet and overcome the opposition of the unbelieving age. And by so doing he acted the rational part, adapted means to ends, like God, contenting him-

self with teaching the sublime principles of Natural or UNIVER-
SAL RELIGION.   We mean, by the latter proposition, a Religion
adapted perfectly to the requirements of the human heart and
mind, and therefore natural, and essentially universal in its character, to meet the needs of universal Man.   It is no argument
against this view of the Christian Religion, that its principles have
been so grossly misunderstood and misrepresented by those who
have professed to believe and teach them.   The Youthful, undeveloped mind of the Church of past ages accounts fully for all
errors of judgment, and apparent contradictions in profession and
practice.   For the Democratic Philosopher of Nazareth regarded
Man in his cosmopolitan, and not in his national relations.   His
prescient mind recognized the grand level of Humanity, Man as
children of the Divine Father and Mother God, and he was
able, consequently, to address his Gospel of love broadly to the
common needs of the whole Human Family of every condition
and of every period of time.

In the clearer light of the Reasoning Age of the Church and
World, which is rapidly advancing, the Master's comprehensive
intellect will be seen and acknowledged, because the millions
of Christendom will then be more intuitional, will possess more
of the Mind that was in Christ Jesus, through which to interpret
his character and teachings.   At that progressed period, there
will be less discrepancy between the faith and life of the Christian Church than there is at the present time.   And in that intuitional-intellectual age of humanity the words that the Master so
thoughtfully and tenderly spake to his beloved disciples will convey a deeper meaning to the believer——I have many things to
say unto you but ye cannot bear them now.   And that remarkable utterance, that he frequently made after addressing a multitude, will be better understood——He that hath an ear to hear,
let him hear——let his heart and mind be enriched by understanding.   Alas, that so few, of all who have been instructed in
his Divine Religion of Nature, have been able to comprehend
and practice what they professed to believe.

We have said that the intuitional character of the mind of
Christ was a prominent reason why he has been so little appre-

ciated intellectually. And we wish to say, in this connection, and thereby render tardy justice to the opposite sex, that Woman's mind has a relative intuitional action, and this is one reason why she has not also received her full measure of appreciation through the ages. The cultivated intellect, trained to reason inductively, by slow methods of demonstration, cannot fully comprehend the nature of the intuitional mind, as we have before stated. Standing firmly on its material plane of thought to which it has laboriously ascended, it naturally undervalues the the rapid action of the intuitional and deductive order of mind, that swoops down from the lofty plane of cause to declare possible results with all the assurance of knowledge. And so the scholars declare that Woman "jumps at conclusions" in argument, and judges of future results from present conditions, independently of cause and effect, even where subsequent developments of principles and of facts show that her conclusions were correct, and her predictions founded in reason. They call her judgment a "guess;" her foresight a "wonderful hit." And, yet, they understand that both the "guess" and the "hit" involve cause and effect—are actions of the subtle reasoning mind.

The Philosophers accredit the male half of creation with intuitional or inspirational power, and call it of the highest order of intellect, which, in truth, it is. Because the power that enables man to comprehend a principle more clearly and quickly, shows his mind to be in nearer and truer relations to that principle. But they are not prepared to admit that woman can exercise any higher action of intellect than to "jump at conclusions,"—because of their inherited prejudices of sex, and for the additional reason that woman has not yet acquired, as generally as man, the formulæ of logical argument, and cannot state the process by which she reaches her conclusions. If she be educated, she can and does follow the rapid logical action of her own mind; but if she be ignorant, she can simply say that she "knows," or the familiar "because," common to the uneducated of both sexes, while yet she may be conscious of strong mental action on the questions presented to her understanding. Ah! the savans do not yet see that the reason *why* woman can "guess," is because she has more of the *intuitional mind* that was in Christ Jesus. And this is also a solution of the acknowledged truth, that she loves the Master more than man, and can better understand and practice his Divine Gospel of self-abnegating love.

But in the coming age of Reason, when the Church and World shall have grown into the likeness of Christ, when they shall have become spiritual and intuitional-intellectual, like the Master, woman will be better understood, and will receive her full measure of appreciation. Then there will be no more disputation about woman's rights, and woman's sphere. For the great idea of that glorious day will be—HUMAN RIGHTS—without regard to sex, race, color class, or condition. And mankind will universally enjoy the largest civil, political and religious liberty under Christian Republican Institutions. In this higher state of knowledge and freedom, women will move as naturally in her appointed sphere as the planets revolve in theirs; beautifully filling her prescribed niche in the Temple of the Most High.

And then the scales of prejudice will fall from the eyes of men, and they will perceive the divine in woman's nature, and her true relation to the Deity—which has remained a secret since the foundation of the world. For then they will see and acknowledge, with amazement at their former blindness, that the great God that inhabiteth Eternity is male and female. And they will understand that when He spake in the beginning and said —Let *us* make man in *our image*, after *our likeness*—He made them male and female, after the image and likeness of the Divine Father and Mother God. This is the only logical conclusion to be drawn from the premises; notwithstanding that theologians have taught the people for centuries that the Universal Father spake to the Son on this great occasion of populating a new creation to revolve in its eternal circles. Had He really addressed these remarkable words to the Son, the logical sequence would have been the production of a race of males. But man was created male and female, after the image and likeness of the Dual Godhead, and the divine marriage of the Heavens instituted on earth, the union of the twain as one flesh, symbolic of the higher marriage of the soul.

And when Mankind shall have progressed so far that they will be able to perceive these elevated truths and to acknowledge woman as the representative of the Universal Mother, even as man is the representative of the Universal Father, then the *true marriage*, a union of the affections and intellect of two admitted equal companions, will indeed be consummated below, and the sons and daughters of Time will in verity bear the image and likeness of the Divine Father and Mother God. Is it not written in the volume of Inspiration, as well as of Philosophy—I have said, Ye are Gods; and all of you are children of the Most High?

It is a remarkable fact of History that the thought of the World has always been many thousand years in advance of its practice. And Man is ever nearer the truth of Nature than he himself believes. Lo! for centuries the most exalted virtues have been represented by Female Divinities. Ah! a Higher than Mortal Power holds the reins of Universal Government, marking the distinctive epochs of time by stirring events; and lifting high the symbols of coming truths to the World, as signposts by the pathways of the ages, to intimate their true nature and direction.

But man's exceeding joy in discovering the Mother God through the Divine in woman will be attended with humiliating and sorrowful reflections. It will be painful to his pride of intellect, as well as to his affections, to know that, in his strong practical tendencies, in his absolute self-hood, and boasted power of reason, he recognized only himself in the Godhead, and so worshipped a Male Divinity, unregardful of the Divine Mother, Comforter, or Holy Ghost, ever present in the subtle and elevating influences of the beautiful of earth and heaven, and in the persuasive and sustaining power of tenderness and love.

And when it shall be seen that woman, in her sacred office of Maternity, represents the Divine Universal Mother, then these remarkable words of the Master will strike home, with thrilling import, to the understanding of Mankind: All manner of sin and blasphemy shall be forgiven unto men, but the blasphemy against the Holy Ghost shall not be forgiven unto men, neither

16

in this world nor in the world to come.   And such is the inevitable result, because the sin against woman,—the representative of the Divine Mother-God,—will be inherited by her offspring and leave its eternal impress upon their natures.   It is the sin unto death, the effect of which extends beyond the grave, that no prayers can remove, no repentant tears wash away.

And because of the practical tendency of the minds of men they will never regard women as equal and independent human beings with themselves, until they see and believe in the existence of the Divine Mother God as well as the Divine Father. And Science must demonstrate the proposition clearly before they will permit themselves to accept fully this marvellous truth of Nature, and before they will be able to comprehend the grand level of Humanity—Man, male and female, in the image and after the likeness of the Dual Godhead.   And when they shall see and believe, and shall reflect upon the fearful humiliations that women have borne in silence for ages, and upon the thorny paths that they have traveled in patient endurance, striving all the while to be contented and cheerful, and to do good to those who have (often unintentionally) crippled their powers of body and mind, and rendered their lives sorrowful and desolate; THEN there will come a strong and overwhelming reaction in their favor, and, in the earnest desire to fully redress their wrongs, men will do them *more* than justice.   And then the very significant prophecy of Jeremiah will be literally fulfilled: The Lord hath created a new thing in the earth, a woman shall compass a man.

For in that radiant day of Humanity, the heart and intellect of man will expand to give woman larger place.   He will admit her as an equal worker, companion and friend in all the pleasures of life.   She will descend with him to the mineral realms, and wrest the truths of Science from the heart of Nature.   Together they will explore unfrequented wilds, and learn the marvellous secrets of the Animal Kingdom in the grand Cathedral Forests.   Hand in hand she will walk with him through the flowery fields of literature, and climb Parnassean hights to the lofty abode of the Muses.   She will stand by his side in the hallowed Temple of Art, invoking the beautiful of earth, and sea, and air, and of the wondrous human soul, to illumine her canvass and marble, aad her creations will live and speak to the heart and mind of future generations.

And man will not only admit woman's *right* to political franchise as an individual and citizen of the commonwealth; but he will earnestly desire it as needful for the highest benefit of the State. He will call for her to sit within the folds of her Country's honored flag in the high councils of the Nation; and will mantle her with ermine, and appoint her place among the Judges of the people. Indeed, a number of the most enlightened and progressive minds of the present time have already accorded to woman any business position that her abilities and education render her competent to fill. And, even now, she is called to the polls by one of the most distinguished clergymen of the United States. Ay, Henry Ward Beecher has declared from pulpit and rostrum, that it is not only woman's *right*, but her imperative *duty* to stand there by the side of Father, Husband, Brother or Son, and drop her vote into the great Ballot-box of Liberty:

> " To fall,
> Light as a snow-flake on the sod,
> Yet, execute a freeman's will,
> As lightening does the will of God."

The call of this large-natured, humanitary divine, struck like a clarion note on the ear of our nation. City responded to City, through the length and breadth of the land, awaking echoes in all the villages of the plains and valleys. And ocean shouted to ocean across the vast American Continent:——Equal and universal liberty on earth for all the sons and daughters of the Most High.

The opening of the ballot-box to woman will not induce her to leave the consecrated world of the affections and the paths of domestic life in which she has so long lived; but it will infuse into her life an element of practical power which she can use for high and noble objects. It will have the tendency to stimulate her intellectual and moral faculties, to broaden her sympathies, and to increase her love of Country and of Humanity.   And it will also elevate her self-respect, and self-governing power, which have been greatly depressed through the continued injustice of man.   Then she will be better able to defend herself from undisciplined and aggressive passion; and to protect the opposite sex from the abuse of their affectional nature.

When woman can say the word "Sesame!" to the ballot-box, then the doors of attractive occupation will fly open before her, and the avenues of honorable industry will excite her ambition, and attract her away from the trifling follies of life into the higher paths of knowledge and wisdom.

And when this long-wished for day shall arrive, then both man and woman will see that the true marriage relation is pure and holy; and that the office of maternity is a sacred endowment of Heaven.   And it will be seen and acknowledged, for the elevation of mankind, that the Creator could not have appointed, at the beginning, an *inferior sex* to perpetuate the Human Family, without having violated His own eternal law of progress.   And the All-Powerful, All-Wise, and All-Perfect could not be inconsistent in action.   It is a well understood physiological principle that the higher and more perfect the creature of any class or species of the animal kingdom, the more superior will be its offspring.   And it is also an established fact, that *conditions* exert a powerful influence upon structure and intelligence, through the whole range of animate nature.   It must follow, consequently, as a logical sequence, that, if we would have a highly organized and superior race of human beings, we must obey the requisite laws of improvement.

At an advanced period of social development, man will not only admit that antenatal conditions make indelible impressions on the fœtus, affecting the character of the yet unborn, and moulding the form in correspondence therewith ; but he will earnestly co-operate with woman, in providing favorable conditions for the development of the human offspring, whom the All-Father inspires with his own breath and endows with His own immortality.

Oh ! then, marriage will indeed become a holy sacrament,

and great will be the joy of maternity.   Woman will no longer
bring forth children in sorrow ; and there will be no unwelcome
little one in the family circle to reproach either parent for un-
dervaluing the highest trust of Heaven—an innocent and immortal soul!   Oh! then—thank God! there will be no more pitiful, homeless wanderers in His beautiful world, to die of lingering starvation under the very shadow of Christian churches,
or to run in the dark alleys of sin until their feet are soiled with
the mire, their lives corrupted with its malignant contagion, and
the light of their higher natures extinguished in crime.

It has been said, in the early part of the present Chapter, that
the advanced Reasoning Age of the Church and World, that
grasps principles, observes relations, and prophecies results, is
pressing rapidly forward.   The truly inspired workers of this
glorious day of Reason will adapt means to ends, like God, for
His name will be written in their FOREHEADS.   Verily, it will be
an Age of marvellous intellectual and moral achievement.   Civil,
social, and religious movements, as aforesaid, will go forward
with accelerated power.   Even now the great work of Christianizing the World, through the agency of enlightened Reason, has
been commenced in earnest.   Serfdom has been abolished in
Russia, and Slavery in North America, and in some parts of
South America, as preparatory measures in the Government of
God.   For Christianity is but another name of pure Democracy,
which implies Universal Liberty, Equality and Fraternity for all
the sons and daughters of the Most High..   Where the Spirit of
the Lord is, there is Liberty and Love for all the Human Family.   It is the Divine Spirit, acting through an *enlightened reason*,
that is to accomplish the great work of regeneration in the heart,
and renovation in the life of the World.   Ay, social, civil and
religious institutions are already being remodelled after the
heavenly order.   Law, Medicine and Divinity have felt the impulse of a quickened reason, and are moving forward.

The Navy of the United States has abandoned the inhuman
practice of flogging men for trifling offenses, because it is at
length seen that they grow rapidly worse, instead of better, when
subject to the irrational and degrading punishment.

17

Through the wise counsels of Horace Mann, the public schools of our Country have also set aside whipping for trifling offenses, and instituted, in place of the ferule and rod, moral punishments which are humane, and far more effective for subduing ebullitions of passion in children, and the unadjusted physical energy that rebels against authority, manifesting itself in endless varieties of fun and mischief. A few Old Testament teachers, as well as Clergymen, continue still to hold Solomon's rod threateningly over their schools and congregations; for they do not yet SEE.

Through the influence of the enlightened minds of Doctors Gall and Spurzheim, the unfortunate victims of insanity are no longer bound in straight jackets, and confined in narrow dungeons, as in former ages, and obliged to submit to cruel flagellation, which increased their fearful malady, until reason became hopelessly dethroned, and they were irrevocably lost to themselves and to society. But they are now treated with considerate kindness, and by means of amusement and attractive occupation, diverted from the one engrossing subject of thought, in order that the over stimulated faculties, which have induced the unbalanced condition of their minds, shall have time to rest and react until equilibrium be restored.

The cruel and inhuman treatment of State prisoners has also been greatly modified within the past few years, through the humane influence of Dorothea L. Dix. The cheering light of day, the healing breath of heaven, and a few crumbs of intellectual food, have found their way into these dark, damp, and demoralizing cells. But it yet remains for advancing Reason and Humanity to convert our State prisons into schools for instruction, where the unfortunate inmates may learn their duty to themselves, to their fellow beings, and to their Creator; and where they may also acquire a knowledge of some useful and attractive occupation, adapted to the capability of each, so that, when the hour shall arrive for them to mingle again with their fellows, their feet may be lifted entirely out of the mire, and set in clean paths. The action of punishment will then be altogether reformatory and enlightening, instead of corruptive and benightening.

The name of God was written in the "forehead" of Theodore Parker and Thomas Starr King, and they SAW, and comprehended the profound significance of the Word: In God we live, and move, and have our being. Their great hearts and minds were filled with the Master's divine "enthusiasm for Humanity,"and they were instant in season and out of season, teaching the people to see, and to venerate the divine in their nature that they were clouding with sin, or burying in the rubbish of the world. The name of God is written in the " forehead " of Beecher, of Frothingham, and of Chapin, and they too, SEE, and are filled with "enthusiasm for Humanity." And their words have vitalizing power; going forth from earnest hearts and minds, they strike home to the affections and understandings of the people, even as the lightening flies directly to its mark. The result is that the churches of these inspired men are always thronged with sympathizing hearers, and humble seekers after light and truth from above.

Livingston was touched on the " forehead" by the finger of the Almighty, and his religion became enlightened by his reason. He SAW. Then he comprehended the important meaning of the Revealed Word to Man: First, in the order of God, is the natural; after, that which is spiritual; and, acting in harmony with the word of inspiration, and with his own intellect, he wrote back from Central Africa to the English Board of Foreign Missions, who had sent him thither, recommending the establishment of Trading Posts across the entire Continent, fro m the Indian Sea to the Atlantic Ocean, which posts should be connected with reliable Commercial Houses in Europe; showing, at the same time, the entire practicability of the enterprise. Through such measures he proposed to unite the Material Interests of the various native tribes,—to establish laws for mutual protection of life and property among them,—to encourage habits of provident industry, and to stimulate the spirit of enterprise, and thus prepare the way for the permanent establishment of Schools and Churches. He believed that these Institutions for enlightening and elevating could thus, and only thus, be effectively protected from injury, in case of warlike disturbances among the allied Tribes, and hostile invasions of savage neighbors.   It was a grand rational and inspired plan of operation which would have accomplished the missionary work of ages in a limited number of years.   But the creed-bound Board of Foreign Missions DID NOT SEE.   That Board pronounced the inspired idea a worldly scheme, opposed its adoption, and reproved the chosen Instrument of Deity.   Yet, ideas that have been sent forth to Man, with the endorsement of Reason and of Heaven, will not be forever dishonored on earth.   Another generation of Man will act on Livingston's plan; and his labors will not have been in vain.

Bryant, Whittier, Lowell, Longfellow, Elizabeth Barrett Browning, and a few other noble poets of the present age, have been touched on the "forehead" with a live coal from off the altar of truth, and they SEE, and are filled with the divine afflatus, with the dear Master's "enthusiasm for Humanity."

Horace Greeley, William Lloyd Garrison, Wendell Phillips, Lydia Maria Child, Lucretia Mott, and Thompson of the British Isles, have been touched on the "forehead," and filled with rational enthusiasm for humanity.   They SEE.   They led the Grand Army of Reform majestically forward on the battle-fields of Freedom, and sent electrifying bombs of "Moral Suasion" within the strong entrenchments of Slavery, that struck the soul of Despotism with terror.

And there are small numbers of earnest workers, men and women of heroic souls, in every department of humanitary labor, who have been touched on the "forehead," whose Religion has been enlightened by their Reason, and who have proved successful workers and advocates of truth.   To have a Zeal for God according to Reason and Knowledge is the acme of human endeavor.

If disheartened Teachers were able to leave the old hackneyed methods of forcing truths through established grooves, and to look up with inquiring minds for Divine assistance in their labors, they would also SEE.   For is it not written: *Ask* and ye shall receive; SEEK and ye shall find; KNOCK and the door shall be opened?   And they would be able to leap the difficulties of the present hour, and to establish their principles in the hearts and minds of the people, receiving encouraging sympathy and co-operation from their contemporaries.   When the ministers of the Gospel SEE, as well as believe, they will adapt their methods of instruction to the nature of Man, and will inevitably reach the hearts and minds of the Millions and inspire them with the same truths, and the same burning zeal for labor in the vineyard of the Lord.

Do any inquire: What will be the peculiar or marked character of the Second Christian Era after it shall have culminated in meridian glory?   Let To-day speak and answer :—It will be eminently Spiritual and Intuitional-Intellectual.   Such is the response of the Present from the most elevated point of human observation which overlooks the Past, and observes the progressive movements of the ages, and where their lines of direction are projected upon the grand future of Humanity.   Ay, the various races of Man will then have grown into the likeness of Christ, and become Spiritual and Intuitional-Intellectual, like him.   The Master himself taught this truth by striking and beautiful illustration, when he said to his disciples :   I am the Vine, and ye are the branches.   The Vine and its branches are *one*, and bear kindred fruit.   And every vine may be known by its own peculiar fruit.   In anticipation of the coming Day of Humanity, Science, Art and Religion are now waiting to receive the baptism of the Holy Ghost and of fire.   And when they shall receive this baptism of FIRE, the Priests of their Altars will then become loving and devout worshippers of the Divine Father and Mother God.   Under its kindling inspiration Science will ere long safely navigate Sea and Air ; will drain the malarious marshes, and convert them into fruitful gardens ; will exalt the valleys and make the rough places plain, preparing a royal highway for the Brotherhood of Nations.   And Divine Art will enchant the soul of Humanity with more perfect creations and become an agent of power in producing social order, peace, and harmony.   The while, in accordant action, the various Religions of the globe, like confluent waters, will merge into ONE—in a pure Christian Democracy—under the controlling influence of Spiritualistic Rationalism.

It is a well understood principle of Philosophy that physical growth is the result of physical exercise; intellectual growth, of intellectual culture; and that all development obeys a uniform law of unfolding.   Spiritual advancement forms no exception to the universal order of progress.   A Spiritual Religion must culminate of necessity, in obedience to its own law of growth, in a spiritual direction, and must bear its own peculiar fruit.   A running review of the Church of God on Earth, from the call of the patriarch Abraham to Abraham Lincoln, justifies the conclusions of Reason and Philosophy.   And it is logical to infer, that as mankind grow more and more spiritual and intuitional, they will become more and more open to the influx of truth and light, from the Divine Creative Spirit.

And they who have grown into the likeness of Christ, and become spiritual and intuitional-intellectual, will beget offspring who will inherit the same peculiar order of mind; and our humanity will at length reach the full stature of men and women in Christ Jesus.   If any doubt the spiritual and intuitional-intellectual tendency of the present age, over that of past ages, let them observe the children born in Christendom within the last few years, and compare them with former generations.   Large numbers of children, at the present time, see disembodied spirits and converse familiarly with them without either surprise or fear, because to the manner born.   And the children of the present, manifest a remarkable development of Intuitional reasoning power.   For there is a spirit in man, and the inspiration of the Almighty giveth understanding.   All who will investigate the subject will be convinced of the truth of the proposition.   The Book of Nature is open.   They who run, may read; if they do not willfully blind their eyes.

In past centuries, the difficulty of achievement has been so great, in both physical and moral fields of labor, that it has given rise to the following adage: It is one thing to plan, and another to execute.   But in the advanced reasoning maturity of the world, after the Christian Religion shall have become universal, and the popular mind intuitional—for this will then be a general, instead of an exceptional character of the human intellect—both physi-

~cal and moral forces will move so grandly forward, that it will appear to be *one thing* both to plan and to execute. In that coming day, there will be as much accomplished in a year as there was formerly in an age. And then the true significance and justice of the Master's parable will be seen, in his comprehensive view of progressive humanity. In the parable to which we allude, he likens the kingdom of Heaven to a vineyard, in which laborers were engaged to work at various hours of the day. When the Lord of the vineyard summoned them at evening, to pay them their wages, he gave to every man a penny. They who commenced labor at an early hour, supposed that they would receive more; but he gave to every man a penny, in accordance with the principle of eternal justice. For if those who came earlier, labored longer and harder, they did not accomplish as much as those who came later, even at the eleventh hour. Because, in the world of mankind, which is represented by the vineyard, the capability of executing increases in an exact ratio with the advancement of reason and knowledge. And so it is written: The last shall be first, and the first last.

We have shown from Sacred History that the Church of God on earth has been marked by two distinguishing Epochs, or Religious Dispensations, the early inauguration by Abraham, in its season of Childhood; and the subsequent one by our Lord Jesus Christ, in its period of Youth; and that both of these important events were attended with marvellous spiritual phenomena and revelations from Heaven. The later Era was more signally marked by spiritual manifestations than the former, because of the increased growth of spiritual truth in the world. But spiritual phenomena have not been confined to these two distinctive periods in the history of the Church. Ministering Angels have ever waited at her consecrated Altars to keep alive the holy, sacrificial flame of love in the hearts of the people, and to stimulate the spiritual developement of Man through the dark physical ages of ignorance and sin. God's Church on Earth rests upon this Spiritual Foundation. It underlies both the Israelitish and the Christian Dispensations, which are ONE in the vast plan of infinite progression, and of universal adaptation of truth to human conditions and requirements.

And, now, in the reasoning Maturity of the Church, as in its
Childhood and Youth, these remarkable Spiritual Phenomena
have appeared, for the third time, but with an accession of
power—because of the still farther progressed spiritual development of the present age—and are sweeping, like a flood, over
the earth, breaking away the barriers of infidelity, and renewing, with unanswerable facts, the Gospel promise of immortality
to the family of Man.   This power is of God.   It heralds the
Second Advent of the Master, in the reasoning Maturity of the
Church and World, in which period his sublime Gospel of Love
will be accepted with the *understanding*, as well as with the
heart of Man.   We could as easily roll back the mighty waves
of Ocean, borne onward by resistless winds, as we could stay
the mightier Spirit Forces that control the winds and waves,
when they are sent forth on their mission of power and blessing
by the Supreme Ruler of the Universe.

It is no argument against the high Authority of the Spiritual
Phenomena of the times to say, that they are dangerous to society, that they have produced insanity and moral dereliction.
All the great principles of truth that have grown into the heart
and mind of the World were once pronounced dangerous to society, and their Apostles fanatics and insane persons, who were
persecuted and tormented often unto death, being regarded as
enemies, instead of Saviors of the Human Family.   Much ab-
erration of intellect has resulted from false presentations of the
Christion Religion, and much moral evil from the example and
influence of unworthy professors and hypocrites.   And yet, we
would not expunge the Church for such reasons.   If there be
danger to society through ignorance of the laws which govern
Spirit Phenomena, the more imperative becomes the duty of
Christian Teachers to investigate spiritual facts, upon which the
Christian Religion is based, and to instruct the people how to do
the same with benefit, instead of injury.   But at this present a
very large proportion of Teachers in the Church either ignore
Spirit manifestations altogether, or pronounce them to be wholly
of the Devil.   And by so doing they declare to the reasoning
age that they are incapable of taking a philosophic view of the

growth of spiritual principles in the Church and World through the centuries, of meeting the logical results in the present, and of stating them fairly to the questioning minds of to-day. They permit their own peculiar prejudices and experiences to bias their judgment. And they will lose the respect and confidence of thinking minds, outside as well as inside of Church organizations, if they continue in this irrational course. Because intelligent men and women know, from facts of history, from general observation, and from personal experience that such is not the truth. And they also know, from Reason and Philosophy, that God's laws are uniform and universal through the wide range of matter and of spirit; and that the Divine Parent does not permit good to exist to the exclusion of evil; nor evil to prevail to the exclusion of good. They believe in the philosophical action of the Spirit Phenomena, as of all other forces in Nature. They cannot admit that these peculiar Phenomena of the present are alone exceptional in their development to the universal order of cause and effect, and to the general manifestations of both good and evil in the world. Let the tares and wheat grow together until the harvest: Says the Revealed Word to Man; and the Revealed Will in Nature speaks with a significance equally wise and profound, through the continuous growth of lovely and useful plants. together with injurious and poisonous weeds; and through the production of harmless and serviceable animals in common with the destructive and venomous. It is clear to thinking minds that, if good spirits can return from the Valley of the shadow of death, evil, or ignorant, undeveloped spirits can also return by obeying the same laws of communication; these are alike open to all who are able to improve them. There are no distinct rules made, nor conditions provided, by Heaven for different classes of the Human Family, outside of each individual's own ability and high Court of Conscience. He maketh His Sun to rise on the evil and on the good, and sendeth rain on the just and on the unjust. Such is the policy of God's Government.

And thinking men and women believe, further, that evil has its mission on earth, as well as good, otherwise it could not exist. Man is stronger and nobler for contending with difficulties,

18

and individualizing himself in truth.   The Human Family are required to be watchful against temptation, because there are besetting sins that may lure into forbidden paths and lead astray. They are required to work out their own salvation with fear and trembling, because there is error and evil to overcome ; and if they are proud and self-sufficient they will not seek humbly for the help which cometh from above, that can alone aid them in the difficult work.

" He that is born is listed, life is war."

From the cradle to the grave, it is a moral contest between the false and the true; between the open foes of truth, who challenge us abroad, and the more subtle and dangerous enemies of the soul, who ambush in the coverts of self-love and indecisions at home.

The Chnrch can find no valid argument in favor of neglecting to investigate Spirit Phenomena, in the fact that " Free-lovers" have become believers, and still continue to advocate their abominable sensualities; nor, because Spiritualism has found adherents among sinners of every shade of villainy, from that arch-apostle of Ecclesiastic Saintship, Brigham Young, down to the lowest saint of the catalogue, who attract—in accordance with the universal law that like attracts like—Spirits of a kindred order from the other world, who pronounce evil good; and good, evil.   Many persons were possessed of devils, or evil spirits, in the days of the Master.   And Jesus himself is said not only to have cast out legions, but to have empowered his disciples of that, and of every age, to do the same.   And there are no sweeping anathemas in the New Testament, pronounced against Spirit manifestations, because devils had power to appear on earth, as well as Moses and Elias.   But, quite the contrary: St. Paul exhorts the followers of Christ to seek earnestly after spiritual gifts, enumerating those most to be desired.   He wisely counsels all to try the Spirits, to see what manner of Spirit they are of; and to prove all things, and hold fast that which is good.

Neither can the Christian Church find a valid excuse for her neglect of duty, in reference to this subject, in the fact that the

Spirit Phenomena of the day appear, to a very great extent, outside of her organizations. The law of growth demands that such should be the case. Conservative organizations are always unfavorable to progressive movements. The first action of such bodies, is to *reject* new principles without investigation, however much of truth they may contain; even when the truth presented is also the same in kind with what has already found acceptance. And it is so, for the reason that the minds of the people who compose them, have been narrowed by the *special form* of presentation. This is one reason why the Philosopher of Nazareth established the Christian Religion among the lower classes, outside of the Hebrew Church, and of conventional society. He wished that it might have an opportunity to thrive, as well as to become radical and democratic. The Church is required to meet all principles and conditions as they may exist in Christendom, in the understanding and loving spirit of the Master. It is her imperarive duty to show the people how to investigate spiritual facts, in order that their souls may be enlarged and enriched by the true influences, and protected against the false, and that they may be able to render a reason for the faith that is in them.

The widely spreading Spirit manifestations of to-day are loud calls of the Master to the Church in her maturity, to investigate Spiritual Truths with the reasoning intellect. For the Reasoning Age of the world is rapidly advancing, and she must show the philosophy of her faith, or she will be swept away by the increasing army of Materialistic Rationalism. The present, as we have already shown, is the period of Demonstrative Reason, (which constitutes it, eminently, the Age of Invention,) and there is a universal tendency to reject all principles of truth that cannot be submitted to logical demonstration. Ay, if the Church does not awake to this truth, she will become a dead letter in the world. Now is the accepted time, and now is the day of salvation. Let her arise and show that she is alive and in earnest. Let her shake off the trammeling forms of past ages, and draw fresh and kindling inspiration from the ever-present Deity, and send forth her spiritual life in burning lava streams from the central fires of God's truth, that shall electrify and warm the heart of this cold

Rationalistic Philosophy.   Ay, let her labor unceasingly to demonstrate Spiritual Truths with unrefutable arguments.   She stands face to face with facts; let her examine, and build up for the All-Father and All-Mother a beautiful and holy Temple of Spiritual Philosophy that shall reach far above the clouds of human error and sorrow into the clear light of Divine Truth; and the smile of the Godhead will rest upon it; and it cannot be overthrown by all the Materialistic Rationalism of all the ages.

When Spiritual Truths shall find acceptance of the enlightened intellect of the Church and World, they can never more degenerate into superstition, as in former ages of ignorance and darkness, in the Childhood and Youth of Mankind.

We often hear it boldly asserted by the Materialistic Rationalists of our day, that Christ introduced no new principles in ethics, and was no greater than other moral reformers who preceded him.   They tell us that Zoroaster and Confucius taught the immortality of the soul, and the practice of the same exalted virtues, and that they have drawn more followers after them than the man of Galilee, and exerted a more widely extending influence than he.

Assertion is an easy and a convenient method of stating opinions, but it is not always the most effective and reliable.   If we turn to the records of history and compare the Pagan Teachers of ethics with the Democratic Philosopher of Nazareth, and observe their peculiar methods of presenting truth, and the effect upon the human mind of the truths presented by each, we shall then be able to arrive at just and logical conclusions in regard to the comparative value and influence of their respective teachings.   The power of any truth must be measured by its effects. We may learn the magnitude of a luminous human soul by its capacity to receive and to transmit the light which it borrows from Heaven.

It is true that Pagan Philosophers taught the doctrine of immortality.   Yet, they gained but a partial view of the subject, and hence treated the grand generic truth specifically ; in verity, monopolized the universal law of Intelligent Nature in favor of the male half of creation.   They were unable, from their peculiar standpoint of observation, to view broadly human relations and conditions, past, present, and prospective. They aimed, undoubtedly, to be equally just to each sex, but failed of the mark through limited mental vision, and ended with being merely generous to their own. Indeed, woman was too much for the Pagan Philosophers. They could not comprehend the intuitional quality of her mind ; and, judging man to be the dominant sex in the order of creation, they naturally ranked her beneath him And they took not only a partial, but an inverted view of the character, mission and destiny of woman. Living in an age of the world when the animal nature of Man was in the ascendant, they confounded the beautiful and sensuous with the purely sensual, and measured woman by her animal, instead of her intellectual and moral powers, regarding her as the special minister of the passions, and as a lovely, artful tempter to entice man to wander from the paths of virtue and wisdom. And so they limited her sphere to the office and duties of maternity.

Ah! the Pagan Philosophers did not comprehend the Divine Unity of all Intelligence, did not recognize Man, male and female, in the image and after the likeness of the God, Male and Female ; and consequently they could not see the common origin, level, and destiny of the great Human Family. For they possessed not the spiritual requisites of character, and woman's hour had not fully come. The rough places of the earth were not made smooth before her ; nor the harmony of the physical, intellectual and moral elements inaugurated, which is to distinguish her era in the luminous Day of Reason, when mankind will be in closer sympathy with Nature, and there will be a more general application of universal principles.

But, we repeat, it must not be forgotten that Pagan Philosophers were partially developed men, belonging to a partially developed age; and that, as a consequent, their philosophy was but a partial observation and statement of general principles, and a partial application of universal laws; and that their methods of teaching were also partial and did not address and reach the whole nature of Man, nor the whole Human Family. They had received from their own, and from other times, the bias of sex; and were bound by traditionary forms of religious faith, and their prejudices controlled their judgment.   They were powerfully influenced by the first Religious Dispensation of Law and Authority, or special revelation of the Divine Father God in the Childhood of the World; and, notwithstanding their belief in a plurality of gods, the great I AM of the Hebrews, in solitary glory and light, unapproachable by mortal man, deeply impressed their minds, which were more strongly affected by the sublime than the beautiful in Nature, and gave direction to their religious sentiments.   And, because of their faith in Masculine Supremacy in the abode of the immortal Gods, their partial view of the grand truth of eternal life was a logical necessity.   They argued themselves into the belief that, in that Paradise of male blessedness and power, as in the council chambers of earthly monarch, woman would not be permitted to enter.   It is true that there were exceptional cases in her favor.   But she could not appear there in the vestments with which she was clothed at nativity by the God of gods.   She was required to robe her spirit, through some magical process, which the Philosophers themselves did not comprehend and could not state for her instruction, in the male habiliment, in direct violation of the very truth of Nature for which they were pleading.

And, for the reason that the Pagan Philosophers took this limited and erroneous view of the character and influence of woman, they deprived her of a voice in the State, and of an equal interest in the remunerative industrial, and the speculative pursuits of the ages.   And so woman, equally endowed by Nature with man, intellectually and morally, was confined to domestic and religious fields of labor, and to the direct cultivation of her affectional, apart from her intellectual, qualities.   And this limited action of her powers has tended to develop in her character more heart than intellect, and more of the sentimental and ideal, than of the practical and executive.   And woman's subordinate position in the past has forced her to subject her native independence of character, and to implore for a small share of the results of man's industry and position of power—rarely to aid herself, individually—but for the benefit of helpless infants, to feed, clothe and educate; for the sacred privilege of aiding the unfortunate; and for the high uses of intellectual and religious culture and social elevation.

And, now, woman, in the reasoning age of the world, and the nineteenth century of the Christian Religion, after long periods of crippled powers and limited spheres of action; after having been condemned by Pagan Philosophers and Legislators to the disheartening and stultifying position of continual dependence, cursed with the almost maddening necessity of planning continually, without the command of material means to execute, and thus relieve the tension of purpose; and after all the fearful suffering of the past from a stinging sense of injustice toward her, which she has been powerless to prevent; she is informed, by a modern Christian Teacher, who represents large numbers of men in power in both Church and State, that she must continue in the same path of humiliation and trial through her earthly existence; because *he* has discovered that she is not only in a "subject condition," but also "in a subject nature," which disqualifies her for holding positions of power and influence. But the Doctor wishes to be very kind to the subordinate woman that he, not God, has created, and promises her—much in the same style that a crying babe is presented with a sugar-plum to soothe its grief—that she shall be rewarded for the injustice and tyranny to which she has been subjected on earth, by becoming man's equal in Heaven. But the Doctor does not show any reason for this compensatory conclusion of his argument, and of woman's destiny. He does not show *how* her whole nature will become changed, by merely casting aside its garment of flesh, and his subordinate sex will be at once equal to his superior sex, on the more elevated plane of existence.

The learned Doctor points to woman's vail, as a symbol of her subject character and condition. The vail implies *concealment*, but not subordination. Woman's noblest and best friend, the Democratic Philosopher of Nazareth, uplifted the vail when he bestowed on the daughters of God the baptism of the Holy Ghost and of fire. And thenceforth woman has been recognized by the seer, as the representative of the Divine Mother, even as man is the representative of the Divine Father. And, among the nations of Christendom, the vail is no longer regarded as a conventional necessity. There woman's true relation to man and Deity is only concealed from those who are governed by tradition and prejudice. But the chain around woman's neck, and the bracelet about her arms, are striking emblems of her yet enforced subjection.

Dr. Bushnell presents to his readers the woman of the past, under the influence of all her circumscribed conditions, and her disabilities for place and power, because of her lack of educational advantages—of that intellectual training, which alone qualifies man for exalted positions, by putting him in possession of his own faculties, and teaching him the application of these powers to definite ends—and affirms that she is helpless and dependent by nature, and, consequently, incapable of commanding. The peculiar manifestations of woman's character, under conditions of enforced ignorance and servitude, he thus judges to be the normal expression of her nature. But while it is true that the historical woman exhibited the *natural results of her peculiarly limited conditions;* it is also true, that very different results would naturally have followed had she enjoyed the same personal freedom and civil liberty as man—the same opportunities for acquiring knowledge and broadening her understanding—and the same stimulating influences of a noble career before her, with the world for her sphere of action, in addition to the nursery, drawing-room and kitchen. Knowledge is the test of capability between man and man, and Reason is the arbiter; and the same high powers should sit in judgment between man and woman, instead of tradition and prejudice.

It would be monstrous to Reason, for an Enlightened Nation, to show her results in the arts and sciences, and comparing these with those of an illiterate, undeveloped people, to conclude therefrom that she was more highly gifted by Nature than the other whose native endowments were yet latent forces in heart, mind and soul. When Britain was a barbarian, she would not bear comparison with the cultivated Roman, and was regarded by the latter as an undeveloped child, to be restrained andguided by superior intelligence and wisdom. But when the great enlightener, Knowledge, walked forth in sublime freedom on her island shores, her aspirations were kindled, and her intellect was enlarged, and she rose to majestic stature, and commanded the respect and admiration of the Ancient Mistress of the world.

Dr. Bushnell tries to persuade himself and his readers that woman's habit of pleading and imploring for the end she would attain is another mark of her "subject nature." He does not see that it arises from the obstinate fact that she is powerless to command, by reason of her circumscribed position and limited resources. And because woman is able to endure dependence, injustice and tyranny, without complaint and often with cheerfulness—with a force of purpose that would be termed *philosophy* in man—the Doctor brings this strength of her nature to bear against her as a weakness by which to prove her "subordinate" character. He cannot see that woman's apparent willingness to love and cling to man through all phases of tyranny, and through every degree of error, immorality and crime, is because of her peculiar relations of wife and mother, and the responsibilities connected with these, together with the hard pressure of social conditions, and the closed avenues of remunerative occupations. And it is also a necessity to woman to preserve her love for man, in order that she may retain her self-respect in the close relation she sustains to him as wife. Without affection, life with him would be but legalized prostitution, and an unendurable burthen. And so she tries to palliate and excuse his errors, tries *not to see* this, or that, fault of character, hoping that he is really better than he seems. He is her husband—the father of her children —he is human still—he cannot be utterly vile. If she should cease to love and care for him he *might* sink into lower depths of evil, and she would feel herself responsible for his fall—her love *might have saved him.* The while she struggles on, striving to be cheerful and courageous for the sake of the dear little ones —for the sake of the friends whom she loves—for the sake of her Religion, which is like an anchor to her soul, reaching within the vail and connecting her with immortal joys, unclouded by

19

disappointment, sin and sorrow—she would render it attractive to others, that they might also share its hope and consolation.

Woman can, indeed, submit to personal abuse, and can endure torture of soul, as well as body, until she feels as if her own proper self had been crushed out of her being ; but she cannot see her children destitute of bread, and ignorant and degraded in the world ;—she cannot see the husband whom she clothed in her maiden purity, with ideal perfection, and vowed before her God to love and cherish through life, go down the dark ways of sin and death without placing herself as a barrier in his path, even should his reckless hand be uplifted against her in violence.

It would be equally as rational for the Doctor to infer, because the slave loves his master, even under the stings of the lash and all kinds of injustice, and often appears happy and cheerful under such conditions, that therefore God created the African to be the slave of his fellow man, as for him to conclude that woman's acceptance, in past ages of ignorance and helplessness, of a subordinate position in society, is an indication of a "subject nature." HABIT, as well as necessity, exerts a powerful influence upon individuals and classes. So true is this in the estimation of mankind that it has passed into a universal adage: Habit is second nature. The poor captive learns at length to love his chains; not because they limit his freedom, and cripple his form, until the iron enters his soul; but for the reason of long, familiar association; for the reason that the human being is so constituted by Deity that he will turn in extreme conditions in every possible direction for aid; for one ray of light to relieve the oppressive darkness; for one point of interest to attract the weary eye; for one familiar sound to vibrate on the listening ear; and if he can establish no sympathetic relations with his fellow beings, he will strive to adapt himself to his lonely condition, and become intimate with his inanimate and gloomy surroundings. Byron's Prisoner of Chillon declares, in confirmation of this truth,

> The very walls and I grew friends.
> So much a long communion tends
> To make us what we are. And I,
> Even I, regained my freedom with a sigh.

Indeed, Dr. Bushnell has been able to take but a very narrow view of his subject, through pride of dominant sex, faith in traditional falsities, and the strong prejudices of education. Under these unfavorable conditions for philosophic thought and righteous judgment, he would hold woman in subordinate positions, even though she were better qualified than man for places of trust and influence: "Only for the look of it!"—to quote his own language ; and because of an impassable gulf of cause and effect, which, fortunately for the opposite sex, is of his own creation, instead of Heaven's ordination. The Doctor has not only wronged woman by his partial views and illogical conclusions, but he has done injustice to himself as a reasoning man, and also to the class of minds in sympathy with the opinions which he represents.

We find excuses, naturally, for Pagan Philosophers, in the pioneer conditions of the human race, and in the limited and despotic tendencies of institutions and governments under the ancient rule of Might. They lived at a period of time when material manifestations of power were grander than intellectual and moral. He who ranked highest in physical achievement was the superior being to both man and woman. But, in proportion as the various faculties of heart, mind and soul unfolded in the Human Family, as the World progressed towards Maturity, the mental view gradually changed ; and, now, the intellectual and moral powers are grander and more God-like, to the enlightened reason of Mankind, than physical forces ; and it becomes more difficult to find excuses for those, claiming to be Philosophers, who treat broad principles in a prejudiced and partial manner.

It is interesting to note from the pages of history that woman has ever ranked proportionally higher in society with the increase of knowledge and the fuller development of reason ; and has received a juster measure of appreciation with the progress of Christian civilization, ascending rapidly in the social scale, when offset by the refined weights of enlightened opinions. Democracy has succeeded Despotism in the world, through the influence of the profound Gospel of the Philosopher of Nazareth, which is, as we have already shown, a clear, forcible and con-vincing statement of the Religion of Nature. And the many subtle forms of Despotism which have insinuated themselves into the social and religious, as well as civil, life of the world, will pass away before this glorious Christian Democracy, this ris-ing Sun of Righteousness. It will penetrate tyranny and error with its positive living power, and exhale them from the moral world, even as the beams of morning gather up the malarious fogs of night that have lingered in the pleasant valleys of Nature, dissipating them with warmth and brightness. The overcoming of evil with good is a grand principle of intelligent as well as of material creation.

Ay, we can truly apologize for Pagan Philosophers. At their times of ignorance, God winked; but, light having come into the world, Christian Philosophers remain without excuse. The people feel that they have a moral right to demand that they shall be truer to the truth of Intelligent Nature than ancient sages, and draw more logical deductions in their speculative theories of human life; because they have superior points of ob-servation on the ascending pyramids of the centuries, they have the accumulated *data* of all the ages to aid them in forming more correct opinions, and in presenting clearer and fuller state-ments of general principles.

The people of Christendom are indeed disappointed, when they sit down to enjoy an intellectual feast, that has been pre-pared for them, by a caterer of accredited ability, to find that mere skeletons of dead theories have been dragged forth from the tomb of the past, and re-served with modern condiments for their delectation. They look in vain for living bread to satisfy the hunger of the soul, and for the pure water of life to quench the thirst of the Spirit, and go forth to their labor, pining still for the words of truth and life, that are not written in the books of the philosophers. They are weary of blind, partial Paganism, and call earnestly for far-seeing, far-reaching, and all-embracing Christianity. They believe that they shall find in it, alone, the true liberty of the Children of God; the Spirit itself so witness-eth with their spirits. They know themselves to be circumscribed by the *special forms* in which it was presented in the Youth of the Church, and feel painfully the limitations of their creeds; and they implore the Teachers of the age, to give them a more rational, and a higher interpretation of its elevating, democratic principles. Where is the God-like soul, aglow with Human and Divine Love, that, recognizing the progressive nature of Man, and the demands of the Reasoning Age, will be able to liberate the masses of Christendom from the dead formulæ of their faith with the living word of inspiration?

The partial views which the wisest and most intelligent men of past ages have taken of general principles, and the false conclusions at which they have, consequently, arrived, may serve to illustrate to the people of the present the exceeding folly of holding fast to the philosophy of early times, and to the traditions of the Fathers, as the ultimate of truth ; and of bringing enlightened Reason into abeyance to blind Authority. For, although there were many truly inspired Teachers in the past, it should not be forgotten, that they were inspired for their own day, and its peculiar requirements, and not for our time, with all its increased needs, because of its changed and enlarged conditions.

It is curious to observe, as the wheels of thought revolve, that what was uppermost in one epoch of the world, will be at antipodes in another. A modern Philosopher was recently tracing the physiological law of progressive creation, which shows that each species of animals, in the ascending scale, bear on their forms some one organ in an incipient stage of development, which is perfected in the next approximately higher species. Pausing, suddenly, he placed his hands impressively on his heart, and exclaimed with the enthusiasm of a new idea: What mean these intimations of woman on the form of man? Ah ! maybe we are to become *women* in that other state of existence. And thus the Christian Philosopher has turned the table on the Pagan, and woman is avenged.

It is true that, in addition to the Pagan Philosophers' partial statement of the truth of immortality, they elaborated an elevated Code of Morals, many principles of which are kindred with the truths taught by the Philosopher of Nazareth; in the generic

20

sense, that all truth is kindred, emanating as it does from one Source, and being adapted broadly, as it is, to one end, the development of created intelligence; the while radiating from the centre to the circumference of the universe, and scintillating in beauty, power and glory through all Nature, animate and inanimate.

And the Pagan Philosophers were not only partial in their observations and statements of truth, as we have already shown, but their *methods* of teaching were also limited. They did not address the *whole nature of Man*—did not appeal to the *heart* as well as to the *mind* of the people. They were coldly ethic, and could not feel the full, deep throb of Humanity's great heart. The male and female principle throughout material nature was recognized by them, but the Divine Mother of the Human Family was unseen. For the baptism of the Holy Ghost, and of the sacred fire of purifying Love, was not bestowed on them, to burn, and glow, and warm the whole intellectual and moral being. Their minds were under the dominion of masculine supremacy in the Universe, and they were more on the external and demonstrative, than the spiritual and deductive plane of Thought. They addressed the reason of mankind at a period of human progress when that noble power of the mature Man was feebly developed, and the popular mind incapable of responding intelligently to the appeal. The letter of their philosophy was recived on authority and prevailed in the world, aided by legislative enactments; but there was but little inspirational life in the formulæ to stimulate the soul of the believer and render its obligations effective in moral action. And for these reasons, their truly remarkable and advanced systems of ethics, if we consider the age in which they wrote, could not receive, and have not, yet, received a full measure of appreciation from the nations for whose improvement they were written.

It is a curious and an interesting feature in the history of the progress of ideas, that the writings of Pagan Philosophers have been obliged to pass over to Christian Nations in order to receive a just estimation. This is so for the reason that the latter are more fully developed, intellectually and morally, as well as humanitarily, through the inspirational influences of their religion, and its direct tendency to a pure Democracy, which not only recognizes Man fraternally, but truth broadly, as a unit of many parts, a comprehensive whole. Christion Nations are, consequently, the first to feel the influence of the luminous day of Reason, which is now dawning on the earth; and the first to gather up the rationalistic ideas of all the ages and *re*-present them to the world. The Materialistic Rationalism of Christendom may indeed be regarded, as we have already stated, as the culmination of Heathen Philosophy. But a clearer understanding of universal principles, and a fuller comprehension of the common origin, level and destiny of Man, male and female, lead the Rationalists of the Reasoning Age of the World to reject the ancient philosophers' partial theory of immortality; and they aim at more consistency by cutting off the *whole Human Family* from a life beyond the grave.

And thus we learn that every new age is overshadowed by the receding one, and feels its influence rest upon it, like a wondrous spell. The deep mystery of its exit and silence lends a charm to the productions of those noble beings who have survived the departing ages, and perpetuated their existence through all time in imperishable creations. Admiration of their exalted genius is heightened by distance; love drops a vail over their human weaknesses, and recognizes, with a sympathetic tear, the brotherhood of Man.

And the student of History enters upon his difficult task with reverent tenderness, like one who exhumes the form of his honored and beloved dead. And he soon becomes deeply interested in the times in which they lived and wrought for posterity. And, as he gathers up the many links of the chain of Reason which unite the ages, and the various races of Man, in one grand Human Family, he imbibes the while, unconsciously to himself, the materialistic conditions of those early periods; and loses, proportionally, at the same time, the increased spiritual truth and light of the present; and, finally, returns to the progressed nineteenth century infidel to the grandest truth of Intelligent Nature—Man individualized and immortal. And they who read his writings, by coming into close *rapport* with his mind, catch a portion of the same subtle influence with which he became imbued while in sympathy with the more material ages,—and are controlled by it, in their turn, for a limited season, depending upon the reactive power of their minds and their adaptation to philosophical principles.

This tendency of the human mind to be impressed and influenced by associate intercourse, may be clearly illustrated by common observation and experience. Numerous examples are annually furnished of persons who go abroad to a foreign country, or into remote sections of their own, where they notice existing evils which at first shock their moral sensibilities ; but they become gradually accustomed to the prevailing condition of things,—lose sight of the evil,—enter into sympathy with those who practice it,—and, finally, end by defending and practicing the same themselves. And they are able to persuade their friends residing in other parts of the land, who are in close sympathy, or kindred relationship with them, that this peculiar evil is, after all, a real practical good. The parties appealed to soon become the most strenuous advocates of the evil in question, by a curious law of blind, partizan zeal ; in which the abettor is influenced to the use of more offensive language, and to the adoption of more violent measures in its defense than the real actors themselves. Because such persons do not feel individually responsible for either the existence or continuance of the wrong ; and hoping selfishly to derive some advantage therefrom, either directly or indirectly, they throw the weight of responsibility on others, and rush fanatically on to unseen consequences.

But the rapidly increasing army of Materialistic Rationalism is destined to be of short duration in the world, for two important reasons : first, the great law of Human Progress, which involves higher and yet higher development of the mental powers, will challenge it, step by step; and, second, the Spirit of the Reasoning Age, which takes clearer and fuller views of man's spiritual nature and relations, will lead off, more and more strongly as the age advances, in the direction of Metaphysical Philosophy, until it will finally be arrested altogether in its forward march, and its leaders will be led captive by Spiritualistic Rationalism. The present day is only a point in human progress, which we have already termed the early manhood of the race.   It is the peculiar period of development in the individual being, in the nation, and in the world, when the Reasoning Powers are quickened, and act more fully with the perceptive and constructive faculties of the mind on the material plane of life, ultimating themselves in inventions for the improvement of physical conditions.   And the Age of Invention is pre-eminently the Age of Demonstrative Reason, and of Inductive Philosophy.   But as the Reasoning Age advances, point by point, with its broader and more comprehensive grasp of general principles, the higher deductive Metaphysical Philosophy will follow in its own succeeding order.   Yet, that which can be made tangible to the senses, and evident to the intellect, will attract the popular mind more powerfully for a limited season.   The material resources of the earth are everywhere exciting increased attention and action, preparatory to the investigation of higher principles.   Land and sea combine to aid the active spirit of material enterprise.   REASON is laboriously at work with Science in the mineral stratifications of the earth, analyzing the very structure of the globe, to learn the chemical principles of which it is compounded, in order to render such knowledge available to man.   And she will, ere long, successfully navigate the air, as she ascends triumphantly from the material to the spiritual plane of thought, and will carry the enlightened millions forward as she advances in her car of glory, until Spiritualistic Rationalism shall at length prevail on Earth, even as it does in Heaven.

Verily, verily, the Pagan Philosophers were partially developed men, partial in their views of intelligent nature, and partial in their modes of presenting those views to the world.   But Jesus Christ, the great Democratic Philosopher of the World, was a full-orbed human soul, a grand Spiritual, Intuitional - Intellectual and Harmonial God-Man.   In him dwelt all the fullness of the Godhead, as the representative of the Divine Father and Mother of Humanity to their earthly family of sons and daughters.   Being in harmonious relations with himself, physically, intellectually, and morally, he was, as a logical sequence, in harmonious relations with Material and Intelligent Nature, and a perfect medium of Deity. And he exhibited a fine equipoise of being, in all his comprehensive teachings, through all his marvellous life of use and power and love. Viewing from the lofty altitude of Cause, the triune relation that every son and daughter of Time sustains to Deity, he extended his arms, in fraternal love, and embraced the whole Human Family in the broad principles of Natural Religion, including all in the life beyond the grave. And so it is truly written: Life and immortality are brought to light through the Gospel. For, be it known unto you, O! disciples of Zoroaster and Confucius, that Christ did not teach immortality as a reserved right of either sex, or as a reward of good behavior; but as a grand, eternal truth of Intelligent Nature, open alike to every individual member of the Human Family as a child of Deity, even as are all the beneficent influences of the material world.

And because the Master possessed a grand generalizing mind, and great loving heart, he was able to make a comprehensive statement of Human and Divine relations, and to address his teachings to the whole human being, to the heart, and to the mind, and to the soul of Man. And, as his perfect system of morals is founded in the principles of Intelligent Nature, it is broadly adaptive to human capacities, however limited or exalted, and to all degrees of human development, of all ages of the world. The individual of one talent, who is unable to comprehend the Gospel intellectually, can, yet, draw nigh to the Divine Father and Mother God, through the Mediative Son, with newly awakened affections of his *heart* and be filled with joy and love. And the larger nature, endowed with ten talents, like St. Paul, can approach nearer to the Deity, through his quickened intellect as well as affections, and be filled with peace and blessedness, *seeing*, while feeling the beauty and sublimity of the marvellous truths that inspired the Teacher.

Ah! it must be admitted by the reasoning mind that Pagan Philosophers, with all their breadth of intellect, were yet partial in their developement, and consequently in their power of perceiving universal truths and relations, and in their methods of presenting them to the world.   It most be admitted that they addressed the *mind* of Man at an age in human progress when the reasoning powers of the millions were yet too feebly developed to respond intelligently to the appeal; but they did not address the HEART of Humanity.   They did not touch the quick of the soul and kindle its immortal aspirations.

But the Democratic Philosopher of Nazareth struck home to the very source of existence, the Spiritual life of Man, and unsealed its fountain of living waters.   He penetrated to the consecrated altar of the affections, and engraved his precepts on the human heart in letters of light.   And He appealed with direct and marvellous power to the REASON, and to the *moral sentiments* of the people for the ratification of the principles which he enforced upon the affections.   And He addressed also the CONSCIOUSNESS of the human soul, which is the highest intuitional action of all its combined forces:—Why even of yourselves judge ye not what is right?   But although the Church has lingered long in her Youthful paths, and REASON has been slow to respond to the Master's appeal; yet the *heart* of Christendom has answered with tears of exultant joy for eighteen centuries: I feel!—I believe!—I rejoice !   And the awakened Reason will ere long cry aloud to Earth and Heaven: I see! I know! I believe! I accept the Gospel of Intelligent Nature with all my heart, with all my mind, and with all my soul!   I believe in God the Universal Father, and in the Holy Ghost the Universal Mother, and in the Mediative Son, both human and divine, the representative Man of the intellectual and moral ages.   I believe in the common origin, level, and destiny of Man, male and female; and in the sacred brotherhood of Nations, and the divine unity of all Intelligence.   I believe in immortal life beyond the grave: For He hath abolished death by his own glorious resurrection.   I subscribe joyfully to my dear Master's creed of the Church Universal: Love to God, and Love to Man! I stand firmly by the Constitution of the great Democratic Republic of Earth and of Heaven!

Such has been, and such is, and such will ever be, the renewing and vitalizing power of the inspired and inspiring Gospel of Christ.   Truly, Christianity must increase in the world, while Pagan Philosophy must decrease with the advance of Knowledge and Reason.   And we find that the Church of God has ever been enlarging, instead of diminishing, with the growth of ages, because the principles of Christianity are adapted broadly to the whole nature of Man.   They admit of no distinctions of sex, or of color, or of class in the Human Family ; they regard no degrees of either natural or acquired ability, or of moral conditions of purity and of degradation.   For they are all-embracing, like the beneficent influences of the material world.   They extend upward to the highest abode of the blest, and downward to the lowest abyss of the fallen.   The language of the author of Christianity is: Come unto me ALL ye who are weary and heavy laden, and I will give you rest.   Christ hath opened the door of the Kingdom of Heaven for all to enter who are willing to live its life of use and love.   It is not a place, but a condition of the soul.   Its throne is in the *heart* of the believer.   It is peace and joy of spirit, that passeth understanding, in sweet union and communion with Deity.   It is to be ONE with Christ in God.   All have attained it who are able to say, with the full assent of heart, mind and soul: Not *my* will but THINE be done.

If we would find the difference between the teachings of Christ and of Pagan Philosophers marked still more significantly, we must observe the clear distinction that exists between the civilizations of Pagan and of Christian countries.   For religious principles affect the character of Nations as well as that of individuals.   The religion of any people determines, indeed, both their intellectual and moral status.   We perceive, at a glance at Heathen countries, the lack of the inspirational and vitalizing influences of the Christian Religion.   The people are centuries behind those of Christendom in the mechanical and fine arts, in literature and science, and in the principles of government.   In the land of Confucius, where it is estimated that one-fourth of the Human Family reside, his disciples still continue to teach the irrational theory, that women, who beget offspring with immortal souls are destitute of souls themselves, their office in the economy of Nature being, simply, to give birth to Male Heirs of Immortality ! Ah! the injured spirit of Maternity will in some hereafter be avenged ; and that Male Kingdom will send forth an agonizing cry for its Mother. But no marvel at the fearful lack of Justice, Reason and Common Sense among a people who have indulged in the demoralizing practice of polygamy for thousands of years. The wrong done to human affections perverts the heart, and blinds the understanding of both man and woman.

Pagan Moral Philosophy is an abortion. It is a meagre, dwarfed and mutilated body without a soul. It does nothing for the spiritual nature of man, male and female. It degrades one-half of the human family, whose important office is to re-create and perpetuate the human species, below the other half who frame the laws, thereby demoralizing, instead of elevating humanity through the high and God-like office of Creation. It is speculative theory; but it is not Philosophy. For Philosophy is the eternal truth and justice of God, revealed in material and intelligent Nature, in the fine equipoise of all things, and nice adaptation of means to ends, in every department of creation, which ever tend, from the widest diversity of parts, to produce the most perfect and harmonious whole. It admits of no limited views, nor prejudiced conclusions. Its exponents must be able to take a comprehensive survey of material, and of intelligent nature, and to make a clear and logical statement of principles and of their relations and ultimates, from the high altitude of cause, which overlooks the world of effects. And thus far in the history of man, only one, in whom dwelt all the fullness of the Godhead, has been able to do this for the Human Family.

Pagan Philosophy is the cold light of intellect without warmth, like the beautiful yet transient Aurora Borealis of the evening. Christian Philosophy is the union of the affections of the heart with the convictions of the understanding, which evolves both light and heat, like the Sun of the morning; therefore its author has been appropriately named: The Sun of Righteousness. One was given to illumine the children of the night

21

of time; the other, to make glorious the meridian day of perfected humanity.

The Rationalism of the present is not, as many of its leaders maintain, a development of the progressive enlightenment of the people of Christendom; but simply, as we have already attempted to show logically, the culmination, or flower of Pagan Moral Philosophy, which is obliged, through the normal action of principles in Intelligent Nature, to come forth to the light of the Reasoning Age, because it is itself a plant of reason, in order that it may not only enjoy its highest development, but may exhibit, at the same time, its true qualities and character, and be examined and correctly classified by the Moral scientists of the day.

We would render our idea clear to the popular mind by familiar illustration. As the different seasons of the year, in their successive order, are needful for the devolopment and perfection of the germs of plants in the Material World, even so in Intelligent Nature, various successive periods of human progress are required for the full unfolding of the immortal germs of thought. They, too, must be nurtured and perfected by the unseen, yet powerful influences of Autumn's penetrating gales and Winter's silent frosts. And they must also enjoy their Spring of quickening power, when the life principle shall strike root deeply in the soil of mind, and send forth leafy branches; and their genial Summer, when the buds of promise shall become fragrant blossoms. The ethics of the Pagan Philosophers, being addressed to the Reason of Mankind in the ignorant Childhood and Youth of the World, when this power was but partially developed and feebly operative, remained in a quiescent state, during long Autumnal and Winterean ages; its germs of thought could not be attracted to take root in barren, uncultivated soil of mind. But about the period of the French Revolution, at which time the world began to progress more rapidly from Youth towards Maturity, and the popular mind to advance in intelligence, the latent reasoning principle commenced also to develop more fully and to manifest itself strongly, on the plane of Demonstrative Reason, in Materialistic Rationalism. Pagan Philosophy began then to take root in more favorable soil, and to thrive, naturally, outside of the countries where its principles were enforced by the authority of the ruling powers. And, now, it is flowering in Materialistic Rationalism all over the enlightened globe.

But it should be carefully noted that Pagan Philosophy has come to its season of flowering in the TRANSITIONARY PERIOD of the Reasoning Age of the world; it could not blossom in the glorious meridian Day of Humanity, when earth will be filled with the knowledge of God. And the present time is favorable to the culmination of old errors, as well as to the growth of new truths. Because society is in strongly active and reactive conditions. The people are being impelled forward in one direction by radicalism, and drawn backward in another by conservatism, while yet they are rapidly approaching the terminal points where extremes meet, and the common origin, level, and destiny of Man will be seen and acknowledged.

And now, that Pagan Philosophy is everywhere flowering and filling the moral atmosphere with its aroma, let the Church look to her Tree of Life, of the Lord's own planting, and see that it is carefully nurtured and putting forth the immortal blossoms of Spiritualistic Rationalism, and that the finer and more subtle pollen of the latter falls upon the seed-vessels of the former, and impregnates them with the true life principle; then, when the golden Autumn shall arrive, the fruitage of both will be Christian instead of Infidel.

When the Church shall receive a full baptism of Reason, which will be attended with a *re*-baptism of the Holy Ghost and of fire, then there will be a universal revival of Religion in the world, and the Gospel of the Democratic Philosopher of Nazareth will be accepted of all nations. But, before that day of inspired prophecy shall arrive, she will have gained a philosophic standpoint of thought and action, from which she will calmly and dispassionately review the past, and separate the chaff from the wheat of the creeds of her Childhood and Youth. And she will return with renewed life and joy to Revelation, to the Spiritual truth and light that was rejected in the Transitionary Period, when she strove to shake herself free of error, and will *re*-construct her Religious Formulæ reverently, on the higher plane of Philosophy, adjusting the truths of Revelation and of Science in the clearer light of Knowledge.

The Reasonin Age of the World will culminate in the Harmonial, in the glorious Day of the Church Universal, when the Nations shall learn war no more ;—-when all will understand, and love, and practice the Gospel of the Prince of Peace, from the least even unto the greatest ; when the great congregation of the grand Cathedral Earth will joyfully accept one Lord, one Faith, one Baptism, and one Father and Mother God over all, guiding and controlling in Infinite Wisdom and Love the united Brotherhood of Nations, the vast Christian Republic of the World.

CHAPTER VII.

*Behold, the Tabernacle of God will be with Man; and they shall
be His people, and God Himself shall dwell with them, and be their
God.*

What pen can adequately portray the glorious future of Humanity? Who is able to trace on the fly-leaf of the present dis-
sonant and Transitionary Period of Human Progress the gran-
duer, beauty and perfection of the Harmonial Years, when the
various races of Man, enlightened by Knowledge and guided by
Reason and Love, will form, as in a sublime Oratorio, a perfect
arrangement of parts, and the full chorus of redeemed Humanity rise from earth in unison with the harmony of Heaven?
Who can fully estimate what will be the fruitage of the ages
whose trees of varied knowledge have only yet put forth luxuri-
ant leafage and the opening buds of promise ?

But we know, as certainly as that effect follows cause, in uniform and universal order throughout the wide range of Material
and of Intelligent Nature, that the quarternion seasons of the
year will continue to succeed each other in the future as they
did in the past, renewing seed-time and harvest, and that they
will continue to develop higher forms of vegetable and animal
existence as they unfold in ever-perfecting beauty and power.
And we know, also, that the different stages of Human development in the Individual being, in the Nation, and in the World
of Man, are obedient to the same law of Progress in their own
advancing order.

Each generation, treading on the heel
Of generation, sends a grander peal
From the great March of Ages, swelling on
To blend the interests of Mankind in one.

And Revelation enforces the teachings of Philosophy with marvellous power. Lo! it is written in the Volume of Inspiration concerning the glorious Harmonial Years: They shall teach no more every man his neighbor, and every man his brother, saying, Know the Lord: for they shall all know me, from the least of them unto the greatest. I will put my law in their inward parts, and write it in their hearts. * * * * * And they shall be my people, and I will be their God. And thus the faith and hope of the Christian World is strengthened in the final triumph of truth and right, over error and wrong; and of knowledge, reason and love, over ignorance, prejudice and every phase of excess and evil.

And there never was a period in the history of Christendom when the encouraging lessons of Philosophy and Revelation were more needed than at present, during the transition of the Church of God from the unquestioning faith of her Childhood and Youth, forward to opinions the growth of rational conviction. And such is the case because the radical changes that needfully attend the Transitionary Period necessitate a chaotic condition of society for a limited season, or, until the Reasoning Age shall be fully inaugurated. For Reason is a powerful element of *change* in the human mind, as well as a great *adjustive force* to bring order out of confusion; and it is everywhere active in the present progress of the world towards its maturity, as we have already shown, throwing off old conditions and taking on new, that are more favorable to harmonious development. It demands a thorough review of the Christian Religion, a higher interpretation of its truths, and, as a consequent, an entire reconstruction of its formulæ of doctrine, and a new presentation of its principles to the Reasoning Age. And revolutions in the Church involve revolutions also in the State, in Institutions and Governments which have been the outgrowth of Christian civilization in the past. Reason is actively at work, even now, remodelling these in order to establish them on broader foundations of Human Rights, on the eternal principles of liberty, equality and fraternity.

And during these revolutions, and the attending chaotic condition of society, the Church will suffer loss, humiliation and sorrow. For the love of many will wax cold through lack of faith in vital Christianity;—and Rationalism will sweep like a flood over the earth;—and rank infidelity to God and Man will smite with the fist of wickedness;—and vice and crime will more than ever appear to abound; and evil to array itself against good with unblushing front and fanatical diabolism. Because the Satanic powers of earth, seeing the Divine Spirit of Truth abroad to thwart their plans and weaken their control, will make furious haste to accomplish their hellish purposes, knowing that their rule is swiftly passing away.

We have stated in the early part of our work, that the order of advancement in the Church, and in the World, bears a close analogy to the unfolding powers of the individual being through the various stages of infancy, childhood, youth, maturity, and the fullness of years. And we have shown that this natural order of development has marked the history of the Man, and of the organized Church of God, from the infancy of the Human Family— at which time instruction was orally communicated to them by angel ministers of the Divine All-Parent;—forward to their early childhood (at the period of the call · of the Patriarch Abraham, a Medium of the Almighty Father,) and the religious Dispensation of Law and Authority;—forward to their Youth or heroic and affectional age of the First Christian Era of Love and Free-Will;—and forward to the present Transitionary Period of the Reasoning Age or Second Christian Era, when the Son of God and Son of Man is again to be " revealed" in the maturity of the Human Family. A second revelation of Christ, and of his sublime Gospel of Love, is a demand of eternal justice, as well as of the Reasoning Age. It is important that his *character* should be measured by a higher standard of judgment than has yet obtained in the World; in order that he may be able to complete his twofold mission in the Natural and in the *Spiritual*—his Gospel being addressed to two distinct periods of human development, Youth and Maturity.

And we have stated that Jesus Christ was a Spiritual, Intuitional-Intellectual, and Harmonial God-man, and a grand type-man of human capabilities and destiny. And we have shown, from the history of the past, that his nature was imperfectly understood, and his Gospel but partially comprehended by the Church, during her Youthful age of the first Christian Era, and for the reason that the mind of the age was partially developed. And we have drawn conclusions, from the teachings of Philosophy, as well as of Revelation, that the character of Christ, and the principles of his profound religion, will be more fully understood and appreciated during the Reasoning Age that is now dawning on the Nations.

In proportion as the Christian Church and World have progressed spiritually, the people have grown more and more into the likeness of Christ; from which fact we may logically infer, that in proportion as they shall continue to advance in wisdom and virtue, and in the knowledge of God, they will continue to grow into the similitude of His Son, until they shall possess the same mind that was in him, shall become Spiritual, Intuitional-Intellectual and Harmonial. And we have called upon the reader to test the truth of these propositions for themselves, by glancing at the Spiritual and Intuitional-Intellectual growth of Christendom, during the past eighteen centuries, and by observing the striking and rapid development of the Intuitional Power in children of the present time, over those of preceding generations. Yet, not until the Harmonial Age of Humanity shall arrive will mankind perfectly understand the Harmonial Mediative Son of God, and truly practice his Divine Gospel of Nature. For not until that period of human development is attained, can we hope for a nice balance of the physical, intellectual and moral powers of man, male and female, and a broader and clearer perception of the truths of Intelligent Nature, by reason of knowledge widely diffused among the masses of society, as well as through the elevating and inspirational influences of the Christian Religion. *Then* there will be unity in Individual and in National character; and mankind being themselves harmonious, will be in perfect rapport with the truths of Nature, and, hence, ONE with the great

Moral Philosopher of the World, and, like him, AT ONE with Deity.

And after man and woman shall have grown into the simili-tude of the true Son of the Godhead, after they shall have be-come Spiritual, Intuitional-Intellectual and Harmonial, then, like him, they will also be perfect mediums of the Divine Spirit. And they will be able to see, and to hold converse with their dear departed ; and with the mighty heroes of past ages ; and with the spirits of just men made perfect ; and with Jesus Christ himself, the Mediator of the new covenant to Man.

Ah ! we commiserate the barren condition of the Rationalist who has silenced the pleading voices of his spiritual nature;— who feeds only on the husks of the world and starves his soul, when his Father has bread enough and to spare ; whose mental vision is bounded by earth's visible horizon ;—who has argued himself into the belief that human beings *alive with the Spirit of Creative Intelligence*, move, like the seasons, in circles ; and die, like the vegetables, after they have completed their little round of years. We pity the Rationalist who is unable to see with the Christian Philosopher that, while human beings move in circles, they move also in a continuous series of circles, which rise in an ascending spiral to the throne of the Infinite One, including all the various members of the Human Family, of every grade of intelligence and virtue ; in progressive and eternal unity.

The different eras of human progress have left alike their phy-sical and moral impress on the face of the earth, and the char-acter of its inhabitants. And we may logically assume that the progressive epochs of the future will be obedient to the same universal law of cause and effect ; and that, as the Human Fam-ily approach Maturity through the unfolding faculties of mind and heart, their labors and achievements, under the fuller guid-ance of reason and the moral sentiments, will be grander and grander, and the record of these, in their own order, will also be stamped upon animate and inanimate Nature in ineffaceable lines of beauty and power.

In glancing backward through the vista of years along the highway of departed centuries, we observe the records of the phy-

22

sical ages, rising in melancholy grandeur above the crumbling tombs of the Pharaohs.   There the Childhood of the Human Race culminated in collossal monuments, which continue still, after the lapse of thousands of years, to boldly challenge material destiny, and bid defiance to obliterating Time.   These massive and solemn piles are expressive of the peculiar ambition, knowledge and power of the Children of our Race, and of the longings of their natures for something beyond this limited existence,——for an earthly immortality.   And there the timid hand of incipient Art traced upon the marble palaces of their dead, angular and grotesque shapes of undeveloped Humanity ; and registered the names, the deeds, and the aspirations of their heroes,

" In hieroglyphics elder than the Nile."

We turn thoughtfully from monumental Egypt to view with sentiments of blending pity and admiration the classic lands of Greece and Italy.   Those lands of fable and of story are closely linked in history, and blended in the mind of its student ; for the reason that each Nation, as the wheel of destiny revolved, inherited the other's treasures of knowledge in the successive order of its rise and fall.

Of Egypt Greece first learned her alphabet,
And Rome of Greece, alas ! as her sun set,

In those regions of romance the Youth of the Human Family culminated in higher forms of art.   The temples of ancient Greece rose in marvellous symmetry and grace in honor of her immortal Gods, and they were elaborately ornamented with fanciful forms of the spirits of earth, and of sea, and of air, and with the statutes of mythic heroes, many of which still live to speak to the present age from the tomb of past greatness.

After ancient Rome was redeemed from Paganism by Christianity, and the aspirations of her people were awakened by a Spiritual Religion, magnificent Cathedrals succeeded her Temples of Idolatry, ascending in more complicated and artistic forms of beauty and majesty, crystalized anthems of praise to Jehovah, the God of gods !

. And as the Human Family continued to advance toward Maturity there was a fuller and more varied development of human faculties, which had remained latent during the crude physical ages, awaiting their own appointed hour of unfolding. The higher sentiments of the soul sought for more perfect expression in poetry, painting and music, striving to portray, in the harmonies of verse, color and sound, the ever-growing harmony of progressive Humanity. And in this unfolding power of Human capabilities, the future shall be as the past, and much more abundant, because of the greater increase of knowledge to enlighten and enlarge the human heart and mind, and the fuller development of Reason to guide aright.

And, as we cast our mental eye abroad upon the present dawning Day of Reason, and mark the active manifestations of operating principles, and their lines of direction, and then turn to the page of Revelation and glance at the inspired prophecies relating to the present Era, and confirmatory of its intellectual and moral rising glory, we draw conclusions from both Philosophy and Revelation, that the Reasoning Age of Man will culminate in Institutions and Governments founded in the principles of Natural Religion, taught by the great Democratic Philosopher of the World; and that all the various races of Man that populate the globe will become an enlightened brotherhood of Nations.

In that remarkable passage of the Word where the Almighty Father addresses the maturer and more enlightened children of Earth in the following expressive language—Come now, and *let us* REASON *together*—He clearly points to the advanced Day of Humanity, announcing its progressed condition in the strong and beautiful words of the context—Though your sins be as scarlet, they shall be as white as snow; though they be red like crimson, they shall be as wool. Father, we believe, help thou our unbelief. We confidently know when we see Earth's vernal carpet spread before our footsteps, and inhale the aroma of unfolding leaf-buds, and listen to the joyous songs of birds returning from their winter journey, that the glorious Summer of Nature is near; even so, Father, when we look abroad upon thy Intelligent Creation and observe the manifestations of an active Reason everywhere at work on the physical structure of the globe, developing conditions of greater convenience and comfort in material relations; and also engaged on the higher intellectual plane, unfolding vital principles of truth to Man, then we know surely that the season is drawing nigh for the fulfillment of Thy promise in reference to the Day of Reason, when there shall be a clearer understanding of, and more perfect obedience to Thy holy laws, when the sons and daughters of Earth, like Thy Mediative Son, shall be in full rapport with Material and Intelligent Nature. And then, indeed, will Truth spring out of the earth, and righteousness look down from heaven, as redeemed Humanity walks abroad in the true liberty of the Children of God.

Ay, we confidently believe, that when Mankind shall put forth the same determined energy in grappling with moral questions, as they already exercise in controlling material interests, and Reason shall fully examine the relations and consequences of human actions, the people will be influenced to shun every evil way, and the crimson sin of shedding a brother's blood, until they shall become as stainless as snow;—and that when Reason shall clearly view the beauty, holiness and freedom of the higher law, and see that wisdom's ways are ways of pleasantness and all her paths are peace and joy, they will be constrained to obey lovingly the simple requirements of Heaven, and will grow in grace and in the knowledge of God, until they shall become as white as wool.

In view of the past history of the Human Family, which shows the progressive tendencies of man, the Millennial Day, or an Age of Harmony on earth, is a logical necessity. For it is a natural sequence of perfectly unfolded faculties of heart, mind and soul, in the advancement of the Human Race. And we may also learn from the nature of the individual being, who is a representative of his kind, that it becomes a philosophical result of man's progressed maturity. For man is an epitome of all things of Earth and Heaven, and, consequently, as we have already stated, adapted, in both his physical and spiritual organization, to all the truths of Material and Intelligent Nature; and he needs must love the highest when he sees it clearly, because he is adjusted to that condition when he is fully developed, physically, intellectually and morally, and is able to ascend, in the glorious freedom of a child of Deity, the lofty heights of cause, and view all questions, independently of the prejudices of education, in the strong light of God-like Reason. Many centuries ago, Revelation anticipated the deductions of Philosophy, and proclaimed this truth in prophecy, to stimulate the hope of the Nations, during the dark and cruel physical ages of ignorance, error and crime.

The prescient minds of all countries and of all ages have been alike inspired with, and sustained by, this elevating truth, in their herculean labors to reorganize society on broader foundations of Human Rights, of equal and eternal justice, for every member of the Human Family. But during the Childhood and Youth of the world, the prescient Children of Genius were always misunderstood and persecuted by the undeveloped millions that they endeavored to enlighten. Their noble efforts were denounced ambitious; and their advanced theories of social order, Utopian and harmful to mankind. And they have been dragged without the camp, and tortured and slain by the very people that they were seeking to elevate, and for whom they would willingly have sacrificed their lives, to redeem from ignorance and its consequent error, superstition and suffering. Alas! that the world has never recognized its Saviors until after it has crucified them. Truly, the radiant light of Heavenly truth is darkness to unanointed eyes.

We have shown that the Age of Reason will culminate in Institutions and Governments founded on the principles of Christianity, or Natural Religion; because the knowledge of its elevating truths and their adaptation to the highest development of Humanity will be widely diffused over the Earth. Ay, and then Science will go forth on the wings of the wind and reveal the secrets of the Material and Intelligent Universe to the listening Nations. Divine Art will accompany him in his car of glory, and embody the truths of Nature in immortal creations. And a New School of Art will be established, as far transcending the Schools of the Old Masters, as the meridian sun exceeds in brightness its early rising glory. The partial development of the Human Family, during the Childhood and Youth of the World, necessitated a partial unfolding of the creative faculties. But in the Reasoning Age of Humanity the mind of Man will receive a fuller baptism of knowledge and a commensurate measure of power. And a New School of high Art will as naturally follow the *re*-awakened intellectual, moral and religious sentiments of the millions, as the light of day succeeds, in eternal order, the darkness of Night. The Sentiments are the source of the high aspirations, and answering inspirations, of the human soul. It has been truly written that Art is the handmaid of Religion. She brings her earnest students into close rapport with Nature, and elevates the hearts and minds of those who receive, and of those who impart, her divine lessons.

It is rational to presume that the New School of Art will be inaugurated in the most enlightened part of the globe, where the quickening and inspirational power of the Christian Religion will be more deeply felt, and fully operative; and where knowledge will be more widely diffused among the millions, to stimulate and elevate the popular mind and create a demand for works of taste and beauty. And so we confidently assert that the New World is destined to become the seat of the New School of Art. And the preparation for this important event has been advancing in the United States with the rapid movements of the centuries. For, in this part of the globe, there was established, in the wisdom of the Divine Councils, the new and more liberal Church of the Era of Reason; here the doors of the Public School were thrown invitingly open to the children of every Nation—to the Youth of the whole World! And a great awakening light, a grand Intellectual and Moral power, has already gone forth to the ends of the earth, as a glory and a benediction to the inhabitants thereof, from the Public School! And from the Church of the New Jerusalem of prophecy, the City of the God of Heaven and of Earth.

There are many inspired Artists at the present hour in the United States whose labors have already crowned their brows with victorious wreaths, and reflected honor upon their country. But their works are only a prelude to the coming glory.

Far greater marvels Art will yet reveal,
When her bright Angel breaks another seal;
The true apostles of the beautiful
Upon this soil will found a New-World-School
Of Art subjective, to the soul-life true—
No rival of the Old—Art born anew
Of new conditions, holding all the truth
Of all the Schools in its profounder youth;—
A broader School, result of freer laws
And wider knowledge of effect and cause,
Among the millions it shall represent
In all their features on this Continent.
Under self-rule and education Free,
Enlightenment, the growth of Liberty.
For, as the culture of the New-World mind,
By all its Institutions free and kind
Is all-embracing, after Nature's plan,
And contemplates the good of all the Man.
So will that mind unfold to Nature true,
And of her laws obtain a clearer view.
As friend, in harmony with friend, doth know
The other's thought, ere yet the word-notes flow,
So, to the soul responsive to her own,
Nature's profoundest marvels will be known;—
The tenderness and strength of her great heart;—
The wond'rous life inspiring every part;—
The bending Heavens low whisper to the Sea
That wakes the deep response—eternity !
The all-pervading soul through matter's range;—
Rest in unrest, and permanence in change.

In the advanced Day of Reason, after Science shall have learned how to subdue the unfriendly forces of nature, and to convert them into powerful agents of use and blessing to Man, the stern and sterile states of human ignorance, and of poverty and degradation will be universally ameliorated, and the conditions of social life more generally equalized. And then Free Trade and Equal Rights will not be spoken in the ear of listening Nations to disappoint their hope. Commerce will stretch forth her hand and gather the "golden fleece" of both the Orient and Occident, and distribute the bounties of Providence among the inhabitants of every quarter of the globe. The Polar Regions will share the fruits of the Tropics, and the cereals of the Temperate Zones. But the millions of earth will receive benefits far more valuable than material riches. They will be blessed with the accumulated wealth of knowledge of all the ages; and with the higher benediction of the Christian Religion, which will reveal their exalted relation to the Divine Father and Mother God, as children and heirs of imperishable treasures, and their consequent kinship with the whole Human Eamily as brethren. And it will awaken hope, kindle aspiration, fill their souls with immortal light and love, and convert the present dark ways of life and death into an attractive journey to the land of the beautiful.

The Harmonial Age will be Earth's most glorious season of fruitage, of intellectual and moral fullness, beauty and perfection. The Human Family will then have grown into the Likeness of Christ, and become Spiritual, Intuitional-Intellectual and Harmonial; and, like him, perfect Mediums of the Divine Spirit. And they will finely exemplify the Christian Religion in their lives, in their laws and in their Institutions. In that advanced day of Human Progress there will be no elaborate and cumbrous Plan of Salvation of man's device, as at the present time, to perplex and dishearten earnest seekers after truth, acting as bolts and bars to prevent their entrance into the fold of the Good Shepherd. The simple and sublime Creed of the Church Universal of the promised Day of Humanity will be— Love to God and Love to Man, male and female, made in the image and after the likeness of the Divine Father and Mother.

The Church of that Day will see in the clearer light of Reason and Philosophy the true and natural relations existing between Man and Deity, and the attending obligations resulting from these high and holy relations of Love. And the statement of these Religious mysteries of the centuries, by the expounders of ethics in the Harmonial Age, will be in accordance with the simple and direct teachings of Revelation and Philosophy, which are the only reliable exponents of Intelligent Nature.

Let us turn to the Law and the Testimony, and declare briefly what these statements will be, and what the religious belief of the sons and daughters of God, when they shall have been redeemed from ignorance and its attending errors, when

Science shall have learned the gamut of Nature, and can run the Scales of her Laws, and there shall be full development of the physical, intellectual and moral faculties of Man, and attending harmony between the forces of Material and of Intelligent Creation.

God is the great spiritual, uncreated intelligence of the Universe; the Creator of all things, animate and inanimate; in whom all created intelligences live, and move, and have their being. He has endowed organic matter with sex, and the various species of plants, and of animals, of every class and order, with power to reproduce their kind, after their own peculiar forms and qualities.

Spiritual or essential qualities have figure or shape which they impart to matter, moulding it after the divine pattern ordained by Heaven for each distinct and peculiar species. For in the true order of Nature, the highest principles are everywhere the governing forces.

The existence of man, individualized, male and female, spiritual and intelligent beings, made capable of comprehending the thought of God in Nature, are indications of a Dual Creator, male and female. And all the various classes of animal and of vegetable existences, throughout the globe, are also indices of the Dual Godhead. The mineral kingdom forms no exception to the universal teaching of Nature.

And as man is endowed with powers of mind which enable him to acquire a knowledge of God through the works of creation, it is manifest that these powers must be kindred with the Creator's own—differing only in degree (otherwise man would be unable to comprehend the laws of Nature,) and that man, possessing the attributes of Deity, must, necessarily, be *informed* by them, and *re*-present the form of the Divine Creative Intelligence of the Universe. And Revelation sustains the teachings of Philosophy.

In the beginning, the Almighty Father said unto his co-equal and co-eval companion of Eternity, the Divine Mother God: Let us make man in *our image*, after *our likeness*. So GOD CREATED MAN, MALE AND FEMALE, IN THE IMAGE OR FORM, AND AFTER

23

THE LIKENESS OR SPIRITUAL AND ESSENTIAL QUALITIES of the All-Father, and the All-Mother.

Man was sent into the world a helpless infant, IN A STATE OF INNOCENCE AND OF IGNORANCE, unconscious of his high origin and destiny. The God-like powers of his nature were latent, and awaited development through the stimulating influences of knowledge. He was endowed with an organism and constitution adapted to the conditions and requirements of two spheres, the material and spiritual.

And, as man inherited, as a child of the Intelligent and Informing Spirit of the Universe, like qualities of mind and soul, he is capable of comprehending the laws of matter and of mind, and thus of acquiring a knowledge of God through the wide range of Material and of Intelligent Nature. And, as he must ever remain a child of Creative Intelligence, he is a responsible being, and accountable to the high Tribunal of Heaven for his actions.

And thus man was created a Religious being, and placed in the grand Cathedral, Earth, to learn of God, to individualize himself, male and female, in the truths of Material and of Intelligent Nature, in order that he might be able to return to the high Spiritual source of his existence, at the close of his earthly career, IN A STATE OF INNOCENCE, WITH KNOWLEDGE, recognizing himself fully as a child of Deity, and rendering loving obedience to the laws of both Material and Intelligent Nature, of which he is the grand *ultimatum*.

And man is required by Heaven to improve his abilities and opportunities to the utmost of his power. This requisition of Deity is clearly taught by the Mediative Son of God, in the parable of the talents; and confirmed by the teachings of Philosophy in the economic use of forces.

And, in accordance with the Divine plan that man should unfold and grow through the acquisition of knowledge, the Creator bestowed on him for an immortal inheritance, the two marvellous keys to knowledge—Love and Labor—which would enable him to unlock the arcana of Nature, and appropriate her rich treasures of truth and wisdom.

And in the morning of creation Man, male and female, were

introduced into the Garden of Eden by angel attendants.   And Adam and Eve became ONE DUAL-FAMILY-HEAD, through the appointed sacrament of marriage, forming a precedent of Human alliance on Earth, after the order of the Divine Marriage of the Heavens.   And in that consecrated hour of Union the *keys of knowledge* were given to them by the All-Father, in the following words of direct command : Be fruitful and multiply, and replenish the Earth, and subdue it.   This command could alone be obeyed through Love and Labor.

The sacred TRIUNE relations—Father, Mother and Child—followed the consummation of the marriage of the first earthly son and daughter of the Father and Mother God, and established, on the Natural and on the Spiritual planes of existence, on Earth and in Heaven, the eternal and holy Natural and Spiritual Family Trinity.

And thus in the beginning, in the beautiful Garden of the East, God's Infant and Unorganized Church, or Family of Man, was first established, and in the profoundest truth of Nature—the Sacred Family Trinity.   And Man, male and female, were instructed orally by angel ministers, there, on the consecrated altar of the vast Cathedral, Earth, under the magnificent dome of Heaven. They were there taught their relations to the Divine Father and Mother God as children,—to each other as brethren of the same Human Family,—and to the great coming generations of Man,—and carefully instructed concerning the obligations attending these high and holy relations.   And during the period of Infancy, which included an unknown number of ages, of which we have but limited data, the people continued in a passive state of infantile innocence and ignorance.   But they were receptive of the truths of Natural Religion, revealed to them by angel ministers of the Divine.   Yet, at that early period of time, the Human Family had but little intellectual ability to assimilate truth, and thus acquire growth; they could be only guided spiritually, from point to point, like infants, until the latent forces of their nature should gradually strengthen and unfold, in obedience to progressive law and order.   Many of the spiritual truths taught in the Infancy of the Human Race remain, to this day, with the simple and philosophic Brahmins of the East, the most precious of inherited traditions.

But at length, in Heaven's established plan of progressive development, the Human Family arrived at the Transitionary Period from Infancy to Childhood, when they began to manifest intenser activity on the animal plane of being. The Children of Earth were now required to learn the Alphabet of Material Nature, and commence to outwork practically the great problem of life on the physical sphere of existence. During this period of external activity, they lost, to a great extent, their finer spiritual perception and receptivity. And this Second Era of Human unfolding has been termed, in consequence, "The Fall of Man from his first estate of innocence and purity." But it was simply a natural and needful departure from the early condition of Infancy and passive innocence; such as we constantly recognize and accept in the individual being, who is but a representative of the Human Family in the aggregate.

A Religious Dispensation became necessary, now, for the Human Family; one that should succeed the former system of oral instruction instituted by Heaven as best adapted to their primitive, infantile state. The busy, erratic Children of Earth required organization and Leadership on the material plane of action. And hence the Organized Church, with the written Law and the Authority, was introduced by inspired men, who were appointed by Deity to take the place of angel teachers and guides. And, as the people were active, thoughtless and impatient Children, forgetful to-morrow of the lesson of to-day, with undeveloped minds, incapable of perceiving clearly and retaining associate truths, therefore it was ordained, in the wisdom of the Divine Councils, that their instruction concerning Deity should be distinct, direct and forcible, adapted to their childish condition. And so the ONENESS OF THE GODHEAD was strongly impressed on their volatile minds, to concentrate and focalize thought, in order that they might be able to learn of God. And all the sublime epithets of Deity were employed by their inspired Lawgivers and Prophets to attract their mental eye, and to awaken awe of Jehovah the Eternal Father, God, dwelling in solitary glory and power and majesty, and in light inapproach-able. The doctrine of the FULLNESS of the Godhead, taught by Christ, would have had the tendency to diffuse, rather than to concentrate thought; therefore that higher knowledge awaited their riper age. The low physical development of the Chil-dren of the World was also another reason why they could not be instructed in the mystery of the Holy Ghost, or Divine Mother of Humanity. That Revelation of the Heart of Deity was too interior and holy a truth for their active and restless minds to comprehend. For only in the silence of the reflective human soul, seeking earnestly for the baptism of Divine Love, can the still voice of the Comforter come, to lead into all truth.

And the Organized Church of God of the Childhood of the World, like the unorganized, infant Church of Eden, was es-tablished in the profoundest truth of Nature—the sacred Family Trinity. We learn from the Testimony that, at the birth of Isaac, Abraham, Heaven's chosen inaugurator of the Hebrew Dispensation, was required to cast out into the wilderness his illegitimate child and its mother, the bond-woman and her son; in order that this most essential and holy truth might be pre-served, intact, in the History of the Church, and clearly set forth to the World.

During the world's long period of Childhood, it was inevitable that the Human Family should acquire knowledge by slow and laborious experience. And in going forth into untried paths of enterprise, they would often stumble and fall by the way, or wander from the true course of progress, or down the fearful steep of crime and ruin. Yet, this was not the result of loving and choosing evil in preference to good; but through impatient haste, ignorance of the right, and often because of the perplexing circumstances by which they were surrounded, and the attending difficulty of choice. But the sorrowful experiences, errors and crimes of one age became the monitors and aids of another, act-ing as milestones along the path of the centuries, to enable the Children of Earth to turn their feet towards the King's royal high-way of truth and life.

And at different points of the journey of the Human Family

through the wilderness world, and often when the hour appeared darkest, and there were none to aid, the ever-watchful, pitying Heavens would send forth prescient men, of the divine order of Genius, possessed of great loving hearts and luminous minds, to lighten the way, and aid the wandering Children of Time to return to God. They were moral watch-fires upon the mountains of the Lord, to warn the enemies of right that the soldiers of Truth were armed and vigilant; and to encourage the weak and feeble, and strengthen the faith of the doubting.

But the intervals were often long and dreary between these great lights of the world. Yet, it was not because Heaven was unmindful of the needs of Earth; but for the reason that the Human Family were unprepared to receive higher principles of truth, not having appropriated past lessons of instruction. The wise husbandman does not sow his fields with fresh seed before the growing grain comes to its full head and bearing, and is ripe for harvest; seed sown in occupied soil, would yield no increase, and there would be misapplication and waste, instead of fruitfulness and blessing. It often required ages for advanced ideas, evolved from the prescient intellect of one Child of Genius, to ripen in the heart and mind of the World, and prepare the Human Family to receive still higher truths from more comprehensive teachers. Too much light becomes darkness to eyes unaccustomed to the sun. Man and woman are required to *search* after the pearls of truth. They must unlock for themselves the doors of knowledge in the hidden arcana of Nature, through Love and Labor, and thus work out their own salvation, while the Divine Spirit of Truth and Love works in them and by them.

It became the high office of Love to recreate Man in the image, and after the likeness of the God, Male and Female, and to learn, through her ever-active and tender sympathy, the temporal and spiritual needs of undeveloped Humanity, and to provide conditions adapted to their requirements. It became the mission of Labor to learn the governing principles of Material Nature, and thereby to develop the resources of the Earth, and SUBDUE IT; to expel all deleterious influences therefrom, or convert them into agencies of use and blessing to Man; to drain the malarious marshes,—elevate the miasmatic valleys,—and cause the waste places of Earth to bud and blossom as the rose. But, in the dark physical ages, Love and Labor were held in bondage to Ignorance, and obliged to suffer the agonizing pains of lingering martyrdom. Yet, even in her enforced and cruel prostitution and suffering, Love mitigated the severity of Labor; and even in his fearful degradation and abject servitude, through ignorance and undisciplined passion, Labor rendered more easy and attractive Love's sorrowful journey.

[Ah ! Fellow-traveler of Earth, Love must always suffer when she is made subservient to gross, unhallowed passion ; because she is of divine origin, and appointed by Heaven to the highest uses—the reproduction of the Human Family in the image, and after the likeness of the Divine Father and Mother God. The consciousness of degradation presses painfully upon her spirit. In the present Transitionary Period of the Reasoning Age of the World, in which there is a continual breaking away from the tetherings of past ages of unquestioning faith in Authority, there is everywhere a tendency to independent thought, to opinions the growth of rational conviction, and to the assertion of individual liberty. The limitations of the old regime, in reference to the relations of man and woman in the Family, the Church, and the State, are now more deeply felt than ever before in the history of the World. And a yet indefinable consciousness prevails in society that there is a great inequality and injustice in the marriage relations, which ought to be remedied. Man is accorded too much liberty ; Woman, too little. But, unfortunately for the interests of both sexes, many who seek to change the present relation, and institute freer and more equal conditions, do not recognize Love's high ideal of—Freedom in Law. They seek to liberate themselves from the old bondage by instituting License in its place, Love's worst enemy, under the name of " Free Love ;" and they bind themselves to a far more degrading slavery than that from which they are seeking to escape : the bondage of hurtful lust. And these unbalanced persons draw many weak-minded followers in their train, and lead them down the fearful steep of vice and ruin.]

And thus we learn from the past History of human progress that, through Love and Labor, hand in hand, and heart in heart, and through painful experiences in wrongdoing by reason of ignorance, which led to repentance, and earnest searching after, and final understanding of the right, the Family of Man continued to struggle forward until they approached their next higher Transitionary Period from Childhood to Youth, and required another Religious Dispensation, adapted to their farther progressed condition. Then Heaven, ever responsive to the needs of the Children of Earth, sent forth the grandest Leader of the ages, one IN WHOM DWELT ALL THE FULLNESS OF THE GODHEAD, to establish the New Dispensation of Love and Free-Will to Man.

During the Infancy of the World the Human Family were instructed orally by Ministering Angels. But there have been but two prominent Religious Dispensations given to the Organized Church of God on earth—which Church is the conservative and executive Body of the Moral World, whose duty it is to carry into effect the principles of His Spiritual Kingdom—the Dispensation of Law and Authority, or special revelation of the Divine Father God in the Childhood of the World; and the Dispensation of Love and Free-Will, or special revelation of the Divine Mother God in the Youth of the World. Yet, there have been numerous Religious Creeds through the centuries, among the various nations of the earth, which may be regarded as offsets of these main branches of the tree of Knowledge of Good and evil in the Garden of the Lord. And these differing creeds serve to illustrate the degrees of development or enlightment that have existed among the various Nations of the earth at different and remote periods of time. The Hebrew and Christian Dispensations exhibit the distinct *individuality* in UNITY of the Dual Godhead, Male and Female.

The Hebrew Dispensation of Law and Authority, which was on the more material plane of thought and action, being adapted to the undeveloped and erratic Childhood of the Human Family, was attended with numerous forms and ceremonies, and restrictions for discipline and guidance, and with many typical propitiatory offerings and sacrifices, addressed to the external senses; all of which were compulsory, and to be performed in a *visible* Temple, and in a specified locality.

The Christian Dispensation of Love and Free-Will, which was adapted to more advanced states of society, to higher spiritual and intellectual conditions, included two distinct periods of human progress: the Heoric-Affectional, and the Rational— for it was addressed to the Youth and the Maturity, or to the Heart and the Mind of the World. A visible Temple in a specified locality, with attendant imposing forms and ceremonies, to impress the mind through the visual organs, and to fix the attention of undisciplined Childhood, were non-essentials of the later Religious Dispensation. Its venerated author, the high Representative of the FULLNESS of the Godhead, himself declared that, neither at Jerusalem nor in the Mountains of Samaria were the chosen people thereafter to worship the God of Heaven and of Earth; for MAN was thenceforth to become the Temple of the Living God ; the Human Heart, the consecrated Altar on which to offer acceptable sacrifices in Spirit and in truth, and the Human Mind, with all its breadth of understanding and its wealth of knowledge, the humble minister and attendant there, in the presence of Deity.

The Hebrew Dispensation of Law and Authority, which required the exercise of *unquestioning faith*, because the people were ignorant, undeveloped children, and reason was latent and inoperative, tended toward Autocratic Governments and Monarchical Institutions; as the teachings of the ages plainly indicate.

The Christian Dispensation of Love and Free-Will, adapted to a higher spiritual and intellectual plane of human development, to the Youth and Maturity of the Church and World, to the periods of awakening reason, and broadening knowledges of the principles of Material and of Intelligent Nature, ever tended more and more rapidly, with the progress of Christian Civilization, towards Democratic forms of Government, and Republican Institutions—toward universal Liberty, Equality, and Fraternity.

And, yet, these two Dispensations do not conflict the one with the other. The latter naturally succeeded the former in the di-

24

vine order of progression.   The dear Mediative Son of God assures us that his mission on earth was *not* to destroy the Law and
the Prophecy; but to fulfill.   And in reviewing the past History of
the Human Family, their peculiar stages of progress, and the requirements of each epoch, we learn the beautiful and touching
truth that, the Hebrew Dispensation of Law and Authority was
also one of Divine Wisdom and Love to man.   The fact is clearly seen in the perfect adaptation of the principles involved therein to the needs of Humanity.

That the Dispensation of Law and Authority is also one of
Wisdom and Love, may be strikingly illustrated by the tender
relations of earthly parents and children.   The deepest tone of
love in the heart of the parent for the helpless little one, is the
truest and holiest touch of Nature, and it leads to the exercise of
that law of discipline, and that authority to enforce it, which will
ultimate in the highest good of the latter, independently of the
wishes of the unreasoning child, who becomes often enraged at
denial, even when it desires most what would prove in possession the worst enemy of its happiness.   One moment a razor,
with a keen, shining blade, attracts its attention, and it wishes to
possess the dangerous instrument, and shave its dewy chin, as
papa shaves his beard.   Another moment the child's restless eye
lights on a looking-glass, and it will cry until it becomes ill with
determined impatience to possess the glittering thing, which it
wishes to strike with its toy hammer, and to see the cunning boy
in the mirror strike at the same moment with his little hammer.
It rebels against the restrictive law and authority which withholds
the coveted amusement.   The parent is unkind, every one is unkind who will not gratify its wishes.   And in its ignorance and
impatience it cannot appreciate the watchful, tender love that
prevents it from mutilating itself in its blindness.   And truly, in
the sight of the observant Angels, in their divine ministrations
to Humanity, men and women are but children of a larger
growth; for, like children, they often complain most bitterly because of the withholding of a present *seeming good*, which would
eventuate in the most harmful of evils.

The Law and the Authority were given by Moses ; but Grace

and Truth came by Jesus Christ. He was the Mediative Son of God, and Son of Man, chosen of Heaven to stand between the Divine Father and Mother, and the divine Humanity ; and to take of the Deity and to show it unto the Church and World, that the world through him might be saved from its ignorance and consequent sin and suffering. Ay, who came to teach the sublime and elevating truths that each son and daughter of Time, while forming a Sacred Trinity on the Natural plane with earthly parents, forms, also, a holy and eternal Family Trinity on the Spiritual plane with the Divine Father and Mother God. And although they may be orphans and outcasts on earth, may be poor, desolate and abandoned by Man ; they are still Heaven's legitimate and well-beloved children ; and in the Father's house are many mansions prepared for them. And he came clothed with power from on high to baptize the Human Family into their true generic name—Children of God.

And this sublime Mission to Humanity inspired the whole heart and mind and soul of the Mediative Son of God. And he labored with burning zeal that electrified the listening multitudes, to reveal unto them this marvellous knowledge, and to impress *their* hearts, minds and souls with the ever-present, pitiful and loving care of Heaven. With fervid eloquence he sought to kindle and purify the affections of Man, to exalt and enlarge the mind, and to awaken immortal aspirations. The Mediative Son would uplift the whole human being, and the whole Human Family, to the Divine Author of life. And he would attract the millions of earth by love, as pleading, tender and pitiful as a mother's for her erring child, and thus lead them gently forward and upward, renewed and purified from the dross of their sensual nature, to the spiritual Source of their existence. He would bring Man into perfect AT-ONE-MENT with God.

And our dear Mediator was willing to suffer, the just for the unjust, that he might the more effectively attract the attenion of the World to the elevating truths of his Gospel of Love, declaring to his disciples in the sublime faith of his Mission: If I be lifted up I will draw all men unto me. And so he laid his perfect and glorious life of use, and power, and love a Free-Will offering on the altar of Humanity. And he ransomed mankind with his own most precious blood from the bondage of the physical ages of ignorance, of degraded Labor and Love, by kindling their affections anew with the purifying flame of heavenly love, by awaking the aspirations of their minds to know more of the truth of God revealed in Nature, animate and inanimate, and thus enlarging and elevating their whole being.

And thus the dear Mediative Son ransomed Mankind with his own most precious blood. For without the shedding of blood there could be no remission of sins, in the dark and cruel physical ages of ignorance, and of unquestioning faith in authority. And such was the case, because the masses of the physical ages were infants and children. They were on the material plane of thought and action, and received their opinions as children receive their elementary lessons of instruction. Reason, the great adjustive power of the human mind, was undeveloped, as it is in infants and children, and consequently inoperative. And their only direct mode of resisting new ideas, which appeared to them to conflict with truth and with old doctrines, received on authority, was to take the lives of those who advocated them. They knew of no other mode of protecting their time-honored and cherished opinions from innovation. And they verily thought, in the blindness of their ignorance, that they were serving the cause of Right when they destroyed the Teachers of new and higher truths than they were capable of perceiving. They believed that the Reformers' special doctrines would perish with them in the grave. They could not comprehend that an idea once spoken in the ear of the World becomes a living and immortal creation; and that the new truth must challenge the old error, and thenceforth awaken an irrepressible conflict between the false and the true.

The Mediative Son of God himself understood this condition of the ignorant, undeveloped mind, and, in the true spirit of philosophy and of Heavenly love, apologized for the cruelty of the Jews toward their inspired teachers and prophets of the past, and then present, in the following words of wisdom : I wot that through ignorance ye did it as did also your rulers. And, in his departing hour of mortal agony upon the cross, He cried aloud in pitying sorrow for the intellectual and moral blindness of his persecutors : Father, forgive them, for they know not what they do. How sublime in its divineness was that spirit of philosophy and of Heavenly love that aided him, while suspended between Time and Eternity, and while suffering the most excruciating physical torture, to view calmly his relations to the great principles for which his life was being sacrificed, and to the people who were engaged in crucifying him ; and that enabled him to exercise, in such an hour, tender pity for their intellectual and moral darkness, praying the Father that their sin of ignorance might not be recorded against them.

In the last hour of impressive destiny, when the dear Mediative Son exemplified to the world the value of His GOSPEL OF PEACE AND GOOD WILL TO MAN, he must have realized more fully than ever before its great importance, viewing its elevated and elevating principles in the clearer light of the better world that was dawning in glory on him, and have felt more painfully how great a blessing his beloved people were casting away, and how bitter would sometime be their waking, and their repentant sorrow. And so the Divine Man cried out, in anguish of spirit for his ignorant brethren : Father, forgive them, for they know not what they do.

Ah ! the Jews would not have crucified the Mediative Son of God had they recognized him and the import of his mission. But Ignorance has ever been, through all the ages, and still is, conservative, arrogant, aggressive and cruel. It laughs at the grandest principles of Truth which it is incapable of comprehending, as most amusing folly, when those principles do not conflict with cherished opinions received from Authority, but if they touch a deep-rooted prejudice, or a traditional creed, inherited from a long line of Ancestors, or of Apostles, then it will spring, like a tiger bereaved of its young, to rend remorselessly, and to destroy. Enlightenment has been of slow growth in the world, because ignorance and its hosts of errors and prejudices have proved formidable enemies. Progressive ideas have been the nurslings of stormy centuries, baptized in the precious blood the Martyrs of Humanity.

Our great High Priest, who could be touched with feeling for our infirmities, and had a clear understanding of our conditions and requirements, was no partial Mediator to effect but a limited ATONEMENT for the Human Family. For all power was given to him in Heaven and on Earth; and at his marvellous nativity he was proclaimed, by the angelic host—Man's universal Savior. Glory to God in the highest, on earth peace, goodwill to Man! For unto you is born this day, in the City of David, a Savior which is Christ the Lord. Again, it is written in the volume of Inspiration: The kingdoms of this world shall become the kingdoms of our Lord and Savior Jesus Christ. For he must reign until he hath put down all rule, authority and power that is not of God. Lo! he was crowned with the diadem of Heaven; although he wore the cruel thorns of earth in mockery on his glorious brow.

Unlike all other Kings of earth the royal Christ of God went about doing good, in the true spirit of his divine mission to humanity, preaching everywhere to Spirits in prison, both visible and invisible to man. For, in the comprehensive view of the great Democratic Philosopher of the World, all spirits on the earth and in the spheres are alike in prison who do not comprehend their true relation to the Divine, as children, and to the divine Humanity as brethren.

And the Mediator's mission on earth is not yet accomplished. His life is a continual offering and sacrifice for the ignorance, errors and sins of man. He himself assures us of this wonderful truth when he declared to his beloved disciples: Lo, I am with you alway, even unto the end of the World. And so long as there shall remain one poor, sinful and suffering son or daughter of Adam to be redeemed from the dark prison of ignorance and the bondage of hurtful lusts, through the divine Gospel of Life, Light, and Love, so long will Christ's Mediatorial mission continue in the world.

But a full and perfect AT-ONE-MENT has been effected for every son and daughter of man, who has felt in the soul the true baptismal name—Child of God. It is of little consequence whether this elevated state of feeling has been attained through the direct teaching of the Mediator, or of some Christ-like Spirit, a faithful worker in the vineyard of the Lord; it is enough that the son or daughter experiences the blessing, and lives the Redeemer's life of use and love. And Christ is no longer a Mediator for such a ransomed child; but a glorious companion and friend. How touchingly he reminded his disciples of this beauful truth: Ye are my *friends*, if ye do whatsoever I command you—if ye strive to be perfect, even as your Father which is in Heaven is perfect. And all such sons and daughters of Deity, friends of Jesus, who seek earnestly to live his life of use and love, become *a part of the Christ power* in the world, and aids to the Mediative Son of God in completing its full and perfect redemption. Because they help to elevate mankind from the physical and sensual plane of existence to the spiritual and divine. They form the Advance Guard of the Soldiers of the Cross, who go before to proclaim the Millennial years to the expectant nations, when earth shall be filled with the joyful hallelujahs of the Heavens.

Again, we repeat, such will be the religious teachings of the Moral Philosophers of the Harmonial Age of the Church Universal; and such the belief of the sons and daughters of God in regard to the relations of Man to Man, and of Man to Deity. The Utopian speculations of the Philosophers of all the centuries were preludes struck upon the Harp of Time to the sublime Anthem of Man's complete redemption from ignorance and consequent sin and suffering. They were thrilling prophecies of the coming Harmony, of the long-expected Day of Humanity, when the vast globe should become a brotherhood of Nations,—when Man and Woman should become Spiritual Intuitional-Intellectual and Harmonial, like the representative Christ-Man, the Democratic Philosopher of Nazareth, and, alike, equal citizens of the great Christian Republic of the World.

The attractions of the human mind are proportional to its destinies. In glancing over the records of the Family of Man in their progress from Childhood to Maturity, we observe that their Ambition first seeks expression in material forms; and that, as they rise in the scale of knowledge and virtue, it strives to manifest itself on the higher intellectual and spiritual planes.

For ambition is a progressive and immortal element of mind that will not be not be satisfied until it reaches its highest mode of expression. And, hence, the early attempt of the Children of the World to climb on granite walls to Heaven, is a prophecy that, in another age, and in another higher spiritual form, they will yet attain the height of their ambition.

We learn from Biblical History that, in the Childhood of Man, in the darkness of the physical ages, after the waters of the Flood had swept away the inhabitants of the globe, saving righteous Noah and his family ; that the descendants of Noah, who increased rapidly in numbers, dwelt contentedly together on a plain in the land of Shinar. And as soon as they began to realize the strength and power of numbers, and to feel the indefinable yearnings of their spiritual nature for something beyond the limits of their material existence: They said one to another; go to, let us build us a city, and a TOWER, whose top may reach unto Heaven; and let us make us a NAME.

And, at the time that they began to construct the impossible Tower, they all spoke one language—it was the language of Ignorance. But as they proceeded with the Tower, the builders increased in skill, each according to his own degree of native ability, producing a greater inequality of intelligence and power among them. And THEN arose angry contentions for precedence in the work; and the progress of the building was arrested through a confusion of tongues. For not in the intellectual and moral night of Time could a Tower rise from Earth into the perfect Day of Knowledge.

That colossal enterprise was an early attempt of the Children of the World to express in a grand material form their immortal aspirations. But Man cannot perpetuate eternal principles in perishable creations ; nor climb to Heaven by physical achievement. To the unreflecting millions of earth the unfinished Tower of Babel will ever remain a monument of the childish ignorance and assumption of the people of that early age. But to the Christian Philosopher it is typical of an hour of fulfilment, when a Tower will indeed rise from Earth in symmetrical beauty to Heaven. Ay, the early abortive attempt of Man to scale the Heavens contains a promise of future effort and fruition.   It is prophetic of a day when the Human Family shall learn through Science to speak one language,—the language of Knowledge; and when they shall learn through the Gospel of Christ to practice one Creed—the Creed of Love. For then there will be union and strength, instead of confusion of tongues, and weakness among the Nations.   And THEN the inhabitants of Earth, possessing *one mind* through Knowledge, and *one heart* through Love, will indeed be able to ascend empyrean heights and baptise their souls in the glory of Uncreated Light.

At a later period of Human Development, IN THE YOUTH OF THE WORLD, an attempt was made by the leaders of the Church of God to climb to Heaven on a Tower of words, unaided by spiritual and divine Wisdom and Love.   And the Prelates of the Roman Catholic Denomination of God's Church said one to another: Go to, let us build us a city, and a Tower, whose top may reach unto Heaven; AND LET US MAKE US A NAME.   And they constructed an elaborate *plan* of *salvation*, a complicated mesh-work of creeds, that should rise in an *infallible* Tower of strength from the abyss to the zenith, upon which all Nations might ascend to Heaven, if they would repeat the formulæ of words and walk along the narrow line of Doctrine.   But they laid its corner stones in ignorance, instead of Knowledge; and supported its foundation with Death and Hell.   And they placed *an earthly Holiness*, the Pope, upon its capital, to overlook the empires of the World, and constrain her citizens to fall down and worship·the image that they had set up, in place of the God of Heaven and of Earth.

But at the dawn of Humanity's Day, the opening of the New Christian Era of REASON, the unstable edifice of creeds, cemented with the untempered mortar of selfish ambition, shook to its deep and perilous foundation.   A confusion of tongues arrested the builders; and they were scattered, like the ancient people of Shinar, over the face of all the earth.   The cunningly devised Tower of words is now falling to decay; while the Pope is trembling with fear and apprehension, endeavoring vainly to stand

25

steadily in Serene Holiness upon its toppling capital. He has lost, forever, his ancient prestige of infallibility; not even the Ecumenical Council have power to reinstate him. The world has moved forward.

But in the advanced ages of Knowledge, Reason and Love, when men and women shall have grown into the likeness of the Mediative Son of God and become Spiritual, Intuitional-Intellectual and Harmonial, THEN shall the united Denominations of the great Christian Republic of the world be able to construct, in verity, a glorious and imperishable Tower of noble, humanitary deeds, that shall rise in sublime strength and symmetrical beauty to the abode of the immortals. And the sons and daughters of Earth will behold the Angels of God descending and ascending its golden stairway, in fulfillment of Jacob's prophetic vision.

It shall be called the TOWER OF HARMONY. Its broad foundations will be laid in Knowledge and Reason; the Creed of the CHURCH UNIVERSAL—Love to God and love to Man—will be engraven on its corner stones; and on its ascending spiral will be inscribed, in letters of light—Holiness to the Lord. And Jesus Christ himself, the author and finisher of the Christian's faith, in whom dwelleth all the fullness of the Godhead, will stand in glorious Majesty upon its summit,—radiant with the smile of Deity, while declaring to his disciples, yet extant in time, in tones of ineffable tenderness and love: Lo, I am with you alway!

In that MERIDIAN DAY OF HUMANITY—" Behold, the tabernacle of God will be with Man, and they shall be his people, and God himself shall dwell with them and be their God. And God shall wipe away all tears from their eyes; and there shall be no more death, neither sorrow nor crying, neither shall there be any more pain : for the former things are passed away." Amen. Hallelujah ! HEAVEN AND EARTH ARE FULL OF THY GLORY ! Amen. Hallelujah ! Let the whole Universe respond : Amen. Hallelujah !

Part Second.

AN APPEAL

CHURCH OF THE LIVING GOD,

OF

EVERY NAME, THROUGHOUT THE WORLD.

———————

The Law was given by Moses; but Grace and Truth came by Jesus Christ.

Ye are not come to the Mount that might be touched, and that burned with fire, nor unto blackness and darkness and tempest, and the voice of words; but ye are come unto Mount Sion, and unto the city of the living God, the heavenly Jerusalem, and to an innumerable company of angels, to the general assembly and Church of the first born, which are written in Heaven, and to God, the Judge of all, and to the spirits of just men made perfect, and to Jesus the Mediator of the new covenant; whose voice *then* shook the earth: but now he hath promised, saying, Yet once more I shake not the earth only, but also Heaven.

CHAPTER I.

THE REVEALED WORD OF GOD TO MAN, AND THE REVEALED WILL IN MAN.

In the beginning was the Word, and the Word was with God, and the Word was God.

And the Word was made flesh and dwelt among us, full of grace and truth.

In him was life; and THE LIFE *was the light of man.*

It has been stated, in the First Part of the Teachings of the Ages, that the position of the Organized Church in the world, corresponds to that of the Legislative Body of the civil government of a nation. It is the conservative element of society, and the executive branch of God's Moral Government, whose duty it is to hold its sacred principles of truth in trust for the sons and daughters of earth, and to disseminate them over every part of the inhabited globe. And, in view of the elevated relation which the Church Militant sustains to the Church Triumphant, as the expositor of the Divine Law, and also to the world of Man, as moral Teacher and guide;—and in view of her present relation to the Reasoning Age of the Human Family, and the demand of the people for a REASON FOR THE FAITH THAT IS IN HER, for a philosophical statement of the Christian Religion;—we earnestly appeal to God's Church of to-day, for a careful review of the Creeds of her Childhood and Youth, and for a higher reconstruction of her formulæ of doctrine. And we appeal to her, to test her principles and practice more thoroughly by the Revealed world of God to Man, and the Revealed will of God in Man. The mind of the Reasoning Age reaches forward and upward, and it is the sacred duty, as well as privilege of the Christian Church, to ascend before to the summit of Zion, where she can receive and reflect upon the waiting millions, the light of knowledge and the warmth of love from the great Spiritual Sun of the Universe.

The Revealed Word was given to the Human Family as a guide of life in the Childhood and Youth of the World, before the children of Earth were capable of comprehending either their own nature, or their true relations to their fellow beings, and to their Creator. The Old Testament came to their capricious, erratic and ignorant CHILDHOOD, to restrain, discipline and direct. The many special rules and prohibitive enactments which it contains, for the regulation of conduct in all the varied relations of life—(which show the fearful misunderstanding and perversion of natural laws that existed in those early physical ages,)—were given in words of peremptory command, adapted to the undeveloped condition of the childish mind. The Law demanded unquestioning faith and implicit obedience. Its authority was the highest. It issued from the Throne of the Invisible, the King of Kings, who inhabiteth Eternity. It was a direct challenge to the imagination and spiritual nature of Man, to soar in search of the Divine. And it awakened the latent sentiments of veneration and sublimity, filling the human soul with mysterious awe of the greatness and majesty of God.

The New Testament was given to the YOUTH of the Church and World, as we have already shown, and was adapted to the farther progressed condition of the Human Family. Man was no longer a nomad of the wilderness, but a law-abiding citizen. His capabilities for receiving and understanding truth were enlarged. For he had been favored with the instruction of inspired teachers and had gained the experiences and growth of ages. He had entered upon his heroic and affectional Youth—his era of adventure, of reckless daring, impulse and passion.

But Man was still on the physical plane of thought and action, and required a visible guide, one possessed of an elevated moral nature and a comprehensive intellect. One who could lift high the standard of Truth to rally all his sentiments for Right, and give direction to their growing power. The All-One saw and supplied the need. Lo ! the Word was made flesh and dwelt on Earth ; the truth of Heaven became incarnate. And to the enthusiastic Youth of Man was given the lofty example and Leadership of a God !

Now, the appeal was no longer to Arms ; but to Principles. The moral conflict superseded the physical, of the Hebrew Dispensation ; as saith the Apostle : The weapons of our warfare are not carnal, but mighty through God to the pulling down of strongholds ; casting down imaginations and everything that exalteth itself against the knowledge of God, and bringing into captivity every thought to the obedience of Christ. For we wrestle not against flesh and blood, but against principalities, against powers, against the rulers of the darkness of this world, against spiritual wickedness in high places.

On the Christian Banner is engraven in broad generalities the whole sum of faith and practice.

Life and immortality are brought to light through the Gospel of Christ, who abolished Death by his own glorious resurrection.

Thou shalt love the Lord thy God with all thy heart, and with all thy soul, and with all thy mind. This is the first and great commandment. And the second is like unto it : Thou shalt love thy neighbor as thyself. On these two commandments hang all the law and the prophets.

The fruits of the Spirit of Love are love, joy, peace, long-suffering, gentleness, goodness, faith, meekness and temperance. For they that are Christ's have crucified the flesh with its affections and lusts. And by their *fruit* ye may know them.

Christ, the great Democratic Philosopher and Teacher of Natural Religion to the World, uplifted the whole Human Family to his own high level, declaring them to be children of a Common Parent, and praying them to be one with him, *even* as he was one, or at-one, with the Godhead; in other words, to accept with all their heart, and soul, and mind, and to practice the divine Humanitary principles of his Gospel of Intelligent Nature. And Christ himself was the grand type-man of human capabilities, and Heaven's appointed Leader, not only of his own, but of all future time, until Man and Woman should become like him, Spiritual, Intuitional-Intellectual and Harmonial, filled with the Knowledge, wisdom and love of the Divine—at-one with God.

And Christ must reign until he hath put all enemies of the Godhead under his feet. And when all things shall be subdued unto Him, then shall the Son also himself be subject unto Him that put all things under him, that God may be all in all. And then, Earth and Heaven in harmony, the Mediative Son having accomplished his mission, will be united under the acknowledged Government of the INVISIBLE ONE who inhabiteth Eternity—the Divine Father and Mother God.

By the Revealed Will of God in Man is meant the various faculties of mind and heart with which the munificent All-Parent has endowed the Human Family, and which naturally seek for expression and take definite direction when unchecked by false educational influences. These faculties are the same in kind with the Deity's own, differing only in degree. They constitute Man, in verity, Children of God. They interpret clearly the true significance of the Word: And God created Man in his own image, in the image of God created he him, Male and Female created he them. And it is through these wonderful powers that the Human Family are able to understand the thought of God in the works of creation. For like only can appreciate like. And it is by the education or development of these Heaven-endowed faculties of heart and mind that Man can be brought into rapport with spiritual truths, and with the principles of science; or, in other terms, with the laws of God in the universe of matter and of mind. And, consequently, under right educational influences, the Human Family become intellectual, moral and spiritual, self-poised and self-governing.

And these faculties of mind and heart are a constant challenge from the Invisible to Christian Teachers, to awaken them to careful study of the Revealed Will in Man, in order that they may better understand how to co-operate with the All-Parent in developing the immortal germs of existence.

26

The world is continually renewing its yonth.   And Infinite Love speaks through each coming generation: "There is a new race, begin once more;" develop the whole nature of man and woman in order that they may become harmonious in character, and, as a consequent, in true and perfect relations with material and Intelligent Nature.   Upon the normal unfolding of these faculties of mind and heart depends the virtue, usefulness and happiness of each individual member of the Human Family, and the true progress of Society; while their non-development, or misdirection, is the fruitful source of human wretchedness, poverty, vice and crime, and causes the general demoralization and disorganization of communities and Nations.

And, in view of the Nature of Man, inherited from Deity, we appeal to the Church of to-day for a recognition of each and all of the marvellous faculties of mind and heart with which the Divine has endowed the Human Offspring; and for effective action in the development of these God-like powers.   We can as easily set aside the passions of Man as the affections; as easily extinguish the sentiments, as the varied tastes which manifest themselves in the love of the beautiful of earth and Heaven; and as easily expunge the reasoning powers, as either class of human faculties.

The most that any religious sect of Christendom can accomplish, is to *suppress* these invaluable natural gifts of God to his children.   But it should not be forgotten that a fearful responsibility rests upon that individual, or that class of individuals, who would suppress, rather than develop human capabilities.   For suppressed power is volcanic in its nature, alike in the moral as in the material world; and will eventually burst forth in far extending and destructive eruptions, filling whole communities with consternation and terror.

Ay, we appeal earnestly to the Christian Church to recognize Man, male and female, as God made them in his own image, or form, and after his own likeness, or essential qualities; and not attempt to stultify or dwarf them in any one of the varied powers of their being.   Let the Church take her stand by this undeniable truth, that God's man and woman are nobler creations than any School of Theology could form, however erudite it might be, or however comprehensive in its principles. Let her study carefully and reverently these representative persons of Deity, in order to learn the Revealed Will of Heaven in regard to their nature and the requirements of that nature which is inscribed on every faculty of mind and heart; remembering that the study of man is, in verity, the sublime study of God himself.

The fearful doctrine of total depravity, taught by the Church, which causes one to regard his neighbor with suspicion, and to mistrust his highest motives of action, grew out of the unnatural suppression and abuse of Man's Heaven-endowed faculties, during the ignorance and darkness of the physical, or experimental ages; but not out of the nature of Man. Yea, let God be true, but every man a liar.

It is well to remember in our estimate of what has descended to us from past centuries, that the World has been a physical Infant—a capricious, ignorant Child—an impulsive, arrogant Youth —and that it has not yet received its credentials as a profound reasoning man. We of the nineteenth century are just beginning to realize, from our higher point of observation on the ascending pyramid of the ages, how comparatively limited have been the knowledges and experiences of the past from which to draw reliable data for philosophical deductions. And we are yet unable to measure the sublime capabilities of human growth and power in the direction of knowledge and of understanding. And for these reasons we should strive to wear our *opiinons* lightly, even as a mantle that may be changed with the increasing temperature of knowledge, and not as a Knight his armor, to challenge every passer by to strike fire with the flint of argument. But our *Christian principles*—Love to God and Love to Man— should be cherished deeply in heart, mind and soul, in order that our whole physical, intellectual and moral being may be grandly moved by them to comprehensive Humanitary action.

CHAPTER II.

A good tree cannot bring forth evil fruit, neither can a corrupt tree bring forth good fruit. Wherefore by their fruits ye shall know them.

Wo unto them that justify the wicked for reward! As the fire devoureth the stubble and the flame consumeth the chaff, so their root shall be as rottenness, and their blossom shall go up as dust.

Having briefly stated in the preceding Chapter what we intended to convey to the mind of the Reader in the terms— the Revealed Word of God to Man, and the Revealed Will in Man—let us glance at the different Denominations of the Church of God, and observe where they stand in regard to the Revealed Word, that requires, broadly, Love to God and Love to Man ; and the Revealed Will that demands development and action in the direction of the faculties with which the Creator has endowed the Human Family. But, before entering upon our proposed plan of treating the Church of to-day Denominationally, and testing each sect by the Revealed Word and the Revealed Will, let us first take a running review of the past history of the Roman Catholic and Protestant branches of the Church, in order that we may be able to observe more clearly their present relation to each other, and to the outside Family of Man.

Let us first glance at the Roman Catholic, or pioneer branch of the Christian Church: The Prelates of this Denomination claimed, in the Youth ot the Church, and still claim in her Reasoning Age, to be the only true successors of St. Peter, and to hold the keys of Heaven and of Hell, with power to open wide the gates of Paradise to all believers in their special forms of doctrine ;

> The ever-during gates, harmonious sound
> On golden hinges turning ;

or, to unlock for heretics, doomed by their anathemas to endless perdition, the gates of fearful Erebus ; when—

> On a sudden, open fly,
> With impetuous recoil and jarring sound,
> Th' infernal doors, and on their hinges grate
> Harsh thunder.

This pioneer branch of the Christian Church has been a great power in the Earth.   In its early purity, love of the Word, and zeal for God, it entertained the sublime idea of Christianizing the World, and of becoming THE CHURCH UNIVERSAL.   Its devotees journeyed over barren deserts and trackless wastes of Ocean to establish the True Religion, with an indomitable will that conquered unprecedented difficulties, and a faith and courage that triumphed over the most adverse circumstances.   And it erected churches and cathedrals, and elevated the symbol of its faith in every part of the inhabited globe.

Its organization was perfect.   Its policy for enlarging its numbers and increasing its power was uniform and persistent. And, had it remained true to its early, inspirational idea, it could not have failed of becoming THE CHURCH UNIVERSAL.   Ay, had it retained the same purity and simplicity, the same earnest love of truth, and zeal in its promulgation, which characterized it in its early history (when the Catacombs of Rome were filled by the persecutions of the Pagans with devoted sons and daughters of God, who could die of lingering starvation, be sawn asunder, or perish at the stake, rejoicing in tribulations, but who could NOT renounce the blessed truths of the Gospel of Christ,) THEN it could not have failed ; or, had it put forth, in after ages, when it had attained numbers, power and influence, half the energy to propagate Christian Principles—Love to God and Love to Man—that it exerted to enforce Ecclesiastic Dogmas

on the people, *nolens volens*, and often with the most fearful tortures of body and soul; THEN it could not have failed.   Oh, no !
For then an innumerable company of Saints and martyrs, far
exceeding that which Elisha saw in vision drawn out upon the
boundless fields of ether, would have been marshalled on its
side by the King of Kings; and all the combined forces of
Earth and Hell could not have prevailed against it.

But, alas! in proportion as the Roman Catholic Organization
increased in numbers and wealth, and advanced in position and
influence, it receded from the vitalizing and elevating principles
of the Gospel of Christ; and, consequently, lost its attractive
and regenerating power.   The true Christian Religion is so perfectly adapted to the spiritual needs of human beings, that,
whenever it is addressed to the heart and understanding of Man
in an earnest and loving spirit, it will not fail to draw the people
to its green pastures and beside its fountains of living water, and
to·appease the hunger and thirst of the soul.   But thinking men
and women refuse to be driven by the sting of the lash, like
dumb animals, and tethered there.   Nature rebels.   They must
be attracted thither by the *beauty of holiness*, and gently per-
suaded by loving influences to enter the Heavenly Pastures and
enjoy the glorious liberty of the Children of God.

Coersive measures are opposed to the constitution of Man,
and to the pure and Liberal Spirit of Christianity, which the Divine All-One adapted to the nature and requirements of the
Human Family.   And they who use such to propagate the
Gospel of Love, will signally defeat the end they would attain.
For coersion arouses a spirit of resistance that waits only on
opportunity, and will eventually decimate the organization that
adopts them.

Through pride of success, the earnestness of Rome for the
truth of the Gospel degenerated into vaulting ambition that
o'erleaps itself.   It strove to *Doctronize*, rather than *Christrianize*,
the World; and so missed the mark.   In its haste to proselyte,
that it might advance more rapidly in numbers and power, it
stepped back from the progressed Youth to the Childhood of
the Church of God, of less enlightened ages, and engrafted

upon the living Christian Church many of the dead forms of the Hebrew Religion.   And in order to render itself acceptable to heathen nations, and thereby increase its communicants and extend its influence, it borrowed doctrines from the Pagan Schools, corrupting the purity of the Gospel of Christ.   The Invocation of the Virgin and of Saints naturally followed this prostitution of its integrity.   And, because of the mental darkness of the age, and the materialistic tendency of the undeveloped mind, the Christian Religion degenerated quickly thereafter into another mode of image worship or idolatry.

Many devout Ecclesiastics of that period were strongly opposed to these corrupting innovations.   The Roman Power arrayed itself against them and became an unrelenting persecutor of the most elevated and earnest Leaders of its own Body. And, in proportion as Rome vastated itself of Spiritual Life, its lust of TEMPORAL POWER increased, until at length it aimed at UNIVERSAL EMPIRE, instead of *universal Christianity*.   That was the fatal rock on which its hopes were wrecked.   Then arose angry contentions among its Prelates about who should be greatest, and fierce and deadly animosities that followed their unfortunate victims beyond the grave.   During this period in the history of the Church the body of Pope Formosus was dragged out of the tomb by Pope Stephen Seventh and thrown into the Tiber.   But retribution was not slow in following this inhuman act.   Pope Stephen was shortly after taken to prison, where he was strangled by another Prelate, equally as ambitious and cruel as himself.

In the early part of the tenth century, the power of the Pope was greatly augmented by forged decretals.   And this fresh acquisition of influence, unrighteously obtained, had the tendency to stimulate personal ambition more and more, and to greatly increase feuds and deadly strifes among the Ecclesiastic Body; eventually the Papal Crown could only be won by either force or bribery.   Popes warred against Popes with furious hate, while accusing each other of the most inhuman and abominable crimes; each one claiming to be the only *true successor* of Saint Peter, while the large portion of their number resembled that repentant apostle in but one unenviable particular—their vehement and blasphemous denial of the Philosopher of Nazareth in almost every act of their reckless and profligate lives.

And in proportion as Rome wandered from the Revealed Word of God to Man, and the Revealed Will in Man, it adopted measures for enlarging its numbers and influence, opposed alike to the truths of Nature and of Revelation   The Celibacy of the Priesthood was now enjoined by that Church, in order that the undivided interest of the Clergy might be given to its unscrupulous system of proselyting and of espionage, unsoftened by the gentle and ameliorating influences of woman.   And thus the Christian Church, the Bride the Lamb's wife, was represented by the Prelates of her corrupted Religion, as a stern, Masculine Bigot.

Few, comparatively, of the clerical body were able to remain true to their vows of celibacy; and the measure proved an element of weakness instead of strength to Rome.   All violation of natural law must inevitably produce a kindred result.   It is truly painful to think of a class of men with the natural affections Heaven bestowed in wisdom and love crucified within them, leaving their animal passions—(undisciplined by the responsible and elevating ties of husband and father, and all the stronger because of the check placed upon their legitimate expression)—to become grossly sensual, aggressive and cruel.   Yet such was the condition of the Roman Priesthood, during the darkness of the middle ages.   Outraged Nature was fearfully avenged in the increasing licentiousness and impurity of both the Ecclesiastic Body, and the laity; and the consequent decline of Papacy.

Rome continued to grow more and more tyrannical, avaricious, and cruel, until it culminated in power and corruption, it has been estimated, about the central period of the middle ages. After it had filled the measure of its prosperous days, its fall was rapid and full of horror.   Because as soon as it began to fear a decline, in consequence of the general disaffection among its purest and best adherents, it adopted a *policy of expediency* for preserving and extending its rule, limited only by the impossible.   And, at length, in the blind and fanatical *furore* of alarmed Despotic Power, Rome established the fearful INQUISITION, which shocked the moral sentiments of the enlightened World. And thus tyranny and torture became a part of its organized system of religion, for restraining and constraining the human body, mind and soul. And so Rome, opposed itself to the great essential Democratic truths of the Gospel of Christ, which are—LIBERTY AND LOVE—and became Anti-Christ, cutting itself off from the possibility of universal acceptance; and by the very measures that were adopted to attain that end. And such a result inevitably followed. Because, as before stated, coersive action is opposed alike to Nature and to Revelation. There is a bound that tyranny cannot pass without arousing a spirit of resistance in human beings, commensurate with its own power, that will eventually liberate them from its thraldom.

But Rome was hard to resist, for it was the dominant religious power of Christendom, and claimed absolute control over the temporal as well as spiritual affairs of the people. And the struggle was long and bloody. It would paralyze both heart and brain to portray the fearful persecutions and ingenious tortures by which the Lambs of Christ's Flock were crucified without mercy, in the name of the Christian Religion, whose *Alpha* and *Omega* is LOVE, by the wifeless, childless and pitiless Priesthood. On the lintels of the doors to the Fold of the dear Redeemer of the World were inscribed in letters of light—LOVE TO GOD AND LOVE TO MAN—but upon the threshold was stamped, in characters of blood—Torture and Death for Heretics.

Yet, we should remember, in reviewing the fearful record of the Church, that this was the period of her heroic, affectional, and unreasoning Youth. Man was everywhere reckless of life in enterprises that enlisted the feelings and passions; for the popular mind was undeveloped, and had not been imbued with the highest aims and uses of existence. The educated few were still controlled by precedence and prejudice, alike in Church and State; and entertained no respect nor humanitary love for the groping millions whom they continued to hold in the bondage of ignorance, believing it to be safer for the populace than knowledge. And so the benighted masses, driven forward in the dark, reflected back no light to guide their guides, and the

27

latter continued, for ages, blind leaders of the blind ; and both the clergy and laity were unable to see the gross inconsistency that existed between their profession and practice.   To-day, we live in the dawn of the Reasoning Age of the Church and World. Knowledge has greatly increased, and the Christian Religion is receiving a higher interpretation.   The Church, viewed as a whole, is wiser, and her practice better ; but are there no inconsistent professors and leaders in the present ?   Judge ye.

AURICULAR CONFESSION naturally attended the Inquisition. Through its agency the officials of Rome enlarged their system of espionage, learned all the secret thoughts and transactions of the people, and acquired a more complete control over their actions and conscience.   Now, they could be swayed at pleasure by the Priesthood, like reeds shaken of the wind.   This system had the tendency to check effectually the normal exercise of the Reason of Man, and to hold the mind in a state of weak irresolution.   Auricular Confession furnished, alas! many innocent victims for the torturing Rack, and supplied the insatiable flames of the Stake with innocent and heroic martyrs, the purest and noblest sons and daughters of the Divine Father and Mother God.

BIBLE PROHIBITION followed after Auricular Confession.   The people were strictly forbidden, under heavy penalty, to read the Holy Book.   This measure was all the more remakable, because it exhibited a reckless disregard on the part of the Clerical Body for the high authority by which they professed to be governed; for it was in direct opposition to the command of the Author of Christianity to his followers of every age of the world: Search the Scriptures; for in them ye think ye have eternal life : and they are they which testify of me.   The policy was an additional attempt to check thought and inquiry in regard to the true significance of the sacred text, and to prevent the popular mind from reasoning upon matters of religion ; and thus to render the intellect of the people entirely subservient to the Ecclesiastic power. And through such measures the Roman Denomination of the Christian Church became at length the REASON and CONSCIENCE of its members.   And when the great regulating forces of the human soul, Reason and Conscience, are in the keeping of the Clergy, or of any class of men, or women, it is a deplorable condition for individuals, as well as for nations.

If any think that we have stated the case too strongly, let them turn to countries where the Roman Catholic Religion has been the dominant Power for centuries—Italy, Spain and Mexico furnish illustrations in point—and observe the general demoralization and mental darkness of the people. He that spake as never man spake hath said : A good tree cannot bring forth evil fruit ; neither can a corrupt tree bring forth good fruit. Wherefore by their fruits ye shall know them.

The Prelates of Rome wrapped the worshippers at God's altars, body, mind and soul, in swaddling bands, and guided them by leading-strings, like infants, whithersoever they would. They were reduced to a condition of the most abject slavery. In this helpless state of subjection and puerility PENANCE was instituted for the correction and discipline of the people. For, now, it was an easy matter to persuade them that it was meritorious to lacerate and torture the body for the good of the soul. And so, in the Roman Catholic branch of the Christian Church, Penance for moral dereliction was made the substitute for repentance and contrition of soul for wrongdoing ; externalizing still more and more the worship of God, with whom a contrite spirit is the *only* propitiation for sin, and the voluntary devotion of heart and mind the only acceptable offering.

And as the people were in a condition of *enforced childhood*, which was induced by dwarfing the natural and noble qualities of mind and heart bestowed by affluent Heaven, it was but a meagre and miserable apology for human existence, sensual, helpless and rayless. Poor, smothered souls ! They were tortured and paralyzed, instead of being kindled and inspired by the electric spark of Divinity. For when the marvellous faculties of the human being are wrapped in a napkin and buried in the earth of the physical nature, they become a blind force in the soul, creating morbid, indefinable and ceaseless yearnings that cannot be appeased. Freedom ! Freedom ! ! is the agonizing cry of the Spirit of Man, struggling vainly against its enforced limitations, while it feels the expansive power of the Infinite moving through the deep of its nature.

The physical world was then, as it is ever, beautiful and bright in God's vivifying sun and air. But it rendered darker, by contrast, the realm of thought and feeling that had been desecrated by a despotic, unscrupulous and corrupt Priesthood. Under such depressing religious influences the human soul was rarely lighted, saving by transient gleams from a brighter world, glancing athwart the valley of the shadow of death. The condition of Cloistered Devotees was even more favorable to individual happiness than that of the mass of worshippers. For their peculiar habits of life were conducive to spiritual growth and MEDIUMSHIP; and the monotony of existence was often relieved by moments of strange exaltation, ecstasy, and enrapturing trance, that elevated them awhile into a freer, purer atmosphere, leaving upon their minds an ineffaceable impression of brightness and beauty.

The Roman Catholic Denomination continued to degenerate more and more, and to depart farther and farther from the true principles of the Christian Religion; until at length its Prelates, in their unregenerated and infatuated selfhood and lust of rule, arrogated to themselves the PARDONING POWER, which proved a fearfully demoralizing agent in their hands. Through this policy the Church became, in verity, an *abettor* of the worst offenses against society. It SOLD LICENSES for the commission of crime, in anticipation of the deed to be perpetrated; and, thus, leaping the chasm between the inception and the execution of the crime, it became *particeps criminis* with the offender.

But Rome's increasing venality, its use of power for selfish and wicked ends, and its torturing persecutions of those who were striving for elevated Christian lives, aroused, at last, among the incorruptible few, a spirit of burning indignation and vehement PROTEST, that all the ingenious tortures of the Inquisition, and all the withering flames of the Stake could not suppress. And PROTESTANTISM culminated at length in the Reformation of the Sixteenth Century, under the strong and determined leadership of the earnest and devout Luther, Calvin, and Melancthon. It was the early dawn of Humanity's Day. The dark ages retreated slowly into the night of years. Thank God!

And thus Rome was taught by humiliating and painful experience, that the many artificial measures which it adopted to increase its numbers and influence were powerless to enlarge and perpetuate the Church of the living God. Its unnatural methods served only to galvanize the corpse of a church into a momentary and painful mimicry of life. That which the Roman Catholic Denomination needed, in order to increase its numbers and influence upon an indestructible foundation, was vital Christianity. It required purity of soul, devoted Love to God and Man, and burning zeal for the truth; for such alone are the Christian's weapons of warfare with which to attack the strongholds of Satanic Power, and to bring rebels against the government of Heaven into subjection and loving obedience to the King of kings.

And thus the Roman Catholic branch of the Church lost its ancient prestige, and fell from the height of its ambition, never more to rise a Dominant Power in the world. About the period of its decline, the ORDER OF JESUITS, founded by St. Ignatius de Loyola, an ardent devotee of Rome, sprang into existence, and put forth almost superhuman power, hoping to resuscitate its enfeebled Body, rebuild its waste places, and restore its pristine glory. And the members of that peculiar Order still continue to go forth on their remarkable, self-imposed Mission, baptized with the spirit of martyrdom, pledged to endure fatigue and hunger, the chilling cold of Frigid Zones, the burning heat of Tropical climes, and even Death itself, in any form of terror, should it be considered important for the interest and advancement of the cause which they have vowed to sustain. They compass sea and land to proselyte, energizing every faculty of heart and mind in order to learn all the peculiar phases of human nature, and to acquire the subtle diplomatic power through which they may be able to adapt themselves to the infinite varieties of the *genus homo*. And, armed with knowledge, penetration, patience, and suavity in mode, they weave about their victims fine tissues of motives and arguments, persuading them that the only way to Paradise is through the door of the Roman Catholic Sect.   And thus they attract unsettled, restless men and women, whose hearts have not been established upon the Rock of Ages, luring them on and on, like the deluding light of the *ignis fatuus*, until they are hopelessly bewildered and lost in complicated meshes of creeds and dogmas.

The Order of Jesuits, in the United States of America, includes many persons of intellect and learning, who are wily politicians, as well as acomplished *diplomates;* and if their power to execute were commensurate with their ability to plan, strange and startling events would be announced in the daily news of the nineteenth century.   But Man proposes, and God disposes.   The World is secure from the terrible despotism of universal Ecclesiastic sway, because HE is the Omnipotent Ruler of Earth and· Heaven, and will delegate the Supreme Power to no man.

By their strenuous and persistent labors, the Jesuits may succeed in erasing the hand-writing upon the walls of Rome——MENE, MENE, TEKEL, UPHARSIN——but they cannot avert the inexorable decree of Destiny.   The Roman Catholic Denomination can never regain its lost position by any human effort, however ably directed.   THE WORLD HAS MOVED FORWARD.   Rome stamped the seal upon its own doom, when it corrupted the purity of the Gospel of Christ, became ambitious of Temporal Power, tyrannic, avaricious and cruel; and when it exchanged the Olive Branch of Christian Democracy for the Crown of the Ecclesiastic Autocrat, and issued its fearful *autos-da-fe* through the scathing lips of the INQUISITION.   For, then, it enslaved and cursed Humanity, instead of enlightening and blessing.   Ay, it dwarfed and enfeebled the Human Family, instead of rendering them self-governing and harmonious in character, like the great Exemplar of Christianity, and leading them grandly forward, on the broad plane of universal principles, into the glorious Liberty of the Children of God.

But, during all the corruptions, intolerance and bloody persecutions of the Roman Catholic Church of the past, God did not leave himself without a witness.   There were many individual examples of elevated piety, which were as lights shining in a dark place, to encourage the hope of the doubting, and show to the World that the holy flame of Heavenly Love was not totally extinguished on earth. Among these illustrious sons and daughters of God, all will recognize the noble and devout Fenelon, Thomas A. Kempis, and Madame Gion. The glory of their illumined lives still radiates from the zenith of the moral Heavens through the night of Time in rays of undiminished splendor. And there were large numbers of true and earnest Christians in humble paths of use and duty, whose daily lives were like living streams that wind through the lowlands, keeping the meadows green, while reflecting back the brightness and beauty of the bending Heavens.

Ah! had the Roman Catholic Denomination of the past been a distributor, as well as a conservator of knowledge; had it been as spiritual and humanitary, as it was ambitious of worldly power and cruel; THEN, what splendor would have radiated from its domes and turrets! how noble and glorious would have been its record on Earth, and in Heaven! But, *now*, alas! its history must ever be a sorrowful one to every true disciple of Christianity. The fearful Ecclesiastic Tragedy that it enacted for ages, stained its chancel with the precious blood of its purest and most devout worshippers, and filled the Middle Ages with funereal groans, whose mournful echoes have not yet died away in the depth and darkness of Cathedral Dungeons.

And could the Roman Catholic Denomination of the United States, even at this day, unite Liberty with Order in its government, could it shake off its crippling creeds and dogmas and adopt the broad platform of the Christian Church Universal,— Love to God and Love to Man,—and labor for Humanity with a zeal according to Reason and Knowledge, meeting the requirements of enlightened society, and of the Reasoning Age of the Church and World,—THEN its light would break forth as the morning ; and the Nations would flow unto it ; and its numbers would be as the stars of Heaven, or as the sands upon the sea-shore, innumerable.

But, if it continue to keep its people in the darkness of the physical ages, trammeled by the creeds and dogmas of the early

Childhood and Youth of the Church—now that she has reached
her maturer years, and the New Christian Era of Reason is
dawning upon the World ;—if it continue to take charge of the
conscience of its members through AURICULAR CONFESSION and
special guidance, and to weaken their understanding by claiming the right to reason for them ;—if it continue to disregard the
Revealed Word of Heaven which requires, broadly, Love to
God and Love to Man, together with the fruits of love, charity
for and fellowship with other Christian Sects of every name that
labor in the Vineyard of the Master ; if it continue to ignore, or
to oppose, the Revealed Will of God in Man, by either checking
the development of the minds of its people, or failing to give
earnest attention to the full unfolding of their God-endowed faculties (upon which faculties depend their knowledge of themselves, and of their true relations to their fellow-beings, and to
their Creator) thereby depriving them of that intelligence and
self-governing power that would elevate them in the scale of
being and enable them to acquire and maintain independence
of want, and would likewise afford them powerful protection from
moral irregularities and crime;—and, if it still continue, while
forming a part of our noble Republic (that opens freely the doors
of her Workshops, Schools and Churches to the wide World of
Man, without reference to either religious sect, or nationality,
inviting all to share the blessings of munificent Heaven) to stand
as an ISOLATED, ACCRETIVE, and POSITIVE POWER in the State, but
not of it—(because opposed to the genius of our Republican Institutions, which it seeks to undermine by its subtle policy, the
while elevating itself above all earthly rule, and rulers, through
its false claims of supremacy, on account of antiquity, and of the
true apostolic succession and power, recognizing but one Papal
Head, that assumes to receive delegated authority from Heaven
to represent the Eternal God and to rule the nations of Earth)—
taking but little interest in the great progressive movements of
our Age and Country, that are revolutionizing society, saving to
watch with eagle gaze, from turret, spire, or dome, the political
chess-board of the Nation, in order to seize the ripe moment to
swoop down from its eyry and make some move favorable to its

own exclusive, sectarian policy;—THEN, its doom will fall from Heaven in a day when it looketh not for it, and in an hour when it is not aware. And the mighty waves of Human progress, surging from the great Ocean of Eternal Truth, will sweep over it, and the strong under-current that engulfs error will bear it back to the tideless waters of oblivion. And its grand Cathedrals, that have attracted the admiration of the Nations, will stand as everlasting monuments OF WHAT IT WAS—AND MIGHT HAVE BEEN.

The foregoing doom is not announced in the spirit of Prophecy; but with the voice of Philosophy. It speaks from the actual. Let us make a brief *resume* of the data from which its conclusions are drawn.

By the system of ESPIONAGE in the Roman Catholic Denomination, which engenders fear and bondage among its members;—by PHYSICAL PENANCE, for *moral dereliction*, which acts upon their mind as an offset against the sin committed, and serves to weaken the moral sense;—by AURICULAR CONFESSION, which places their *conscience* in the keeping of the Priesthood;—by ABSOLUTE AUTHORITY, which claims the right to exercise REASON for them, thereby enfeebling their understanding;—and, by all the superficial and despotic measures which it adopts for its own ambitious ends, which dwarf and degrade the human being, the Roman Catholic Power produces, everywhere, among its members, inward vastation and outward constraint, reducing them to a condition of perpetual childhood. There is no growth.

The people themselves are so closely united sympathetically with the power that holds them bound, that they fully believe in the right of the Ecclesiastic Body to exercise the unwarrantable authority. And this near relation of the people to the Priesthood brings them into rapport with the intellect of the latter, and they receive from the clergy, unconsciously to both parties, the insensible, yet positive magnetism of their minds, and in this way gain a vague, general idea of the policy of Rome, which policy they aid also, without premeditation, in carrying forward; even as the current of a river increases the speed of the row-boat that plies its oars on the inflowing tide. Thus the clergy

28

and laity are united in action: and the people aid indirectly in forging the chains that enslave them.

There are two large and distinct classes of believers in the world.   One is composed of ignorant, unreflecting persons, who receive opinions from authority, by an exercise of the will power;   the other class includes the educated and intelligent, who are unable to embrace opinions, except from the convictions of Reason.   The large mass of Roman Catholics are composed of the former class.   Their minds are undeveloped, blind and superstitious.   They remain alway children.   It is true that they have the mature physical growth of men and women, but——

> " They must be measured by the soul ;
> The mind's the standard of the Man.''

The character of the mind of the mass of this Sect, like that of its Ecclesiastics, is dogmatic, absolute and unteachable; and it cannot be otherwise; for the reason that, in addition to the strong, yet imperceptible influence which the intellect of the latter exerts upon that of the former, the *will power* of the people is constantly stimulated and kept in an active state, as they receive their opinions through the exercise of this faculty, instead of Reason; being obliged to rely entirely on authority for their social and political, as well as religious creeds.   And they are unable to be either much impressed, or influenced, by outside enlightenment; because of their sectarian restraints and prejudices on one side, and on the other, by their lack of development, and, conseqeently, capacity to perceive and appropriate the good about them to their intellectual and moral elevation.

This dogmatic and absolute condition of mind increases as the people advance in years, by reason of the continuous influence of the Ecclesiastic Body; and the laity, being filled with it, throw it back, in their turn, upon the Priesthood, together with an influence from their own unreflecting erratic minds, which tends to equalize mental and moral conditions, and to render their autocratic leaders still more absolute and dogmatic.

And thus the Priesthood and the People are pre-eminently one; and form a strong concentrative, active and re-active, *force* in our Republic. And this sect is becoming more POSITIVE and powerful every year, through accretion. The community outside of the Roman Catholic Denomination is NEGATIVE to this POSITIVE POWER; for the reason that knowledge and enlightenment are not concentrative, but diffusive in their action, like sunlight, air and moisture, and all the beneficent influences of Nature. And there must always be imminent danger of collision in a community where there exists this strongly isolated, concentrative, accretive and positive power, industriously and insidiously at work in its midst, for definite political and religious ends, unconnected with, and inimical to, the general welfare of the country.

And the danger must, inevitably, be greater to the *positive*, than to the *negative power*; for the reason that the former is naturally encroaching and aggressive in character, because it is an absolutism that does not admit of compromise; and will, eventually, provoke resistance from the latter, which, being more extensive and powerful, must at length neutralize its force, and restore the normal condition of enlightened and progressive society; which is a community of individual aims and interests, all tending toward general effect, toward public peace and prosperity; even as the various parts of a sublime anthem unite in producing the most perfect harmony.

A storm in the physical world will serve as an illustration. It is an effect of an operating cause, which is an unequal, or inharmonious condition of the atmosphere. Nature endeavors to restore the lost equilibrium by creating an active condition of the elements. The positive clouds continue to accumulate power, until they bocome highly electric; then they are attracted toward the negative clouds in the distance, and this flying artillery of the skies sweep through the fields of air, and charge upon the negative forces in reverberating thunder. They are dismembered by the shock and dissolve to tears that fall upon the earth in benediction. Nature is appeased with returning order, and the unvailed Sun looks down once more from the heights of ether in rejoicing approval of restored harmony.

CHAPTER III.

SEARCH THE SCRIPTURES ; *for in them ye think ye have eternal life : and they are they which testify of me.*

God is a Spirit : and they that worship him must worship him in spirit and in truth.

Protestantism appears to have been the growth power of the Christian Religion of the past ; even as war has been the developing agent of Nations. One announced the individuality and Spiritual Freedom of the Man ; the other, the individuality in unity and political independence of the Nation.

Yes, Protestantism burst the bands of Ecclesiastic domination, and asserted before Earth and Heaven the Spiritual Freedom of the Human Soul. It claimed the right of each individual being to address the All-Parent in his own behalf, using his own form of words, independently of the authority of the Priesthood, and in accordance with the direction of the Author of Christianity : Enter into thy closet, and when thou hast shut the door, pray to thy Father which is in secret. And the Protestant branch of the Church repudiated the numerous forms and ceremonies of the Roman Catholic Denomination, on the plea that they occupy the mind with the *externals* of worship, and thus prevent *interior* action and development, or the regeneration of the soul. Protestant Sects sat aside, consequently, in their formulæ of faith and practice, THE INVOCATION OF THE VIRGIN AND OF SAINTS—CELIBACY OF THE PRIESTHOOD—AURICULAR CONFESSION—EXCLUSIVE RIGHT OF THE CLERGY TO READ AND INTERPRET THE SCRIPTURES—together with PENANCE and the PARDONING POWER. And they strenuously maintained the *right* of each individual member of their Body to read the Word of God for his own edification ; and, to the care of his conscience, and the liberty of worshipping the Creator in accordance with its dictates.

And, thus, Protestantism removed the REASON and CONSCIENCE of the people from the keeping of the Priesthood, while charging home upon its members with startling emphasis their high responsibility to the ETERNAL ONE for their sins of omission, as well as of commission ; thereby stimulating the highest motives of the Human Being, and elevating the standard of right action. And so this progressed branch of the Church of the living God purged itself of the innovations and corruptions of Rome ; and the Christian Religion was re-established in its simplicity and purity. Freedom to worship God in accordance with the dictates of conscience, and the stimulating influence of vital piety, produced a marvellous change in individuals and in society. The devout Protestants of the Reformation believed, with all their heart, and mind, and soul, in the literal word of Revelation : The Kingdom of Heaven suffereth violence, and the violent take it by force. And, in their direct and indivertible earnestness of purpose, they would seize upon the very horns of God's Altar, and draw inspiration from the Eternal Source of existence.

The mind of the succeeding ages enlarged under the electrical influences of the REFORMATION ; so radical, energizing and expansive was that power which had been gathering force through long periods of oppressive Ecclesiastic sway ; and the wonderful possibilities of the human intellect were perceived and acknowledged for the first time in the history of man. Undying aspirations were awakened, and immortal genius shone forth from the moral heavens in constellated splendor. The Seventeenth Century was luminous with the brilliant galaxy of stars of the first magnitude.

> Thy Monuments of deathless fame arose,
>   Prouder than Egypt's in her Pharaoh's days,
> Or Grecia's Temples in sublime repose
>   Above the murmuring crowds that thronged her ways—
> O, Europe, then ! Vast Monuments of Thought,
>   Immortal aspirations, rose to Heaven,
> Whose spirit columns richly were inwrought
>   With priceless gems of mind thy God hath freely given.

This sublime awakening of the intellect and moral nature of Man was a grand prelude to the rising glory of the New Christian Era. It was indeed the resplendent dawn of Humanity's Day, the Herald to the waiting nations of the Reasoning Age of the Church and World.

But it is painful to chronicle that the Protestant branch of God's Church, which was born of persecution and torture, became, in its turn, after it had acquired numbers and influences, a stern, uncompromising bigot. Intolerance was its fearful birthright, and it was true to its lineage. But, fortunately for its spiritual growth and for the spread of the Christian Religion in the world, Protestantism contained within itself elements which were corrective of Ecclesiastic tyranny and of the supremacy of Creeds; and the days of its persecuting spirit were limited to the peculiar period of despotism at which it sprang into existence.

Many able writers have believed and stated that the annals of Protestants would have shown as many Martyrs as those of the Roman Catholics, had the former Body been equal in numbers and power to the latter. But more deeply reflective and unprejudiced minds cannot assent to the proposition; for the reason that the World progresses, and Protestantism is one of the results of the advancement of ideas. Christian nations were more enlightened at the period of the Reformation than they had previously been; and enlightenment is a powerful modifier of prejudice and intolerance. And SPIRITUAL FREEDOM was also one of the cardinal doctrines of Protestants; in opposition to the teaching and practice of Romanists. THE PROTEST POWER has acted as a safety valve to the whole Body of Dissenters, preventing sudden and alarming outbursts of Religious excitement. It is a gate without a Clerical key in the enclosure of the Christian Flock, through which the Lambs of Christ's fold can go in and out and find pasture.

Protestantism must, in verity, ever be regarded as the precedent of liberal and enlightened Christianity. Its Denominations possess great advantages over the parent Sect, which has no progressive element in its organization, but remains, in every

land and age, the same unyielding Conservator. Our Democratic institutions, which awaken a deeper humanitary feeling
and create a more liberal public sentiment, have the tendency to
check its persecuting spirit, and will in the course of ages mod-
ify its policy—(if Rome do not succeed in becoming the dominant political as well as religious power of the United States,
in accordance with the ambitious aims and the numerous efforts
toward their accomplishment, which that power is at present vigorously engaged in putting forth in every industrial, educational
and political avenue of our country; as may be clearly shown
from the reliable statistics of the day, as well as from the strategic movements of political parties. What means the twenty
thousand armed Fenians in the City of New York, alone, playing,
ostensibly, an expensive *game at patriotism*, which the Ecclesiastic Body professes not to approve, while it *does approve* of the
arming? Were it otherwise, the Fenians would be at once dis-
armed; and that Rome knows full well; for he understands far
better than a looker on in Christendom the absolute control that
he holds over his worshippers. Let him answer that question
to the people of the United States.) But the advance of this
Sect towards Liberal Christianity must be exceedingly slow, because its system of espionage over every grade of its Priesthood
keeps the entire Body in a cold shiver of apprehension; and
this condition of mind weakens the moral sentiments and is,
consequently, unfavorable to the reception of new and progressive ideas. And it is greatly to be feared that, before Rome can
become more receptive of enlightened religious opinions, his
power will be broken in the United States by the violent antagonisms that his encroachments will awaken.

We have stated the proposition that War has been a developing agent among the Nations. In this capacity it has also been
the pioneer of the Christian Religion, and prepared the way for
the acceptance of its grand principles of Peace and Good Will to
Man. War, in asserting the individuality and independence of
nations with the sword, either captured, or enslaved the conquered; and by such measures it became an organ of enlightenment to both hostile countries, and thus awakened a power

stronger than itself, that will eventually disarm betligerent nations, and prepare the way for the great Christian Democracy of the World. For the captives of War carried with them into foreign lands the peculiar features of their own civilization, which enlarged the knowledges of their enslavers, and created a broader humanitary sympathy. Kindred effects were also produced upon the conquered nations by the final return of these captives to their native land. New arts and sciences were introduced, which exerted an influence upon their social, civil and religious institutions, imparting a fresh impetus toward higher enlightenment. And thus it is written in the Volume of Inspiration: The wrath of Man shall praise Thee.

Long continued seasons of peace were unfavorable to human progress, during the physical and more experimental ages of the World, because of the undeveloped condition of the mind of Man. the limited amount of general information, and the comparatively small numbers of persons with fine reasoning intellects to lead the ignorant, waiting millions forward. The mental and moral status of the people were necessarily low; and their laws, the exponents of their enlightenment, were, consequently, highly restrictive and unfavorable to advancement. An outside pressure was needful to break inside barriers, and make inroads upon one of the worst forms of despotism, ignorant conservatism, and to quicken the torpid life of the masses.

With the newly aroused heroic spirit of resistance to foreign aggression upon *national rights*, there was also awakened a clearer perception of personal liberty, and the inalienable rights of Man. And thus individual ambition and aspiration followed in the wake of National pride and independence. Enlightenment was the natural result of repeated conflicts, with the attending increase of knowledge from abroad, to enlarge the popular mind, and the enforced intercourse with strangers in close household relations, to lead to an exchange of the amenities of life, and thereby weaken national animosities.

And thus we learn from the Teachings of the Ages, that the tendency of War, all through the ignorant Childhood and the unreflecting Youth of Mankind, has been toward the—EQUALIZATION OF KNOWLEDGES——THE MODIFICATION OF NATIONAL AND RE-

LIGIOUS PREJUDICES—THE ELEVATION OF THE TASTES AND SENTI-
MENTS OF THE PEOPLE—AND THE GENERAL ADVANCEMENT OF SO-
CIETY.

And so, at length, long desired Enlightenment came to bless
the World, in obedience to its own progressive law. But it is
none the less a benediction of Heaven. It was directed in the
providence of God that the United States of North America
should reveal to the Despotisms of the Old World the SELF-
GOVERNING POWER OF THE INDIVIDUAL MAN, and his adaptation to
Republican Institutions.

The World had grown weary with waiting. Its ear was
pained with the agonized cry of suffering Humanity:—" Watch-
man, what of the night?—WILL Liberty come with the dawn?—
How long, O, Lord! how long!" When, lo! Columbia's sons
and daughters called aloud to the peoples that sat in darkness :
" The dawn is breaking !—The Eagle hath soared from his
eyry !—Liberty is abroad !"

> " And Freedom!—Freedom ! ! was the answering shout
> Of Nations, starting from the spell of years."

Enlightenment tarried long, because the Family of Man were
loath to leave the faith of the Fathers, and the peculiar teaching
and impressions of early years, and launch their bark on un-
fathomed waters of Truth, with immeasurable depth below and
above, and infinite space around them. It is alway hard to un-
learn early prejudices and errors of opinion.

> The fancies of our youth, and riper years, forsooth,
> Long cherished in the heart, though we grow wiser,
> We treasure still, tenacious as the miser.
> At length we start from our delightful dreaming—
> And find our sterling treasures only *seeming*—
> And our opinions change ; yet, keen the pain
> Of disappointment, and we strive in vain
> To reconcile our *feelings* to the change
> Our *reason* sanctions.

The settlement of the New World by our Pilgrim Fathers,
and subsequent Declaration of Independence of the Mother
Country, and establishment of a Democratic form of Government, quickened the soul-life of the World, imparting a grand

29

impulse toward higher social and civil conditions.   Invitations
to our Western Eden, to a land of Liberty and abundance, were
sent abroad over the earth.   Commerce bore them swiftly forward on the wings of the wind, wherever she unfurled the dear
old Stars and Stripes, as a benediction to the Nations.

> And as the message flew from man to man,
> From heart to heart a thrill electric ran;
> They felt, in every land beneath the sun,
> The mystic chain that links mankind in one
> And Emigration's mighty human tide
> Set toward our land from Peoples far and wide.
> They came in thousands from the Celtic Isles,—
> And from the Northman's rude and cold Defiles,—
> From dreamy Italy —and sunny Spain,—
> And many a German city, vale and plain,
> Commingling like the waters of the Sea,
> And pledged themselves to God—and Liberty !

Our Country was formed of the purest, freest and best people
of every Nationality under Heaven.   It is true that our Pilgrim
Fathers brought with them much of the intolerant spirit of the
Old World; it was the legacy of despotism that they had inherited from their own and other times ; but they did not entail it
on their posterity.   For they established the PUBLIC SCHOOL to
enlighten their own children, and the youth of the world ; which
beneficent Institution will eventually liberate them forever from
every form of Civil and Ecclesiastic Despotism.

The causes of war, among peoples progressed beyond the
savage state, may be attributed to their different degrees of enlightenment.   It may, indeed, be broadly stated that foreign
wars have resulted from different degrees of enlightenment
among different Nations ; and civil wars, from like cause, in different sections of the same country.   And this is so, for the reason that men, belonging to different nations, or to remote sections of the same country, are unable to view political questions,
and divergent interests, from the same intellectual and moral
standpoints ; hence, uncompromising assertion of either national
or sectional policy and interests on one side—determined resistance on the other—and subsequent meeting of belligerent
armies.   Nations who have progressed beyond the necessity of

war have often felt obliged from principle to engage in hostilities with benighted peoples, in order to prevent the triumph of Barbarous, over Enlightened Institutions.

In proof of this proposition we may cite the past history of our own country in relation to its foreign and domestic wars. There could indeed have been no civil war in the United States had it not been for the Institution of Slavery, which prevented one Section of our country from becoming as broadly enlightened as the other. A large portion of the Slave States was cut off from receiving the enlightening and elevating influence of the PUBLIC SCHOOL (which was established in every village and township, and in every district in the cities of the Free States), for the reason that a greater part of the territory of the South was divided into plantations of many miles in extent, which were cultivated by Slave Labor. There were not many large cities, and but few small towns and villages; and, consequently, there was no large industrial middle class of intelligent Mechanics and Farmers, who owned the soil that they cultivated, and the tools with which they wrought, as at the North, to demand the PUBLIC SCHOOL as their right as American Citizens. But, instead of such, there were three and a half millions of Slaves, who were prevented by law from learning to read; and two and a half millions of a " Rolling Population," or nomadic class of people, too poor and worthless to care for instruction; and these, together with three millions of the Aristocratic Class, two hundred and sixty thousand of whom were Slave owners, constituted the entire population of nine millions. This small population of the Slave States was scattered over a territory vastly greater in extent than that occupied by the twenty-one millions of the Free States.

The Rolling Population, or " poor white trash," as they were contemptuously termed by the slaves and their masters, because of their poverty and helplessness, constituted a class of men and women that existed in the Slave States only, being an outgrowth of the " Peculiar Institution." They were deprived of the blessings of education, and of the healthy mental stimulus of self-respecting industry by the unfortunate circumstances of their condition, which was even more deplorable than that of the slaves themselves; for the reason that the former class were composed of the *superior race*, degraded by the existence of servile labor in the community; while the African Slaves were elevated by association with their Anglo-Saxon masters, and by the industrial pursuits in which they were engaged. The Rolling Population were too proud to work, because labor was not honorable: and, being too poor to dispense with it, they obtained a meagre and precarious subsistence, by either squatting upon the borders of large plantations and gathering the voluntary contributions of the soil, or by hunting, fishing, or stealing, as opportunity offered, or conditions of want pressed upon them.

And thus we find that two-thirds of the entire population of the Slave States—the rolling population and slaves together, constituting six out of nine millions—were in a state of extreme ignorance and degradation. This large percentage of undeveloped minds lowered the standard of enlightenment, year after year, at a rapid ratio—because of the greater increase of Slaves and Rolling Population over the Aristocratic Class of citizens—until the average enlightenment of the South fell very far below that of the North, with its twenty-one millions of Freemen.

The industrial classes of the Free States, which enjoyed the advantages of the Public School, and the compensations of honorable labor, acquired knowledge, self-respect, self-governing power and independence; and became large consumers, as well as producers; thereby greatly increasing the commercial interests of the United States with foreign Nations, which has rendered our Country widely known and respected abroad. Throughout the Northern section of the United States:

> Labor is honored and rewarded well.
> And a large Middle Class in virtue dwell;
> The bone and sinew of our youthful State;
> Brave, self-respecting, and with hope elate,
> And great ambition for their native land,
> And for its honors, *they* may yet command.
> And these producers, aspirants for fame,
> Are large consumers; hence, our Nation came
> The grand Commercial Centre of the West,
> With power to succor all the Earth's oppress'd—
> Ay, and she does! Turn to our lists Marine;
> Stand on our Piers and watch the moving scene.

Lo! from the Old World Emigration pours
Her living currents on New England's shores
And great Manhattan's. See! they sweep along;—
Where toil competes with toil the strangers throng;—
In waves, on waves, our thoroughfares they flood—
The exiled ones and poor of noble blood—
The working classes of three-pence per pay,
Half famished on the miserable pay—
Paupers, and Convicts.—pariahs of all
The Monarchies that curse our rolling Ball:
Dejected. dwarfed in soul and body. too,
They come, their life and manhood to renew!
It were a sight most pitiful to see,
But for the promise born of Liberty.
The Almoner of Heaven our Country stands,
Extending to the WORLD her helping hands.

The contemplation of the beneficent and humanitary Institutions of the United States kindled our patriotism for a moment. Let us return to our subject. The two hundred and sixty thousand Slaveholders who represented the three millions of the aristocratic class of citizens in the South, needed to exercise—in view of their relation to the six millions of degraded human beings—vigilance, skill and force, to restrain, constrain and direct the whole. And thus the Slave States became, of necessity, a strongly POSITIVE, CONCENTRATIVE and ACCRETIVE POWER in the Federal Government. And in the early part of our history as a Nation they began to demand *special legislation* of the General Government, because of the peculiar difficulties and diverse interests of their Domestic Institution. The Free States acceded, reluctantly, to these demands ; for the reasons that it gave to the former an unfair advantage in the Federal Government, and involved, year after year, a greater extent of free territory in slave labor, which served to strengthen the institution of slavery. And it was through the repeated concessions of the Free States that the Slave States grew more strongly SECTIONAL, and increased in their demands for still farther extension of territory, and greater *political privileges.*

And the political influence which the Slave States wielded in the Republic—founded in *property representation,* instead of numbers, as at the North—had the tendency to fill them with pride and an inflated sense of power, until at length they verily believed themselves to be far superior to the Free States, which had, unfortunately for the tranquillity and honor of the Nation, elevated them to, and sustained them in, their false position in the STATE, the North being far more powerful in numbers, wealth and knowledge than the South.   And thus it occurred— by reason of the unjust acquisition of territory, and of power established on the false basis of representation in property, instead of in numbers—and through the long-continued exercise of irresponsible domination over large numbers of men and women, held as chattel property, and entirely subservient to the imperious will of their owners—as well as through the pernicious influence of the subjection of the many by the few (an anomaly in a Democratic Government,) and also through the deteriorating action of so large a percentage of uneducated and degraded human beings upon the whole mass of society—(who had neither the ability to improve their condition, nor to effectively resist the encroachments of the Absolute Class, nor to redress their wrongs)—that the Slave States grew disregardful of HUMAN RIGHTS, and exceedingly arrogant, unjust, and aggressive.

And they became, consequently, year after year, a more strongly POSITIVE, concentrative, accretive, sectional and despotic power in the Federal Government.   And their representatives at the capital of our Nation resorted to political strategy, bribery, imprecations and threats, in order to advance SECTIONAL MEASURES, opposed to the higher interest of the General Government, such as could not have been carried by Statesmanship and honorable legislation.

The Free States, being broadly enlightened, were in a *negative* relation to this *positive* power; and, for the reason before stated, that knowledge is free and diffusive in its character and action.   A vast inequality existed between the mental and moral status of the Northern and Southern sections of our country, owing to the peculiar Institutions of each; consequently, both looked at the broad principles of Right and Justice, and of National policy, from very different standpoints. And while the liberal and Democratic Institutions of the North were ever tending forward to greater enlightenment, the Aristocratic Institutions of the South, which were necessarily sustained by force, were retreating as rapidly backward toward barbarism. And thus these opposite sections of the same country diverged farther and farther each succeeding year. The result was, that they became less and less able to understand each other, while they continued to grow more strongly antagonistic. At length the Slave States entirely lost their national pride and patriotism, ceased to sympathize with the Federal Government, and became thoroughly SECTIONAL. And now, they aimed to use the STATE as a tool merely to advance sectional, ambitious aims; the while charging vociferously upon the North the very sectionalism that had become their uniform policy.

The Free States remonstrated earnestly, using the Christian's powerful weapons, moral suasion and philosophic argument. But the Slave States opposed this enlightened method of redressing wrong, with canes, bowie-knives and revolvers. And this mode of resistance accorded with the genius of their institutions, which modeled, to a great extent, the character of their citizens.

And when the Slave States, the minority, finally lost control of the reins of Government for one Congressional Term, through the Election of Abraham Lincoln to the Presidency, by a large Republican majority, they became enraged; and resolved, *en masse*, either to secede altogether from, or to destroy the Federal Government; and to establish upon its ruins a Governmental Structure of Oppression, that should have—in the infamous language of Toombs of Gorgia—"SLAVERY FOR ITS CORNER STONE;" instead of Human Liberty and the RIGHTS OF MAN.

Ah! they forgot, in their unjust anger and vindictive passion, WHO holds the reins of Universal Empire. They forgot that God himself colonized our Country with the purest and noblest sons and daughters of earth, that HE might have a home for his oppressed and exiled children of every land; and that HE inspired its lawgivers and rulers to found Institutions for enlightening and blessing Humanity, as beneficent as air and sunlight, and all the free and glorious influences of Nature. In the phrenzy of their thwarted, selfish ambition, they lost their men-

tal and moral equilibrium, became unreasoning fanatics of oppression, and fell from our magnificent constellation of States,
while striving with Herculean effort to wrest the balance of even-
handed Justice from our Nation, and turn the scale of Divine
Liberiy, in favor of human bondage.   Alas! they rushed blindly,
madly, against the thick bosses of Jehovah's buckler; the while
praying the dear Redeemer of the world, whom they were crucifying afresh in outraged, suffering humanity, to prosper their
unrighteous cause.

The storm-clouds of War gathered darkly and threateningly at
Sumter!   The POSITIVE FORCE charged upon the NEGATIVE—and
fierce lightnings flashed from the artillery of death in reverberating
thunders!   But ere the echoes of that fearful challenge of the
South had died away in the ears of our Nation, the Slave States
became a desolation.   The result could not be otherwise.   If
God be on the side of Human Freedom, who can stand against
HIS legions?   All the grand old heroes and martyrs of Liberty of
all the ages went forth from the North with our great National
Army of enlightened freemen, and conquered Oppression in the
name of Humanity's God.

And thus that POSITIVE, CONCENTRATIVE, SECTIONAL and AG-
GRESSIVE POWER in the STATE, which strove for ascendency and
sectional rule, in opposition to the higher interests of the General Government and of Republican Principles, was at length
broken by its own blind, selfish and irrational policy, and became its own destroyer.

Every evil contains the elements of its own destruction.   And
the Almighty Ruler of the Universe uses the agents of wrong as
instruments through which to redress the wrong, and often by
the peculiar methods that they adopt to perpetuate it in society.
Human plans and efforts are powerless before the counterplots
of Heaven.   The terrible crime against Humanity of which our
Nation was guilty has been expatiated in human blood.   For,
without the shedding of blood there can be no remission of sin,
when the people are blinded by passion and prejudice and become fanatical adherents of error.   And the precious blood of
the noblest sons of the State was poured out as freely as water

upon the earth, and burning tears of agonized affection flowed forth and mingled with the crimson tide. It was a priceless ransom of the Slave, and an everlasting vindication of Human Liberty. The North suffered equally with the South; foi she was an accomplice in the crime against man.

Uncompromising justice is appeased. Industry and Science have already gone forth from the Cradle of Liberty to restore the waste places of belligerent armies. The Public School will everywhere follow their lead. Knowledge will eventually be equalized, and harmony restored on the broader and more enduring foundation of HUMAN RIGHTS.

We have set down nothing in malice. All sections of our well-beloved Country are equally dear to our heart. We have simply sought to show the philosophy of events in our past history, and to illustrate, by the sad experience of our Nation, the truth of a former proposition: that *civil war* is the result of different degrees of enlightenment in different sections of the same country. It is our hope to awaken thereby the popular mind to the following facts : *that institutions which favor ignorance are destructive of republican principles;* and that the perpetuity and power of our Government, and the growth of civil and religious liberty in the world, depend upon the general diffusion and equalization of knowledge. And, in view of these vital truths, we desire to call the particular attention of the Christian Church to the educational interests of the Christian State; for it appears to us that her obligations in the case are very clearly and strongly defined. The Church has also an important, unfulfilled duty to perform for the Ballot Box of the Nation. She must see to it that intelligence is made the basis of suffrage. This is of vital interest to the life of our Republic; and it is the only consistent and rational policy that can be adopted by a government founded in the supposed intelligence and consequent self-governing power of the millions. At present the ignorant vote of the Nation controls the Ballot. And this is the reason why *drunkards* and *prize-fighters* desecrate the Halls of Congress, consecrated to GOD AND LIBERTY, and sacred to the memory of the illustrious Fathers of our Country. But we will linger no longer on the

30

subject in this connection, as we propose to return to it in another; and pass on to our yet unfinished theme.

Had the Clergy of the different Denominations of the Christian Church, *both* North and South, have done their duty fearlessly and faithfully, in the early part of our history as a nation, slavery would have been abolished peacefully then, as it was at the North; the Public School would have taken the place of the Peculiar Institution, the people would have become enlightened, and there would have been no civil war.   A few of the clerical body, the most earnest in the cause of HUMAN FREEDOM, might have suffered martyrdom for principle; but the wholesale slaughter of our Nation would have been avoided.

Several years prior to the civil war of the United States, there had been much angry disputation and animosity manifested at the annual meetings of the Clergy of various denominations North and South; because one cherished evil existed in the latter named section of our country, which members from that part were too sensitive to hear disapproved, even while they admitted that *slavery* was a sin against God and Man; for the reason that their congregations were composed of Slaveholders, and many of their own number held property in Man.   And, finally, wishing to escape altogether from the reproof of their contemporary Clergy, and from the false and unpleasant position of being obliged to condemn themselves in the thing that they allowed, they resolved to quiet the question at once, by pronouncing the *evil* GOOD.   Watchmen upon the Southern walls of Zion took fresh observation of the land of Ancient Canaan, and noting that the Hebrews of the ignorant Childhood of the Church and World held their fellow-men and women in bondage, they concluded therefrom, and declared to the world, that Slavery must be regarded as a Divine Institution; amazing reflective minds of the nineteenth century with the irrational assertion.   And they exhausted their Biblical lore in trying to substantiate the truth of the monstrous proposition, and to appease, with their unscriptural, as well as unphilosophical arguments, their own conscience and the troubled spirit of many of their people,

The Clergy North, exposed the weak sophistry of their cun-

ningly devised fable, by arguments drawn from the same Sacred
Word, which were clear, forcible and convincing ; but this had
the tendency to exasperate and humiliate their Southern brethren
still more and more, for they had not only determined to believe in the Divinity of Slavery themselves, but they had resolved
that the Clergy North should also believe, or at least accept the
theory without controversy;—failing in this, they next determined
to place themselves beyond the reach of either argument or ad-
monition. They revealed clearly to the Church and World, by
their remarkable sensitiveness and irritability on the subject of
Slavery, that the specious arguments which they had wilfully
maintained in its favor had not given repose to their own conscience, whatever might have been the influence upon the people. They hoped that they had set the vexing question at rest
forever when they pronounced Slavery a Divine Institution, and
attempted to hide the Monster Evil under the very hem of the
dear Redeemer's garment. But there was enough Christian
Democracy left in one Nation to ferret the wicked nursling
of despotism. Thank Heaven. It is painful to trace, that the
spirit of slavery conquered at length the peaceful and loving
Spirit of Christ, and various sects of the Christian Body parted
asunder; the Ecclesiastic records of the day chronicling the Denominations North, and the Denominations South. But the dis-
affected clergy could not rend, by their denominational antagonisms, the seamless robe of the Redeemer of the World. And
the truth of that beautiful emblem of fellowship and unity on
earth, will be fully realized in the coming ages, in the perfect
oneness of the CHRISTIAN CHURCH UNIVERSAL.

It is safe to predict that both PROTESTANTISM and WAR have
nearly completed their missions. The time is not remote when
the Christrian Church will be rent no more by dissension; and
when Nations will no longer cut the Gordian Knot of politics
with the sword; because KNOWLEDGE and REASON are to be the
great regulating Powers in the maturity of the Church and
World. They will sit in a Synod of the Chiefs of the various
Christian Denominations to unravel difficult questions of faith
and practice, that have existed acrimonious disputations in the

past, and to expound the divine laws of Liberty, Unity and Love which constitute the Church of God ONE on Earth, even as it is in Heaven. And this noble twain will rise in a CONGRESS of NATIONS to disentangle the complicated wires of State polity; and to establish a chain of commercial intercourse that shall link together all the near and remote countries of the Earth, uniting the material interests of the whole Human Family; and that shall diffuse and equalize knowledge, and prepare the way for the great Christian Democratic Republic of the World.

But before society can attain to this progressed condition the Church of God has much earnest labor to perform. And by far the most difficult part of the work will be to renovate her own Body; for she has vastated herself of spiritual life and become cold and inanimate. While reviewing with profound sorrow the lifeless and lamentable state of the Christian Church of to-day, we are forcibly reminded of Ezekiel's vision of the Valley of Bones: Lo, they were very dry! And we cannot forbear questioning with the ancient prophet of Israel: Can these bones live? The context is hopeful. The breath of the Lord is able to revive, and renovate all things.

Having made a running review of the Roman Catholic and Protestant branches of the Church of the past, we propose to the Reader to glance with us at the prominent Denominations of the Church of God of the present, scattered throughout the United States and throughout the World, and observe where they stand, and what is their position in regard to the REVEALED WORD OF GOD TO MAN, AND THE REVEALED WILL OF GOD IN MAN; and also in regard to the Democratic Spirit of the Gospel of Christ, and to the requirements of Progressive Humanity.

It has been stated in the first part of the present work that Jesus Christ was the first great Democratic Philosopher of the World, and the Teacher of Natural Religion to Man; in other words, that he was an exponent of the Divine Gospel of Intelligent Nature, the principles of which are perfectly adapted to the peculiar nature and requirements of Man, male and female, and, consequently, to the progress of the human race in virtue, happiness and the knowledge of God. For Christ appealed to the intellect and to the affections of the Human Family by direct command, as well as through the Philosophy of his religion, calling upon the people to awake and engage in the active service of Deity:——Thou shalt love the Lord thy God with all thy heart, and with all thy soul, and with all thy MIND, is the impressive and comprehensive mandate of Inspiration.

And it has been also stated that the Christian Religion is the purest and broadest Democracy. It recognizes one God, Godhead, or All-Parent, as the high and only source of created intelligences ; and hence the oneness of the great Human Family. It endows each individual being with power of becoming a King and Priest unto the Divine Author of existeuce. All who desire to enjoy this elevated distinction in the Kingdom of Heaven are able to attain it through obedience to the Divine Law of Love, and by yielding the beautiful fruits of the Spirit of Love, as did our dear and perfect Exemplar.

The Christian Church is a UNIT. It has many members, and but one Body. It may be termed, indeed, a Family of Children with different names, adapted to the peculiar order of minds, but of kindred interests in time and in eternity. For the various Denominations of the Church differ from each other in non-essentials only. They have one Lord, one faith, one baptism, and one Father and Mother God over all, blessed forevermore.

And, consequently, the true Christian Church is essentially Democratic. Where the Spirit of the Lord exists there is freedom for all. And the normal outgrowth of the Democratic Christian Church is the Democratic Christian State and Republican Institutions. Where such a result does not follow, CHRISTIAN CHURCH is a misnomer ; for it does not bear the legitimate fruit of the Gospel of the Son of God. They who are true Freemen in Christ are children of the light and cannot walk in darkness and in chains. It is the direct influence of spiritual liberty to stimulate the mind to larger growth, and produce mental freedom ; and hence, civil and political freedom succeed in a true Christian community, as a logical sequence, as certainly as that the day follows the night.

Ay, the Christian Religion is the purest Democracy ; but the Church has become antipodal to its principles. Turn with us to view her various denominations and behold their anomalous position. The members of the different Christian Sects must bear with us while we attempt, in the most loving spirit, to show them how they appear to earnest seekers after truth outside of Church Organizations. We are aware that our task is a difficult one, and that, even should we hold the picture up to nature, it will not be accepted as a true delineation ; for the reason that each denomination has a peculiar standpoint of its own, and, consequently, is incapable of taking the same observation of itself that others take of it who have a different and more remote position and are uninfluenced by the same opinions and prejudices. Christian Sects, like individuals, are also far more lenient, each towards itself, than they are capable of being toward other sects, or than outside parties are able to be, who stand and measure the Church as a whole by the high and holy standard of the true Christian faith and practice, by the great humanitary laws of the Mediative Son of God.

In viewing the moral standing of different Christian Denominations we do not overlook the encouraging truth that there are many individuals in every Sect who are earnestly striving to exemplify elevated Christian lives. Happy is the man, or woman, who is able to conform in all things to the requirements of the Gospel of Love ; and happy is the Sect that condemneth not itself in the thing that it alloweth ; for unto such the Holy Spirit will be manifested, as it is not manifested unto the unbelieving World.

CHAPTER IV.

THE CHURCH OF GOD OF THE PRESENT VIEWED DENOMINATONALLY.

THE ISRAELITES.

If the casting away of the Jews be the reconciling of the world, what shall the receiving of them be, but life from the dead?

The Church of God of every name is one on Earth, even as it is in Heaven. Before glancing at the prominent Christian Sects of to-day, let us take a cursory view of the Hebrew Church, which was the pioneer of the true religion in the Child-hood of the World, and observe its present relation to the De-nominations of Christendom. The Jewish Church may in verity be regarded as a constituent part of the Gentile; for its foundation, which was laid deep and broad in the physical ages, is also that of the Christian Church. And when the Chief Cor-ner Stone was laid in Zion it rested on that enduring foundation. And the glorious superstructure of the Church Universal of the intellectual and moral ages of the World, will rise upon it in symmetrical beauty towards Heaven.

In that memorable hour when the dear Mediative Son of God sealed his divine Mission to Humanity with his warm life-blood, which fell in crimson streams of love upon the earth, that immortal flowers of faith, hope, and charity might bloom below and make beautiful the ways of life and of death for the children of men, THEN the New Christian Dispensation to the Youth of God's Church was signally marked by the rending of the vail of the Temple of the Old Hebrew Dispensation. For the Temple of Solomon symbolized, as did also the forms of the Jewish Religion, the higher spiritual worship of Deity that should succeed the imposing ceremonies of the ancient Church, which were addressed to the external senses of the undeveloped and ignorant Children of the World.   THE VAIL OF THE TEMPLE WAS RENT IN TWAIN; for Man was thenceforth to become the Temple of the living God, consecrated, with all the powers and faculties of being, to the presence and service of the Divine.

And the rending of the vail of the Temple was also a fore-shadowing of the destruction of the Holy City, which was fear-fully accomplished by Titus, a Roman General, in the seventieth year of the first Christian Era.   The conservative character of the Jews rendered severe discipline needful for their develop-ment and progress.   The belief in the advent of a *temporal King*, who would liberate them forever from an irritating foreign yoke, had taken radical possession of their minds; and so they hardened their hearts against the Philosopher of Nazareth, who declared that *his kingdom* was not of this world.   They required to be uprooted, to be wrenched forcibly away from old associa-tions with the Religion that had been adapted in the providence of God to the condition of their undeveloped Childhood, in order that they might be eventually made receptive of the ad-vanced truths taught by Christ, and become willing to accept the Spiritual Freedom which he came to impart, in place of the temporal power and glory toward which they had been looking forward for ages, in the selfish hope of gratifying their national pride by a signal triumph over their oppressors.   Their chastise-ment has been terrible.   But strong characters require strong measures to move them.   And this was the way appointed of Heaven, by which the pride of their nature should be subdued, and they become prepared to accept the broader Humanitary Religion of Love and Free-Will to Man, of the FULLNESS OF THE GODHEAD.

The unbelief of the Israelites in Jesus Christ as their Messiah, opened the door of the Christian Church for Gentile nations to enter in and receive the benediction of the light, liberty and love of the Gospel.   For, had the ancient Church accepted Christ, the Jews would have believed themselves to be more peculiarly than before the Chosen People, and would have become more conservative than ever, and isolated themselves and their advanced truths more completely from the outside world. In the masterly argument of St. Paul to the Romans on this interesting topic, he shows clearly to the Church and World that: Blindness in part is happened to Israel until the FULLNESS of the Gentiles be come in. But the *fullness of the Gentiles* could not come in until the knowledge of the living and true God should be broadly disseminated over the earth, to prepare the way for the comprehensive Gospel of Intelligent Nature taught by the Mediative Son of Deity. And thus we learn that there were weightier reasons in the mind of Jehovah for dispersing the Children of Israel over every inhabited part of the globe, than merely chastisement for national offenses, with its corrective influences, and the introduction of the Christian Religion among the Gentile nations by whom they were immediately surrounded. Ay, the Children of Israel were appointed by Heaven, for a term of ages, to be the Pioneer Church of the living God to the idolatrous nations of the whole earth. Their peculiar and striking characteristics as a people fitted them pre-eminently for the important mission.

The Christian Church of the past, in blind zeal for her Religion and its Author, has reproached and persecuted the Jews for rejecting and crucifying the Messiah. And by so doing, she set a mark upon their foreheads that has invited the hostility of heathen nations and whetted the sword and poisoned the arrows of their malignant enemies. And, while occupied with this partial view of the subject, the Church has overlooked the most important as well as interesting feature in their history—the GRAND MISSION for which they were dismembered as a nation, and dispersed over the face of all the Earth, even as at this day. She has failed to observe that, in the Youth of the World, as in its Childhood, the Israelites were still the Chosen People of Heaven, to pioneer the knowledge of the living God, and sow broadcast, over the inhabited globe, the seeds of the *true* Religion.

In their second Exodus they were the pioneers of a Spiritual Kingdom through an inhospitable wilderness world, that did not recognize the Divine Origin and Unity of Humanity, and

31

the great brotherhood of Man. And in their wanderings, again, as in the former time, they were guided by a cloud, or concealed providence, by day; but, in their night of doubt, apprehension and sorrow, a pillar of fire proclaimed the unseen presence, power and glory of their Almighty Friend and Guide. And again, as in their early wanderings, a Red Sea was interposed between them and the haven of rest, that they were wearily seeking. Now, alas! it was a fearful sea of blood, and their hearts failed them with dread and consternation. But the crimson tide parted asunder before their advancing footsteps toward the New Jerusalem of prophecy: The joy of the whole Earth.

Gradually, like the breaking of morning over the mountains of the East, a clearer light has been dawning on the nations; and the persecutions and proscriptions of the Israelites have been slowly passing away before its benign influence. For the long period of eighteen hundred years the Chosen People have been silent, unobtrusive, and yet patient and conscientious teachers of the ONE INVISIBLE, ETERNAL, OMNIPOTENT, OMNISCIENT AND OMNIPRESENT JEHOVAH, the God of gods. And all the while they were unconscious of their high calling to disseminate the elevating knowledge of the living God among the idolatrous peoples of the earth. Had the Israelites been acquainted with the grandeur of their mission they could not have performed it as acceptably to God, and as effectively to man. for they would not have labored with the same earnest, humble and contrite spirit that has marked their history. Because, that had they acted under the recognized influence of the high authority of their mission, they would have been self-asserting and arrogant, and awakened greater antagonism against themselves and their religion.

Ah! the individual and the nation in the fulfilment of their destiny are ever greater in their relative positions and relations than they themselves can know. For it is only by retrospection that they can see the peculiar niche that they were appointed to fill, and be able to estimate the value of their humanitary service to their own and to future generations. And, beyond the boundaries of time and sense, there are innumerable spirit existences, influenced by and influencing, in turn, their actions;

each one standing in the proper place and sustaining a relative value to the whole vast sum of being. Indeed, the results of human effort in any moral direction cannot be fully estimated by man ; for they extend too broadly, strike too deep, and ascend too high into the immeasurable of Infinite Power and Eternal Existence.

The remarkable dispersion of the Israelites throughout the globe for the fulfilment of their important mission, accords with the promise of the Almighty Father to the Patriarch Abraham in the Childhood of the World: In thy seed shall all the nations of the earth be blessed. The promise is yet but partially realized. The Jews have acted, thus far, only as an *entering wedge*, in the social structure of the world, to prepare the way for the introduction of the higher Evangel of the FULLNESS OF THE GOD-HEAD of the Church Universal, of the Reasoning Day of Humanity. And the wedge is small and almost imperceptible. But, through its means, truth, like the grain of mustard seed, has been implanted in the heart and mind of the people, to grow and thrive under the fosteringcare of Heaven, and bear abundant fruit.

The Jews have nearly completed their mission. We may rationally infer that such is the fact, from the gradual cessation of hostilities toward them, and their increasing popularity among the nations with whom their lot has been apportioned. The seal of the New Era is already broken, and the Reasoning Day of the World will ere long reveal a marvel to the inhabitants of the globe. The Israelites will be seen casting aside the ancient symbols of their faith, and accepting the long-expected Messiah in the true spirit of his Gospel of Love and Free-Will to Man, while receiving its divine baptism of the Holy Ghost and of fire—the baptism of the FULLNESS OF THE GODHEAD.

Through these marvellous providences, revealed in the history of the Israelites, the people are taught that, in the administration of God's Government of *equal justice* to Man, He causeth the wrong of one people to become the blessing of many ; and the consequences of that wrong to a nation, to act as healthful discipline to bring it back again to the paths of righteousness ;

thereby exemplifying still farther to the World that all nations are alike objects of His Parental care ; and that the active and reactive forces of His sublime economic Government of Equal Justice and Love, have a dual power of use and blessing, while moving grandly forward to the development of immutable principles by progressive ages, rather than by the limited periods of generations.

And thus, for the greatest good of the greatest numbers, it was decreed in the wisdom of Deity that the magnificent Temple of the Old Dispensation with all its hallowed associations should be laid waste, the Holy Land become a desolation, and the Pioneer Church of God scattered far and wide over the face of the earth. For eighteen centuries the Israelites have bowed meekly beneath the heavy burden of lifeless forms, intently gazing on the types and shadows that have been antityped for ages, chanting their solemn ritual in an unknown tongue far from the land of their inspired Teachers and Prophets, while waiting patiently, in the dim light of other days, for the Messiah to come and restore again the Kingdom to Israel.

During their long exile the Israelites have been forced, by the peculiarities of their situation to become usurers among the nations. For, in the hope that they would eventually return and rebuild the waste places of Palestine, it has been their policy to engage in such remunerative business as could be readily closed, and their poperty rendered at once available for any emergency. The continued persecutions to which they have been subjected and the extortions that have been practised on them among foreign nations, have also tended to limit them to few occupations ; and caused them, in the exercise of self-protection, to become watchful of others and shrewd in their business relations, and often miserly in their habits. And, again, in their later wanderings, as in the olden time when they were strangers in Egypt, they have borrowed jewels of silver and jewels of gold, and spoiled their oppressors, while preparing to return to the promised land of their Fathers.

But the scales are beginning to fall from their eyes ; for, lo! the Reasoning Day of Humanity has already dawned upon the earth, and the Second Christian Era of the Church Universal is even now inaugurated;—and the Mediative Son of God is near, waiting to perfect his glorious mission,—to gain the assent of the Reason of Man to the truth of his Divine Gospel of Intelligent Nature. Listen to the dear Redeemer's appeal to the mind and heart of the Age : Behold, I stand at the door and knock : if any man hear my voice, and open the door, I will come in to him, and will sup with him, and he with me.

But, alas ! the Denominations of the Christian Church are in the condition that the ancient Hebrew Church was at the period of his first advent ; they are cold and torpid in their Religious forms, so that they cannot hear the voice of the Good Shepherd when he calleth them by name. It may be that the Israelites, who are slowly awaking from the blind unbelief of ages, will be the first to hear his voice, in the New Era of Reasoning Christianity, and to open the door, and enjoy with him the feast of love and reason to which he so tenderly invites them ; and that they will accept their long neglected Messiah, who was despised and rejected of their Fathers, with loving, contrite hearts and understanding minds. And then will the Jews, in their turn, reap the fruit of Christian labor, be graffed into their own Religious Tree on Gentile branches : For God is able to graff them in again.

The fearful persecutions and sufferings of this Pioneer Church of God have caused its members to become unostentatious and humble in spirit. And the Jews have won the toleration of many nations by the moral character of their people, as a body, and by their persevering worship of the God of Israel under the most adverse and trying circumstances. They take particular care to train their youth to virtue, and to provide for their own poor. Indeed, there is no Religious Denomination extant whose record is equally free from pauperism and crime.

And the Hebrew Church has been purified during its protracted exile from many of the gross evils of its early, ignorant Childhood, prominent among which were *Polygamy* and *Slavery*, and become, in this respect, an example for the Church of the New Dispensation, which, having lost the vital glow of its Chris-

32

tian Democracy and Humanitary love, has turned back from the progressed enlightenment of the nineteenth century to the dark physical ages of the Old Dispensation, to find, in the social practices of a people *then* scarcely removed from barbarism, precedence and authority to justify its indulgence in sensuality and oppression.

We look forward with confident hope to the day when the Israelites who have been purified in the fires of adversity will enter, with one heart and one mind, the temples of the Christian Church and become a great regenerating power. For they will gather together in the fold of Christ with the inspiring enthusiasm of fresh converts to his Divine Gospel of Peace and Good-Will to Man, and rekindle the torpid life of the Church by the vitalizing power of their newly awakened faith and love ; and they will co-operate grandly with her in the active and practical service of God and Man through the glorious Reasoning Day of Humanity, the Era of the Church Universal. For if the casting away of the Jews be the reconciling of the World (through their missionary services) what shall the receiving of them be but life from the dead ?

And whether the Israelites will return to rebuild the ruined City of their Fathers—as large numbers in Christendom believe, and as the recent proposition of the Rothschilds to purchase Jerusalem appears to foreshadow—or whether they will remain and fraternize with the nations among whom they have lived and labored, yet remains a mystery. But we have the testimony of Revelation, which is confirmed by the movements of the present age, that they will inquire the way to the Christian's Zion, with their faces thitherward, saying : Come and let us join ourselves to the Lord in a perpetual covenant that shall not be forgotten.

THE ROMAN CATHOLICS.

He that hath an ear, let him hear what the Spirit saith unto the Church: I have somewhat against thee, because thou hast left thy first love. Remember therefore from whence thou art fallen, and repent, and do thy first works; or else I will remove thy candlestick out of his place. If the light that is in thee be darkness, how great is that darkness.

The Roman Catholic Denomination, or pioneer branch of the Christian Church, is a stern Autocrat and Lords it over God's heritage, ruling his people with a rod of iron. This religious Sect constructs magnificient Cathedrals and adorns them with the most beautiful and expensive creations of Art; but it robs the hireling of his wages, to work its miracles of architectural splendor. And it binds heavy burdens and grievous to be borne, and lays them on men's shoulders; and dwarfs the human soul with ignorance and with superficial forms of religion. The query naturally presents itself to the reasoning mind, in viewing its costly edifices;—is the All-Parent better pleased with these than He would be with enlightened and liberal worshippers at his Altars? The churches of this Sect are freer to all classes of people than those of other Denominations, with a few exceptions; and, yet, while its assemblies are more decidedly Democratic than others, its doctrines and government admit of far less individual liberty of thought and action.

And the Roman Catholic Denomination constructs beautiful Temples of Learning; but not for the purpose of developing human beings broadly, in accordance with the Revealed Word of God to Man, and the Revealed Will of God in Man, which demand the normal exercise and unfolding of the combined powers of heart, and mind, and soul; for these Institutions are simply *doctrinal nurseries,* the hot-beds of Romanism; general knowledge and enlightenment are everywhere held subservient in them to restrictive mental discipline and sectarian formulæ. The great Apostle of the Gentiles exhorts believers in the Gospel of Intelligent Nature to Leave the first principles of the doctrine of Christ, and go on unto perfection. But the Roman

Catholics make no progress, as a sect, in the divine life. It is always a pioneer, dwelling just on the borders of the promised land of light and liberty, but never entering there to enjoy the inheritance to which the sons and daughters of God are entitled by their divine birthright. For their freedom of thought and of action are limited by doctrines and dogmas; and their spiritual life is choked by the external forms of religion; in the observance of these they are instructed to look for the saving grace of the soul; and in the letter of the creed, for the essential knowledge.

And the Roman Catholic Denomination founds public Charitable Institutions more extensively than other Sects, in order to extend its power and influence; but it organizes *pauperism*, as well, by granting permits to beggars to go from door to door, displaying rags and deformities, thus to earn by human degradation a pitiable subsistence; a certain percentage of which moneys is to be paid over to the Fathers, to aid in sustaining these Public Charities. But, fortunately, this system of licensing beggars is not as extensive in the United States as in countries where the Roman Catholic religion is dominant. The Seat of the Papal Throne literally swarms with paupers, done up in unclean rags. Uinterested men and women, in viewing the squalor and degradation of the masses of Rome, would say that the curse of Heaven appears to rest upon the people who claim to enjoy the blessing of the Pope. These poor, miserable apologies for human beings hover, like birds of ill omen, about the entrances of grand Cathedrals, dedicated to the worship of the Universal Father, to prey upon the bits and pennies of strangers with pitiful moanings and incoherent mutterings. And yet, those costly edifices contain wealth enough in their deep vaults, in valuable relics and solid silver statues of canonized saints, to enrich the Nation that is impoverished in order to supply this useless, unproductive treasury. Verily, the Lazzaroni of Italy are a striking commentary on the charitable and industrial institutions of the Roman Catholics of that country; it reveals clearly to the World that Ecclesiastic principles are very different from Christian.

True Christian Charity, directed by enlightened reason, would establish public workshops, to give employment to God's poor, enable them to earn a self-respecting livelihood, and uplift them from their helpless and demoralized condition.   And it would organize also Public Schools to disseminate the light of knowledge and develop their mental capital, in order that it might become, not only an advantage to each, individually, but a benefit to society.   The pennies that such redeemed sons and daughters of God could spare from honest and honorable labor, would have the ring of the true moral metal, and would fall into the coffers of Charity, as a benediction, instead of a curse upon the people.

How strikingly inappropriate sound the following words of St. Paul, when applied to the wretched and degraded Church paupers of Roman Catholic Europe: In God ye live, and move, and have your being! Why! it gives one a twinge of pain in the soul to associate such mentally and morally dwarfed and soiled specimens of Humanity with the great All-Loving Intelligence of the Universe.   And yet, there is not a dignitary of the Roman Catholic Body, (who claims to be intrusted by Heaven with the elevation and redemption of Man,) from the Pope down to the lowest Official grade, more precious in the sight of the All-Parent than these poor tattered, half-starved and debased creations, who are degraded below the level of the beasts that perish by the very religion that claims to redeem and bless them.

The first imperative duty of every Christian Country is to prevent pauperism —establish industrial occupations—and diffuse knowledge among the masses.   First in the order of God is the natural; after, that which is spiritual.   There is an apology for the pauperism and degradation of so large a number of Roman Catholics of the past of the Old World, in the darkness and Ignorance of the Church in its unreasoning Youth; for Prelates as well as Laymen were overshadowed by them; but, now, that light has come into the world, with the dawn of the Reasoning Age of Man, Rome is left without excuse.   It is the Imperative duty of the Papal Government to see that its subjects are enlightened in order that they may become self-poised and self-governing human beings, and, that they have occupations adapted to their capabilities and conditions, to render them self-respecting, as well as self-supporting.

Rome answers the demands of the age, for the enlightenment of its people, and greater attention to their industrial interests, in the solemn phrase: "It is the mission of the Church to save souls." These words sound farcical to the mind of the earnest disciple of Christ, remembering that the policy of Rome has been to *save souls per doctrine, and per force*, while the Volume of Inspiration teaches that: God is a Spirit: and they that worship him must worship him in spirit and in truth;—and that, The Spirit itself beareth witness with our spirit, that we are the children of God;—and that the saving grace of the soul is, To do justly, and to love mercy, and to walk humbly with God;—and that, God is no respecter of persons: but in every nation he that feareth him and worketh righteousness is accepted of Him;—and, finally, that God is love; and he that dwelleth in love, dwelleth in God, and God in him. The physical nature of men and women, and their hearts and minds, must be developed before any saving work is performed for their souls. Although one were to sit solemnly in a gorgeous Cathedral, during every hour of appointed devotion, and although he were to repeat a prayer, or an invocation, on his bended knees seventy times seven, it would not be worship, if the heart were not warm with love to God, and love to Man; and one genuine act of kindness, done for a suffering brother or sister of the Human Family, would outweigh all the unprofitable repetition, even were it conscientiously performed in accordance with the direction of his Holiness, the Pope. Ay, generous acts, done to any in need of human aid, are most acceptable Worship to Heaven. Labor is Worship. Loving obedience to God's laws, from an intelligent understanding of them, is the truest Worship. The normal activity of every God—endowed faculty of mind and heart is the most perfect worship of the Creator, for it is the complete fulfilment of all human obligation to the Divine Author of existence. And the best conditions for this perfect Worship of Deity are the largest liberty of thought and action, under vigorous intellectual and moral influences; for this is the safest and surest way of saving the bodies of men and women from ruinous excesses, or from starvation; and, thus, rendering it easier to save their souls from vice and crime, and society from demoralization and decay.

The Republic of the United States of North America is the nearest approach that any earthly government has yet made toward a perfect system of enlightened Liberty, under Law, for the millions. It was founded in the supposed self-governing power of the people under liberal institutions, adapted to human development. The Fathers of our Country wisely established the PUBLIC SCHOOL, independently of either sect or party, in order that all her citizens of every form of religious faith, and of every nationality under heaven, might become enlightened, self-governing, and self-supporting freemen, and thus avoid the fearful degradation and pauperism of the servile masses of the Old World. And they desired also to perpetuate our great Christian Republic by means of this broad system of popular education and the attending enlightenment of the millions. And, up to the present period in our National History, the Roman Catholics have been the only religionists who have spoken openly against this beneficent Institution. And it is the only sect that has opposed the reading of the Bible in the Public School of freemen, whose Government and institutions are founded on the HIGHER LAW of its moral code; and opposed it too on the plea that the Bible is a *sectarian book*— a proposition which cannot be maintained by logical argument. And, on this false assumption, it has presented a claim in several States of the Union for a private fund, to be drawn from the non-sectarian Public School moneys, with which to establish *directly* a SECTARIAN SCHOOL; a school in which its peculiar construction of the Bible, together with the Catechism of its Order, is to be taught alike to Protestant and Roman Catholic children; and taught moreover for the express purpose of proselyting. But, the small portion of the Bible that is daily read, without comment, by the teachers of the Public School, has no such object in view. And the Roman Catholic Priesthood know full well that no effort has ever been made in this liberal Institution to bias the mind of any child belonging to either of the various denominations of Christendom.

A little reflection will reveal to any reasoning mind the falsity of the proposition that the Bible is a Sectarian Book; for, were it such, the Sacred Text could admit of but one construction, and there would then be, as a logical necessity, but one denomination in Christendom; instead of many, as at this present, all of which claim to hold the true interpretation of the Word. That marvellous Book contains milk for babes, and meat for the strong; for the precious truths therein conserved are perfectly adapted to the varied requirements of progressive Humanity. To the earnest soul of every age that seeks to grow in grace and in the love and knowledge of God, the Word unfolds an interior meaning, which all are not able to perceive, and becomes luminous and sublime in its comprehensive significance. And every one who searches the scriptures—not for the purpose of fortifying himself in his preconceived ideas of doctrine, but to learn of God—will find pearls of great price, adapted to his peculiar necessities; and new and enlivening views of old truths will shine out, like sun-bursts, from the sacred page, and enlighten his whole intellectual and moral being; such is the breadth and depth and height of the Gospel of Intelligent Nature, revealed for the instruction and elevation of universal Man, male and female. And the Bible is not only *not* a Sectarian book; but it opposes directly the narrow and uncharitable spirit. The great Author of Christianity himself speaks unmistakably against it, and teaches the broadest liberality to his professed followers. When a disciple under the influence of blind, sectarian zeal said to the Democratic Philosopher of Nazareth: Master, we saw one casting out devils in thy name, and he followeth not us; and we forbade him, because he followeth not us;—Jesus answered and said, Forbid him not: for there is no man which shall do a miracle in my name that can lightly speak evil of me.

But, we do not touch the core of the matter. The charge of Sectarianism was not made against the Public School because of conscientious religious scruples; wherefore, Reader, ponder well the meaning. That charge was a *direct measure* of Ecclesiastic policy, to cover the *indirect methods* that Rome adopts in order to attain ambitious ends. It was a crafty plan of the Priesthood to occupy the popular mind with a false issue, and thus to divert it from their own insidiously aggressive sectarian movements, and better enable them to use corrupted political influence in order to obtain moneys from the National Public School fund for the purpose of establishing private sectarian schools; and, through these means, to inaugurate, not only an extensive system of proselyting; but also to weaken our strong and broad system of popular Education, by introducing an element of discord; and to increase, at the same time, their own wealth and power by using the public treasury of our Nation for the purpose of establishing Sectarian, instead of National Schools, the edifices of which are to become the exclusive property of Rome; all of these aims being subsidiary to the grander scheme of universal Roman Catholic Rule in the United States.

Should the Roman Priesthood succeed in obtaining a separate School Fund in the States, they would destroy the unity and weaken the strength and power of the Public School of America, which, like the sun, and air, and rain of Heaven, are open to the Youth of the whole world. A sectarian precedent once established, the Jews could present a stronger claim for a separate school fund than the Romanists, in States where the former pay a larger proportion of taxes to the government than the latter; and the Mormons could also present a claim; and we should eventually have the public school of the Protestants—the public school of the Romanists—the public school of the Jews—and the public school of the Mormons—and the Public School Fund, divided and subdivided among these opposing sects, would be wasted, its economic use in unity of action being destroyed, and our great Repblican Government would become a party to Sectarian divisions and animosities, and to the general disintegration of society; instead of the powerful agent of a free and independent people for preserving the strength, solidarity and harmony of our noble Christian State. In the name of God and of Humanity, let us determine that this blighting curse shall never fall on our broad and beneficent system of popular education. The Public School is the Chief corner stone in our Temple of Liberty. Every true American Philan-

33

thropist and Christian should guard this legacy of our Fathers with greater care than he would the most valuable earthly possessions; for its price to posterity is above rubies.

It has been said in another part of this work that Christianity is the only true Religion, because it is the only Philosophical exponant of Intelligent Nature. It reveals the relations of man to man, and of Man to Deity, placing the Human Family on a broad equality as children of the Universal Parent. It is the "leveling up Democracy;" it elevates the Human to the Divine. The natural outgrowth of this comprehensive equality in Christendom—which equality is recognized deep in the soul of universal Man, whether in a savage, barbarous. or enlightened condition—is the Democratic Christian State and Republican Institutions. But the progress of Humanity toward the highest condition of freedom under law, which is the true liberty of the Children of God, has ever been and must continue for a season to be comparatively slow, even under the favorable influences of the Democratic Christian State; because Ignorance is strongly conservative and opposes crude bone and muscle to enlightened opinions, and to new scientific methods of performing labor, regarding these as innovations upon its time-honored usage of plodding; and, also, because Scholastic Knowledge, untempered by the spirit of the Christ's Divine Gospel of Love, is also conservative in its pride of mental superiority, and opposes the enlightenment and enfranchisment of the millions; and THE PERFECT LIBERTY can only be attained by knowledge of, and obedience to, the laws of Material and of Intelligent Nature. A comprehensive system of popular education—a Church of various denominations, independent of the State—and a Republican form of Government, similar to our own, are the grand educating powers that can effect, in process of time, this desirable universal enlightenment and freedom of the people. The world had never seen such benign influences acting together for the greatest good of greatest numbers, after the Divine Order, until the advent of our glorious Republic. But it had witnessed all forms of Civil and of Ecclesiastic Despotism for the subjugation, instead of the elevation of Humanity. And it had also witnessed the misrule of many premature and spurious Democracies, established on the ignorance of the millions, and the supremacy of class—but never before a great Christian Democracy, resting upon the comprehensive Philosophy of Intelligent Nature—THE BROAD EQUALITY, AND INALIENABLE RIGHTS OF MAN—the Organization of an enlightened, progressive, and self-governing people.

The peace and permanence of our Democratic Christian Republic was seriously endangered for many years previous to the inauguration of President Lincoln by a peculiar phase of DESPOTISM that existed in a large section of our Country; a power which was strongly aggressive in character and action, as the past history of the Federal Government clearly shows. But the danger from Slavery is scarcely past when the State is again threatened by the same wily enemy to Republican Institutions in another form, which is ambushed in the very midst of Christendom—Ecclesiastic Despotism.

Let the Christian man and woman extend to Roman Catholics, as to all other religious sects, the utmost charity, agreeing to disagree in the spirit of love, remembering that the Church of God is ONE FAMILY, of united interests in time and in eternity, by whatever specific names her various members may be denominated. And let them extend to the Priesthood of Rome the same liberty to exercise *their* legitimate profession which is awarded to other Clergy of the different religious sects. But while they should strive to practice the broadest Christian charity toward every Denomination of Religionists, they should seek also to obey the injunction of the great Exemplar, and unite the wisdom of the serpent with the loving spirit of the dove, in order that they may not give aid and encouragement to any evil principle. They should be watchful over the whole of God's heritage, and not remain willfully blind to the character, policy, and influence of any organization thereof, remembering that : Eternal vigilance is the price of Religious as well as of Civil Liberty.

Does any one believe that God would not permit the progress of the Church and of society to be arrested in its onward march?

Let the ages speak, and answer.   They teach us, by reiterated illustration, that God works by human as well as divine agencies in his great Family of Man ; and that if his agents are cold and inactive in his service, or if they become ambitious of mere personal distinction and popularity, and are afraid to utter the whole truth and warn the people of their charge of an imminent danger in season for efficient action ; then the millions will be easily led into captivity by the ever watchful opponents of Freedom, and obliged to learn, from their own painful experience in humiliating bondage, the priceless value of Civil and of Religious Liberty ; instead of through the pleasanter, wiser, and more economic method, that of applying the severely earned experiences of former generations.

We have called the attention of the Church more particularly to her Roman Catholic branch, because it is a more isolated body in Christendom, and marks itself strongly by claiming to be the only true Church of God on earth ; while believing and teaching that all other Christian Sects are schismatics and heretics, rebels against its authority and government, whom it has the right to punish as such, and to deprive of personal liberty *ad libitum* until they shall retract, acknowledge Rome as the supreme temporal and spiritual power and worship at its altars. The dogma of Infallibility, which Rome presents to-day for the endorsement of the nineteenth century, is no new manifestation of that power ; it was put forth and acted upon as Ecclesiastic Policy in the darkness of the Middle Ages, at the very period, in truth, when this Sect proved clearly to every reasoning mind of Christendom its human weakness and fallibility, by departing from the truth, simplicity and purity of the perfect Gospel of Intelligent Nature with its broadly Democratic and Humanitary principles, and making use of the most cruel and coercive measures of Despotism, to *force* men and women into an observance of the forms and ceremonies of a Religion of pure Love—the Author of Christianity himself declaring that Love to God and Love to Man is the fulfilling of the whole moral law.

Many persons in the United States smile at the assumption of his Holiness the Pope, remarking that he must be in his second childhood, otherwise he would not render himself absurd to the enlightened world ; and that being the case, and the dogma of Infallibility entirely harmless, they hope that the Ecumenical Council will support it, and please the poor old gentleman! But Pope Pius Ninth is *not* in his dotage.   He is unnaturally stimulated, exalted above measure by a too absolute use of power ;—and he is giddy on the height of the Papal throne that overlooks the world, and he is perplexed by the complicated machinery of his temporal and spiritual government ;—and fatigued with the abortive effort of striving to hold the Kingdoms of the World and all the glory thereof in one hand, and the Kingdom of Heaven, with its great spiritual interests, in the other ;—and his mental vision is clouded by religious prejudice, so that he can neither see nor understand himself nor his surroundings ; now, believing himself to be a man, weak and erring, like his fellows, and *now*, a God, that is not to be measured by their standard of judgment;—but he is *not* in his second childhood (although he evidently believes that all the rest of mankind are children born to obey his *dictum*) and through all the peculiar phases of his existence he is still Rome— ETERNAL ROME—whose policy is unchangeable.

The Dogma of Infallibility means something.   It has a background plan of action whose labyrinthic marvels are only seen by the projectors of the revised measure.   Infallibility is the fulcrum on which Rome intends to rest the lever of AUTHORITY by which it hopes to move the World.   But the fulcrum will prove an abrading saw, the friction of which will break the Lever of universal sway in twain.   The marvel is that Rome can hope so much of so weak an agent, and dupe itself so entirely.   But Rome does not see that, while it has been dreaming of Universal Empire and striving to devise means by which to ascend to the pinnacle of its ambition, the World has outgrown its Childhood and Youth, and entered upon its Reasoning Age, and that, in approaching maturity, the Human Family have lost faith in the exclusively "divine rights of Kings,'" or of Priests ; for the idea of DIVINE RIGHTS has broadened with the increase of knowledge and wisdom until it embraces Humanity.   He who would be leader among men in the Mature age of the World, must

34

make good the claim, by superior intellectual and moral powers, and by the greatness of his human love.

The Protestant branch of the Church may clearly see, that while such is Rome's position and policy toward the other religious sects of Christendom, reciprocity of feeling and loving Christian fellowship cannot exist, neither can there be any broadly united action in Humanitary labor. And Rome asks not, indeed, for reciprocal relations with any other sect—it *demands* CONFORMITY to doctrine and to dogma. The toleration and Christian charity of to-day must all come from the Protestant denominations who represent the liberal and progressive branch of the Church; for they are in a more favorable position to practice these exalted principles; and hence it becomes their imperative duty to show forth kind consideration and charity, and the love that maketh not ashamed; but they should not act blindly and without careful discrimination. Self-protection (not selfishness) is a higher law of Intelligent Nature than self-abnegation. In order to be able to render effective service to others, we must keep ourselves in healthful conditions, physically, mentally and morally, and not permit our vitality to be drawn unresistingly away by any species of vampire which may desire to feed on the vital principle and show no sign, saving the slow but sure decay of that which fosters its strength and power. One may manifest the fruits of the spirit of Christian love, without encouraging the growth of any evil principle in the Church.

Rome is more than willing that Protestant denominations should supply its nunneries and religious, nurseries of learning with pupils from their various orders, a large proportion of whom become proselytes of its faith, and through these means replenish its hungry treasury, enlarge its numbers, and strengthen its influence; for this aids directly in promoting its design of ages in regard to the United States. And the present is a favorable time for Rome to increase in numbers, wealth and power, because the moral World is in a transition state, passing from one period of development towards another and higher, towards maturity; and the Church is, consequently, advancing from her Youthful era of unquestioning faith in authority, forward to *her maturer age of* REASON, and of rational conviction in reference to principles of faith and practice; and, while she is in this unsettled, reactionary condition, she is enfeebled therefrom and more easily acted upon by the uniform and determined leadership of that Power. The Roman Catholic laity are less impressed, mentally and morally, by the stimulating influences of the times, because their reason and conscience are in the keeping of Rome, and they do not progress, as a whole, out of the Youthful condition of unquestioning faith in Ecclesiastic Authority; and, being habituated to restrictions upon thought and action, they do not perceive their limitations, and are not irritated by them. And so this Sect has the appearance of being more alive at present, in the United States, than other Denominations, while it enjoys, in verity, far less spiritual life than they. Another reason for its seeming life, in addition to the above, may be found in the fact that Rome is ambitious of TEMPORAL, as well as of Spiritual Power, and that it has an active policy for the accomplishment of this end, putting forth intense energy in the State, in order to acquire numbers, wealth and political influence. The Protestant sects are not seeking to found an empire; they declare, with the great Democratic Philosopher of Nazareth, that their Kingdom is *not* of this world, but they seek one to come, whose maker and builder is God. And they depend on the spiritual life of society for an increase of numbers and greater prosperity; and, consequently, suffer from the influences of the *transitionary period*, which is unfavorable to the increase of spiritual life and power.

The milder and more rational forms of doctrine, which the advanced Protestant Denominations have introduced, from period to period, under the broadening influences of increasing knowledge and reason, appealing with persuasive argument to the *understanding* of Man for the recognition of Gospel Truth, has drawn upon them the epithet of " milk-and-water Sects," from the Roman Catholics, who continue to dwell in the mental realm of the physical ages, under the shadow of The Mount that might be touched, and that burned with fire, under the blackness, and darkness, and tempest, and all the superstitious terrors of the Old Dispensation; so that they do not see that Protestant.

Sects are progressing more rapidly than they toward Mount Sion and toward the city of the living God, the heavenly Jerusalem. And again, as progressive Christians advance in the upward journey, and pass from youth to maturity, they lose the fire and passion of, early years, and the angry persecuting zeal for God, that is not according to knowledge and reason; but they gain an abiding faith in eternal principles that cannot be shaken by all the anathemas of Rome, and all the persecutions that human ingenuity can devise; and they repose more calmly in the Infinite Love, and strive more earnestly and patiently to work out the great principles of the Gospel of Intelligent Nature, in Love; and not in *violence*. External Nature, in clouds, and storms, and tornadoes, is fiercely grand and terrible; but she is not weak and insipid at the deep calm of noon, when her meridian sun projects no shadows from her forest pines and mountain peaks upon the living landscape that shares equally the benediction of its fructifying power. And the human mind, in its high noon of maturity, free from sectional and sectarian proclivities and prejudices, viewing principles broadly and calmly from a lofty altitude of thought with the clear eye of enlightened Reason, is grand and God-like in the profound stillness of its self-poised existence.

We have called the particular attention of the Church to its Roman Catholic branch, because it aims in the present, as it aimed in the past, to become the Church Universal, in which the State is to be merged, as the finite, in the Infinite; and because it is the only Denomination in our Country that believes that it holds the right, by a higher than human authority, to control the civil Government of a Nation, and to overthrow it (if it be powerful enough) when such government becomes prejudicial to the interests of Rome; and because it believes that its members owe a higher allegiance to Rome than they do to either their native or adopted land; and, farther, because this Sect is the only one in the United States which strives persistently, in conformity with these views, for political power and ascendency in the State, in order that it may be eventually able to grasp the reins of government and distribute its patronage and treasury. Ay, Rome of to-day believes, as sincerely as mediæval Rome believed, that it has a higher than human authority for exercising both Temporal and Spiritual Power wherever it erects a Cathedral, and it only awaits the ripe moment for action. None must understand us to say that both the Clergy and Laity of Rome are *alike* ambitious of obtaining political power in order to establish Ecclesiastic rule in the United States; we simply believe that the laity desire to see their Denomination become the Church Universal, because they regard it, in accordance with their teaching, as the only true Church of God, and consider faith in its doctrines as essential to the salvation of the soul. But the *sincerity* of the laity of Rome in aiding its prelates to force their doctrines and dogmas and Ecclesiastic Power upon our Nation, would not compensate our millions of freemen for the loss of civil and religious liberty.

Many persons, who have not carefully observed the peculiar character and action of the Roman Catholic branch of the Church, may regard the present view as a mere chimera of the imagination. Let statistics speak to such in direct and forcible utterance. In eighteen hundred and sixty-six an appropriation was made by the Legislature of New York to the various religious societies of that State, amounting in the aggregate to one-hundred and twenty-nine thousand and twenty-nine dollars; the Jews and Protestants, united, who form a very large majority of the population of that Commonwealth, received from this large sum the small amount of four thousand and eight hundred dollars; all the rest of these public moneys was paid over to the Roman Catholics to enrich their private, sectarian institutions. The City of New York controls, politically, the State; and it is not amazing that a small minority of the entire population should have received twenty-five times more of the public moneys appropriated to religious societies than was apportioned the large majority, when we learn farther, from statistics, published in the New York Herald of that period, the remarkable fact that nearly all the municipal offices of that City were held by Roman Catholics. The following is a copy of the published list: Sheriff, Register, Controller, City Chamberlain, Corporation Counsel, Police Commissioner, President of the Board of Councilmen, Clerk of the Common Council, Clerk of Supervisors, five Justices of the Courts of Record, all the Civil Justices, all the Police Justices but two, all the Police Court Clerks, three out of four Coroners, fourteen-nineteenths of the Common Council and eight-tenths of the Supervisors.

It may be readily seen from the foregoing statistics that the Roman Catholics, who are in a small minority, compared with the other religious sects in the aggregate, must have put forth united, persistent, and indefatigable effort in order to have produced such stupendous results. And it evinces clearly that they have already a strong hold of the political wires, and understand how to pull them vigorously for Denominational and Ambitious ends.

We have called the particular attention of the Church to its Roman Catholic branch, because that ORGANÍZATION is strong and powerful, and its plan of action as systematic, deep, and comprehensive, as human intellect, stimulated by worldly ambition, and love of power, could possibly devise. Rome is a unit. It has the same mainspring of action the wide world over, and tolls out the passing hours of time to the measure of Universal Empire. It plans, and works, by the ages. That which cannot be done towards effecting its object in one century, Rome determines shall be accomplished in another, the while it labors silently on, amassing wealth, and acquiring numbers and influence. The whole World is included in its plans of Empire, and the United States of America is designated on its Chart as the future seat of the Papal Throne.

The power that Rome already exercises in the New World, of which the foregoing may serve as an illustration, is conclusive evidence of its perfect Organization, and of its systematic and persevering action. And the marvellous and bold coup d'etat of December eighteen hundred and fifty-two, when France, sensitive, enthusiastic, liberty-loving France, was suddenly transformed from a Republic into an Imperial Power by the " Presto! change!" of the chief Magician, furnishes a striking elucidation of Rome's yet powerful Organization in the Old World. Napoleon himself was as much surprised as his subjects at the sudden change of fortune which deprived France of liberty.   But it was not Rome's love for Napoleon that placed a crown on his brow, and mantled him in the imperial purple of Kings; it was Rome's fear and hatred of Republican Institutions that gave France an Emperor when she desired a President.   For Rome preferred to rely for support on the plighted faith and gratitude of one ambitious man, rather than on the sympathy and love of the large numbers of its laity under a liberal and enlightened form of government.   In a recent conversation with a friend on the affairs of Church and State, reported in the public press, the Pope quietly reminds the Emperor that he holds the Crown of France, by the same tenure that He retains his Tiara; which spoken in forcible English implies that, "The power that makes can, also, unmake a King."   Napoleon knows, full well, that he is not a free man, and dare not pursue an independent course to-day, whatever might be his desire, or conviction, were that course of action to be directed against the interests of Rome.   And this powerful Organization has adopted a policy of expediency, limited only by the impossible.   It believes and instructs its teachers that "the end justifies the means," when that end is either the temporal, or spiritual, prosperity of the Roman Catholic Organization.

Had the various Protestant Sects united and organized strongly in the United States for broad and effective humanitary action, exercising *reason*, as well as *faith*, in and for the principles of the Christian Religion—Love to God, and Love to Man—then their power would have been infinitely greater to-day than that of Rome; for, under the electric influences of vital Christianity, they would have moved the heart, the understanding, and the soul of the people to action; because the Gospel of Intelligent Nature, in its unadulterated truth, is a pure Democracy, which is perfectly adapted to the Nature and needs of universal Man, and has power to stimulate all the noble faculties of his being.   And when it is received in the heart and mind of man, in its purity, it commences at once its renovating work, and converts the rudest natures into "gentle-men" and women, through the potency of its divine regenerating Love.

We have called the particular attention of the Church to her Roman Catholic branch, for the reason that under its present policy and action, it is a disintegrating, instead of a strengthening power in our Democratic Christian State; as it is entirely opposed to Republican principles, and uses all the power and influence that it acquires under the fostering care of our Country to undermine and weaken her Institutions. Its Prelates strive persistently to convert our broad political and liberal educational systems, and the freedom of speech, and of the press, into agents of Rome, by which to work covertly, and openly, when it dare, against these inherited rights and liberties of American citizens. The late Bishop Hughes, of New York, lectured publicly in that city against our Republican Institutions. And other dignitaries of Rome in the United States have denounced them in severe and sweeping terms of disapprobation. Rome is opposed to Republican Institutions, because they endow the masses with too great liberty of thought and action, and under such influences they are not easily converted to its religion of forms, and made subjects of its restrictive government. Rome is opposed to *popular education*, because it enlightens the people broadly, enabling them to exercise their reasoning powers, which are the highest attributes of mind bestowed by Heaven, and this is fatal to all old-time creeds and dogmas that cannot stand the test of rational argument. It has never been the policy of Rome to educate the millions in any country where it has been the dominant power; for it assumes to be the *reason and conscience* of its subjects, and understands well that an ignorant, unreasoning community is more easily controlled by its Priesthood than an enlightened self-governing people.

But Rome pursues a different course in the United States. Here it multiplies schools in every populous district; and a large proportion of the thousands of Protestant children which annually attend these doctrinal nurseries, become Roman Catholics. It was a masterly policy for Rome to become an Educator in the Republic of the United States. whose greatest strength lies in her PUBLIC SCHOOL; to adopt her educational system, in order, through

that system, to weaken her power, by using it as a means of proselyting her citizens, and of converting them into subjects of its
government. It has been, indeed, the uniform policy of that
Power, in every age, to turn the weapons of its enemies against
themselves. We have used the term *enemies* in its application to
principles; Republican Institutions—which imply the rule of the
many instead of the few—the greatest good of greatest numbers
—the self-governing power of the enlightened millions—and the
broad equality and brotherhood of Man—are the most formidable opponents of Ecclesiastic Despotism. It is curious and
wonderful to observe Rome of the Old World, dying slowly of
tithes and of superficial and restrictive forms of religion and government; yet, resuscitating its failing strength in the New World by
feeding on the vigorous life of an uncorrupted people; to observe
it deliberately burying its riches there, in deep vaults with the
decaying forms of other generations, while actively engaged in
replenishing its empty coffers with the gold and silver freshly
dug from the hidden mineral treasures of the United States.

Should the Roman Catholic Denomination in the United
States succeed, through its present extensive system of proselyting, in becoming numerically greater than the aggregate of the
other religious sects, it will then wield a stronger political influence in the Federal Government than they, through which to
control a larger proportion of the National patronage, and of the
Public moneys; and, then, Rome will claim to be THE STATE!
as well as THE CHURCH;—and such has been its ambitious aim
ever since we have had an existence as an independent People.

What then?—what then? THEN, instead of being a Nation
of freemen, blessed with a progressive form of government which
recognizes the divine Rights of Man, blessed with a great Christian Democracy which is a benediction to the Nations of earth,
we shall be cursed with the worst system of tyranny that ever
oppressed Humanity—Ecclesiastic Despotism.

What then?—what then? THEN, in addition to the loss of
civil and religious liberty, the freedom of the press, and the freedom of speech, the people will lose the liberty of thought and action, and become the mere puppets of an *ism*, Romanism.

35

What then?—what then? THEN will follow the gradual but sure decline of business enterprise, and the loss of intellectual aspiration, attended by a fearful atmosphere of moral death, like that of modern Rome, which is more suffocating than her gloomy Catacombs of decay; for the torpidity and stillness of that atmosphere of death is contagious, it oppresses one at the heart until he pants unconsciously for breath, and wonders why his spirit is thus burdened in far-famed " Italia's" balmy air, and under her beneficent and beautiful physical influences. But while he pauses, marvelling, the voice of injured Nature breathes in the mournful music of the winds: It is the lingering death of the highest attributes of the human soul that renders Rome more gloomy than a sepulchre, to the unfettered and liberty-loving man and woman of every nation.

What then?—what then? THEN, Ah! then, the stagnant waters of human existence will ripple once more with the breath of the Infinite One, passing over and moving them to action! And then will follow a low suppressed cry from the indignant heart of enslaved Humanity, feeling the inspiring influence of the Divine presence in the deep of its spirit awaking unutterable yearning for the *true liberty* of the children God. And, then, these kindling aspirations of the human soul will take form in independent efforts for civil and religious liberty; which will be attended, again, as they were in the past, by persistive and bloody persecutions of the earnest minority of true-hearted men and women who can, and dare, no longer breathe the blighting atmosphere of Ecclesiastic Despotism. And they will put all the force of their immortal being into action, to rend the bonds of error which enslave them; regardless of neither death, nor life, nor angels nor principalities, nor powers, nor things present, nor things to come; nor of aught on earth, nor aught in heaven, saving God and the Divine Liberty of His children. And the awakening aspirations, and responsive inspirations of the Human Soul will be attended again, as they were in the past, by a mighty moral revolution, commensurate with the powerful forces of the human heart and mind in united and determined action. A Reformation broader and grander than that of the sixteenth century will sweep over the earth from the Infinite Ocean of Truth, and bear away, per force, the refuge of lies.

But is the Church of God willing, is our Nation willing, that the fearful Tragedy of Ecclesiastic Despotism that saturated the lovely plains and valleys of the Old World with human blood shall be re-enacted on the soil of the New? Has not mankind suffered enough already from the horrible persecutions of religious Intolerants and Bigots? One would imagine that even Despotism's self might be surfeited with the crimson tide, and cry—Enough! he has already drank such deep potations from the bleeding heart of Humanity. In the dear and sacred name of the Divine Father and Mother God—the God of *justice*, as well as of Liberty and Love—let us have FREEDOM? Let all the Protestant Denominations unite and resolve, as the soul of ONE, to preserve our great Christian Republic intact, to preserve civil and religious liberty for ourselves, and for our children, and for our children's children, to remotest generations! Ay! and then the benediction of our Republican Institutions will extend until it embraces the whole world. Behold, *now*, is the hour for united, peaceful and effective action! Behold, NOW, is the day of salvation! In a few years longer we may not be able to preserve our Liberties without bloodshed. Rome is already armed; and our Government permits its legions to parade in the streets of the great metropolis of the Nation, twenty-thousand strong, and to make an occasional raid on Canada; blind to the fact that it is simply a childish by-play, permitted by Rome, in order to delude our people, and the *ranks* of Irish citizens, with the idea that these men are armed to demand their rights of England! But Rome's Prelates know better—and the Centre-heads of the movement, also, know that it is a miserable artifice; they understand well that these raids are but the prelude to another and a deeper tragedy. It is time that the artifice should be exposed, in order that the calamity may be prevented by our Nation. If another mob break loose from the civil authorities of New York, there will be an army of disciplined men to let out the life-blood of her citizens in wholesale slaughter. The avenues of travel are even now all in the hands of this army. New York has indeed already lost her Liberty; but she may regain it peacefully once more, if her sons and daughters will awake to the danger in season, and be willing to do their whole duty to themselves and to their Country. Let all true Americans, whether native born or adopted citizens, be early and late at the POLLS, and see to it that the patronage of our government is not monopolized by any religious Denomination. And let them look to the interests of the PUBLIC SCHOOL, and not permit any encroachment on that beneficent system of popular education, by any sectarian movement. And let them look to the general interests of the Church, and the State, and guard carefully the cherished liberties of the American Nation.

We have neither prejudice against, nor uncharitable feeling toward the Roman Catholics; but we wish all the religious sects of the United States to share equally the benediction of our Republican Institutions. We desire to preserve our civil and religious liberty by holding the Church and State intact, in order that there may be healthy action and reaction between these two Bodies, which represent the conservative and radical forces of God's earthly Government. We desire to see Religion, Reason and Knowledge, a divine sisterhood, move forward hand in hand toward the harmonial years of Prophecy, when The *knowledge* of God shall fill the earth, an intelligent understanding of His laws through all Nature, animate and inanimate, instead of the less profitable knowledge of creeds and dogmas.

Rome forgets, while striving for supreme rule in Church and State, that God's Church is not a Temporal, but a Spiritual Power; and that it is not a narrow-minded Sectarian, but a broad, democratic Humanitarian. Neither Romanism, nor any other *ism*, nor *schism*, is such stuff as God's Church Universal will be made of. That Church of the Reasoning Age of Man, and the grand Harmonial Era of the World, will not be the deformed outgrowth of ignorance and superstitution, but the perfect Offspring of Reason and Knowledge. Its leaders will not then strive to limit and control, but to enlarge and liberate the human mind. They will seek to endow the people with freedom of thought and action, requiring only loving obedience to the great Law of Love—the Christian's only rule of life. The Church Universal will be, like a city set upon a hill, radiating the glory of Heaven. Each individual member thereof will be lighted from within, The law of God being written on the Heart, instead of engraven on Tables of Stone, or on the Tablets of the Ecumenical Council. Ay, each Son, or daughter, of the Most High will be a self-poised, reasoning existence, understanding and cherishing the sublime and beautiful truth, that he sustains a similar relation to Deity that the sunbeam sustains to the orb of day; that he is ONE with Christ in God; for in his soul burns a living ray of the Spiritual Sun of the Universe, to light and guide him forward and upward toward the source of Infinite Existence from which he sprang, forever and forever.

The Government of the Roman Catholic Organization is, we repeat again in closing, Autocratic and Despotic in character; its policy is Ecclesiastic, instead of Christian; and it diverges as far from the *true democracy* of the dear Redeemer's Gospel of Intelligent Nature, as Hades from Heaven. But what saith the Spirit to the Church concerning this branch of her heritage: Thou hast a few names even in the Roman Catholic Denomination which have not defiled their garments; and they shall walk with me in white: for they are worthy.

MARGINAL NOTE. Since the preceding was written, the Pope has lost his Temporal Power. But the Prelates of Rome assure the people that the policy of their Church still remains unchanged, and that his "Holiness" will in due time become once more the HEAD of the Nations; because God himself entrusted him with both the civil and religious government of Earth. The FORTY SECRET MILITARY SOCIETIES which had sprung up within the last few years in the Catholic Denomination (enumerated in the Catholic World, a leading organ of Rome) intimate rather strongly the carnal means that the Pope proposes to employ in order to regain his lost political position. The same Paper which furnishes the above information, does not leave us in doubt in regard to the line of action they are to pursue. It says:—"Catholic associations, in order to be victorious must pass over the dead body of this powerful enemy. There is no other way." It points out the enemy—the "Reformation," or its fruits—Protestantism. Not a very pleasant prospect for the liberal sects of Christendom—if Rome rises to power!

In whatever country on the face of the earth that there is a Catholic Denomination, which believes in the Temporal Power of the Church of Rome, there must also exist two forms of civil government, or, a State within a State, in which Rome claims the higher power. This assumption of the latter naturally awakens antagonism, and sooner or later the government becomes, like a house divided against itself—it cannot stand. But, fortunately for society, every evil contains the element of its own destruction. It will soon become a mooted question in political circles of the United States:—

Can a man be regarded, in verity, as a CITIZEN of a Republic, while he owes, at the same time, a higher allegiance to another government of a different form, which claims precedence in authority and power?

36

EPISCOPAL CATHOLICS.

He that hath an ear, let him hear what the Spirit saith unto the Church : I know thy works, that thou hast a name, that thou livest, and art dead. Be watchful, and strengthen the things which remain, that are ready to die: for I have not found thy works perfect before God. As many as I love, I rebuke and chasten: be zealous, therefore, and repent.

The Episcopal Catholic Denomination is a haughty Aristocrat, stately, serene and cold. It claims with the Roman Catholic Sect, antiquity—a direct line of Apostolic Succession from Saint Peter—and to be THE CHRISTIAN CHURCH. And it erects, also, costly edifices of architectural beauty for the worship of the God of Heaven and of Earth, whose symmetrical towers and spires appear to ascend to the All-One, in a continual anthem of praise.

But it opens not the doors of these magnificent piles to God's waiting poor; and they famish and thirst for the bread and water of life, under the very shadows of the spires that point Heavenward. Neglected by the Church, and uncared for by society, they hunger also for daily food, and shiver in the snows of Winter for the lack of protecting raiment, while many of their numbers have not where to lay their heads. And having no attractive home of rest below, it would be precious balm to their weary and wounded spirits to be able to enter God's earthly sanctuary, and learn from loving Ministers at His Altars, that they are not the less children of the Divine, because of their poverty, ignorance and suffering; and that there is a beautiful mansion not made with hands, preparing for them in the All-Father's home of love on high.

The cordial invitation of the Revealed Word to Man is truly inspiring: Ho! every one that thirsteth, come ye to the waters, and he that hath no money, come ye, buy and eat; yea, come, buy wine and milk, without money and without price. But this proud, statuesque Aristocrat requires the weary and heavy laden millions to stand upon the order of their coming. Knowledge

of the conventional rules of Society, and conformity to the standard styles of dress and manners are important requisites for in-
suring a gracious welcome to the Table of the Lord.   For this
religious Body is a fine exemplar of deportment, its manners
are unexceptionable; but, they are after the fashion of the World,
and not after Christ; it is more regardful of position, wealth
and refinement, than of the spirit and temper of the Gospel.

The Episcopal Catholics appear, in verity, to the looker-on in
Christendom, to seek more earnestly to convert the people to
Episcopacy than to the broader principles of Christianity, the
Gospel of Intelligent Nature.   Like the Roman Catholics, this
denomination establishes sectarian schools, and sectarian chari-
ties, to increase its numbers and influence; and, like that religious
Body, it is careful in the observance of times and seasons,—of
Holy Days,—of Church fasts and festivals,—and of all the ex-
ternals of devotion.   But there is more of form than heart in
this mode of worship, and the great loving Intelligence of the
Universe is not thus propitiated.

Is not this the fast I have chosen, saith the Lord? to loose
the bands of wickedness, to undo the heavy burdens, and to let
the oppressed go free, and that ye *break every yoke ?*

Is it not to deal thy bread to the hungry, and that thou bring
the poor that are cast out to thy house ?   When thou seest the
naked that thou cover him ; and that thou hide not thyself from
thine own flesh ?   Then shall thy light break forth as the morning, and thine health shall spring forth speedily: and thy righteousness shall go before thee; and the glory of the Lord shall
be thy re-reward.

Ah! in the advancing Era of Reason and Knowledge, the
promised Day of Humanity in the full maturity of the World,
that Denomination will be recognized as the true Church of
God which is the most consistently Christian, which is all aglow
with human and Divine Love, and that exemplifies its love in
broad humanitary deeds.   And, of those who minister at God's
consecrated Altars, they only will be regarded as being in the
line of the true Apostolic Succession who are endowed with the
largest share of the knowledge, wisdom and love of God—who

have been baptized with the spirit of Christ—whose lips have been touched with a live coal from off the altar of Eternal Truth. For, only such sons and daughters of the Most High are able to stimulate the latent powers of the human soul to action. They are to the moral world, what sun, air, and moisture are to the physical,—grand vitalizing and generating forces; and only such are able to quicken the torpid professors of religion, who know the Master's will, but are either too indolent to do it, or too much occupied with the passing fashions and vanities of the world. And only such Watchmen on the walls of Zion are able to awaken and resuscitate the dead in trespasses and sins, uplift their feet from the mire, and lead them tenderly forth into green pastures, and beside the still waters of salvation. And only such true Apostles of the Divine are able to electrify the people, and kindle their hearts and minds with the scintillating sparks of Heavenly love, with the living flame of pure devotion, inspiring them with fervent zeal in the service of God and Humanity. The earnest-hearted Cowper has truly said: "They who would make us feel, must feel themselves." And, verily, they who would quicken the souls of the millions, themselves must be inspired of Heaven.

Alas! for the Episcopal Catholic Denomination; it has lost the vital glow of Christian Democracy, its earnest, loving and quickening spirit, and degenerated spiritually until it has almost become a Denominational fossil. But it is, notwithstanding, far in advance of the Roman Catholics. Its Laity are more generally enlightened, and its Clergy more progressive and liberal than they. And, as a religious Body, it exercises broader charity towards other sects of Christendom, and inclines to greater reciprocity in humanitary labor. And, yet, it stands too coldly aloof from other Denominations included within the dear Redeemer's seamless robe of love; and fails to approach the high standard of Christian Democracy.

But what saith the Spirit to the Church concerning this branch of her heritage? Thou hast a few names, even among the Episcopal Catholic Denomination, who have not defiled their garments; and they shall walk with me in white: for they are worthy.

LUTHERANS, PRESBYTERIANS, CONGREGATIONALISTS.

He that hath an ear, let him hear what the Spirit saith unto the Church: I will give unto every one according to his work. Remember therefore how thou hast received and heard, and hold fast and repent. And he that overcometh, and keepeth my work unto the end, to him will I give power over the nations.

The Lutherans, Presbyterians and Congregationalists are also Aristocrats, filled with spiritual pride, intolerance and bigotry. And they, too, construct expensive ornamental churches, and establish Sectarian Schools—and Sectarian Charities—rather than humanitary; while the poor famish daily for food, and for the bread and water of life eternal, under the shadow of these costly Temples, dedicated to the service of the munificent Father. And they, likewise, Pay tithe of mint and anise and cummin, and have omitted the weightier matters of the law, judgment, mercy and faith. And they, also, indulge in envy, strife and jealousy, and in bitter animosity toward other denominations of the Christian Church; because they, like other religious sects, have lost their first love, and their early humility and charity, and become ambitious and worldly.

These denominations do not assert themselves to be THE CHRISTIAN CHURCH, and strive to establish a claim to the regular Apostolic succession, as do the Roman Catholics, and Episcopal Catholics ; but they declare with austere emphasis to all other religious sects: THIS IS THE WAY; WALK YE IN IT. The Plymouth Confession of Faith is the tether that limits their pasturage to the lowlands of creeds; and they stint their souls with meagre fare, while the green fields of truth, flowering in celestial beauty, lie open before them, and the mountain heights of Zion rise in grandeur beyond, gushing with living water, and bright with the smile of God, to attract them onward and upward to higher levels of truth and knowledge.

There are men among their Clergy, like Henry Ward Beecher, that possess great reasoning minds and loving hearts, who kindle with our dear Redeemer's "enthusiasm for Humanity," and long to embrace in their fraternal arms the whole Family of Man, and uplift them from their weakness, suffering and sin, and establish their feet upon the Rock of Ages.   In moments of religious exaltation, these grand souls, feeling within their bosoms an infinite joy, and a longing for freedom, break away from their tetherings, leave the ground-work Plan of Salvation devised by man, to enjoy for awhile the glorious liberty of the children of God, to take in full draughts of inspiration from the overflowing fountains of Heavenly truth and love.   But these poor timid Sects take alarm at their daring.   Their ideas of *religious propriety* are shocked.   They are afraid that, in some way or other, the "*cause* may suffer injury."   They have lost faith in the power of Divine Truth to guide those earnest Christians aright, who have been endowed from on High with a double portion of the Spirit of Christ.   And they stretch out unholy hands to steady the Ark of God.   They send forth spurred hunters of the Flock, mailed in creeds, on swift steeds of Sectarian Policy, to lasso and corral the inspired servants of the Most High God, and pin them down again to the old tethering ground.

Alas! that they who are blessed with a fuller measure of the loving spirit and Heavenly wisdom of the Mediative Son of God, should become Marks for Sectarian Sportsmen.   Is it so, indeed, among these Denominations, that the true disciples of the Master are to be hedged about forever with a cumbrous Plan of Salvation of human construction, to weaken their power and limit their usefulness?   Are they always to be rallied round a standard of creeds; and, thus, cut off from the lofty heights of principles, and from broad Humanitary views, through which the Church can alone grow in grace and in the knowledge of God, and thus be transformed into the likeness of Christ?

More than eighteen hundred years ago, Christ himself taught the broad, general principles of faith and practice, which contain the true germs of soul-growth ; and he endowed his disciples of every land and age with the liberty of the Universe of Truth; in order that they might learn of God.   The elaborate Scheme of Salvation is a labyrinthine wonder, when compared with the great Teacher's statement of Human obligations to the Divine. Sorrow for wrong-doing is the only required sacrifice for sin; and, Love to God, and Love to Man, fulfills all the requisitions of the Moral Law, preparing the Human Family alike for the Earthly and the Heavenly Societies. Ay, the Democratic Philosopher of Nazareth placed no other barrier in the way of any truth than the natural limitations of the capabilities of human beings for receiving and understanding its comprehensive principles. He that hath an ear, let him hear,—were the Divine Teacher's oft-repeated words to the multitudes who thronged to him for instruction and blessing.

The Lutheran, Presbyterian and Congregational Denominations have lost the vitalizing spirit of Christianity, and fallen into a fatal lethargy in the by-paths of traditional religion. What impending judgments of Heaven will arouse and inspire them with life again? No marvel that they stumble and fall; for they are no longer children of the day of *spiritual illumination;* the darkness of unbelief has blinded their eyes. These Denominations are limited by a narrow and rigid Sectarian Policy, which is entirely antagonistic in its character to pure Christian Democracy.

But what saith the Spirit to the Church concerning this branch of her heritage? Thou hast a few names even in the Lutheran, Presbyterian, and Congregational Denominations, which have not defiled their garments; and they shall walk with me in white: for they are worthy.

CALVINIST BAPTISTS.

He that hath an ear, let him hear what the Spirit saith unto the Church: I counsel thee to buy of me gold tried in the fire, that thou mayest be rich; and white raiment that thou mayest be clothed, and that the shame of thy nakedness do not appear; and anoint thine eyes with eye-salve, that thou mayest see. To him that overcometh will I give to eat of the tree of life, which is in the midst of the Paradise of God.

The Calvinist Baptist Denomination is a self-righteous Pharisee. It says to other sects of the Christian Church, through its policy

and action: Stand by; I am holier than thou.   I fast twice in a
week.   I pay tithes of all that I possess, for the support of the
Gospel in Heathen lands.   I alone understand correctly the
oracles of God.   I believe in the Trinity, in the Atonement, in
Baptism by immersion, in Foreordination, in Election, and in a
literal hell of fire and brimstone for all out of Christ.   I am of the
elect—thank God!—and commune only with " brothers and sisters of the same faith and order."

And, yet, strange to relate, this Denomination believes, more
fully than any other, in the total depravity of human nature.   It
declares from its pulpit, in mournful, dirge-like tones, that, " There
is no good thing in man; that, His days are few and full of evil
from the cradle to the grave; that, He goeth astray as soon as he
is born, speaking lies; that, From the sole of the foot, even unto
the crown of the head, he is full of wounds and bruises and pu-
trifying sores."   But, fortunately for the Baptist, the doctrine of
election is a loophole through which it escapes from the fearful
consequences of so much original sin.   Truly this Sect appears
to find, in the frequent confession of its extreme depravity, a
marvellous quietus for its conscience.

A relative of the Author, who was a deacon of the Methodist Episcopal Denomination, once attended a Baptist Confer-
ence Meeting.   On his return home his wife inquired if he had
been pleased with the services.   " I was greatly amused," he replied.   " One member after another related his experience, and
ended with telling us that he felt himself to be a poor, miserable
sinner, more depraved and vile than any other, and entirely unworthy to be present with his brethren, entirely unworthy to be
called a child of God.   Finally, the Parson rose and responded meekly, that he was truly happy to find such a
blessed union of feeling among the brethren.   But, for my own
part, I was surprised by such confessions of wickedness, and felt
thankful to escape unharmed from so large a company of sinners."

The Baptist is hopelessly sectarian, because he believes in the
efficacy of doctrines to save souls, rather than in the earnest
efforts of men and women to conform to the requirements of
the perfect Law of Love, and thus to work out their own salva-

tion, while the Spirit of Truth worketh in them, and by them. This Denomination appears, indeed, to be born of creeds, instead of the Holy Spirit.   And while it is engaged in endless disputations about the *letter* of the Gospel, it loses sight of its beautiful loving *spirit*, and so fails to apply the principles of Christianity to its own regeneration, that it may, in very deed, be born anew.

Hear what the Mediative Son of God saith of the *new birth:* The wind bloweth where it listeth, and thou hearest the sound thereof, but canst not tell whence it cometh, or whither it goeth: So is every one that is born of the Spirit.   Nicodemus said unto him, How can these things be? Jesus answered, Art thou a master of Israel and knowest not these things?   Ah! there is many a Nicodemus in modern Israel who cannot comprehend the spiritual birth of the soul.   They who are born of the Spirit are children of the light, and cannot walk in gloom and darkness.   The Spirit itself beareth witness with their spirits that they are born of God.   While they who are born of doctrines live in fear and torment, trembling at the very names of Death and Judgment.

In order to illustrate the importance of the Creed to this Sect, we will relate an incident that came under our own observation.   A lady friend of the Baptist Denomination, being dangerously ill, a committee of visiting sisters was appointed to wait on her, in accordance with the custom of the society, in order to learn, and report the condition of her mind in view of death and judgment.   Entering the chamber of their invalid friend and sister in Christ, with sternly solemn faces and cold, formal manners, they stood by the side of her dying bed and addressed her in the following words: " Dear sister, we learned that you were near the confines of the tomb, and called to inquire about the state of your immortal soul: Do you feel yourself to be comfortably established in the good DOCTRINES of our Church?"   Not one word was spoken concerning the rest of the soul in the promises of the Heavenly Parent; not one word was spoken of the peace and joy in believing, and of the happiness and glory of the life beyond the grave, to comfort and sustain the departing sister on that untried journey.

37

"Say, ye cold-hearted, frozen formalists,"—in the final struggle of the soul with its mortal frame,—in the last hour of dissolving nature, when flesh and heart fail and the soul must go alone to its Creator,—in that trying hour in which our dear Redeemer himself cried aloud in agony—My God! my God! why hast Thou forsaken me?—will CREEDS then become a firm staff to lean upon?—will they conduct the weary traveler safely across the valley of the shadow of death? And, when he reaches the gates of the Celestial City, will he be questioned in the Assembly's Shorter Catechism in respect to his knowledge of *doctrines?* Will he not, instead, be interrogated in regard to Christian *practice.* Hast thou fed the hungry, and clothed the naked? Hast thou been ears to the deaf, and eyes to the blind? Hast thou been strength to the weak, and faith to the doubting? Hast thou been comfort to the mourner, and hope to the despairing? Hast thou removed the stumbling stones out of the way of the stranger? Hast thou been a lamp of truth and knowledge to those who sat in darkness? And if he can truly reply: Father, I have endeavored thus to do Thy will; then shall he hear the joyful sound: Well done, good and faithful servant; inasmuch as thou hast done it unto one of the least of these my brethren thou hast done it unto me; enter thou into the joy of thy Lord. The righteous shall shine as the sun in the firmament, and they who have turned many to righteousness, as the stars, forever and ever.

Truly, it appears marvellous to a thoughtful looker on in Christendom that any educated person, capable of reading and comrephending the Gospel of Intelligent Nature, should believe that mere faith in doctrines could possess " saving grace;" because faith may exist independently of Holiness of heart, without which no man can see the Lord. The doctrine of Atonement for sin is a will-o'-the-wisp to all who do not strive daily and hourly to walk in the footprints of the Mediative Son of God, and lead his devoted life of good works, purity and love.

Alas! for the Baptist. The severity of its creed has struck in, and benumbed the soul-life. And it appears more like a solemn petrifaction of humanity, than a warm vitalized Body, aglow with Love to God and Love to Man. It seems, indeed, to the outside world, to possess a heart of stone, instead of a heart of flesh with its kindling affections, and so it has but little attractive power to draw men and women into the Fold of the Good Shepherd. When we turn from this rigid Sect toward the great Democratic Philosopher of Nazareth whom it professes to serve, imitate and love, what a wonderful change of feeling is produced in our hearts, minds and souls; how they expand and glow under the beneficent influence of his broad humanitary love. Hopeful and cheering indeed is his voice to the toil-worn millions of Earth: Come unto me all ye that labor and are heavy laden, and I will give you rest. Take my yoke upon you and learn of me; for I am meek and lowly in heart; and ye shall find rest unto your souls. For my yoke is easy, and my burden is light.

The Baptist has been so long occupied with the *form* of Godliness that it has lost the power thereof, and become a stern and frigid Sectarian, instead of a live Christian Democrat.

But what saith the Spirit to the Church concerning this branch of her heritage? Thou hast a few names, even in the Calvinist Baptist Denomination, which have not defiled their garments, and they shall walk with me in white: for they are worthy.

THE QUAKERS.

He that hath an ear, let him hear what the Spirit saith unto the Church. I know thy works, and charity, and service, and faith, and thy patience. Because thou hast kept the word of my patience, I also will keep thee from the hour of temptation, which shall come upon all the world, to try them that dwell upon the earth. Notwithstanding, I have a few things against thee; be zealous, therefore, and repent.

It may be said of the Denomination of Quakers that it was *once* alive; but now it, too, is cold and inanimate. The Costumer has proved a fatal enemy. She has fastened herself upon this Body, and, like a vampire, fattened upon its vital currents, until it has become a mere skeleton of a Christian. And she has dyed it so long in monotonous drab that it appeares scarcely more alive than the dull earth that the color symbolizes

And Original Sin has proved a Lion in the way of this Sect when it would ascend the mountain heights of Zion, causing it to journey onward in a state of fear and apprehension, and to mistake the tuneful voices of Nature for the roar of the monster, and wander farther and farther from the summit of its aspiration. At length it reached a waste devoid of verdure, where it pitched its tent—in the morning twilight of Humanity's Day— in order to lead a severe life of self-abnegating duty, and thus propitiate the favor of Heaven, untempted by the tuneful sound of harp or lute, or the joyful language of many-colored flowers.

This Denomination has silenced so long the sweet voices of Nature, which speak to the soul in music and color, that they have almost ceased to appeal to the spiritual perception of its members for a recognition of their peculiar service to Man, which is to teach him a lesson in the beautiful, the harmonious and the perfect, in order that his heart, and mind might become accordant with universal Nature.

The combinations of various colors, and of sounds, produce, each, a distinct harmony; and the peculiar harmonies of both are allied to every other harmony ; even as solar systems are to solar systems, uniting in ONE the grand universe of God. Humanity is ONE of many shades and tones, as are color and sound, and was created to form a spiritual harmony which should include all other harmonies, rendering peaceful, beautiful, and perfect the wide realm of Intelligent Nature. The Church of God is ONE, on Earth and in Heaven, although composed of many names; and it is intended that the whole Human Family should unite in her Universal Anthem of praise to Jehovah, and learn to accord with the music of the higher spheres. More than eighteen centuries ago the Heralds of Deity were sent forth to proclaim to the Nations the inspired words of that Universal Anthem: Glory to God in the Highest, on earth peace, good will to Man. But the Church has not yet set them to the music of the spheres.

The natural fondness of Man and Woman for colors and

musical sounds, and the evident care of the Creator in providing for the gratification of these tastes, teach an important lesson in the philosophy of God's Government; namely, that He adapts means to ends through the wide range of material and of intelligent Nature, that human faculties are adjusted to the truths of the external as well as the spiritual World—in other words, that Man is adapted to Nature, and Nature to Man—and consequently, that the Human Family may acquire a knowledge of the Universal Father through His works, by loving, earnest and careful investigation.

All the varied powers of mind and heart and soul are the REVEALED WILL OF GOD IN MAN; and they who would obliterate either one of them, would attempt to defraud Man of his legitimate inheritance, of his glorious birthright as a child of Deity, and do violence to the Divinity who created them all for use and blessing. Obliterate, did we say? No finite being can do that to the least of the heaven-endowed powers of Man. These faculties may be checked and stifled in the soul by sectarian bigotry, or by false systems of education, until the human being fails, as at present, to be recognized as a Divine Creation; but they can never be obliterated—thank God!

Fortunately for the human race, Nature is stronger than blind Proscription, and will eventually triumph over her enemy. In the present Reasoning Age of the World, all unnatural restraints upon human faculties and actions will be weakened by every new-born generation. And a very important change is near for the Silent Society. Already the gay young Quakers conceal their bright colors and pianos in the attics of their dwellings, after the older members of the family have become deaf and dim-sighted by years; and the Night only sees, and listens to their protest against proscriptive bigotry. But the day will soon be jubilant for them, with liberated song, and bright with the beautiful harmony of colors.

There is hope in the great progressive future for the Quakers. And yet, it is saddening, and even pitiful, to see the goodly company of Friends, sitting, year after year, on the hard benches of their plain Houses of Worship, crucifying the flesh, and wasting

38

the fire of the spirit, while praying for an illumination which can never bless their longing souls; because they have silenced so many of the inspirational qualities of the mind through which the Divine Father and Mother speak to their sons and daughters of Earth.   It is impossible for the Friends to receive aught, saving occasional and transcient gleams of light from above, so long as they set Man's munificently endowed nature aside, and seek for God's grace, while rejecting His natural gifts, which are the only legitimate channels through which it can be communicated to their souls.

How long must it be before the Christian Church of every name will learn the important truth that it is not Nature that requires to be subdued in Man; but the perversion of Nature, through ignorance, that needs correction, and the irrational use. or, rather, abuse of the faculties bestowed by Heaven.   Nature requires development, alone—opportunity.   EXCESSES are the bane of the human race and the corruptors of society; the antidotes of which are, Knowledge, Reason, and an enlightened Conscience.   Increase the light.   Cultivate the seeing faculties of human beings; instead of striving to destroy natural endowments, because evil sometimes results from the abuse of them. Men and women are often cut off in the midst of their years by a *coup de soleil;* and they frequently fall into the sea and are drowned;—would it not be folly to attempt to punish Nature for these accidents, by striving to drain the Ocean, or to strike the meridian Sun out of Heaven?   It were as easy to destroy the physical as the spiritual powers of the universe; and equally as wise to attempt to annihilate the one, as the other.   The Sun with its many beams, and the Sea with its numerous arms, are the great dispensers of light, heat, and moisture to the earth; and the heart and mind of Man with all their varied and associative faculties, bear a kindred relation to the moral world that the former bear to the physical—they are grandly renewing and vitalizing forces.

The most powerful agents of Heaven for good may be converted, by Ignorance, into the most fearful instruments of evil. But the fact, that evil *may* come of good, furnishes no rational argument for attempting to destroy the good; for that would prove an abortive effort to correct a lesser wrong by committing a greater. We must admit, indeed, that all evil is but the perversion of good, so long as we believe that God is the great positive Good of the Universe, and the Author of all things of earth and heaven. Evils are His monitors to the sons and daughters of men, to warn them that either they do not understand, or that they willfully disobey His Laws, and must beware of consequences.

And, since the Christian Church is not prepared to suggest to Deity any new and higher type of Man, male and female, than His own image and likeness—as recorded in the written Volume of Inspiration—let her be content to accept the human heart and mind as Infinite Wisdom and Infinite Love have created them; and seek to learn their highest laws of development and use, in order that she may be able to magnify the lives of her people and double their measure of usefulness and blessing.

Human Nature has borne, and is capable of bearing, a vast amount of ill treatment; for she has Protean power; if you snub her to-day, she will spring up to-morrow in some other form and laugh you to scorn. And she has an able Voucher for her ability to take care of herself, if you develop and let her go free—the Infinite God.

One would say, on viewing the Denomination of Friends at its religious meetings, attired in its plain dress, and adorned with its Sabbath-day countenance, chaste and meek, that it does not appear to be at all worldly-minded; and yet, no other Denomination of the Christian Church is more so, in verity. But its worldliness is peculiar to itself. It lives in a world of *drab*, within the world of colors, and there it wastes as much precious time, in the selection of a particular shade of drab by which to express its *degree* of renunciation of the outside world, as they waste who live in the latter, and adorn themselves with all the gorgeous colors of the rainbow.

The ostentatious display that this religious Sect makes of its spiritual attainments through the shades of its drab, and the cut of its garments, is an offensive reproach to other Denominations. If the Friend were more spiritually alive than other sects are, if it had more earnestness and zeal for truth and for the spread of the Gospel of Peace and Good-will to Man, than others have, its assumption of a holier and more useful life, through the externals of dress and color, would be the more excusable. But, alas! the Friend has the same greed of gold, and the same fondness for luxurious living, that other Sects manifest, and the same devotion to the external forms of worship, together with far greater *spiritual pride*, which is more hopelessly incurable than any other form of evil in the Christian Church. And, while this Denomination has the seeming of a broader and higher CHRISTIAN LEVEL than other Sects have, its social rules are equally as stringent as theirs, and its Christian Democracy quite as impeachable.

But, what saith the Spirit to the Church concerning this branch of her heritage? Thou has a few names, even in the Quaker Denomination, which have not defiled their garments; and they shall walk with me in white: for they are worthy.

THE METHODISTS.

He that hath an ear, let him hear what the Spirit saith unto the Church. I know thy works: behold, I have set before thee an open door, and no man can shut it: for thou hast a little strength, and hast kept my word, and hast not denied my name. To him that overcometh will I give to eat of the hidden manna, and I will give him a white stone, and in the stone a new name written, which no man knoweth, saving he that receiveth.

The Methodist Denomination enjoyed, for a long period of time, a higher degree of spiritual life than other Christian Sects. But, with the increase of numbers and of influence, it became, year after year, more and more sectarian, lukewarm and worldly; until it has at length formed, like other Denominations, a Procrustean Bed of Creeds, upon which all its members must be stretched, and dwarfed of their legitimate proportions of soul-growth and life.

In its early history this Sect depended upon the Inspirational Influences of the Holy Spirit for the success of its cause, rather than upon the ability and intelligence of its clerical body. And, then, its growth was marvellous, resembling the rapid increase of the early Christian Church, under similar inspirational influences. In later years it has put forth laudable efforts to educate its Teachers, and the youth of its congregations, and to attract men of mark to its pulpit, where the fire of genius once burned brightly, and still radiates light and soul-warmth ;—for Wesley and Whitefield " still live," and labor. In those immortal sons of God were united a great mind and heart, that were enriched by knowledge ; and they were filled with exalted enthusiasm for the Divine Gospel of Intelligent Nature, and with the dear Redeemer's burning zeal for the spread of its elevating truths over the earth: The glowing eloquence of their language took the people captive. Their inspired genius was truly electrical in its action, leaping from heart to heart and kindling the flame of devotion in the minds of the listening multitudes that thronged them for instruction.

The *inspirational life* of the Methodist Denomination has not kept pace with its increase in knowledge; which it should have done, in order to vitalize its formulæ of truth, and render it more effective for the regeneration of the soul, and for true progress in Christian principles. The consequence is, that this Sect tends more and more toward the externals of worship, and becomes more strongly bound by the special forms of its faith. For it is conscious of the loss of spiritual life, and seeks to supply the divine afflatus by stricter observance of the formulæ of its religion. And it demands a tangible creed, a plan of salvation that can be folded up, and put in the pocket, as a kind of *lien* on the life to come, and a security against death and judgment; or, that can be worn as a shield to ward off the attacks of opposing Sects.

The early assumption of plain dress by the Methodist, has also proved deleterious to its spiritual freedom and progress, by drawing lines which have become occasions of stumbling to weak-minded professors of religion; and which have the tendency to give importance to non-essentials of worship, and thus to lead the thoughts of the people still farther away from higher spiritual good.

The following relation of an interesting incident, bearing upon the subject, will serve to point our meaning. Two lady members of the Methodist branch of the Church, who had been intimate friends from childhood, and in the habit of sharing each other's joys and sorrows, listened one Sabbath evening to an able and eloquent discourse on practical Christianity. Mrs. A——— was of the severe style in dress and manners. She set her face as a flint against all human weaknesses, and all sins of both omission and commission, alike indiscriminately, as well as against all innovations upon the prescribed rules and habitudes of her Sect. Her friend Mrs B——— was quite the opposite in character and appearance, being remarkably graceful and affable, and uniformly cheerful and charitable.

Mrs. B——— was charmed with the sermon, and early Monday morning paid a visit to her friend Mrs. A———, in order that she might renew the enjoyment of the discourse by sharing it with her friend in review. "Dear Martha"—she exclaimed, on entering the dwelling of Mrs. A———, —"I am unusually glad to see you to-day! I could not wait patiently until breakfast was over, I was so desirous of hearing what you would say of that truly inspired sermon. For my own part, I never listened to a discourse so refreshing to my soul. Why, do you know it seemed to lift me above my own little self so entirely, that when the Speaker said with great earnestness: The fields are all white for harvest, but the laborers are few—I felt that it was a direct appeal to me, and could scarcely refrain from crying aloud—Dear Lord, send me forth to labor in thy vineyard—what wilt Thou have me to do? Oh! was it not really inspiring?"

"My dear Mary"—solemnly responded Mrs. A———, "I must acknowledge that I did not hear a single word of that sermon."

"Is it possible! How unfortunate! You must have been very ill; indeed, now that my attention is directed to your face, particularly, I see that you are not looking at all well to-day."

"I am quite as well as usual, be assured; but I must be frank with you, Mary—*you* were the cause of the trouble, you spoiled my sermon."

"I spoiled your sermon? I am greatly surprised, and unable to conjecture how it could be possible—please explain."

"I had resolved to go and tell you all about it, just as you entered the door. Well, as soon as I was seated in Church, I glanced over to your pew to see if you had come; and there you sat, like a Queen, in your rich furs, with an ostrich plume in your beaver, and your gold chain and amulets all shining in the light; and it came over me with a fearful foreboding, that your love of dress and show was a temptation of the Devil, and that it would cause you to backslide from grace, and lose your precious soul at last. And I could not help thinking also of the bad example that you are setting, by your worldliness, to the younger members of the Church; and so you see, dear Mary, that I could neither see, nor hear, nor think of anything else, all meeting time."

"Can it be possible! I do most sincerely wish, dear Martha, that you could really think and care as little about dress as I who am so unfortunate as to disturb your devotions. But, I fear that you will think my condition more hopeless than ever, when I tell you, truly, that dress is a part of my religion. Do not appear so shocked—listen—you will understand *why*, after I have related my experience on the subject. You will remember that I united with our society when very young. At that time, I was told by the older members that it became my imperative duty to adopt the plainest style of dress, in order to set a good example for others. I followed the advice for several years; but did not feel at ease, and in harmony with myself in the severe style of dress; and a very large portion of my time was occupied with the subject. It pained and humiliated me to find my thoughts so unprofitably engaged, when I really desired to become unworldly and useful, and to advance in the Christian life. At length I determined to investigate the question fully, to study dress as a principle, understand *why* I was constantly troubled about it, and remedy the evil if possible. After an earnest and careful review of the question, I came to the following conclusions;—that *dress* is simply a manifestation of NATURAL TASTES, implanted by Heaven ;—and that the uneasiness which I experienced, in reference to the subject, was attributable to the fact that I was continually opposing these natural tastes.   And I reflected farther that, as the Creator himself is the Author of these tastes, human beings have a moral right to their cultivation and enjoyment.   And, thenceforth, dress became a part of my religion."

" I have stated the proposition broadly.   Natural tastes must of necessity be modified in their expression, to a considerable extent, by the prevailing fashions of the day, and by the conditions and circumstances of the people.   But all persons exhibit marked peculiarities in reference to dress, which are inherited, and which do not result from the mere incidents or accidents of life and of fortune.   As an illustration of my meaning:—some men and women delight in all bright colors; others are better pleased with the various shades of drab.   Many fancy simple styles in the cut of garments ; others admire the more elaborate and ornamental.   Men and women of culture and refinement require fine textures in the materials of dress ; others, again, are equally contented with coarser fabrics.   Earnest and truthful persons cannot wear bogus jewels, laces, and inferior furs. such as please large numbers,—they prefer to go without either if they cannot possess the genuine articles.   And all are equally satisfied and at *rest* in regard to dress and appearance, who are able to conform most nearly to their peculiar tastes.

" I aim always to express in dress my highest idea of what is appropriate, beautiful and becoming in material, texture color and style, seeking to combine, as far as possible, economy, use and beauty.   At each season of the year, when it is needful to give attention to the subject, I devote a short time exclusively to dress; after my taste is satisfied, then I have no farther thought or care about my costume, saving when I attire myself for an occasion, and my attention is required in reference to selecting the most suitable apparel; then I experience a pleasing sense of fitness and harmony; for the reason that there is an accordance between the internal and the external, and my nature, in this respect, is correctly represented.   And, dear Martha, the Divine approaches very near to me in the beautiful, the harmonious, and the perfect, filling my whole being with unutterable peace and joy, and love."

It is not difficult to determine which of the two friends was nearer the Kingdom of Heaven, the one of the severe, or of the ornamental style of dress. If we take the Master's words as the guide of our judgment we must decide in favor of Mary ; for He declares that the Kingdom of Heaven is within the human soul. It is not a place; but a state of the affections and intellect in harmony, in reference to the truths of Intelligent Nature; it is a sweet repose of the spirit *at-one* with God.

The Methodists err greatly, also, in opposing the natural and innocent amusements of the young. But they do not pursue this blind policy alone. The Lutherans, Presbyterians, Congregationalists, Baptists, Quakers and Friends are equally guilty of perpetrating the same wrong against Nature. The Pulpit utters its voice against amusements ; the religious Press concurs, and reiterates the admonitions of the Pulpit. The Clerical Body of the Christian Church do not appear to understand that God has endowed the *genus homo* with many faculties of mind and heart beside those of either a purely religious or business nature ; and that human beings have as many needs as they present peculiar phases of character. They do not appear to comprehend, in verity, the philosophy of Human Nature, as manifested in the relation of the various faculties of heart and mind, and as exhibited, both in the simple and in the combined action of these powers. And they do not recognize the Divine Creative Mind in the *diversity*, as well as in the *quality* of these faculties ; neither do they see that the Revealed Will of God in Man requires the development of all human powers ; nor, that the most healthy condition of body and of mind, and, consequently, the highest human happiness, is alone attainable through the fullest exercise and unfolding of these powers ; nor, that it is only through the full play of them all that Man can become harmonious in himself, and, as a consequent, in truer relations with material and Intelligent Nature—*at-one* with God.

Diversion, with its attendant rest, is as useful as labor to the

39

human organism, to relieve over-tasked powers of body and mind, and enable the individual to adjust the complicated physical machinery and keep it in running order. If the grand motive powers of Intelligent Nature, heart and brain, are employed *too long* in any given direction, the parts thus abused become weakened thereby and incapable of healthy and vigorous action. Rest is quite as needful, after exhaustive mental effort, as after protracted physical exertion ; because the organs through which the mind acts are material and become fatigued by labor. And it is a well understood principle that, if one class of faculties have been long, or severly tasked, the brain will be relieved and rested by bringing another class into activity. But if a person permits himself to become so intensely absorbed in any pursuit that he will neither afford himself adequate physical rest, nor vary his occupation, in order that the equilibrium of his faculties may be restored ; then his mind will eventually react, and he will either turn with dread and loathing from the pursuit that he once loved, or become partially insane for a season, or imbecile and hopelessly demented. Some minds are so constituted that they can bear the pressure longer than others ; but an abnormal, kindred fate awaits all, at last, who neglect the required diversion and rest. The reaction will be in proportion to the strength of the natural powers and the pressure that has been placed upon them. And the brain will react in the direction of the most prominent qualities of the mind which have been held in check. The class of religious faculties form no exception to the general rule.

Those persons who have been endowed by Nature with large reasoning powers of mind which have been held subject during their childhood and youth to a religion of unquestioning faith, will react from it in their maturity, and become extremists in Rationalism, or Infidelity. If the spiritual quality of their minds be also large, they will react again, later in life, after maturer reflection, in the direction of the faith of their youth, and seek to reconcile Reason and Revelation in the elevated and enlarged spirit of Christian philosophy. The present age furnishes numerous examples in proof of the proposition.

A striking instance of the reactive nature of the human mind, which may serve the purpose of illustration, occurred not many years ago in the Western part of the United States. A " revival preacher" of the Methodist Denomination, who had been an itinerant lecturer for many years, and who was remarkable in the pulpit for earnestness and pathos, was addressing on one occasion an audience which was literally bathed in tears through the influence of his impressive and touching eloquence. At the highest point of excited interest, the Speaker suddenly paused—glanced a moment at his weeping congregation, and then recited, in tones of mirthful levity, the following snatch from Mother Goose's Melodies:

> High diddle, diddle!
> The cat played the fiddle!
> The cow jumped over the Moon!

After this novel *denouement*, the unfortunate man retreated behind his desk, presenting the most crest-fallen appearance imaginable to the amazed and indignant audience; for, they were dropped so suddenly from the height to which he had elevated them, that they experienced, mentally, the sensation of a humiliating fall. But the Speaker was more painfully affected than his hearers by this sudden revulsion of feeling. He felt that he was left a moral bankrupt, that he had lost his precious religion—lost his honored position in the Church—and lost his only means of subsistence, in one miserable moment of infatuation. But he did not see that he was suffering the penalty of a violated law. He had abused his religious faculties for years, had forced them up to an exalted point of action, and held them there by a determined effort of the will; reaction was the inevitable sequence. In the deep humiliation attendant upon loss of confidence in himself, from which he suffered more severely than from the reproaches of society, he believed that God had forsaken him suddenly and forever. His clerical brethren declared that the Devil had taken possession of him. The people, whose sympathies he had so often awakened, outraged in their most cherished and sacred sentiments, pronounced him a shameless hypocrite, and fancied that he had been amusing himself, through all the past years of his ministry, by playing upon their feelings.   And there were none to pity.

This man was naturally mirthful and humorous.   He possessed fine analytic powers of mind, and saw objects and principles in strong contrasts.   In early life it was his delight to surprise his associates with practical jokes, and covert humor.   After his mind became interested in religious subjects, he learned to believe that these natural qualities resulted from a frivolous and depraved nature, and determined to subdue them.   But Nature rebelled in his hour of mental exhaustion, and laughed at the impotency of the will to hold them longer in subjection.

We cannot fail to notice the provident care of Heaven, in endowing this unfortunate man with those lighter elements of character, to relieve the tension of serious thought, and lessen the stress of feeling; and, had not a false system of religious education prevented their legitimate expression, they would have aided him in preserving a nice equipoise of mind; and would not have reacted to cause their possessor to appear a ridiculous trifler with sacred subjects, and to destroy his character and usefulness.

A large proportion of the Denominations of Christendom cut themselves off from innocent amusements, fearing that it is sinful either to countenance, or to indulge in them; and that even a desire for such is the prompting of a depraved heart and mind. But, fortunately for mankind, Nature is stronger than Proscription; large numbers of persons will leap the barriers of unhealthy limitations, whenever the vigilant eye of the religious Monitor is turned away, and wander off to interdicted places of amusement, and to other fields of literature than those recommended from the consecrated Desk.

Works of romance and fiction have proved the salvation of many a member of the Clerical body, who has been over-tasked in one direction of thought, by relieving the tension of the brain and thus enabling it to recover its healthy action.   When Human Nature is better understood in our Schools of Divinity, the doors of the Opera and the Drama will be thrown open to the Christian Church; and then there will be less Sectarian *cant* than at present, and more of the earnest spirit of true devotion.

We do not wish the Reader to understand us to say, that these amusements will always inspire the religious sentiments of the Clergy and Laity; but, simply, that they will impart elasticity to the mind by leading it into fresh channels of thought, and broadening its human interests and sympathies. And after this expansion of the mind in new directions, and the attending rest of the religious sentiments, the relieved heart and intellect will return to the worship of the Creator with a richer glow of gratitude and love. And the members of the Christian Church will then have a clearer understanding of their relations to their fellow men, as children of the Universal Parent, as well as a nicer perception of the discrepancies between their profession and practice, as an Organized Body ; which will tend to stimulate the Church to higher and more consistent action.

It has always been the aim of the Clergy to keep the religious sentiments of the Laity at fever heat ; and this is one of the philosophical reasons for the reaction which has taken place in the Church, and its present cold and lifeless state. Amusements are as needful to impart animation and a healthy tone to the mind, as sunlight, air and exercise are to invigorate and preserve the vitality of the body.

And we must make a plea for the Dance, as well as the Song; because it, too, has been a prohibited recreation ; when it should have been introduced into our Public School, as an important part of the physical training of the young. It is a healthy, innocent and amusing exercise, which imparts both grace and agility to children, thus combining two desirable elements in their education—use and beauty. For, by the dexterous movement of the limbs, such as may be acquired in the dance, under skillful teachers. many physical difficulties and dangers may be overcome in after life. such as often attend the erratic course of adventurous youth. And, when dancing shall be generally taught in our Public School as a physical exercise, it will not be liable to the abuse of late hours, as it is at present, while regarded as merely a fashionable accomplishment. Grace of motion in the human form imparts to the observer a delight kindred to that experienced in looking upon soft, floating clouds, or the play of Ocean's waves ; and yet, the pleasure is deeper, inasmuch as intelligent beauty affects the mind more intensely than the passive loveliness and grace of inanimate Nature.

The old as well as the young should have amusements adapted to their requirements, if they would preserve the proper balance of their powers.   The members of the various learned professions will not ride as many *hobbies* to the grave, in the prime of their earthly existence, after the Christian Church shall have learned more perfectly Human Nature and its requirements.

But, while making an earnest plea in favor of amusements, we are aware that they are liable to be carried to *excess*, and thus lead to evil consequences ; and that, when such unfortunate results appear, they are then mis-named sinful ; when it is *not* the amusements which are wrong, but the EXCESSES attending their abuse, or misapplication.   And for this reason we call upon the Church to array her power against EXCESSES which curse society, and hold fast to innocent amusements which strengthen and bless.   All violation of law by over-action is. *excess*, and EXCESS IS SIN, whether it be in exhaustive physical exercise, or debilitating sensual indulgence, in either eating, drinking, or passion ; or whether it be in tasking immoderately any class of mental faculties ; because any of the varied powers of Man, stimulated to *excess*, prevent the normal action of his heart and mind, and unfit him for the perfect performance of the duties of life, and the true worship of the Divine Father and Mother God.

It has been said that Nature is stronger than proscription, and that many persons will leap unhealthy barriers, to indulge in needful amusement.   But, although stolen waters are sweet to the thirsting, and bread eaten in secret is pleasant to the hungry, yet, after the craving of Nature is satisfied, calm Reflection approaches closely to the soul, robed in the mantle of religious conservatism, and questions the troubled spirit if it be *right* to appease the craving of Nature with fruit plucked in forbidden paths. And the sensitive conscience, influenced by false religious teaching, will lift up its voice against the offender and cry: Thou hypocrite! And then follows a fearful conflict between the false and the true, while the poor afflicted one strives vainly to justify himself in the innocent amusement which he allowed.

If the Christian Church would not encourage hypocrisy in her members, let her lend her support to innocent amusements, such as spring from undepraved natural tastes, and are needful to preserve the healthty tone of the human body and mind. And let her place her proscriptions and anathemas where they belong, against the fearful EXCESSES that demoralize and ruin society; remembering that the reaction will always be in proportion to the restriction that she places upon her worshippers.

When the Christian Church becomes sufficiently enlightened to adopt a wise policy in reference to innocent amusements, her congregations will be larger, and her members far more earnest, healthy and happy; and then the Christian Religion will become attractive, instead of repellant, to the youth of the land.

We owe an apology to our Methodist brothers and sisters for this extended dissertation on amusements, just as we were on the eve of saying farewell. And, in parting, we would exhort them, in the temper of love, to Prove all things; hold fast that which is good; and to remember that, the letter killeth; but the Spirit maketh alive. We would beseech them to beware of the fatal snare of *forms*, in which the soul becomes entrapped that is not watchful and vigilant.

But what saith the Spirit to the Church concerning this branch of her heritage? Thou hast a few names, even in the Methodist Denomination, which have not defiled their garments ; and they shall walk with me in white; for they are worthy.

THE UNITARIANS.

He that hath an ear, let him hear what the Spirit saith unto the Church: I know thy works, that thou art neither cold nor hot; I would that thou wert cold or hot. Repent; or else I will come unto thee quickly, and will fight against thee with the sword of my mouth.

The Unitarian Denomination is the most liberal religious Sect of the age. And it is also more consistently Christian than other branch of the Church; for its practice harmonizes better with its profession. It has progressed beyond the Religion of Un-questioning Faith in Authority, of the Childhood and Youth of the Church and World; and claims to unite the understanding with the heart in the service of the Divine All-One. But, alas! its affections are, also, lukewarm; they do not fuse with fer-vent zeal and stimulate the intellect to effective action. It exer-cises more brain than heart in the worship of God. It needs Spiritual life and aspiration. It needs to be touched with a live coal from off the altar of Truth, that it may kindle, and glow, and be fully alive in the Humanitary work of the Mediative Son of God. And it needs, also, more faith; it requires to be-lieve that God is, and that he is the Rewarder of all who diligent-ly seek him, and will manifest himself unto such as he does not unto the world.

The Unitarian Sect is equally as ambitious of earthly honors and distinctions, equally as proud and worldly and irreverent to-wards Humanity, as other Christian Denominations; because. like them, it pays more respect to wealth and station than to Man and Woman as children of the Most High; or, to the promulga-tion of the elevating principles of the Christian Religion Like them, it carries the world in one hand, and the Gospel in the other. If it could vitalize society with the spirit of the Gospel, it were well; but, unfortunately, it conforms more to the temper of the World than to the Spirit of its Religion, and fails to im-press the former with the sublime principles of the latter. In very truth, this Denomination lacks vital, and vitalizing piety It does not grow in grace and in the knowledge and love of God in accordance with its blessed privilege.

We have said that this Sect is the most liberal and consistent of the age, because it admits of greater individual liberty of thought and action on religous subjects, than any other branch of the Christian Church; consequently. a larger Humanitary ser-vice is required of it. The exercise of broader Christian charity toward other sects is demanded; and more earnest, patient labor to undermine the prejudices and soften the asperities of differing Denominations of the Church; and thus to harmonize and prepare them for associate Humanitary action in the vineyard of the Lord. Ay, for the very reason that this Sect stands on a loftier plane of the understanding, and a broader platform of principles, and is less trammeled by creeds and sectarian authority, less bound by a traditionary religion, it is in a position to inaugurate more comprehensive movements than other sects, and to invite the co-operation of all Denominations in such movements.

But, unfortunately for the spread of Liberal Christianity, this sect is doing very little for the cause, compared with its ability and power. It is true that its example is worth something to the age, in that it has repudiated the purely affectional religion of the past, with its narrow and irrational theories concerning the nature and the relations of Man and of Deity, and concerning the present and future states of existence, and, in that it professes to unite the Reason with the Affections in the worship of the God of Reason and of Love; but it is so coldly ethic that it does not move the heart of the millions and attract them to the consecrated altars of the Most High. It permits the understanding to operate as a barrier to the affections; instead of a powerful aid, such as Reason should be when the subject is the most important in the interests of time and of eternity, and the highest motives can be presented that ever enlisted the heart and mind of Man. There is a radical mistake somewhere. These things ought not so to be.

The Unitarian Denomination professes to depend on the advancement of knowledge and reason in the world for the enlargement of its congregations ; and yet it is not engaged in enlightening the people in order to effect this desirable object. And, while it relies on the grand Philosophy of the Christian Religion to draw intelligent minds to its organizations, it presents no clear and comprehensive system of this profound Philosophy of Intelligent Nature to the inquiring Age.

The Unitarians are accused, by the professedly Orthodox Sects, of " rejecting the atonement of Christ, of denying the Lord who bought them with his precious blood," and of other irreverences and infidelities to " sound doctrine," which should deprive them of recognition by the Christian Church. And they

40

quietly remain under the ban. They fail to come forth to the
world and show, with burning and convincing eloquence, such as
will electrify the hearts and minds of the listening multitudes,
and energize their moral natures with regenerating power, that
mankind are saved from sin and its consequences, *by living the
life of the great Exemplar*, his life of good works, purity and love;
and that it is not by the *death*, but by the LIFE of Christ, that
Man and Women become *at-one* with God.

And the Unitarians are accused of teaching broad and diffusive generalities, which mean nothing to the unreflecting minds
of the millions, and fail to win either their attention, respect, or
adherence.   It is said that they have no standard truths, like
other religious sects, round which the people can rally and cry —
" Behold! these are my guides, my rules of life ; by these doctrines I fight the good fight of faith, and lay hold on eternal
life."   And it is true that this sect does not and cannot, from its
standpoint of Reason, present the same motives for the worship and love of God that Trinitarians present to the people.   It
can point to no material rewards and punishments beyond the
grave   It can simply set forth such compensations and consequences as result, as a sequence from the lives of the good and
evil here, and harmonize with their character and conditions
hereafter.   It can point to no Hell of scorching heat: " With
walls of fiery adamant, flaming high above all flight of hope,"
to terrify the hoary-headed sinner, and the weak and fearful, and
lead them to hasten into the fold of the Good Shepherd, in
order to escape from the wrath to come;—and no Heaven of
unbounded, sensuous delights, to attract the lover of the beautiful,
and the religious enthusiast, to run the heavenly race, and not
weary; and to walk the lofty heights of Zion, and not faint.

But the Christian Church requires, and the world requires, and
the Cause of Truth requires, that the Unitarian Sect should have
a more distinctive mark of its high calling of God, through
Christ Jesus.   It is its imperative duty to substantiate its claim
to the exalted position it has taken before the Church and World,
as the Liberal and Progressive Christian Denominiation.   It is
called upon to rise to the height of the great argument, and

show *why* the Christian Religion is adapted to Man ; and Man, to the Christian Religion; to show clearly, and forcibly that the Gospel of Christ, which is all embracing, is the profound Philosophy of Intelligent Nature ; and that the Mediative Son of the Godhead, Heaven's illumined Expositor of its sublime principles, is the great Spiritual, Intuitional-Intellectual and Harmonial God-Man—the Democratic Philosopher of the World, and the grand type-man of the Intellectual and moral ages;—for such is the Christian Religion in its fullness, and such is the wonderful man of Nazareth. Ay, the Gospel of Christ covers the whole ground of Human and Divine relations, and of the moral obligations attending these relations. It recognizes Man and Woman as children of the Divine Father and Mother God, thus establishing the holy and eternal brotherhood of Humanity. It would be impossible to present a clearer, fuller, and grander system of moral Philosophy to the heart and mind of Universal Man. And not until these elevated truths of Intelligent Nature are taught widely, and comprehended by the millions, can the Human Family properly understand their relations and obligations to Deity, and become, in verity, *at-one* with God; and not until then will the divine mission of the Mediative Son of the Godhead be fully accomplished.

Behold, now is the accepted time for the Christian Religion to be taught as a grand system of Philosophy, in order to attract and enlist the mind of the Reasoning Age ; behold, now is the day of salvation for the million. Materialistic Rationalism is at work in our very midst, rallying a host of scoffing infidels, and attracting large numbers of partial skeptics to its ranks from among those who have reacted from a religion of unreasoning faith in authority, and wish to take a definite position somewhere on a rational platform. But the latter class of persons are loth to leave the faith of their youth, (for Man is a religious being and and feels intuitively that, when he forsakes Religion, he becomes a moral bankrupt;) they stand at one side and call impatiently to the Church for help; they implore her, in accordance with the earnest exhortation of St. Paul, to render a reason for the faith that is in her, with which they may be able to satisfy the demands of their own nature, and answer the arguments of the opposers of Christianity. It is painful for them to accept Rationalism, a cold negation, in place of the Religion that they once loved. Yet, year after year, they are disappointed, and they become disheartened, and disgusted at length, and fall into the increasing ranks of Materialistic Rationalism ; for they receive from the Church the old-time response of melancholy, canting bigotry:—— " Great is the mystery of Godliness ! Human reason is not to be exercised on the profound subject of Christian faith."

" But what is Christian faith ?"——demands the troubled querist.

" Faith is an act of the soul made spiritually alive,"——replies the Church ; an explanation that requires more than the laborious efforts of an expositor to render clear to an uninitiated mind.

We are living in the transitionary period of the Reasoning Age of the World; and Reason, the great questioner, is everywhere wakening from the slumber of the physical ages of ignorance, and propounding vital questions to the Reverend Doctors of the law. Intelligent men and women can no longer rely implicitly on the authority of either the past, or present, or accept, as the ultimate of truth, a religion of unquestioning faith which they believe to be an irrational, patched up system of theology, handed down from the undeveloped Childhood and Youth of the World; notwithstanding the Church has stamped the seal of Revelation upon the mere *interpretation* of the sacred text by her chosen teachers. Tne *consciousness* of the enlightened mind that seeks after truth must at least approve, as rational, any principles which it is called on to accept as truth, if those principles are too deeply metaphysical to be submitted to the test of demonstrative argument. The God within impels the reasoning mind to seek " to know of the doctrine " that it is called on to believe.

The Trinitarian branch of the Christian Church is not yet prepared to treat philosophically the profound Religion of Intelligent Nature ; because it shrinks from viewing HIM with the eye of Reason, Whom it has been taught for ages to hide deep in the heart and adore as the supreme object of the affections. But with the Unitarians it is different ; they have been in the habit of worshipping the Creator with the reason, as well as the affections ; and it becomes their duty and sacred privilege to present the Christian Religion to the World as a comprehensive system, as the sublime Philosophy of Intelligent Nature. As soon as any Sect of the Christian Church is able to do this for the Christian Religion, then will the Mediative Son of the Godhead be again revealed in great power and glory ; for then will the FULLNESS OF THE GODHEAD, which he came to teach and to represent to the Human Family, be seen and accepted on Earth, even as it is in Heaven ; and the Church militant and the Church triumphant will rejoice together.

But it requires an INSPIRED MINISTRY, in order that the Unitarians, or any other Sect, may be able to do this work so effectively that the heart and mind of the World may be moved and warmed into fuller life by the re-presentation of the divine truths of the Gospel, by the Reason, and to the Reason of Man. For, if the Christian Religion is anything, it is inspirational. The illumined mind can alone throw light on the inspired text, can alone interpret correctly the Philosophy of Intelligent Nature, and reveal it to the World in all its fullness and sublimity, in all its depth, and breadth, and height of love and reason. The mistake has been, in every Denomination of the Christian Church, that it has had but few inspired teachers. For this inspirational power is the very essence of the Christian Religion, and the very substance of its philosophy. It is that divine principle of life which emanates from the central Heart and Mind of the Universe and outreaches to the circumference of Creation, permeating all things visible and invisible to Man. It is that divine principle of life in which the Human Family live and move and have their being, and that infills and overflows the Soul which is *at-one* with God, until the regenerated Son, or Daughter of Deity, becomes superior to all the accidents and misfortunes of life. They who seek earnestly to learn of God, fulfilling all the requirements of the Revealed Word to Man and the Revealed Will in Man, will receive a double portion of this inspirational principle ; for the Father giveth not His Spirit by measure unto them. But, while this inspirational principle is

41

the grand vitalizing power of the Christian Religion, it is the
most difficult part of its Philosophy to explain to those who have
not experienced its elevating influence. It is this that sustained
the early Apostles and Disciples of Christ under all their fearful
persecutions and sufferings, enabling them to rejoice in tribula-
tion.   It is this that sustained the glorious martyrs of Humanity
amid the cruel flames of the Stake, and under the agonizing
tortures of the Inquisition.   It is this that enabled our Pilgrim
Fathers and Mothers to leave their beloved home and country,
with all the comforts of advanced civilization, in order to establish a pure Church of God on the virgin soil of a New World,
and to endure, without complaint, cold, hunger, and hardship,
while surrounded by hostile Savage neighbors and ferocious
beasts of prey.   It is this that has overcome, in all ages of the
World, the impossibilities of uninspired men and women, and
endowed its possessor with power to go forth on His mission of
love to Man, from conquering and to conquer.

This inspirational principle has been, and must ever continue
to be, the cause of revivals in the Christian Church.   And, for
the reason that the fount of Inspiration is Infinite, and that all
who ask, in sincerity and truth shall receive the benediction of
Heaven ; and thus it is possible to produce revivals of religion,
even in the coldest seasons of the Church.   The Mediative Son
hath said :   Where two or three are gathered together in my
name, there am I in the midst of them.   And if a few earnest,
loving souls meet together, and pray for a more special out-pour-
ing of the Holy Spirit, the answer to prayer will soon be visible
in a gradual increase of numbers, until at length the whole community will be profoundly moved.   But the Church has yet to
learn how to attract, and use, the inspirational principle of its religion for the elevation and regeneration of the World.   This
power cannot come to the human soul through creeds and dogmas—it cannot come through an elaborate plan of salvation—it
cannot come through any form of Ecclesiastic Despotism-
There is a spirit in Man, and the inspiration of the Almighty
giveth understanding.

The Unitarians should not only prepare and send forth to the world a comprehensive system of the Christian Religion; but this Sect should also organize a broad Religio-Philosophical Society for the discussion of the Christian Religion as a comprehensive Philosophy, as the Philosophy of Intelligent Nature, revealing the true relations of man to man, and of Man to Deity, and the moral obligations attending these relations. And it should invite the most advanced minds of Christendom, outside as well as inside of Church organizations, to discuss these grand principles in popular language, adapted to the understanding of the millions. Such a society would ere long become more renowned than the Porch of Plato, or the Garden of Epicures; for all the nations of Earth would eventually be represented in it, and become profoundly interested speakers and listeners.

The Unitarian Denomination of the Christian Church should also organize a Liberal Society of its own order in every city of the enlightened world, and attach to the principal congregation of each city a branch of the Religio-Philosophical Society, for the discussion and dissemination of the Christian Religion as the Philosophy of Intelligent Nature. It is the imperative duty of this advanced Sect, to hold the ear of the age attentive to the sublime and elevating principles of Christian Philosophy. Its Leaders should stand on the outer walls of Zion, and proclaim to all creed-bound Sects of every Nation under Heaven, the glorious watch-words of GOD'S CHURCH UNIVERSAL—UNION! LIBERTY! LOVE!—Love to God and Love to Man.

At present, the Unitarian Denomination, while enjoying greater freedom from doctrine and dogma, and greater liberty of thought and action than the Trinitarian Sects, is equally as far removed as they from true Christian Democracy, and, consequently, fails with them to attract the millions to the fold of the Good Shepherd.

But what saith the Spirit to the Church concerning this branch of her heritage? Thou hast a few names, even in the Unitarian Denomination, which have not defiled their garments; and they shall walk with me in white: for they are worthy.

THE NEW JERUSALEM SOCIETY.

He that hath an ear, let him hear what the Spirit saith unto the Church: Behold, I come quickly : hold fast that which thou hast, that no man take thy crown. Him that overcometh will I make a pillar in the temple of my God, and he shall go no more out: and I will write upon him the name of my God, and the name of the city of my God, which is NEW JERUSALEM, which cometh down out of Heaven from my God: and I will write upon him my new name.

The NEW JERUSALEM Denomination bears a very important relation to Christendom, as a Pioneer Organization of the Church of the second Christian Era, or Age of Reason.

It has been said, in a former chapter of the present work, that the New World was opened, in the wisdom of the Divine Councils, for the introduction of the New Era of the Second Advent of the Mediative Son of God to the Reasoning Age of the World; and, also, that Swedenborg was the chosen instrument of Heaven to prepare the way before the inspired Philosopher of Nazareth, and to inaugurate, in the early dawn of MAN'S AGE OF REASON, the Church of the Second Advent, on the higher plane of the understanding.

And Swedenborg was eminently qualified for the exalted mission to which he was called of Heaven. In his theological works he shows clearly to the reasoning mind of the World, by a chain of comprehensive argument, drawn from the truths of Nature and Revelation, the unity of all things of earth and heaven; —that the Spirit-Sphere is the world of Cause; and the material, the world of Effects;—and that, as all things in physical nature were projected from the Creative Intelligence of the world of Cause, and were the product of intelligent thought, they must, therefore, have been created spiritually before they were ultimated in material forms; and, consequently, must have a spiritual significance, each creation corresponding to an eternal truth of the heavens. And he shows farther, that Man and Woman are children of this Creative Intelligence, being endowed with like attributes of mind and heart with the All-Parent, differing only in degree, by which attributes they are capable of acquiring, in progressive order, an understanding of the laws which govern all things of earth and heaven, as they grow in grace, and in the knowledge, wisdom and love of the Divine, through interminable ages; and, finally, that the earth is but a vast Cathedral in Nature, where they commence to learn of God through the great law of adaptive intelligence.

And from these premises Swedenborg draws the logical conclusion, that a knowledge of the laws of the Creator, throughout animate and inanimate Nature, and intelligent and loving obedience to them, is the true Religion of the God of Nature ; and that such is the Christian Religion in its comprehensive significance;—Love to God, and Love to Man, being the required worship of the human heart, and knowledge of and obedience to law, the required service of the human mind. And this view of the subject accords perfectly with the teaching of the Mediative Son of God. And he shows clearly, as a consequent of this truth, that the Christian Religion will become universal infullness of time, when the knowledge of God shall fill the earth.

This great Philosopher states, in an earnest and masterly style, that in view of Man's near relation to the Supreme Author of existence, and to the spiritual and material Worlds of His creation, and in view of Man's adaptation to the knowledges of animate and inanimate Nature,—it becomes the duty of the Human Family to seek devoutly to learn of God, through material and intelligent Nature, as well as revelation; in order that they may be able to conform their lives to the Divine Laws of all things; or, in other words, that they may become intelligent, scientific worshippers of the God of Heaven and of Earth.

Swedenborg shows plainly that worship of Deity with the heart, or affections, merely, is but partial service ; that it is heat without light, zeal without knowledge; and that affection and zeal without intelligence is blind and brutish ; because it will seek to protect what it loves by destroying anything which may appear inimical to it, without either reflection, or mercy ; as the

history of the Youthful, or Heroic and Affectional Age of the
Christian Church, affords striking and painful illustration :—while
in the intelligent, scientific worship of God, conjoined with the
affect'ons, there is light—as well as heat—to broaden and extend
the vista of truth, and reason, to lead the sons and daughters of
time along the illumined way.

And this great Apostle of the New Era of Reasoning Christianity exhorts the Church to leave the former Youthful paths of
unquestioning faith in authority, in the lowlands of creeds, and
ascend the higher planes of the understanding which stretch forward and upward to the glorious world of Cause ; and to go
forth with revived affections, and with renewed strength in the
God-like power of REASON, questioning of all things of Earth
and Heaven :—

" Where shall I find HIM? Angels, tell me WHERE ?"

There is no evidence in the theological writings of Swedenborg that it was his intention to establish a Religious Sect that
should bear his name.   It appears to have simply been the aim
of this truly inspired Teacher to render a higher interpretation
of the Revealed Word than had obtained in the past, to explain
its interior significance, and to show its harmony with itself, and
with all truth ; and so to stimulate the intellect of the Church
to grasp broader pirnciples of the Christian Religion, and to
accept spiritual things with understanding hearts.   And he
sought earnestly to purify the Church of old errors of doctrine ;
and to energize its heart and mind and rekindle its inspirational
power.   Swedenborg demonstrates the truth of his statements,
concerning the glorious reality of the communion of saints, and
of eternal life beyond the grave, by his own mediumistic experiences.

We have made a running review of the Religious Philosophy
of this inspired Apostle of Christianity, in order to show the
stand-point of the Swedenborgian Society of to-day, and its relation to the Church of the Reasoning Age.   The members of
this Body of Christians profess to unite the intellect and affections in the worship of the All-Parent.   But they are, unfortunately, quite as Sectarian as other Christian Denominations, and

not more spiritually alive than they. For, while gazing with admiring awe on the colossal intellect of Swedenborg, and striving to come into rapport with his elevated mind, they lose sight of the broad humanitary spirit of the Christian Religion, and the practical obligations which it imposes. Hero worship is unfavorable to growth in grace and in the wisdom and love of God. Its tendency is to limit the human mind to particular phases of truth, and prevent its expansion into comprehensive and universal principles. All love and veneration is due to so exalted a character as Swedenborg ; and it must be admitted that he is the representative man of the New Christian Era of Reason : but it should not be forgotten that principles are greater than persons. When one loses himself in another's mind, although that mind may be far in advance of the age in which he lives, in many directions of thought, he will sometime feel himself circumscribed by human boundaries beyond which he cannot reach ; but, when one loses himself in principles, he expands without a barrier into the infinite of truth, while consciously enjoying the measureless freedom of THE GOD.

The Swedenborgians, viewed as a Sect, are concentrative, rather than diffusive in their religious character and action. This peculiarity is partly due to their habits of reflection and investigation, which are acquired by turning their attention to internal, instead of external phases of truth; and, partly, to the fact that they are, comparatively, a new Sect, occupied with new views of the Christian Religion, and have not yet been able to pause in their researches into the arcana of truth, and to look forth upon the broad fields of Humanitary labor, and take observation of their vantage ground in reference to other Sects; and thus to note the increased responsibility which their peculiar relation to the Christian World imposes on them. And, because they are still rallying round their beloved Leader, and their outlook from the mountain of Zion is not broadly and grandly Humanitary, they are timid and fearful. They are concerned for Swedenborg's standing in society. They are afraid that HE will be classed with modern spiritualists, or modern spiritualist with him, and that their *cause* will suffer injury. So long as they fear, they will be weak. It is only the courageous in the cause of right, those who have undoubting faith in God and his government, and the final triumph of truth over error, who are strong and invincible; they go forth, clad in the whole armor of God, to glorious achievement.

During the present transitionary period from the Youth to the Maturity of the Church and World, the conservative and radical forces of Intelligent Nature are vigorously at work, and there is everywhere, and will continue to be for a long time in the future, sudden and startling reactions from old principles to new—and the reverse of the proposition, depending on conditions, and the pressure of coming events. And the conservative and radical forces of the age are strongly manifested among the various Denominations of the Church of God. Many are already reacting, from unquestioning faith, to Rationalism and positive infidelity; while others are becoming more and more conservative, and are returning in large numbers to the bosom of the " Mother Church," the Autocrat of Christendom. And the reaction will become stronger and stronger, and will influence larger numbers of the Church, sweeping entire organizations away from their former stand-points of doctrine.

And these radical and conservative forces are already at work in the New Jerusalem Society, producing divisions, and reorganizations, unfavorable to the temporal prosperity of its people. This condition indicates that, notwithstanding its advanced position of intelligence. as a religious Body and its greater spiritual freedom, compared with other sects, there is still much of the old leaven of subserviency to creeds and forms, remaining among its members. If it were not so, there would be no divisions. Because reason and intelligence, stimulated by Christian love, tend to unity in diversity, and to produce the perfect harmony. These God-like powers of the human soul agree to disagree in regard to non-essentials of faith and practice, but to unite broadly and grandly on the divine principles of Wisdom and Love.

We deeply regret, for the sake of example and influence, that this Pioneer Society of the New Christian Era of Reason does not bear the perfect fruit of Spiritualistic Rationalism. Its name

—New Jerusalem Society—challenges the attention of the outside world. It seems to say:—Behold, I show you a more excellent way! And earnest seekers after truth turn to look with inquiry and hope. They regard it closely, to note if it *be* more consistently Christian than other Denominations of the Church. But, alas! they observe that, while it has a name to live, it is also dead.

The New Jerusalem Society should stand as a city set upon a hill, whose firm foundation cannot be shaken, and whose light, shining in constellated glory, sends its cheering radiance far down upon the plains and valleys below, toward whose illuminated height the Chistian Church and World may look, and renew their faith in immutable principles, during the general upheaval of old forms of religions, and of civil despotism, which must inevitably attend the advancing march of Knowledge and Reason. And then, in its brightly shining light, the Church would be able to see more clearly her true position in relation to spiritual truths, and the principles of Science; and in relation to the Second Advent of the Mediative Son of God and Son of Man to the Reasoning Age; and be able to reconcile Reason and Revelation, and reconstruct the Christian Religion on the higher plane of Philosophy.

And when the Church shall be able to take a comprehensive view of the Gospel of Intelligent Nature, then, instead of being a narrow-minded bigot, as in her Youth, desecrating the most holy things of God, through an unregenerate self-hood, and zeal without knowledge, she will be wise and broadly humanitary; will become, in verity, like the Democratic Philosopher of Nazareth, SPIRITUAL, INTUITIONAL-INTELLECTUAL and HARMONIAL; her mind and soul will be open to the influx of scientific as well as of spiritual principles, and she will receive, in the profound calm of her spirit, *at-one* with God, the divinest truths of Nature, and send them freely forth to enlighten and bless mankind, as a benediction of Heaven.

It has been said that the Swedenborgians are the Pioneer Sect of the New Christian Era of Reason, in which the Gospel of the Mediative Son of God will be recognized as the compre-

42

hensive Philosophy of Intelligent Nature; and that the principles of this Gospel are the purest Democracy, being equally applicable to the highest and lowest classes of society, and its obligations alike binding on all the members of the great Human Family, as children of the Divine Father and Mother God. And yet, they are as far removed from the true "leveling up" Christian Democracy, as either of the other Christian Denominations.

But what saith the Spirit to the Church concerning this branch of her heritage? Thou hast a few names, even in the New Jerusalem Society, which have not defiled their garments; and they shall walk with me in white: for they are worthy.

CHAPTER V.

For as we have many members in one body, and all the members have not the same office : so we, being many, are one body in Christ, and every one members one of another.

Awake, thou that sleepest, and arise from the dead, and Christ shall give thee light.

Reader, having taken a running view of the prominent Denominations of the Christian Church, and shown how they appear to an earnest looker on in Christendom, in relation to the Revealed Word of God to Man and the Revealed Will in Man ; let us now consider the Church as a whole, and try her spiritual life still farther by the principles which she professes to believe, applying the test of vital Christianity which the Mediative Son of God himself gave to his disciples when he sent them forth on the sublime mission of Christianizing and elevating the whole Family of Man. " Go ye into all the world and preach the Gospel to every creature: These signs shall follow them that believe; in my name shall they cast out devils; they shall speak with new tongues; they shall take up serpents; and if they drink any deadly thing it shall not hurt them ; they shall lay their hands on the sick and they shall recover."

The Church professes to believe that her Religion is a Revelation from Heaven, introduced to the world and established by wonderful miracles, and remarkable Spirit manifestations, and power; and that this Spirit-life and power have been the peculiar inheritance of God's people in every age, and that they attend the spread and growth of Christian principles as a natural, or logical sequence. The Church teaches, through all her Denominations, that God is an ever-present Deity, the Creator and the Sustainer of all things of earth and heaven; and that He fills all animate and inanimate nature with His presence; and, that in Him we live, and move, and have our being; and that He hears and answers the earnest prayer of His children, imparting freely spiritual life and inspirational power to such as truly seek to be filled with the Holy Spirit.

But, there is marvellous discrepancy between that which the Church professes to believe and teach, and her real faith and practice in relation to spiritual truths. And she presents, in consequence, a strikingly inconsistent character to the world. While she clings to the spiritual facts of the past, she rejects those of the present that are of kindred character and power, and manifestations of the natural growth of spiritual principles in the world. And she quotes St. Paul, as the highest authority in the Church and the clearest expounder of the Christian Religion, when she wishes to teach a doctrine, or enforce a dogma; but repudiates, altogether, the earnest exhortation of this Apostle to the Church to seek after spiritual gifts.

Listen to St. Paul: Now there are diversities of gifts, but the same Spirit. And there are differences of administrations, but the same Lord. And there are diversities of operations, but it is the same God which worketh all in all. But the manifestation of the Spirit is given to every one to profit withal. For to one is given by the Spirit the word of wisdom; to another the word of knowledge by the same Spirit; to another faith by the same Spirit; to another the gifts of healing by the same Spirit; to another the working of miracles; to another prophecy; to another discerning of Spirits; to another divers kinds of tongues; to another the interpretation of tongues. Follow after charity and desire spiritual gifts, but rather that ye may prophesy. But the great Apostle of the Gentiles wisely advises the Christians of his Era to exercise caution in their investigation and use of Spirit manifestations and power; to TRY THE SPIRITS, to see what manner of Spirit they are of; to Prove all things and hold fast that which is good.

There is no liberty in the Chrsitian Church of to-day for the exercise of these spiritual gifts which are our dear Redeemer's own tests of Christian life and faith. And they who are endowed with such gifts guard them carefully from their brethren for fear of misapprehension, persecution and reproach ; instead of using them freely for the spread of truth, and the benefit of those less favored of Heaven.

The Church constantly exhorts her members to attain spiritual growth. and newness of life in Christ Jesus ; but she is startled out of her proprieties when she witnesses the manifestation of this spiritual life among them. Alas! there is no true freedom in Christ within Denominational enclosures, and no broad Christian charity. When an earnest disciple of the Mediative Son of God seeks to cast out devils in his name, if he do not follow the prescribed form of his special order in the work, he is forbidden and castigated ; and no Christ-man is near to say to the blind bigots of sect--Forbid him not.

And the Church not only denies to her individual members freedom to manifest the gifts of the Spirit, to which she exhorts them to attain ; but she presents the curious anomaly of denying the logical results of her own principles—the spiritual growth and fruit of a spiritual Religion. And, it is in consequence of this false position of the Church of to-day, that the spiritual life of Chrlstianity is obliged to manifest itself outside of her Organizations, as in the early days of the first Christian Era ; for the spiritual fruit of centuries cannot be obliterated, even although the Body that nurtured its growth become its most violent antagonist. At that period of the Second Advent, when the Mediative Son shall be again " Revealed" in power and great glory, there will be grander manifestations of the Spirit than the world has ever witnessed ; because there will be a fuller preparation of the hearts and minds of the people to perceive and accept spiritual light and truth from above. And the inspired prophecy concerning the Second Advent of Christ in the Reasoning Age of the World, and the wonderful Spirit power that shall attend that event, will be fulfilled in its appointed time, although the Church should declare against it from every pulpit in the land.

It shall come to pass, saith God : I will pour out of my Spirit upon all flesh : and your sons and your daughters shall prophesy, and your young men shall see visions, and your old men shall dream dreams : And on my servants and on my handmaidens I will pour out in those days of My Spirit ; and they shall prophesy.

The prophetic hour has come.   The marvellous working of the Spirit is visible in the startling phenomena of the times. The grand preparation of Heaven and Earth for His coming is going rapidly forward.   Lo ! the Mediative Son is near, even at the door.   Listen to his loving call to the children of Earth : Behold, I stand at the door, and knock : if any man hear my voice and open the door, I will come in to him, and will sup with him, and he with me.   But, alas! the Church is deaf, and cannot hear the voice of the Good Shepherd ; she is blind, and cannot see the indications of his near approach to his people ; because she is cold and lifeless in her trammeling forms.   While she adheres to the LETTER of the Gospel, she repudiates the SPIRIT that maketh alive, that imparts the power of hearing and of vision.

The Church not only ignores the foundation of her faith, Spirit manifestation and power, denying the possibility of *the signs* which the Mediative Son himself declares shall follow those who truly believe ; but she pronounces the wide-spread spirit manifestations of the present, that are kindred with those that HE enumerates, to be all of the devil.   And she publicly denounces the Mediums of these manifestations, declaring them to be either deluded, or insane, or imposters, men and women of the baser sort ; and does so without discrimination and judgment, and without, in verity, any regard to the facts in question, while possessing no reliable knowledge of their mental and moral states.

Both branches of the Christian Church, Romanists and Protestants alike, denounce the Spirit Phenomena of the present, in the strongest terms of disapprobation.   The Protestant Clergy lecture against them, and write un-Scriptural tracts, warning the people to beware of the delusion, in the best approved *rationalistic* style of the day.   The Pope issues his bulls, declaring them to

be wholly of the devil, and forbidding his people to have anything to do with them. The Roman Catholic Priesthood have
always claimed the exclusive right to spiritual gifts, and to the
power of working miracles: and they do not like to see their
influence weakened. For they understand full well, that, when
laymen and the outside world can exercise the same power,
Othello's occupation will be gone—the Priest will no longer be
the Oracle of the people.

Certes, the rod of Moses, the rod of the inspired prophet of
God, has changed hands; and the Church of to-day holds the
wand of the magicians and conjurors; and she cannot do "so"
with her enchantments, as the true servants of the Divine work
miracles, outside of Church Organizations; because she has lost
her spiritual life and power. The Laocoon, writhing and expir-
ing in the tightening folds of the serpents, is a fitting emblem of
the Christian Church of the present, bound by her network of
creeds, trammeled by the *letter* that killeth. The *creed!* the
CREED! has proved a more formidable enemy to her progress in
spiritual truth, than all the Satanic forces that have opposed her
advancement.

We are aware that it is essential in all new organizations that
the governing principles of such should be presented to the mind
of the people in formulæ, in order to meet the needs of the less
enlightened, and to be deliberately scanned and carefully assimi-
lated. But there is a strong tendency in the human mind to con-
serve its formulæ of faith. Mankind are prone to conclude that,
what they have accepted to-day as sound doctrine, is the ultimate of truth in its particular direction; instead of *one round* only
of the ascending ladder that rests upon the Throne of the Invisible, the Infinite of knowledge, wisdom and love.

And this condition of the popular mind renders it the more
needful that Christian Teachers should stand on an *eminence of
principles*, independent of formulæ, in order that they may be
able to point out the true path of progress to the people; instead
of being corralled with them in the enclosure of creeds, to become blind leaders of the blind.

All truth that the human mind assimilates, enlarges it, and increases its capacity to receive more and more. But if the mind continue to be bound by the *special form*, after the spirit of the truth has been incorporated in the growth of the soul; and if it continue to look backward to Traditionary Religion for Light, instead of forward in the direction of Inspiration, then its vision will be narrowed to a point, by a law of mental as well as physical perspective, and it will be unable to see its own advanced position. And such is the case with the Church of to-day; and she is consequently unprepared to meet the results or growth of Christian principles in the World.

The Hebrew Church was in this condition when the Messiah came to stamp the closing seal on the First Dispensation of Law and Authority, and to break the seal of the Second Dispensation of Love and Free-Will to Man; and to lead the Children of Israel, once more, out of the wilderness of forms and ceremonies into the King's highway of truth and love—into the glorious liberty of the CHILDREN OF GOD But they were bound by the creed of the Fathers, and would not listen to the voice of their Leader. The Christian Church of the present is looking forward as anxiously for the Second Advent of the Mediative Son of God, as the CHOSEN PEOPLE looked for his first coming: To restore again the kingdom to Israel. And, like them, she looks not in the direction of coming, but of receding shadows.

Were our dear Redeemer himself to stand in any pulpit of the Christian Church, on any Sabbath morning, and cry aloud to his professed disciples in the impressive language of Inspiration, would he find faith on earth ? I tell ye, nay, but rather derision. Thinkest thou, Christian Reader, that Christ would be recognized as the Mediative Son of God, and received with joyful, loving hearts by his people, were he to address them in the following words ? I am he that liveth, and was dead ; and behold I am alive forevermore, Amen. All power is given to me in heaven and in earth. Come unto me, all ye that labor and are heavy laden, and I will give you rest. He that cometh to me shall never hunger ; and he that believeth on me shall never thirst ; and he that cometh to me I will in no wise cast out. Would he find faith on earth ? Alas, no ! he would be ignominiously expelled from the pulpit and the altar, dedicated to the Gospel that he died to establish on earth ; the Police would be called upon to take charge of the disturber of Religious Worship. For there is not enough spiritual perception left in the Church to discern that which is of the Spirit, and to bear witness—this is the *very* Christ. Again it would be written : He came unto his own, and his own received him not. And the sorrowful drama of the past would be re-enacted in the Church of the present. Ay, the great Democratic Philosopher of Nazareth would be crucified in the House of his friends.

One of the most prominent reasons for the inconsistent action of the Church is, that her gaze is intently fixed on the past, and she is psycologized by the dwindling point in the distance. And thus she is unable to observe the growth of spiritual truth in the world ; and to note, in the increasing light of the present, the brightening dawn of Humanity's day, of the Second Advent of the Mediative Son of God to the Reasoning Age of the Church and World. But were she able to look forth from higher and broader planes of principles, in the direction of cause and effect, she would not fail to behold the shadows of coming events that are projected upon the opening pathway of the future.

But it is not easy for individuals, nor for collective bodies of men and women, who have been bound by *special forms* of doctrine, from childhood to maturer years, to break away, at once, from their entanglements. Indeed, they are rarely able to comprehend their peculiar condition, which is the first essential thing to understand before they can be prepared to enjoy the liberty of the Children of God, for the reason that the clasping tendrils of belief are intangible. But the loving and pitying Angels see how unsymmetrical the human soul becomes in a network of creeds, and how torpid and lifeless the Church of God is to-day. And they see that she has lost the attractive power of her Christian Democracy, which is adapted to the nature of Man, and can no longer draw the people to the fold of the Good Shepherd.

Alas ! that the Christian Church of the Reasoning Age of the World, has yet to learn this essential thing, that God's truth is not sectarian, but universal. Let the Church arise and lay

43

aside her sectarian garments, even as a Mother lays aside the tiny robes of her infant children, to show to coming generations how limited were her ideas of the Gospel of Love before she grew into the full stature of men and women in Christ Jesus.

Awake thou that sleepest and arise from the dead, and Christ shall give thee light.

CHAPTER VI.

MORMON.

*Because judgment against an evil work is not executed speedily,
therefore the heart of the sons of men is fully set in them to do evil.*

There is a monster evil in the very heart of Christendom, that
causeth the ear of every true man and woman that heareth thereof to tingle.   And the Christian Church is responsible for its existence, and continuance.

Why, think you, earnest Reader, that Mormon, that moral ex-
cresence, that unscrupulous Ecclesiastic Parasite, could have
have fastened himself upon a *live* Christian Church, in the enlightened nineteenth century, and not have been cut off, at once,
with the dissecting sword of God's truth, if the Church had not
been cold and lifeless?   A thousand times, No !

Let us look this Mormon Reprobate in the face and study his
lineaments.   Alas ! we cannot fail to perceive that he is the
legitimate offspring of the corrupt Christian Church; and are
compelled reluctantly to acknowledge the relation.   The Church
has wandered after Gods of gold, and of silver, and of sense, and
forsaken the only living and true God of Heaven and Earth ;
and Mormon is the corrupt fruit of her unholy prostitution.   We
cannot shirk the odious truth.   The pure and true Bride of
Christ could never have produced this grossly licentious Religion-
ist, this striking caricature of the Christianity of the age.

We make the confession with shame and confusion of face.
But we must meet the logical sequence of operating principles

in Christendom.   If the reader will observe carefully the peculiar character and claims of the Mormon he will see more clearly his relation to the parent Church of to-day.   For the Mormon claims, with the Roman Catholics and with the Episcopal Catholics, to be the only true Church of God on earth.   And he professes, with the Orthodox denominations, to " Take the Scriptures of the Old and New Testaments for a rule of life."   Thus he has taken the stand-points of the various Christian Denominations.

Mormon delights more particularly in the Old Testament; because he finds through its pages stronger excuse, in the *habits* of the ancient people, for indulgence in sensual pleasures.   For he is not engaged in learning the Higher Law of justice and mercy, purity and love, enforced by the holy Commandments of either the Old or the New Dispensation, in order to know how to conform more fully to the Divine requirements; but he is occupied in scanning the Bible historically, in noting the peculiar social habits and practices of the ignorant and sensual Children of Israel, during the darkness of the physical ages, before they were redeemed from barbarism.   And he turns from the survey of those times of blind, unreflecting ignorance, with an air of self-gratulation, to speak with the voice of an oracle to the reasoning nineteenth century, declaring triumphantly to the Nations —as though he had discovered some new and grand principle in ethics for the speedy elevation of the World—that the "Chosen People " of Heaven were intended by Jehovah to be the Exemplars of mankind, and that their social system is worthy of all imitation.   And the Mormon practices, accordingly, all the sins of those undeveloped Children of the Physical ages of the World.

Is Mormon unlike the Christian Church of the present in this particular phase of character ?   Is she not engaged in studying the History of the Children of Israel ; instead of the holy Commandments for the regulation of human conduct ?   And does she not also quote the practices, recorded of Israel when he was a barbarian, in defense of her own wrongdoing?   And is she not engaged in searching the Scriptures of both the Old and New

Testament in order to learn how far she may indulge in wrong, in sensual pleasure, and in injustice toward other members of the Human Family, and yet escape the penalty of the Divine Law?—instead of searching the Scriptures for the purpose of learning her whole duty to God and Man, of learning how to walk more closely in the footprints of the dear Redeemer, and to elevate the standard of eternal justice, purity, and love on Earth? Ah! by so doing the Cnurch trails the Christian Banner in the dust, and crucifies the Mediative Son of God afresh, pntting him to open shame.

Let us glance at the recent record of the Church. Not many years ago the English branch of the Church of God declared to the Nations, through the reverberating thunders of her artillery, that it was consistent with " Christian Practice" to *force* the OPIUM TRADE upon China ; and, at a vast expenditure of capital that might have been profitably employed in public works and improvements, and have provided renumerative occupation for God's starving poor ; and, worse than all, at a fearful waste of human life and capability which might have been conducted into avenues of friutfulness and blessing.

A few years later the German branch of the Christian Church became excited in reference to the use of another injurious narcotic, and engaged in its defense with the weapons of intellectual argument. A Diet of the officials of the Church was convened, to examine the *morale* of the question ; and, after elaborate discussion, the Diet announced to the World that the USE OF TOBACCO was consistent with "Christian Practice." And the people continue to roll this noxious weed of sin, as a sweet morsel, under their tongue. And, yet, the members of this representative Body of the Church were aware of the following *facts*, at the very moment that they so decided the question : namely, that persons addicted to the use of Tobacco are, to a greater or less extent, injured by the habit. They were aware that excess attends it, and that morbid cravings displace natural tastes, which demand, in the absence of Tobacco, other stimuli more injurious and fatal in their consequences to the physical constitution; and that the Moral Sentiments of persons who use the article to excess, become weakened and callous, the governing powers of Reason and Will subjected, and the equilibrium of the mind destroyed; and, finally, that Human Beings, with all their Heaven-endowed powers and Godlike attributes, degenerate into the mere slaves of sense—slaves of a poisonous Weed ! And that Diet were aware that a man, enslaved by Tobacco, will purchase the fascinating poison with his last penny, even while his children are hungry for bread, and will steal the small pittance the miserable Mother has earned to keep them from starving, to gratify the morbid craving of his inexorable Master.

Verily, verily, it is a saddening commentary on the Christianity of the age, that, under such circumstances, the Church should pronounce the use of Tobacco to be consistent with " Christian Practice."

At the same time that the branches of the Church in England and Germany were thus actively engaged in disseminating poisons among the nations ; the branch of the Church in the Southern section of the United States of North America, composed of various Denominations, were preparing to defend Slavery at the point of the bayonet. The Pulpit was actively at work with wire-pulling politicians, to break down Democratic Institutions, which were the natural outgrowth of Christian principles ; all the while calling themselves *the* Democracy, in order to deceive the trusting millions ; when they were, in verity, absolute Autocrats and Aristocrats. And many clergymen, of the Pulpit, North of " Mason and Dixon's Line," recreant to God and Humanity, combined with the corrupt press of both sections of our Country, for the avowed purpose of presenting Slavery to the enlightened age as a Divine Institution !—adducing arguments to sustain the monstrous proposition from the practices of a barbarous people. Watchmen on the Walls of Zion employed the Soldiers of the Cross in distributing Tracts among the millions, whose leaves were not for the healing of the Nations. A contagious moral malaria followed the lead of their weak, sophistical arguments, addressed to the religious prejudice of weak-minded men and women, and many became

converts to their miserable subterfuge of lies, which were alike blasphemous to God and to Man.

During this period of moral obliquity, a professional gentleman (who sinned against greater light than many that believed and taught that Slavery was a Divine Institution, because he was born in the Free States, under higher-toned moral influences,) said to the writer : " I have turned over the leaves of the Bible from Genesis to Revelation, and made an unanswerable argument, showing clearly, from the sacred text itself, that Slavery is a Divine Institution !"

"Ah !" we replied, "if it be *true* that you have made an argument from the Bible in support of *human bondage*, that cannot be met and logically refuted by the same high authority; *then* the time has come for the enlightened Nations of Earth to make a bonfire and consume that libel on Humanity and Humanity's God; for He hath written higher principles of right and justice in the heart and mind of the reasoning nineteenth century. But, Sir, you are wrong. The Book of books teaches that God hath made of *one blood* all nations of men to dwell on all the face of the earth ! And Christianity requires men everywhere to love as brethren. Measure for measure, is its rule of equal and eternal justice and love. "As ye would that men should do unto you, do ye even so unto them; for *this* is the Law and the Prophets."

The Mormon gives the Christian Church an encouraging pat when he hears her defense of Slavery, resting on the Bible for its support, and exclaims, patronizingly: " You are right as far as you go; but you do not go far enough; you must admit that Polygamy is also of Divine Authority; you are yet too narrow and limited in your views of Bible truth. We can bring forward stronger arguments from the Old Testament in favor of polygamy than you can in favor of slavery; and you will at length be obliged to agree with us. Consider the subject rationally. Abraham, the founder of the Hebrew Church, and Isaac and Jacob, had a plurality of wives, and David also, who was a Man after God's own heart; now, then, if these chosen servants and intimate friends of the Almighty, who were in constant communion

with Him, were not condemned for the practice, Heaven must
have approved."

The Church is annoyed by the audacious Mormon's defense
of Polygamy from the Old Testament; but when he lays it aside
and looks at the New and higher Dispensation through his polygamic spectacles, declaring that Jesus Christ himself, the incarnation of Divinity, was a Polygamist, the husband of Mary and
Martha, sisters of Lazarus; she is shocked beyond measure, is
outraged in her most sacred feelings and sentiments.   The Church
is painfully humiliated that what she holds as most pure and holy
should be thus openly profaned by the sensual Mormon, this curious and absurd conglomerate of all the evil and good of both Religious Dispensations.   And she cries out sternly to the Ecclesiastic Leader of Utah, in the language of the ancient Pharisee:
Stand by; I am holier than thou.

But it were well to question closely for the purposes of soul-
knowledge and purification;—is not the Christian Church more
offended at the *manner* of the licentious Mormon, than indignant at his crime against Nature and enlightened society?   The
Church does not approve of either legalized, or un-legalized prostitution—the moral sentiment of the age is opposed to both
wrongs against the nature of man and woman—but are not large
numbers of her Body licentious in secret?   Let us probe the
wound.   Do they not go forth in the still and dark night to seek
for the dwelling of the woman void of understanding?   And do
they not entice thither to her chambers of Death, whose foundations take firm hold on Hell, the young, ignorant and confiding,
through the magical words of simulated affection and love, to
gratify their selfish and cruel sensuality?—regardless of the ruin
and desolation of once happy homes?—regardless of the painful
truth that these little ones against whom they offend, can never
again go forth into the pure air of Heaven, innocent and light-
hearted, but must wear forevermore in their souls the stain of
passion not hallowed by love?

We question again.   Do not many Fathers in the Church, who
have gentle and loving daughters, blooming in innocent beauty,
under their own vines and fig-trees, men who claim to be the

guardians of virtue, and the sage protectors of unreflecting youth, commit the unpardonable crime of violating the soul purity, soul sanctity of undefiled virgins with their pestiferous and corrupting lust? Shame on their grey hairs, which have not taught them lessons of wisdom! It were better that a millstone were hanged about their necks, and they were drowned in the depths of the Sea. They know not what they do, nor the fearful retribution that will follow their unholy deeds. Let them remember and tremble in view of consequences, that the sin done against woman, who is the representative of Divine Maternity, is the sin against the Holy Ghost, or Divine Mother of the Heavens, that cannot be forgiven, neither in this world, nor in the world to come; because the sin, in its effects, is transmitted from the soul of the Mother to the soul of her Offspring, and leaves its ineffaceable impression for time and for eternity. And the blight is handed down from generation to generation, involving Humanity; and thus becomes a twofold wrong, a crime against Maternity, and the offspring, Divine Humanity. It is lightly committed; but the consequences are fearful and incomputable.

And, again; do not these Christian Fathers meet at those gilded sepulchres of vice the reckless *roue* of society who pursues sensual pleasures regardless of consequences, and makes no profession of high morality and Christian purity to mask his gross animal excesses. And is it not a stinging reproach to the Christian Religion that it exerts no restraining influence on the lives of these hoary-headed Fathers? And does it not lead the men of mere sensual pleasure, who become acquainted with such, to regard Christianity as a humbug, and its professors as arrant knaves and hypocrites? And while such unworthy members are permitted to remain in the Church, and while many of the clergy, as well as laity, are guilty of such deeds of impurity and darkness, is she in a position to say to the reprobate Mormon :—Cast out the mote out of thine eye !—when, lo ! a beam is in her own eye ?

We observe, farther, that the Mormon is a usurer, and worships the gold that perisheth. He sits a very Crœsus in his harem, claiming the hard-earned tenth of all the labor of the

44

poor, deluded, worshipping "Saints." Does he not resemble in this lineament also the Christian Church of to-day? Is she not a usurer? Are not the courts of her Temples, that have been dedicated to the worship of the God of Heaven and of Earth, filled with Money-Changers' tables? Does not Mammon sit enthroned in her high places, robed in ermine, purple and gold; while Heaven's poor are dying of neglect and starvation in the shadow of her gorgeous Temples?

And, again: the Mormon is proud, arrogant, self-asserting, and altogether *masculine*. Is he unlike the Christian Church in this peculiar feature? Does she not declare to the world, through all the organizations of her various sects, that the Christian Church is a Bridegroom, rather than a Bride, the Lamb's Wife? But the special masculine idea was borrowed from the Pagan, as well as the Christian. The Pagan Woman could not enter Paradise without being metamorphosed into a man; the Mormon Woman is not permitted to pass through the gates of immorality unless " sealed to a man," in a union termed " Spiritual Marriage;" but which is, in verity, legalized prostitution, and a form of that evil which is more desecrating to human affections than any other, and more hardening to the heart of both Man and Woman.

Think, for a moment, sapient scholar of the nineteenth century, of the *moral quality of sex*, ticketing one-half of the Human Family through to the Elysian Fields, and leaving the Mothers, or *re*-creators of the race of Man—who are, at least, equally as virtuous as the other half, and as well qualified for the enjoyments of immortal pleasures—to wander uncared for by the great Creator, in the outer regions of space, or to be hopelessly lost in nonentity! Such theories of a future state of existence are so irrational, so essentially opposed to the teachinsg of both Philosophy and Revelation, that we marvel that they could have obtained in the world, even in the darkness of the physical ages of ignorance ; but, when they are presented in any form to the reasoning mind of the present, they outrage the understanding of the people. In view of such gross absurdities one cannot forbear exclaiming, in the impassioned language of Mark Antony :

O judgment, thou hast fled to brutish beasts,
And men have lost their reason !

But we will pursue the disagreeable resemblance of the Mormon Body to the corrupt Christian Church no farther, saving to note that his government is similar to that of the Roman Catholics—an Ecclesiastic Despotism.   Mormon claims, with Rome, to exercise both temporal and spiritual power over the people : and he issues his Bulls accordingly, roaring bulls, and bullets, too, against all who dispute his supremacy in Utah; in imitation of his contemporary, the Pope of the Vatican.

We are pained and humiliated to find that this infamous Mormon parasite is a caricature of the Christian Church.   But he serves a purpose in the moral Government of Heaven ;   for, by practicing all the social *evils* that existed in the undeveloped Childhood and Youth of the Church, and pronouncing them *good*, he presents a grouped picture of those evils to the Reasoning Age of the Church and World, and they stand out in strong relief against the increased light and knowledge of the present Era.   And the more saintly the Mormon assumes to be with his scores of wives tripping meekly behind him ; some in the early springtime of existence, and others in the hoary winter of age;—mothers and their own daughters all "sealed" to a common level of prostitution,—and the more he attempts to prove from the Bible that polygamy is a Divine Institution, to justify himself for the gross violation of all that is delicate and holy in human affectations, the more monstrous and farcical his position appears to the Reasoning Age.

The picture would be laughable, were it not exceedingly painful to reflect upon the terrible consequences that must result from such unnatural relations to the unfortunate victims themselves, and to their posterity.   The children of such profane alliances will become, alas ! so accustomed in infancy and childhood to the desecration of the affections, that they will reach the physical stature of men and women, demoralized at the very fountain of existence, and unable to perceive the sacred truth of Nature when it is presented to their hearts and understandings.

If it be true, as some persons believe, that Mormon stands

before the world as the precursor of blending Dispensations, of the union of the Hebrew with the Christian Church; the low representative plane on which he lives is a sorrowful commentary on the past and present moral conditions of both Jews and Gentiles.   Fortunately, however, Mormon's life is brief, and will be soon played out on the stage of Time, like the farce that is enacted before the legitimate drama.   The true union of God's People of the Old and New Dispensations, which was prophesied by St Paul more than eighteen centuries ago, will be ere long consummated, on the high intellectual and spiritual planes, in the advanced Reasoning Age of the Church; when the *letter* of Christianity will give place to its pure and elevating *spirit.*

The World is moving forward.   The day is swiftly advancing in which all systems of Religion and of Government will be tested by REASON, in the clear light of KNOWLEDGE.   And these progressive twain are no fossilized antiquarians, to cling to the old with an unrelenting death-grasp!   They smile at USAGE and AUTHORITY, handed down to posterity from the Childhood and Youth of the human race, as precious heir-looms of faith and practice.   All principles that are not adapted to the growth of the living present, they will fling back remorselessly into the rubbish of the past.

CHAPTER VII.

Ye are all the children of light, and the children of the day: We are not of the night, nor of darkness. Therefore, let us not sleep as do others; but let us watch and be sober.

Prove all things; hold fast that which is good.

It has been said, in the preceding Chapter, that the Christian Church is altogether masculine in her organizations and governmental conduct, and that she appears before the World as a Bridegroom, rather than as a Bride, the Lamb's Wife. Indeed, she is so determinedly masculine that she fails to see and understand the true relations of Woman to the Divine All-One and to the offspring, the Divine Humanity; and, consequently, does not comprehend the Philosophy of the principles which she professes to believe, and by which she claims to be governed.

Whenever persons of reasoning minds and liberal sentiments assert that Woman is the equal friend and companion of Man, and an equally important half of the great Human Family, and should be recognized, therefore, by the laws of the land as an individual and citizen, and enjoy like civil, political, and religious priviliges with him; the Church shakes her head gravely and replies that such views are contrary to the Holy Scriptures. And she quotes St. Paul's *dictum* to the claimant: I suffer not a woman to teach, and to exercise authority over man;—as unquestionable proof against her equality with him, and consequent right to enjoy the same liberties and privileges in the Vineyard of the Lord. And the Church understands full well the while that the Apostle's opinion was spoken after the tem-

per of the world, and not after the spirit of the Gospel of Jesus
Christ, and that it was a prejudice of education received at the
feet of Gamaliel; a prejudice which the Fathers of his age had
inherited from the first Dispensation of Law and Authority in
the Childhood of the Church, and from the Pagan Philosophers
of the early Youth of the World.

And the Church of the enlightened nineteenth century wan-
ders deliberately back to the Old Dispensation, and to the Garden of Eden, to find arguments against Woman's natural and
inalienable rights with Man, as Man, as a part of the *genus homo;*
closing her eyes to the accumulated intellectual and moral light
and growth of all the intervening ages, and to the advanced truths
of the New Dispensation, with its clear and forcible presentation
of her claims in the Church to broad equality among the Children
of God.   And the Church declares, with imposing gravity, that
Woman was branded by the Almighty Father, in the beginning,
with the curse of inferiority and submission to Man, for the Reason that *she* was the first transgressor, and led *him* into sin; and
that it cannot set aside the judgment of the Court of Heaven.

Milton, influenced by this peculiar view of the subject, con-
demns his immortal Adam to say, in weak extenuation of his offense:

> " This woman whom Thou madst to be my help,
> And gavest me as Thy perfect gift, so good,
> So fit, so acceptable, so divine,
> That from her hand I could suspect no ill;—
> She gave me of the tree and I did eat.

Very little has been said by the Church of the *curse* that was
pronounced on Man in the same connection; because it involves
the context, which prophecies of a time when the curse shall be
removed, alike from male and female Man, by the *seed of the
Woman,* which shall bruise the Serpent's head; redeeming Man
from servile labor; and Woman from the slavery of blind affections.

And the Church professes to believe that this prophecy was
literally fulfilled, nearly two thousand years ago, in the advent of
the Messiah, and in accordance with the corroborative prophecy
to Mary, recorded in the New Testament: The Holy Ghost, or

Divine Mother, shall come upon thee; and the power of the Highest, or Divine Father, shall overshadow thee; therefore, also, the holy thing which shall be born of thee, shall be called the Son of God. She professes to believe, fully, that the *seed of the Woman*, quickened by the Holy Spirit, produced the Spiritual, Intuitional-Intellectual and Harmonial God-Man, the Redeemer of the World; which was born, not of blood, nor of the will of the flesh, nor of the will of man, but of God. And She teaches that the reign of the Spiritual Adam commenced with our Lord and Savior Jesus Christ, and succeeded the rule of the Natural Adam of the physical and experimental ages.

And, yet, as anomalous as it appears, while the Church assents to the prophecy and its fulfillment, she still enforces, practically, the *partial view* that Man alone was redeemed from the curse of the physical ages of unreflecting ignorance. She refuses, utterly, to acknowledge that Woman was also liberated with Man, through her own offspring, the Christ of God. Because she lives in the limited sphere of thought of the undeveloped past, while dwelling in the progressive present, and so remains blind to the real relations, conditions and interests of the female half of the race of Man. And thus, the Church is weak, when she ought to be strong; she is narrow and bigoted, when she ought to be broad and liberal; and, therefore, is unable to grasp the great Human· Family as a grand *whole*, from the comprehensive stand-point of REASON.

But the facts are before her. Since the rule of the Spiritual Adam, of the intellectual and moral ages of the world, began on Earth, the Serpent's head has been bruised, or the sensual nature of Man, male and female, brought farther under the control of Reason and the Moral Sentiments. And this more elevated condition of the affectional qualities of human beings in Christendom, has been accomplished through the quickening of the higher faculties of mind and heart, and the kindling of the Spiritual and Inspirational powers of the soul, by means of the Mediative Son's Religion of Intelligent Nature, his glorious Gospel of Unity and Love, which reveals the relations of man to man, and· of Man to the Divine Father and Mother God.

Whatever sectarian organizations may believe and teach, concerning the great Philosopher of Nazareth and his doctrines. the results of those broad principles of truth which he died to establish on earth will continue to speak through an unbroken chain of sequences to the mind of the Reasoning Age; and the World will see and believe, even though the Church continue blind. The great work of Man's redemption, consecrated at the garden of Gethsemane, has been going forward for centuries, and will continue to advance with increasing majesty and power until the animal nature of the whole Human Family shall be brought entirely under the control of Reason and the Moral Sentiments, and Universal man, male and female, shall become, each, a consecrated Temple of the God of purity and love, and Earth be filled with the joyful hallelujahs of the Heavens.

It is because the Man of the Church is still trammeled by the traditions of the Fathers, and influenced by the prejudices of education, and controlled by the pride of dominant sex and love of power, that he continues to hold the Woman of the Church in bondage to the Old Letter, and to deprive her of her legitimate rights in the Sanctuary and in Society. And he continues in this unjust course towards her, notwithstanding she has given her whole heart and soul to the Church, and labored with all her mind, and strength, and wealth, to enlarge its numbers and increase its influence;—and, notwithstanding the Church could not be sustained by Man alone, but would disintegrate and fall without Woman's untiring efforts and life of self-abnegating devotion;—and, notwithstanding the Law and the Testimony, and Heaven itself, has set the stamp of Authority on her equal redemption and freedom.

Aside from the religious view of the subject, it appears to be simply rational and just that Woman should enjoy, in the Church which she sustains and renders beautiful and attractive, equal privileges with man, to express her highest sentiments, and have an equal voice in framing and administering the laws. Indeed, the enlightened looker-on in Christendom regards it as a flagrant injustice to Woman, as well as a severe reproach to Man of the enlightened nineteenth century, that all Woman's wealth, education and influence should be brought to bear against herself, to hold her in a subordinate position in the Church, and, consequently, in society, which is governed by her peculiar status in this her own admitted sphere of action.

But this condition could not obtain, if Woman herself were not also enslaved by a traditional religion, so that she is unable to reason *a priori* on any subject connected with the Church and its doctrines ; consequently, cannot see her true relation to it, nor to the Divine All-Parent, nor to the Divine Humanity. Certes, Traditional Religion holds the entire Christian Body in bondage to the Letter. Where the pure and elevating Gospel of the Mediative Son of God is fully operative in the heart and mind and soul of believers, there is newness of life, and spiritual and inspirational power; and where this life of the soul exists, there is liberty for all God's children, male and female.

Let Woman herself awaken then to the subject of her own *freedom in right action*, and equal responsibility with Man for the improvement of the gifts with which she is endowed by Heaven, and become obedient to the voice of the spirit, or the impelling force of her own soul; remembering that God marked out no particular SPHERE for either man, or woman, independently of the revelation of His Will impressed on their hearts and minds, when He created and blessed them, and pronounced His work *good*. The All-Parent said unto both alike : Be fruitful, and multiply, and replenish the earth, and subdue it.

Let Woman remember, with humble gratitude to the Divine Father and Mother, and for sustaining power in right and independent action, that Sarah was Heaven's appointed Mother of the Hebrew Church; and Mary, of the Christian. Let her remember, with holy joy, that the true Church of God is a BRIDE, and put on her consecrated garments of beauty, purity, and love, and go forth to meet the Bridegroom in his coming. The Revelator saw in prophetic vision the renovated Church of the New Christian Era of Reason, the New Jerusalem, descending from God out of Heaven, adorned as a bride for her husband. There was no spot, nor blemish on her consecrated garments. The purification of the conjugal relation in the Church is herein

45

clearly and strikingly prefigured. Let Woman begin, at once, the important work of purification; this is her own peculiar field of labor.

And let Woman learn to look with a philosophical eye, as well as with a discerning spirit, and take in the full significance of the principles by which she has been governed in the past, and is controlled in the present. The allegory of the Garden of Eden, in which Woman is represented as being the tempter of Man and the introducer of sin, suffering and death to the World, is of kindred character with Pandora's Box of Heathen Mythology. The simple statement of this myth without figure of speech involves Man in the evil quite as much as Woman. It appears that her superior beauty attracted him and awakened desire which he did control with reason, and which she did not aid him in controlling, but permitted the sanctity of her nature to be profaned by unlawful excess or abuse of passion; through which the physical natures of both were at length debilitated and corrupted, and disease entailed on posterity. And this obstinate fact, of the entailment of disease through corrupted physical organizations, was the true source of the doctrine of " Original sin." The iniquities of the parents are thus visited upon the children through untold generations.

But while Man and Woman appear, superficially viewed, to be equally guilty before God and Man, her sin is greater than his, insomuch as Heaven has endowed her with a finer spiritual perception of evil; and, farther, because of the consequences to posterity—woman being the appointed Mother of the Human Family, and, as such, exerting a more powerful influence on the character of new-born generations than Man.

In this view of the subject, it becomes Woman's imperative duty to take a stronger stand than man takes, against the licentious proclivities of the age. Let her see to it that she does not pander to the perverted passional nature of the opposite sex, by indelicate exposure of any part of her person in public assemblies, or by languishing looks, or manners, or by any appeal to the senses that might awaken unholy desire. Let Christian Mothers teach their innocent and impressible daughters, that God hath constituted THEM *their own natural protectors*, and that they must not only guard themselves against the undisciplined passions of Man, but they must protect him also in his hour of weakness, when he forgets the nobility of his nature, and would permit the allurements of sense to triumph over his reason and moral sentiments.

And let Woman remember, reverently, that because of her maternal office, as the recreator of the human race after the Divine Order, she stands in nearer relation to Creative Intelligence than man; and that, because of this near relation, she represents more particularly the *spiritual forces* of our dual nature than he; and that Man, with his strong practical tendency and demonstrative reasoning power, stands more particularly on the material plane of thought and action, and, consequently, represents more fully the *physical forces* of our dual nature than woman. In the light of this philosophy, she will be able to see and understand many of the yet unexplained past conditions and relations of the sexes. Thus far in the History of the Human Family, the World has been more on the material plane of development than on the intellectual and spiritual. And this was the legitimate order of its unfolding; consequently, the natural tendency of the mind, during the more physical ages, has been to magnify physical actions and their results, and to glorify itself in them.

In the Childhood of the World, the people piled up colossal monuments to challenge the wonder and admiration of future generations. In the heroic Youth of the World, they erected vast Temples in honor of the successful leaders of their armies, and elevated their heroes far above the millions of Humanity, into the abode of the immortal Gods, in adoring worship of physical daring and achievement!

And in the present, as in the past, the strongest appeal that can be made to the undeveloped mind of either man, or woman, is made through the physical senses. The Roman Catholics understand, and act from this principle. The numerous yearly proselytes of that Sect. drawn from the various Protestant Denominations in the United States of North America, are composed of children who attend their Institutions of Learning, and are in-

structed in the doctrines of that Sect, through the means of attractive pictures which illustrate them, and which are hung on
the walls of their recitation and play rooms for this purpose, and
explained to the teachable little ones by the devoted Sisters of the
faith, in tender tones of venerating love.   The children receive
a permanently sectarian bias, by the time they have learned the
pictures.

And, again, let Woman understand that it was natural that
material manifestations of power should have appeared grander
to the popular mind of the physical ages, than the more subtle
spiritual and intangible; and that Man, as a representative of
material forces, should likewise have appeared to be the dominant power of Intelligent Nature; and that he should have asserted himself to be such, without intending any injustice to
Woman.   For, as a sex, he would not willingly wrong her,
however much he might be influenced in his individaul relations
with her by present social conditions, and by the peculiar prejudices inherited from the Childhood and Youth of the Human
Family.

And let it be remembered that neither the Childhood nor
Youth of the World, nor of the individual man, are the ages
of philosophy; and that Man, as a sex, has been thus far unable
to rise superior to the influences of education, and of traditional prejudice, and to view truth broadly from the comprehensive plane of cause which overlooks the wide realm of
effects.   And, for this reason, he has failed to award equal justice
to Woman, either as a sex, or as a rational and intelligent individual, companion and friend.   And, the mind of the present
Era is so thoroughly imbued with the material and masculine
tendencies of past ages, that it can only see in the direction of
the old masculine channels and act through them.   Even the
professed Christian Philosopher still looks at Woman through
spectacles borrowed of Pagan Sages.   It is true that the Pagan
was unable to penetrate as far into a future state of existence as
the Christian is who admits Woman to Paradise in her own
proper person; but, the latter is still so biased by the narrow
views of the former, that, while he generously accords to her

equal rights in the higher life of Heaven, he obstinately refuses to recognize her claim to equal justice while she remains a resident of the planet Earth.

In consequence of this partial and unphilosophical view of the Human Family, partial and unhealthy social conditions everywhere obtain in the world. We have Institutions of Learning, founded for the benefit of Man only—which are very liberally endowed by the wealth of both sexes—while Woman is equally in need of the educational light which they impart to the youth of the land. And we have large industrial interests, established for Man only; while Woman is equally in need of remunerative occupations to sustain herself and those depending on her efforts for subsistence. And, through all the ramifications of society, there is but a partial application of the principles of social science, and of the deductions of philosophy, and justice is but partially administered. The grand universal principles of truth, broadly gathered from Nature and Revelation for the regulation of human conduct, are nowhere applied to human conditions and requirements irrespective of SEX.

Ay, the Metaphysicians of our day, with all their subtle powers of analysis and synthesis, have alike failed with Heathen Philosophers to measure Woman and define her intellectual and moral status. For the human understanding, on the plane of demonstrative reason, is too low to measure spiritual principles which are operative in Intelligent Nature. Infinite Wisdom and Infinite Love has ordained that that important work shall be performed by Woman. She is required to measure herself by the Divine in her nature while looking up to the hills from whence cometh her help, and ascending to high mental and moral altitudes which touch the lofty sphere of Cause.

Man is busy with his own conditions, with measuring himself by himself, and by his past dominance in the Childhood and Youth of the world; and Woman cannot hope for much help from him until he is able to shake off the traditions and prejudices inherited from the Fathers, and to take his stand on the higher planes of Philosophy.

Lo! the Christian Democrat still declares with the Pagan

Aristocrat: This world was made for Cæsar. The Christian Church concurs.—The Christian State echoes the voice of the Christian Church, and legislates for the benefit of one sex alone. The Christian Press congratulates both the Church and State on their wise and comprehensive views of Nature and Revelation, which reveal the superiority and supremacy of the *male* over the *female half* of the Human Family ! The Church, the State, the Pulpit and the Press are entirely masculine. And the great Creative Intelligence of the Universe, Infinite Wisdom and Infinite Love, appears altogether masculine to the one-visioned, unphilosophical Church and World.

But, fortunately for all the oppressed members of the Human Family, male as well as female, we live in the dawn of a New Era. The World is approaching its maturity. The day of Reason is advancing. Its morning is already luminous with the rising Sun of Righteousness and of Knowledge. All the forces of physical and of Intelligent Nature are vigorously at work to throw off old conditions, and take on new. The subtle Spiritual Powers of the Universe are radiating finer elements of soul-life, from soul-centre to soul-circumference; and these are permeating the mind of the age, and will be manifested ere long in higher types of Man and Woman, and a purer Christian Democracy.

Let woman take courage and labor as she may have opportunity, in every good word and work. Her hour is not yet fully come, but it is swiftly approaching. The Era of Woman began when the Star of Bethlehem announced to the Wise Men of the East the birth of the Enlightener of the World, the great Philosopher of Intelligent Nature—one in whom dwelt all the FULLNESS of the Godhead ; All-Father, All-Mother God.

In the first Christian Era, or Youth of the Church and World, the Gospel of Intelligent Nature was presented to the heart or affections of Man—as we have already shown—then the *letter* prevailed over the spirit of Christianity; but in the second Christian Era, upon which we have already entered, and which is the age of rational religion, the Gospel will be addressed more particularly to the mind, or understanding; and then the *spirit of*

Christianity will prevail over the letter, because the interior truth of the Word will be more clearly seen and deeply felt. Woman will be crowned when the Reasoning Age shall culminate in beauty, strength, and power, and when the Son of God and Son of Man " shall be revealed " in glory to the understanding as well as heart of the Human Family.

The Heavens and the Earth are preparing for His coming. Science is engaged in developing the hidden principles of Nature, and in teaching the Human Family to subdue and control material forces; and the Spirit is revealing the mysteries of the Spirit, and bringing the human soul into rapport with the World of Cause, in order that the origin and unity of all truth may be recognized, and harmony established between the material and spiritual, and the near and remote of human relations. For thus only can the Church and World be prepared for the second advent of the Mediative Son of God, and the re-baptism of the Holy Ghost, or Divine Mother of Humanity. The full baptism of the Holy Ghost awaited, of necessity, the riper age of the Church, and superior physical, intellectual and moral conditions; in accordance with the perfect fitness of associate principles, as exhibited in the Divine Government.

And the baptism of the Holy Ghost will be attended with the *baptism of fire*. For the Church needs purifying. The dross of sensuality, selfishness, and prejudice, must be removed by enlightened reason and heavenly love, before the Divine Mother can be recognized by the human offspring. Truly the heart must be filled with divinest love, ere it will be able to feel her beautiful and gentle presence; and the mind must be open to the influx of celestial truth, ere it will be able to see and acknowledge her individual existence, and accept her tender and holy ministrations.

CHAPTER VIII.

THE ENFRANCHISEMENT OF WOMAN.

Is not this the fast that I have chosen? saith the Lord, To loose the bands of wickedness, to undo the heavy burdens, and to let the oppressed go free, and that ye break every yoke.

The Republican Government of the United States of North America was established on the intelligence, and consequent self-governing power of the people; and must therefore depend upon the enlightenment of the millions for its perpetuity. And, hence, UNIVERSAL SUFFRAGE, on the basis of intelligence, is the only rational and consistent policy for our Nation to adopt, if it would secure public order, peace and prosperity. And it is the only policy which harmonizes with the genius of our free and progressive Democratic Institutions.

UNIVERSAL SUFFRAGE, on the basis of intelligence—requiring the voter to be able to read the English language fluently, and to write legibly—would tend to strengthen the Union and consolidate the interest of the general government. It is a purely Democratic policy; because its requirements and limitations would press equally upon all classes of citizens, and result in the greatest good of greatest numbers.

An ignorant population is easily excited and duped by artful and intriguing politicians, and ambitious, would-be leaders. Its tendency is to split into factions, and to decimate and demoralize itself with perpetual revolutions; particularly where the form of government is Republican. Mexico affords a striking illustration of the truth of the proposition. Ancient Greece and Rome furnish also additional proof of the fact, that ignorant classes of citizens are disturbing and disintegrating elements in Republics. We have tested the truth of the above statement in our own experience as a Nation. And the same principles in operation will produce the same results in the future that they did in the past, and endanger the safety of a government. When the people are unable to read and inform themselves, they are obliged to receive their political creeds on the authority of others, and are unable to judge for themselves of the *true principles of Democracy*, or of the right measures and men to advance these principles, and are quite as likely to vote against, as in favor of, that which they desire to support. They become, in verity, the mere tools of political Leaders, or ambitious Ecclesiastics, who seek for legislative action, favorable to the interests of some political faction, or some peculiar religious sect, irrespective of the broader interests of society.

It is a peculiarity of Ignorance to be self-asserting, domineering and oppressive. It feels itself elevated by holding another class of human beings in a more abject condition than its own. The purse-proud Aristocracy of a land is not more self-respecting and self-gratulating than strong-minded Ignorance with its crude bone and muscle. It will boast that it—"can lick the World!" And it regards refined manners and scholarly attainments as the puerilities of privileged classes.

Knowledge widely diffused among the people tends to a broader understanding of human rights, or Republican principles, and to a more general equalization of material conditions; thus contributing to the harmony of society, and the solidarity of the General Government. An ignorant Republic has no base: It is like an inverted cone that will topple at the slightest pressure. But an enlightened Republic rests upon strong foundations of truth, laid deep and broad in the ages, and cannot be overthrown by civil and religious revolutions.

If the preceding view of the question is correct, it becomes the imperative duty of our Government to offer a premium to intelligence by enacting that she will endow those only with the ballot—in future—who are able to read fluently and to write legibly the English language. This measure could not be re-

46

garded by any party as prohibitive, because it would cut off no citizen, nor class of citizens, from the vote; for the Ballot-Box would be open to all native and adopted Americans on one broad, grand level.   The opportunities for learning to read and write in our Public School, of the day and *evening*, are so extensive, for *adults* as well as children, that none need to be excluded from the privilege.   And private sources of instruction are also so universal, convenient and inexpensive—through the disposition of intelligent ladies, not only to teach the domestics of their own families, but to provide ways and means for those persons, in any and every position, who manifest a desire to learn—that lack of interest in self-improvement, or positive idleness, can alone act as preventives to the acquisition of knowledge.

UNIVERSAL SUFFRAGE, on the bases of intelligence, would prove beneficial to all classes of citizens, but particularly so to the most *helpless*, as well as the most degraded.   It would rectify many evils, to which the former dependent class of citizens are now exposed, and it would act favorably upon the latter class of reckless and improvident men and women, by throwing the weight of responsibility for the improvement or misimprovement of privilege, upon the individual being, thus tending to cultivate directly the self-governing power, so important to the safety and progress of our Republic, while acting through all gradations of Society, as a stimulant to self-culture and noble effort.   A policy so broad and purely Democratic would inaugurate a new era in Republicanism, and a new and true progressive Democracy, a "leveling up" Christian Democracy, sound to the core on HUMAN RIGHTS, would be the glorious result.   And it would eventually challenge the unqualified admiration of the enlightened world.

UNIVERSAL SUFFRAGE, on the bases of intelligence, would render simple *justice* to *Woman*.   It would endow her with the VOTE, which is her natural right as a citizen of the State and as the progenitor of the Human Race.   CITIZEN—did we say?   Woman is not a recognized citizen of the country which she populates.   Our laws ignore the individuality of Woman, the Mother of those who frame them.   They class her, politically, with children, idiots, slaves and criminals. And, like these innocents and unfortunates, Woman has no rights that Man feels himself legally bound to respect; and he measures her by her political instead of intellectual and moral status, in all his business and social relations with her, and treats her accordingly. We speak not now of exceptional cases, but of general usage.

Woman's property is taxed equally with Man's for the support of a government in which she has no voice. Our Nation of to-day, of the enlightened nineteenth century, presents to the world the glaring inconsistency of depriving one-half of its population of citizenship and the power to redress their wrongs through the only available channel, the ballot-box, and then oppressing them with the old wrong of *taxation without representation*, which flagrant injustice called our Revolutionary Fathers of seventy-six forth to the field, to protest, with their swords, their lives and their sacred honor, against the unconstitutional oppression of the Mother Country.

Woman's political rank with children, idiots, slaves and criminals operates against her business interests through all the various industrial pursuits of the age. Fewer avenues of remunerative occupation are, as a consequence, of the low estimation and classification of Woman, open for her activities, and she receives far less compensation than Man for the same kind and amount of labor equally well performed. And this injustice obtains in the community, in view of the well understood fact, that Woman is not as able, physically, to perform the same amount of given labor as Man; and, farther, that she is more liable than he to be left with the entire care of providing for a family of helpless little ones, for the reason, that Man is more exposed to accident than she, through perilous business enterprises, and through decimating wars, which cut down the strong in the midst of their years.

We are sorry to see that our noble contemporary worker and friend, Horace Greely, has taken position against Woman's right to political franchise, on the plea that she herself does not desire to exercise the privilege. It is true that, Who would be free themselves must strike the blow, and that no permanent good can be accomplished for any class of persons who are indifferent to their own interests, while they remain in that negative condition; but should the philanthropist and moral reformer stay therefore the helping hand?   Is one's duty less imperative toward the apathetic and helpless who are exposed to evils, or dangers, of which they are ignorant, or unconscious?

It should not be forgotten, in viewing the general indifference, or even opposition of women to the exercise of political franchise, that they have been educated to their present opinions by the current literature of the age, and also by the public Press, which has been conducted, almost exclusively by men, and which has uniformly opposed their equal political rights, on the ground, that the exercise of such rights would unsex and demoralize them. And it should be remembered, farther, in palliation of women's indifference to their own important interests, that but a comparitively small number, of either sex, are able to look beneath the surface waves of popular opinion, and observe the stronger under-current of deeper principles that rushes ever on to the fulfillment of human destiny, obedient to the mandate of Deity.

It ought not to be expected that women, to whom the Colleges and Universities of the land have been closed, should reason more profoundly than men, to whom these beneficent institutions have always been open for intellectual culture; and that they should be in advance of a public sentiment that the privileged sex has been laboriously creating for centuries; and that they should see more clearly than men the moral influence of the Vote upon the social condition of the people. And yet, strange anomaly of accredited weakness and strength, superior foresight and wisdom are everywhere required of women. Is there not a cause?

We have not taken the pen to make a partial plea for either Male or Female supremacy. We demand not that women shall bear rule. But we appeal to the reasoning minds of the nineteenth century, to say if it be not consistent with the *spirit of truth* that THEY should be in place and power who can best understand and represent the interests of the Age in which we live, whether they be male or female ? We ask if principles are not independent of and superior to sex, and ought not to be so recognized, alike by the materialistic and the spiritualistic Rationalists of the Reasoning Age of the World ?

As before stated, women have been drilled all through the centuries in the belief that the exercise of political rights would unsex and demoralize them. Large numbers of the unreflecting have accepted the proposition as true; and they have a natural repugnance and horror of being unsexed and demoralized. And, while occupied with this formidable objection, they do not see the falsity and injustice which underlies the assumption. But it is none-the-less a lie, and a tyrannous wrong, although women are blind, and although usage and the prejudices of education cause both sexes to view leniently the monopoly of political power by the male half of the Human Family.

But, could the women of America understand that the Vote represents both material and moral power, and that they are really as legitimately entitled by nature to the advantages which it confers as men, and equally as capable of using it for practical ends; *then* they could no longer remain indifferent to the great question of political enfranchisement.

And, could the women of America understand that the Vote in their hands would command for them greater respect and consideration from men, who entertain a profound regard for the material and practical goods of life,—for the Vote and its considerations, citizenship, office and its emoluments, representation in the State, and station in society,—*then*, women would no longer remain indifferent to the question of political enfranchisement. Wealth and its advantages are everywhere highly esteemed among men. But, under the political regime of today, women of wealth lose the benefits conferred by riches. Indeed, wealth is often a greater misfortune than blessing to the daughters of our land; because it renders them conspicuous marks for unscrupulous *fortune hunters*, who simulate the love that they do not feel, and the nobility of nature which they do not possess, in order to win their affections and entrap them for wives. And then these miserable cheats become entitled

legally, not only to the fortune of their victims, but to all the
results of the same; and the wives are powerless to prevent
the sacrifice of their entire property.   And the relative position
of the parties are not changed, although the men may prove to
be weak-minded and incompetent for business, as well as heartless and knavish; while their wives are intelligent, capable of
managing their moneyd interests, and steadfast in moral purpose,
presenting noble examples to society.   This injustice is a flagrant offense against Human Rights, which could not obtain
under our Republican Institutions, if women were endowed with
the Vote.

And could the women of America understand that the Vote
would secure their individual rights, and would constitute them
CITIZENS of their own beloved country (an honor that our Nation
freely confers on the most ignorant and worthless men of
foreign lands, as soon as they are able to reach our shores and
avail themselves of the naturalization law,) and that it would en-
title them to the free use of their inherited property, or hard
earnings, and protect their moneyed interests from direct usurp-
ation and fraud ; *then*, it would be impossible for women to remain indifferent to the question of political enfranchisement.

And could women understand that the Vote would relieve
them from the painfully humiliating and monstrous classification,
politically, with criminals, slaves, idiots and children; and that it
would give them a more commanding position in the Church
and in the State, and, consequently, a wider influence in society;
and that it would enable them to form a truer estimate of their
own measure of power, by giving a freer and broader play to
their capabilities, and thereby awaken a deeper sense of responsibility for their proper direction and use; *then*, it would be impossible for women to remain indifferent to the question of
political enfranchisement.

And could women really believe that men themselves would
be elevated by conferring the ballot on them, insomuch as they
would be relieved from the half-conscious sense of injustice by
witholding it, and would be stimulated to nobler action by associate and competitive effort with them for the advancement of

the highest interests of society; and, that they would learn to regard *human rights* more sacredly by acknowledging theirs, and would, in verity, rise in the scale of intelligence and virtue, in proportion with the political liberty and intellectual and moral elevation of the Mothers and Daughters of our country; *then*, it would be impossible for women to remain indifferent to the question of political enfranchisement.

And could women really believe that the Vote would redress one of the most cruel wrongs of which women have cause to complain, a wrong which may be learned from the Statute Books of every State of our Republic,—that the Mothers of America have no legal right to their own children—when they are *legitimate offspring ; then*, it would be impossible for women to remain indifferent to the question of political enfranchisement. It is well to pause in this connection and glance at a curious fact, the result of our present partial legislation of sex; namely, that women's *natural right* to the possession of her own offspring is only freely admitted outside of the laws. Children born out of wedlock are everywhere recognized as belonging to the Mother, however poor, helpless and unworthy she may be; and she is accorded *the exclusive right of care and maintenance ;* while the father may abandon them at pleasure, or entirely ignore their existence. Again, we repeat, could woman generally become acquainted with the fact that the laws of the United States, as at present framed, expose them to be robbed of their dearest earthly treasures, which they hold by the inalienable right, earned of the God of Nature, during the long months of painful gestation, ameliorated only by the hope before them, and during the fearful pangs of parturition, softened only by the promise of maternity; and, could they believe that the Vote in their hands would ensure them the right to their own offspring; *then*, all the Mothers of our land would demand the Vote of their conntry, which they populate by order of the God of Nations, as their most sacred birthright. Ay ! they would all rally as one against the cruel outrage to Nature, with the thrilling cry of Queen Margaret in the keen, grand agony of her bereaved affections :

> Oh! that my tongue were in the thunder's mouth;
> Then with a passion would I shake the world.

And, finally, could women really know that the Vote would be a mighty lever in their hands, enabling them to right social abuses and wrongs, to equalize labor and its compensations, and to open avenues of attractive and remunerative occupation to the daughters of penury,—who often grow disheartened and despairing under the continued influence of prostrating labor at starving prices, until at length their minds become blurred and demoralized, and any condition of life appears preferable that promises to relieve them from present hunger and debility, and they sink, alas ! into those fearful hells of prostitution that yawn beneath their trembling footsteps—oh ! then, every Mother of America would call so loudly for the Vote ! the VOTE ! !—that the World would resound with the cry; and social and political tyrannies would be shaken to their foundations. And women would accept the Vote from their country with a shout of joy and a prayer of thanksgiving.

The Man of the Church wields enough political influence to endow the Woman of the Church with the Vote the present year, could he awaken to the importance of the question in its bearings upon the social, civil and religious interests of the nineteenth century, and be willing to lay his crown of exclusive suffrage at the feet of Justice.

The Goddess of Liberty is perpetually insulted in America by the mock ovations of her worshippers, who, while professing to honor her, dishonor the sex which she represents. And she stands in sublime majesty among the Gods, pleading with the sons of men in calm and silent pathos for subjected Womanhood, for the recognition of the equal and inalienable rights of the daughters, as well as the sons of our land and world. She speaks with the voice of divine symbolism to Woman, reminding her of her elevated nature and destiny, and stimulating her to seek to achieve true greatness, that she too may be prepared to assume her appointed place among the divinest of Humanity.

Within the last few years, a small number of reasoning minds, of both sexes, have been endeavoring to enlighten the millions on this important question, upon which depends the elevation of the masses and the prosperity of the Nation. Men have been striving, in vain, for thousands of years, to redeem the world from ignorance and its attendant errors, vice and crime; and they cannot hope to succeed without the active co-operation of women in every department of productive labor, and in science, literature and art, and in law, medicine and divinity, and alike in the social, civil and religious interests of the State. And the more enlightened the World becomes, the more clearly it will recognize the truth of the above proposition. For Humanity is a unit. Its interests are one and inseparable.

No class of society is so insignificant that it can be lost sight of, or neglected in its educational or industrial interests, or treated unjustly by the Legislative Body of the State, without injury to the general interests and prosperity of the Nation.

The benefits of our glorious Republican Institutions should not be limited to either sex or class. The highest order of genius often springs from the lowest stratum of society, and by a liberal political policy, and by scattering the seeds of Knowledge broadly, the combined talent of our Republic can be made available to sustain its strength, and power and influence. Every College and University in our land should, like the affluent sun, shine for all; and then these institutions of learning would act upon the popular mind, as that grand disseminator of light, heat and moisture acts upon the earth; they would stimulate the latent powers of the people to productive effort, to put forth leaves and blossoms, so that, when their Autumn shall arrive, it will be, like that of Nature, rich in fruitfulness and blessing.

Since the preceding was written, Rev. Dr. Bushnell has presented a work to the world, in which he opposes the ENFRANCHISEMENT OF WOMAN, on the plea that the Vote implies *governmental power*, and that she is disqualified for the exercise of such power, because, " She is in a subject nature, and not merely in a subject condition."

The Doctor declares, to the surprise of the reflective mind, that—men have always governed the world; ergo, men will always govern the world, even under the most disadvantageous circumstances. Listen to his words: " If twenty women to one man should be the relative scale of births from this time forth,

47

the men would rule the world as completely still as ever. And they would do it, too, by no exercise of force, but only by the look of it." Listen again to the qualifications for ruling which the Doctor claims for his superior sex: " Men's strong and direct base voice signifies rule." Again: " Men originally had the gift or endowment of a larger stature and a far superior muscular force. It may not be a very high distinction, but, such as it is, they have it, and in having it are men. Besides, in this more massive and crude sort of endowments we are to see that, as they are in force, so their force is the housing and expression of their natural authority. It signifies government, or governing capacity and order, and just as impressively the relatively subject nature of women."

Such arguments would have met the approbation of the dark, physical ages of ignorance, where might was the rule of right; but they sound strangely in the ear of the enlightened nineteenth century. *Sound and size* influence the unreflecting minds of children and youth; the mature man and woman are more powerfully acted upon and governed by motives. In the physical dynamics of to-day, loud and harsh tones are not regarded as penetrating and effective as low and fine ones; and the same is also true of moral dynamic forces. Indeed, Dr. Bushnell presupposes, throughout his work, that the Human Family are destined to remain in *statu quo* forever, and, to be impressed and governed in the future, as they were in the past, by imposing external and restrictive measures, and by the noisy rule of crude bone and muscle, as during the Childhood and Youth of the World. But the World, like the individual human being, must enjoy its age of enlightened Maturity, as well as its period of unreflecting childhood and youth; and, in progressing towards its Reasoning Age, its governments naturally change their base of operations, moving forward from the physical plane of restrictive measures, maintained by force; toward the higher moral plane of principles, sustained by arguments, drawn from the fundamental truths of Nature, and eliciting rational conviction. And in this maturer age of the World, HUMAN RIGHTS will be considered broadly, without reference to either sex, or color, or class, or condition. We are now living in the dawn, or transitionary period of this grand Reasoning Age of the Church and World, as we have already shown from the logic of events, when Nations will no longer appeal to the sword for the settlement of vexing questions of State, but to a Congress of Nations, in which enlightened Reason will be the noble Arbiter and Judge. And that Day of Reason will be preeminently the Era of Woman. The world will give her an impartial hearing, then; because ideas will not be measured by sex, as at this present, but by their own specific and generic weight of truth.

We sincerely hope that our fair countrywomen will not be discouraged by this effort of Dr. Bushnell to prevent their enfranchisement. It will not prove a serious injury to their cause, but, quite the contrary, will have the tendency to subserve it, as may be shown from his argument. For, in attempting to prove Woman's "subject nature," and consequent incapacity for governing, he has shown her to possess the requisite elements of character for swaying the hearts and minds of the millions in a remarkable degree, and to be far superior to Man in every quality which must of necessity constitute the true Governing Power in the rapidly approaching intellectual and moral ages of the World.

We are stung and humiliated by Dr. Bushnell's representation of the masculine sex in their capacity as rulers. For the hope of Humanity he should have endowed his Dominant Power of the past, present and future, with more magnanimity, justice and reason; and not have left him to bear sway with the unreflecting, crude bone and muscle, and the ungovernable will of tyranny, which claims *privilege* as RIGHT, and is incapable of being influenced by the Higher Law.

But Dr. Bushnell has given evidence in his work of being a progressive man; and he will undoubtedly be able to exercise, at some future day, a truer judgment in relation to Woman's nature, sphere of action and destiny. He himself informs us, for our encouragement, in the first part of the work under consideration, that he was once bitterly opposed to educating boys and girls in the same school, but that Horace Mann overcame his objections, by showing him practical results highly favorable to the plan of educating them together. And it may be that some other friend of Humanity, gifted with a large heart and comprehensive intellect, like our noble and lamented friend, will be able to influence the good Doctor's opinions on the present important question, and that he will ere long advocate social, civil, and religious liberty and equality for Woman, as well as for Man.

Many persons of education and general intelligence are constituted like unbelieving Thomas; they must have tangible proof of the thing affirmed before they are able to yield their full assent. They believe in Human Rights and impartial Justice, in the abstract; but, when some grand crisis approaches in which a radical change is needfully made, in order that society may be re-established, on broader foundations of liberty, equality and fraternity, they are immediately filled with apprehension and terror; they fear that society itself will be uprooted with the evil, lose faith in God and Man, and, at length, advocate vehemently the *old wrong* to which they have been so long accustomed, declaring it to be safer for society, than the *new right* for which progressive Humanity is pleading. And, thus, when Slavery existed in the Southern States of our country, many persons, conscientiously opposed to property in Man, were yet unwilling to see the "peculiar institution" abolished; because they feared that the Slaves would rise *en masse*, and massacre their oppressors in wholesale slaughter. But experience has proved that their terrors were idle. To-day, the Slaves are Freemen—through the influence of our beloved and lamented President, Abraham Lincoln, one of the noblest martyrs of Liberty—and they meet annually and offer up prayers and thanksgiving to Heaven for their freedom. Verity, verily, we say unto you, timid and doubting brother, or sister man, that the whole history of the world justifies us in the conclusion, that IT IS SAFE TO DO RIGHT, AND TO LEAVE CONSEQUENECS WITH DEITY.

CHAPTER IX.

*He shall speak peace unto the heathen; and his dominion shall be
from sea to sea and from the rivers to the ends of the earth.*

We have said in a former Chapter, that the Age is active and
expectant. The shadows of coming events are looming above
the moral horizon, and leading minds of the day are striving to
catch the significance of these impalpable and flickering prophecies, in order to learn what of promise they foretell to Man.
The Christian Church feels the inspirational influences of the
century, and her watchmen are looking forth from every Denominational Tower to catch a glimpse of the shadows which are
projected from the world of Cause, and to question if they herald
truly the Second Advent of the Messiah to earth.

And we have attempted, farther, to show that the present
Christian Era of the Reasoning Age of the World will mark the
Exodus of God's Church from the wilderness of creeds and forms
of her Childhood and Youth, and her rapid journeyings *forward*
to the Canaan of *reasoning faith*, flowing with the milk and
honey of celestial truth—forward, to a fuller and clearer interpretation of the Gospel of Intelligent Nature, viewed from higher
planes of spiritual progress and broader fields of knowledge.

And we have attempted, still farther, to show that Swedenborg, who was gifted by nature with a comprehensive reasoning
mind, and with apostolic vision and power, and zeal for the
spread of the true Christian Religion over the Earth, was the
chosen Agent of Heaven to inaugurate, in the early dawn of the

Era of Reason, the new or renewed Church of God, on broader and more rational principles of faith and practice, and to aid her in interpreting the marvellous volumes of Nature and of Revelation with a comprehensive and an inspired reason.

Let us now inquire: What is the duty of the Church of to-day, in view of her maturer years of reason and knowledge?—and in view of the relation which she sustains to the enlightened nineteenth century?—and, also, in view of the anticipated advent of the Mediative Son of God, to question if she have rightly improved the talents entrusted to her Youth, and if she is prepared for the re-baptism of the Holy Spirit?

Is not careful self-examination the first imperative duty of every individual member of the Christian Church? My soul, say unto my soul, what doest thou? Art thou a consistent Christian? Art thou thoroughly in earnest, laboring with all thy heart and mind and soul in the great work of redeeming and blessing the World? Art thou truly charitable towards other disciples of the Mediative Son of God, of different names, who are also laboring in his vineyard, seeking to work out their own salvation, and to do good to their fellows? Does thy light so shine before men, that others seeing thy good works are led to glorify thy Father which is in Heaven?

And is it not the first imperative duty of the Church, as a WHOLE, to examine her position and the foundation of her faith. with the eye of enlightened reason, to see if she have interpreted correctly and fully the Oracles of God?—and if her practice harmonize with her profession? Should not the Christian Church question herself closely in order to ascertain if she truly believe that which she professes, in regard to the *inspirational power* of her religion, and the *manifestations* of the Holy Spirit, which the Mediator told his beloved disciples, at the close of his divine ministrations to Humanity, would attend those who should truly believe and teach in his name, as *tests* of the vital power and influence of the Gospel of Intelligent Nature? For the All-Seeing Eye is upon her, and the critical mind of the nineteenth century is actively engaged in scanning her character, and in canvassing the doctrines which she teaches, and the claims which she presents for the acknowledgment of Mankind.

The enlightened reason of the age demands consistency in profession and practice. And the hour has now arrived when the Church of God must either manifest her faith in principles by corresponding works; or become a stumbling stone, instead of an arm of strength, to the travelers of Earth. She can no longer preach a spiritual religion, while rejecting the fruits of a spiritual life, and be accredited with either reason, or sincerity, outside of her own organizations. She must now stand by the principles inscribed on the Gospel Banner, prepared to meet their logical results, or she will be obliged to lower her Colors before swiftly advancing Rationalism, the bold antagonist and fearless enemy of Christianity.

And, in view of this formidable foe to Christ and his spiritual Kingdom,—and in view of the high obligations of the Church to herself as a Religious Body, and to the whole Human Family, for whom she is appointed to hold in trust the Oracles of God, is it not her manifest duty to rally all her various organizations and unite for effective action on the broad, moral battle-field of humanity ? Let narrow-minded prejudice give way, and denominational barriers be broken down in the vineyard of the Lord; and let rank weeds of precedence, envy and jealousy be uprooted from the soil. And let Denomination call aloud to Denomination to arise for UNION and ACTION. Let watch fires be kindled on every mountain top of Zion, and answering signals break forth from every plain and valley, until the moral world shall be all aglow with light. Ay, and let words of electric power be sent into the very bosom of the Church, like bolts of fervid lightning, bolt after bolt, until their reverberating thunders shall shake the Earth and Heavens, and awaken all the sleepers.

If the Christian Church really desires the universal reign of the Prince of Peace, and that the knowledge of God shall fill the earth, she has imperative duties to perform towards each individual member of her various organizations, and towards herself as an Associate Body, and towards the Christian State which is the outgrowth of the Christian Church; and farther on, in extending and intersecting circles, towards the whole Family of Man.

It is the imperative duty of the Church of the Reasoning Age to liberate her members from the old formulæ of doctrine of her undeveloped Childhood and Youth, to set them free from the dead letter of the Word, and re-baptise them in its living spirit;—mindful of the impressive words of Inspiration: The *letter* killeth, but the *Spirit* maketh alive ;—mindful, that the Mediative Son of God himself released his followers of all time from the crippling formulæ of creeds, when he declared that : Love to God and Love to Man is the fulfilling of the Law;—and mindful that the practice of a people is far more essential to the well-being of Individuals and of Nations than the articles of their belief. The world outgrows its political and religious creeds in the progress of ages. Man and Woman are everywhere superior to the constructed platform of their faith, and superior to the books which they indite; because infinite progress towards infinite perfection is their glorious birthright and immortal inheritance. Can we, then, speak too strongly against the inconsistency and folly of Christian Denominations of the present day, holding their members bound to a traditionary religion?

And it is also the imperative duty of the Christian Church, of the Reasoning Age of the World, to liberate Woman from the thraldoms of past ages of ignorance; and to give her an equal voice in the Church and in the State; remembering that Christianity is the purest Democracy, that it recognizes the broadest and grandest level of Humanity. Consistency and Justice demand that both the Church and State of Christendom should admit her equal rights, privileges and citizenship with Man.

It is the imperative duty of the Church of the Reasoning Age of the World, to look carefully after the *physical*, as well as *moral and intellectual* conditions and interests of the youth of Christendom, and the requirements of such conditions and interests; and to encourage early marriages among them by private counsel, and public legislation; in order that the passional nature of Man and Woman may not develop apart from the sentiments, but may be elevated and consecrated by them; and, thus that our sons and daughters may enter into sacred marriage relations with pure minds and healthy bodies; instead of enervated, demoralized and diseased organisms. This is of vital importance to society. A corrupt tree cannot bring forth good fruit. The renovation of the Church must be radical. Her regeneration must commence in the physical. First in the divine order is the natural, after, that which is spiritual. And, when the passional natures of man and Woman are properly cared for, then, the flaming sword that guards the *tree of life* in the garden of the Lord will no longer prove an avenger of violated law, as at present, cutting off large numbers of the Human Family in the midst of their years, but the recognized guard of innocence and virtue. The offspring of God's Church will then inherit clean hands and pure hearts, and will be self-poised and self-governing—in very truth, children of the Divine Father and Mother of the Heavens.

It is the imperative duty of the Church of the Reasoning Age of the World to look carefully after the amusements of the youth of Christendom, to see to it that they are promotive of good health and morals—that they are, in verity, toning to both mind and body.

Ah! the youth of Christendom would never become infidel to the God in whom they live, and move, and have their being, and infidel to Humanity, if the Church fulfilled her whole duty to them in the liberal spirit of supervisory love; if she diffused the light of immortality in her example and teaching;—if she clearly demonstrated the Law of the Spirit of Life by the facts of the past and present;—if she announced human accountability in trumpet tones of encouragement and of warning, showing clearly, from the pages of Philosophy, as well as of Revelation, that human responsibility is everywhere proportional with human capability;—if she taught earnestly and convincingly that *sin* is a violation of Moral Law, to which a penalty is as surely annexed as to a violation of Physical Law, and retribution fearful and inevitable; and that the habitual indulgence in any known sin, however insignificant it may appear, tends to weaken and blurr the moral perception, and prepare the way for the commission of other and greater sins; because evil, like good principles, are associative by the law of kind; they attract each other, they lie in

48

trains, and they lead the irresolute and self-indulgent soul downward, and downward, toward the blackness of darkness.

Alas! that the Church should be worldly-minded, cold, formal
and conservative, when she ought to be intensely alive, earnest
and radical, and prepared for efficient action, ready to strike the
axe of God's truth at every remaining root of evil in his vineyard.
The Church is the Almoner of Heaven to the Human Family.
She is required to attend to their temporal as well as spiritual
needs, and thus prepare them for the reception of higher principles of truth, and richer blessings from on high.

If the Church were really alive and zealous for the propoga-
tion of the Gospel of Intelligent Nature, she would feel herself
to be responsible for every reckless sinner, every degraded pau-
per, and every unfortunate convict in Christendom, and in the
whole world of Man.   And not one member of the great Human Family, however poor, demoralized, and lost to himself,
would remain uncared for and be lost to society.   For, every
city, town and village of the land, and all the remote places thereof, would be viewed as missionary ground, and would be divided
into districts for convenient supervisionary care.   And the various
Denominations of the Church throughout Christendom would
unite and organize a grand executive SOCIETY OF PEACE AND GOOD
WILL TO MAN, composed of concentric societies, or circles, for
comprehensive missionary labor, to provide for the temporal as
well as spiritual interests of the millions.

This proposed Society might be formed of three concentric societies, for convenient and effective united action.   They might
be named the Weekly, Monthly, and Yearly SOCIETIES, or the
Minor, Major, and Grand Circles.

It should be the duty of the GRAND CIRCLE of any State to district the land,—to apportion humanitary labor among the different branches of the Church,—to provide ways and means for
the advancement of the interests of the Society,—and to send
forth agents to other States and to remote Countries for the purpose of organizing similar societies for united Christian labor in
the vineyard of the Lord.

It should be the duty of the MAJOR CIRCLE of any State to establish Intelligence Offices at convenient distances—in every third or seventh district, as might appear advisable to managing committees—which Offices should be in constant communication with each other, for the purpose of regulating the demand for, and the supply of, labor in different sections of the State. And the Major Circles of the various States should be required to communicate with each other quarterly, near the opening of each season, for the above-named purposes.

It should be the duty of the MINOR CIRCLE to appoint visiting committees or distributing agents, for each district, of noble men and women, whose business it shall be to learn the situation and needs of the suffering poor; and to supply this class of citizens with provision, clothing, or employment, accordingly as their conditions may require; without reference to either sex, color, religion or nationality.

The Weekly Society should be required to report to the Monthly Society once in seven days. And the Monthly Society should also be required to report to the Yearly Society once in thirty days.

And it should be the duty of the Grand Circle of the States to call an annual union meeting of the principal Officers of all the Concentric Circles at the opening Month of Autumn, for the purpose of considering the conditions and requirements of the people residing in remote sections of our Country, and for discussing advisory measures for economic and efficient action, as well as for reviewing all questions of vital interest to society.

And, farther, it should be the duty of the Grand Circle to correspond with other Yearly Societies, formed in foreign countries, and to invite them to send delegates from abroad to visit our Annual Society, and report the conditions and needs of the millions living under other forms of Government, for the better understanding of humanitary interests and fuller co-operation with Christian Philanthropists of the various Nations of the earth.

Such Concentric Circles of united action in the Church would perform an important duty for the State, also, by the effective aid they would render in regulating social abuses; in preventing vice from concentrating in stagnant pools to breed crime, and disseminate a moral malaria all through the land; for they would turn the turbid streams, which run into those sinks of iniquity, into healthy channels of labor and productive industry. And these Concentric Circles would protect human beings from the demoralizing lash of jails and prisons, which are, in their present condition, mere nurseries of crime, and prevent the indiscriminate association of hoary-headed villains with youthful neophytes in sin, who thus become initiated into dark and fearful depths of hopeless infamy. For they would seek to have JUSTICE done to all classes of citizens, on broad humanitary ground, without reference to either sex, color, nationality or condition. Because such organizations would act upon His plan: Who causeth His sun to rise on the evil and on the good, and sendeth His rain upon the just and upon the unjust.

And these Concentric Circles would stimulate the political integrity of the Nation, by guarding the Ballot-Box with vigilance, and staying the hand of fraud with effective rebuke. And they would successfully prevent, by the uncompromising moral power of the VOTE, trading, wire-pulling politicians, prize-fighters and drunkards from entering the Halls of Congress as the representatives of the people, thereby disgracing our Country and profaning her sanctuary of Liberty. Ay, and they would forbid, in the sacred names of Right, Justice and Humanity, the ignorant and demoralizing Vote of the State (which is now purchased by party experts with the spoils of Office, and at the ruinous expense of integrity and honor, all that is noble in human nature, to advance the strategic movements of corrupt parties,) from ruling the intelligence, wisdom and virtue of our Nation, by uniform, persevering and determined action against the flagrant wrong. For, they would see to it that Intelligence, *alone,* is made the requisite qualification of the Voter, or the ability to read fluently and to write legibly the English Language; and that the right of Suffrage is universal, excluding no class of citizens, either on account of sex, or of color, or of nationality, cutting off only those who wilfully violate the laws of the land.

And these Concentric Circles would protect the *educational interests* of our Country, and see to it that her PUBLIC SCHOOL is not left to the care of unscrupulous, wire-pulling politicians who would play the part of Judas toward the most sacred interests of the State and of Humanity, if they could thereby advance their own selfish aims of to-day.

And let the Church remember that her strength and permanence, in the rapidly advancing Age of Reason, will depend on the general diffusion of knowledge and the universal enlightenment and enfranchisement of the millions. And, after she shall have organized and set in motion her Circles of Peace and Good Will to Man, for combined and faithful humanitary service, it will become her imperative duty to organize them in other countries, also; and to sow the Public Schools of the United States all over the inhabited globe,—to establish them in the Dark corners of the Earth which are full of the habitations of cruelty, and on the Islands of the Seas that are waiting for His Law. In no other way can she obey, in verity, the injunction of the Mediative Son of God, to preach the divine Gospel of Intelligent Nature to *every creature.* For, the Christian Church would surely rise and take its stand by the PUBLIC SCHOOL; and, thus, Intelligence and Religion would move forward, side by side, elevating and blessing the Nations, and filling the Earth with the Knowledge of God.

But, in order to establish successfully the SCHOOL and the CHURCH, commercial treaties must be made with all the barbarous peoples of the earth, and industrial occupations introduced among them, such as would be best adapted for developing the peculiar resources of the different countries which they occupy; and such as would also forward directly the objects of trade and commerce; and thus their knowledge would become utilized, and they would appreciate its advantages. The greater unity of material interests, resulting therefrom, would prepare the way for social order and harmony. And the uncultivated minds of the people would, through the influences of attractive and productive industry, become more impressible and receptive of knowledge and religious instruction, and thus lighten and render pleasant the laborious duties of Teachers and Pastors.

And these commercial enterprises would eventually become

remunerative and increase the capital of those who might cast their bread upon the waters. And, through such measures, the English Tongue would become the only language of Commerce; and the Gospel of Intelligent Nature, taught by Christ, the universal religion. And then would the wide World indeed become a BROTHERHOOD OF NATIONS.

We are fully aware that the enterprise proposed is of gigantic dimensions; but, the Church of to-day would be equal to undertaking and carrying it successfully forward, if it would resolve to unite and organize for co-operative action. And such an enterprise would attract to its aid all the God-like powers of Intelligent Nature, and all the forces of the physical world that Science has made available to Man. The Telegraph would transmit its fraternal messages from people to people; and Railroads and Steamships bear its ambassadors from country to country.

The discovery of gold in California and Australia bears on the interest of the New Era, and greatly facilitates enterprise. The Pacific Railroad is a powerful aid in bringing the peoples of remote parts of the earth together, and thns inducing concert of interests and action. The living current of travel will eventually set as strongly East as West, and the Orient and Occident clasp hands in fraternal sympathy.

But, if each Christian Sect continue to revolve in its own circumscribed sphere, and, like Diogenes in his Tub, to cry out to every other Denomination—"Stand out of my sunshine"—unmindful of the high duty imposed by the Gospel of Intelligent Nature, to let its light radiate upon all, and to shine with all, in constellated glory, reflecting the light of the great Spiritual Sun of the Heavens, THEN, it will accomplish nothing for the Deity which it professes to love, honor, and obey,—because it will accomplish nothing for the Humanity that He loves,—and will deserve to be cut down, like the barren fig-tree, as a cumberer of the ground.

CHAPTER X.

Master, we saw one casting out devils in thy name; and we forbade him, because he followeth not us. But Jesus said, Forbid him not; for there is no man which shall do a miracle in my name, that can lightly speak evil of me.

The union of the various Denominations of the Christian Church for co-operative labor in the vineyard of the Lord can never be accomplished by controversial argument, for the purpose of establishing points of doctrine. This proposition has been clearly and forcibly demonstrated by the experience of eighteen centuries. And there can never be a general awakening of the Church to the temporal and spiritual needs of the age, and combined action to meet these requirements, until the different Denominations of Christendom learn to exercise a wider charity towards, and to manifest a deeper sympathy with, each other. And this tender humanitary regard and Christian fellowship can only be attained by bringing the various Sects together for the direct purpose of setting aside non-essential differences, and of uniting broadly on the great principles of the Gospel of Intelligent Nature——LOVE TO GOD AND LOVE TO MAN——which divine principles the Mediative Son himself declares are the fulfilling of the law. And it is their duty to meet often together for the preparatory object of discussing the best methods of rendering the religion of love practical through all the ramifications of society.

A frequent exchange of pulpits among different Denominations would powerfully aid in breaking down sectarian barriers in the Church, and in preparing the way for combined action in grand humanitary labor. This measure would be a recognition of the unity of the Church of God, and would tend to cultivate in the minds of both Ecclesiastics and Laymen that Christian sympathy and charity to which we have alluded, and which are essential to union and co-operative action, as well as to vital Christianity.

And it is truly encouraging to observe that a few of the most talented and liberal Clergymen of the present have already advocated the advantages of an exchange of pulpits, and that they practice what they preach. But it is saddening to know that they suffer from Denominational and synodal abuse for striving to establish this freedom in Christ; because they are in advance of the bigotry of the religious world. We cordially extend the right hand of Christian fellowship to Henry Ward Beecher, and to Stephen S. Tyng, junior, and bid them God speed ! It is a great thing to establish even a precedence of Christian fellowship in the Church, in this age of the supremacy of CREEDS. Blessed are they who suffer persecution for righteousness sake; for theirs is the kingdom of Heaven.

Persecution is useful in advancing the cause of Liberal Christianity. It serves as healthy moral friction to rub off the oxyd from the iron hinges of exclusiveness and the bolts and bars of prejudice, the accumulations of darker ages; and Denominational doors will at length fly open through its influence without squeaking until the ears of the people tingle with the rasping dissonance while they are striving to listen to the grand Anthem of Redemption—Glory to God in the Highest, on earth peace, good will to Man.

The occasional exchange of pulpits, for a single Sabbath, would eventually lead to more lenghty exchanges, depending on the condition of pastors and people; and the amount of good that might be accomplished through these means, to both the clergy and laity is incomputable.

The teachings of one man for a consecutive number of years tend, continually, to limit the minds of the people over whom he is installed, to his own boundaries of knowledge and experience; and they cease at length to exercise independent thought, and become intolerant toward those of other sects who differ from them in religious opinions and doctrines.

And the mind of the Pastor deteriorates, also, under the same circumstances. For the reason that, as soon as the people are filled with his peculiar views of truth, they throw them back, in their turn, upon him—such is the philosophical action and reaction of mind—and bind him still more closely to his past conditions of development; thereby circumscribing his sphere by arguments borrowed from himself, and limiting his growth in grace and in the knowledge of God.

And the physical constitution of the Teacher is likewise injured by protracted pastoral duties. For, as he becomes accustomed, year after year, to the peculiar magnetic condition of his audience, it ceases to act as a healthy and invigorating stimulant upon his nervous system; while his intellectual faculties, which are constantly kept at high pressure, through a series of years, to provide varied instruction for the people, tend to exhaust rapidly his physical powers until he becomes languid in body and mind, unable to improve himself mentally, and unprofitable to his beloved people.

But, were the Pastor to go abroad at intervals of every third, or every fifth year, and fill a pulpit in some other State, or Country, for twelve consecutive months, he would be relieved for that space of time from the fatigue of preparing novel discourses weekly, in order to keep alive the interest of his hearers; and he would also be free from the old routine of pastoral duties. Under the new influences, the tension of body and mind would gradually relax, and he would fall into a passive and receptive condition for a season, which would prove favorable to health of body, vigor of mind, and growth of soul.

And the Pastor would widen also his sphere of use by introducing *new elements of thought* among the people who might become the subjects of his yearly ministrations, which would stimulate their minds, enlarge their views of truth, and liberate them from the peculiar limitations of their last Teacher.

And, after the Pastor should have resided for a few months

49

abroad, he would perceive that he himself had grown, while receiving unconsciously the silent lessons of his new surroundings, and that he had become stronger physically and mentally through the invigorating influences of change in his both material and spiritual relations.

The introduction of new ideas among the people, troubling the waters of their spirit, disturbing the old current of thought and feeling, would result in an awakened interest in religious subjects, a more earnest inquiry after truth, and a broader Christian charity. And this peculiar state of the mind of his hearers would act upon his own, kindling anew his spiritual life, until he would become all aglow with Divine and humanitary love, and more zealous than before to "Spread the truth from pole to pole."

And, when the Pastor should finally return to his own people, he would share with them the advantageous lessons of his newly acquired experiences, and learn from them, also, what of truth they had gained during his absence. And this separation of the Pastor from his people for a limited season would enable him to see more clearly their peculiar conditions and needs—even as the lineaments of the human face are more perfectly defined and their relations better observed by holding the mirror at a little distance from Nature—and, thus, aid him in adapting his instructions more perfectly to their requirements.

And, beyond the relations of Pastors and their people, there are still wider social circles and communities to be influenced by such exchanges. Public Teachers in the Church, of commanding intellects and liberal sentiments, should circulate freely and visit points where the forming power of genius is most needed. California of to-day presents a grand field of labor. The four quarters of the globe have been, and are, tributary to the population of that State; and it possesses fine and diverse elements of character, from which to model a superior civilization. The people there are strongly marked and individualized. Acquisitiveness, enterprise and liberty are powerfully operative in the mind of its conglomerate mass of population; and the right kind of educational and of religious influences are needed to inform the whole living body, and to aid in producing social order, elevation and harmony.

In the Spring of eighteen hundred and sixty, a STARK of the first magnitude rose above the horizon of the Western World, and became a great guiding light of the Pacific States. Men and women of all denominations and of all nationalities felt the inspirational glow of his brilliant intellect, kindled by his great oving heart, and paused to do him reverence. But, while they gazed with admiring awe, he culminated in sublime power to the zenith of the moral Heavens, and was lost to their view amid the luminous galaxy of sons and daughters of Deity, who make glorious the Spiritual Universe of God. Alas ! that California should have lost in her youth the grand rallying Leader, who could thus powerfully attract the multitudes of his fellow citizens and inspire them with so true an appreciation of their relations to their God, to their Country and to Humanity, that they would feel ashamed to betray either in the presence of his Loyal Soul.

California needs and demands enlightened teachers and leaders, who are not afraid to introduce " secular subjects " into the pulpit. Indeed, truly inspired preachers of the Gospel regard no subjects as merely secular which involve the principles of right and justice, and the practice of virtue. All human interests are sacred to the far-seeing Christian Philosopher.

Transforming genius makes all themes divine.

When the popular voice cries out: " Secular subjects ought not to be introduced into a Temple dedicated to the worship of God "—*then* the Church may know that there is an imperative call for the treatment of the tabooed question, in order that some far-spreading evil may be arrested in its progress. The Pulpit becomes the stronghold of Satan, when it fails to rebuke the sinner,—when it is too timid to advocate the higher law in the government of the Nation—and to speak out fearlessly against the abuses of public trust,—and against demoralizing sins in high places,—as did the noble and gifted King.

The services of men and women of genius, with large, sympathetic hearts and vitalizing minds, are everywhere needed, and, the more they circulate, the greater amount of good will be effected for society.   Men and women of genius stand on the broad platform of eternal principles.   Superstitions and Dogmas fly from the minds of the people at their approach, as hurtful malaria before the life-inspiring sun and breath of heaven.   Sectarian barriers will always give way before those earnest Souls, who dare to say boldly to a creed-bound age, that Man is greater than his creeds !—that the Sabbath was made for Man, and not Man for the Sabbath; wherefore it *is* lawful to do well upon that day, even if it break the Law of Moses.

Ay, the people always feel large and grow large in the presence and freedom of men and women of great generalizing minds and loving hearts.   They recognize in such sons and daughters of God, the grander tones and forces of Nature,—as the sweep of winds from eternity of ether,—the play of Ocean's illimitable waves,—and the inextinguishable light and beauty of the bending heavens.   In their presence, how insignificant appears the dead letter of a truth, compared with the inspirational glow of its living spirit !   Ah, how puerile is the mere form of doctrine to those who have felt the quickening power of conviction penetrate their souls with the force of the noon-day sun !   What is the chaff to the wheat ? saith the Lord.

Truly, it will be a great triumph for Christianity, when the Watchmen on the walls of Zion see, eye to eye, and can answer the earnest pilgrim who inquires:—" What of the morning ?"—" The mists and clouds of the night of ages are rolling up from the moral horizon, like a mighty scroll, and passing away before the rising Sun of Righteousness.   The allied armies of Christ, composed of every nation, kindred, tongue and people, are marshalled on the field of action.   Union and love !—Fight the good fight of faith !—Overcome evil with good !—are inscribed on all denominational banners; and, one Lord, one faith, one baptism, one communion table for the Soldiers of the Cross ! Great victories have already been achieved over cruel ignorance and prejudice, and sectarian bigotry, envy, jealousy and all uncharitableness.   We are preparing to attack the forces of Rationalism with the sword of the Spirit, double-edged with the philosophy of Gospel Truth."   " Thank God."

But, before the heart and mind of the Christian Church can become accordant, there will be, of necessity, a season of startling unrest, and of strong antagonisms between the false and the true—as we have already demonstrated in the first part of the present volume.   We have there clearly shown, from the progressive unfolding of the Human Family in past cycles of time, and from the logical sequence of events, that the generations of Man, of the nineteenth century, are living in the Transitionary period of the Reasoning Age of the World, and of the Second Christian Era;   and, that, consequently, the present is pre-eminently the season of radical changes in society, of sudden outbursts of popular feeling, and of upheavals amid the foundations of old institutions, social, civil, and religious.   It is a season of fierce Conservative wrath, as well as of furious radical zeal, which will produce everywhere strong action and reaction.   The timid of all religious sects in Christendom will fly for greater security and comfort to the old formulæ of religious doctrine, to the Regime of Authority, (which still requires of its adherents unquestioning faith and implicit obedience,) seeking for rest, *in vain*, beneath the ægis of the Ancient Church of the first Christian Era, of the undeveloped Youth of the World.

And, while reckless and unreasoning reactionists will rush blindly on, striving in impassioned and abortive effort for impossible results, the strong in Reason, and in Faith, and Love toward God and Man, will stand firmly, each in the place appointed by Heaven, and speak to the troubled spirit of the age—Peace !—Be still ! The discordant elements of human passion will pause at their command ; and a grander calm will succeed in the moral world than that which followed His voice in material Nature, when he rebuked the winds and waves that tossed his bark upon the sea of Galilee.   For, hath He not said to his disciples of all time: Greater works than these, which I have done, shall ye do, and because I go to THE FATHER.

And these inspired children of God, the Spiritualistic Rationalists of the Reasoning Age of the Church and World, will reconstruct, from the comprehensive Gospel of Intelligent Nature, taught by the profound Philosopher of Nazareth, a broader and higher platform of Christian faith and practice. Its piles of truth will be driven deeply into the bed-rock of Human Nature, and will penetrate and quicken all the stratifications of society, like shafts of living light sent home to the soul of being by the great Spiritual Sun of the Universe. For the Reasoning Age of Man must inevitably be a season of *reconstruction*, as well as of disorganization; and a period for the forming of new and nobler ties, as well as for the rendition of the old. Because Reason is, as we have already shown, an active, and an adjustive power in the moral world, which observes principles and their relations, and prophesies results from the altitude of *cause;* and will, at the ripe moment in the Councils of Jehovah, move forward to effective action, and bring order out of confusion. Enlightened Reason everywhere follows the lead of Cause and Effect, and co-operates with Deity who speaks to the Human Family in an unbroken chain of sequences.

CHAPTER XI.

THE BAPTISM OF THE HOLY GHOST.

He shall baptize you with the Holy Ghost, and with fire.
I will hear, saith the Lord; I will hear the Heavens, and they shall hear the Earth.

It has been said, in a former Chapter, that the Christian Church was on a more external plane of thought and action in her unreflecting Youth, and consequently, the minds of her people were occupied with the *letter* of the Gospel, rather than with its *spirit*. Ay, the peculiar interpretation of the text, and the special form of worship, engaged the attention of both the Clergy and Laity. And endless controversies arose, as a natural sequence, and angry contentions concerning forms, and concerning various points of doctrine, which were, and still are, erroneously believed to be essential to salvation.

But the Church is rapidly passing through a Transitionary Period and advancing from Youth toward her nobler Age of Reason; and she is now required to leave the dead formulæ of doctrine, and take a higher stand on the living principles of the Gospel of Intelligent Nature, and to cease her acrimonious disputations and juvenile cavilings respecting the non-essentials of faith and practice. The *external* baptism of Water, instituted by John, was a symbol only of the spiritual baptism of the Holy Ghost and of fire, with which he declared that Christ would baptize and purify the Church of God. The immersion of the Church in the full spirit of truth, in the knowledge of the Dual God, the Divine Father and Mother of Humanity——(and hence the universal

Brotherhood of Man)—is the required baptism of her Reasoning Age, in the Second Advent of the Redeemer of the World.

The mind of Christendom is now anxiously turned in the direction of that important event which will be attended, of necessity, with more powerful and wider spread manifestations of the Spirit, and with greater influx of light and truth from above than marked the period of His First Advent; because of the growth of the Church and World for eighteen centuries in the spiritual principles of the Christian Religion. And, in confirmation of this philosophic deduction from the experiences and facts of the past, from the spiritual growth of ages, we have the testimony of the Mediative Son himself concerning his "second appearing," recorded by St. Paul in the impressive language of Inspiration: Yet once more I shake not the earth only, but also heaven. The inspired Watcher sees that the powers of the heavens are even now shaken, and that spiritual fruit is dropping upon the earth, to nourish and quicken the spiritual life of its millions; and that the preparation for his coming in great power and glory is rapidly advancing.

During the past few years of destructive earthquakes, calamitous accidents, and decimating wars, the spiritual forces of earth and Heaven have been signally shaken. Thousands of the Human Family have been cut off suddenly in the glorious promise of youth and in the noble prime of manhood. Beloved husbands, fathers and children have been forcibly wrenched from the strong ties of home and country, and borne—Oh!—where?—arose the agonized cry of the mothers and daughters of the land, weeping for their dear departed ones, and refusing to be comforted, because they were not. Deep uttered to Deep the despairing cry —"Oh!—where?—rending the heavens with importunity of sorrow. And, from the realm of the unseen, yet real, Soul responded to Soul, pouring through the cloud-rifts of grief immortal light, and hope, and love, to appease immortal longings. Words of unutterable tenderness came from the viewless mansions of the air, with dear familiar names, that caused the throbbing heart to pause in hearkening.

And such is the natural manifestation, or philosophic action of the mind of Man, which is immortal in its affections and aspirations, infinite in its capabilities, and in its adaptation to ever-varying and progressive conditions. Because Man is the legitimate offspring of the Spiritual and Eternal Creative Intelligence of the Universe, and his undying intellect and affections are constantly seeking for fuller expression. Ay, it is natural, and therefore philosophical, for human beings to desire to follow the loved and lost to sight beyond the vale which separates the transient from the permanent. And, it is also natural for those who have been suddenly torn away from their dearest earthly ties, to desire to return again, to bind the bleeding tendrils of affection, as well as to receive a recognition from their own beloved ones.

And the sudden rupture of many soul-links on the earth-sphere has a direct tendency to draw heaven and earth together in closer sympathetic relations, and to produce more favorable conditions for wide-spread Spirit manifestations. And there never was a period in the history of Man, when the Natural World and the Spiritual were drawn as closely together as they are to-day, while so many wounded hearts are seeking for reunion with their departed. The facts of the past and present bear witness to the truth of the foregoing proposition.

Let the Sceptic pause and reflect ere he denounce Spirit Intercourse a delusion, the effect of a diseased imagination; for he, too, is human, and may, sometime, feel the agony of desolation, which will wring from his own heart an involuntary cry for one familiar and endearing word from his lost treasures, to soothe the pang of separation; when he, too, will question eagerly of Earth and Heaven in the infinite longings of bereaved affection:—"Do they *love* there still?—O! say—DO THEY LOVE THERE STILL?"

But the spiritual forces of earth and heaven will be more strongly shaken as the Age of Reason and of reasoning Christianity advances. Because, if the Church accept the Gospel of Intelligent nature with the *reason*, as well as the affections, she will recognize Christ and his missions fully and broadly; and such a recognition will involve a fundamental reconstruction of her formulæ of doctrine. For in him dwelt ALL THE FULLNESS OF THE GODHEAD. He represented both the Divine Father and Mother God to their sons

50

and daughters of Time. And this pivotal truth of Intelligent Nature, and of the Christian Religion. which is its exponent, has not yet been seen and accepted by the Church; notwithstanding it was the Mediative Son's divine mission to Humanity to illustrate, in his own character, and to show forth, in his marvellous teachings, this CENTRAL TRUTH of the Universe—THE GOD MALE AND FEMALE;--and to show, as a consequent of this primal truth, the relations of the various members of the Human Family to the All-Parent as children, and to each other as brethren; and the natural obligations of loving obedience to the former, and loving regard to the latter, involved in this dual relation of Man to the Divine All-Parent, and to the divine Humanity.

The student of Science recognizes the Male and Female principle in the very structure of the earth, as distinctly as in higher creations of organized matter that dwell upon and ornament its surface. They are exhibited in the close affinities of mineral substances of opposite qualities, as clearly as in the various and beautiful flowering shrubs and trees which will bear no fruit to reward the labor of the husbandman, if either of these principles be absent; or as visibly as they appear, through the wide range of the animal kingdom, in the universal law of reproduction.

The fruitfulness, beauty and perfection of the Material World depend on the procreating power of the Male and Female Principles of Creation. And they are everywhere engaged in evolving, from lower series of vegetable and animal life, still higher and higher classes of existences, in the divine order of their unfolding.

And the equipoise and beauty of the Moral World in the coming ages will result from an intelligent recognition of the pivotal truth of the Universe of matter and of mind—THE GOD MALE AND FEMALE. Nature teaches the profound doctrine, from centre to circumference. Revelation takes up the marvellous teachings of Nature in harmonious measure, telling us, in confirmation of her silent but impressive lessons : In the beginning God the Father said unto God the Mother, Let us make Man in *our* image, and after *our* likeness. The logical sequence followed. So God created Man, male and female, in the image and after the likeness of THE GOD, Male and Female.

In the Infancy of the Church and World, when Man was in a state of innocence and ignorance, and was instructed orally by angel intelligences, ministers of the Divine All-One, the Human Family were in a passive condition, favorable for receiving instruction and accepting, in simple, unquestioning faith, the profoundest truth of Intelligeut Nature—that Man is the offspring of the Divine Father and Mother God. But, in the active Childhood of the human race, when the organized Church was established among the Israelites, who were the chosen people to hold the Oracles of God in trust for the Nations,—and when the written Law succeeded the oral instruction by angel intelligences,—and inspired men took the place of these attendants and teachers, in order to discipline and direct the growing powers and intense activities of the Children of the World,— *then* the people lost sight of the Divine Mother of Humanity, and of the high spiritual truths which they had been taught in their receptive Infancy; because they were energetically engaged on the external planes of thought and action, learning the simple alphabet of Material Nature; and were unable to perceive and, consequently, to claim their high spiritual relation to Creative Intelligence as CHILDREN OF GOD.

And, so it came to pass in those days that Israel, a representative of the Almighty Parent to the chosen people, was appointed their Spiritual Father for a season, and they were called the CHILDREN OF ISRAEL. The term Father, used in a generic sense, acted as a bond of union between the different tribes of the Hebrews; and they could better comprehend their generic relation to an earthly being of superior intelligence than to a Heavenly.

The Mosaic Dispensation of Law and Authority for governing and directing the erratic Childhood of the Church was, as before stated, a special revelation of the Divine Father, and but a partial statement of the central truth of Intelligent Nature, adapted to the condition and understanding of the undeveloped Children of the World; while, yet, it taught directly, and was intended so

to teach, an important phase of this sublime central truth—the
ONENESS of the Godhead.   For this was the natural and prescribed order of the unfolding of the Human Family in the
knowledge of Deity.

The Christian Dispensation of Love and Free-Will to Man,
addressed to the farther progressed Youth, when the people were
better prepared for the reception of more interior spiritual truths,
was, as we have already shown, a special revelation of the Divine Mother; then, the FULLNESS of the Godhead was first taught
to the ripening heart and mind of the Human Family, by Jesus
Christ, the great Democratic Philosopher of the World.   He was
the only one of all the ages permitted to behold the individuality
in unity of the Dual Godhead; and the only one of all the ages
who was able to view human relations from the sublime altitude
of Cause, and to measure the broad humanitary ground with his
far-extending vision.   At the appointed hour in the Councils of
Deity he was sent to earth, commissioned by the Divine Father
and Mother to baptize the Human Family into their *true generic
name*—CHILDREN OF GOD.   And the baptism of The Holy
Ghost and of fire, with which John, the Inaugurator of the first
Christian Era, declared that Christ would baptize the people, is
the baptism into the knowledge of the FULLNESS OF THE GODHEAD
—All-Father—All-Mother—the Infinite of Wisdom, the Infinite
of Love.

In the physical ages, or Childhhod of the World, the dominance of the animal propensities tended still farther to blurr the
spiritual perception of the people, so that they were unable to
perceive the most sacred. as well as central truth of Intelligent
Nature.   Circumcision was instituted by the Mosaic Church, to
teach that the sensual nature of Man should be checked and
disciplined.   Yet, this external symbol of the denial of passion
appears to have exercised but little power in staying the frightful
abuse of the affectional nature of the Israelites in the early period
of their history.   Circumcision was not introduced in the Christian Church, because her religion was a *higher spiritual dispensation*.   The Church of God had passed on to her more advanced
period of Youth, and the curb of due restraint, needfully im-

posed on the turbulent Children of the World, was removed; discipline, for the regulation of conduct, was no longer enforced on the external plane; it was addressed to the heart and mind of Man, presenting *motives* for right action. St. Paul, influenced by this view of the subject, declares: For in Jesus Christ neither circumcision availeth anything, nor uncircumcision, but faith, which worketh by love.

Yet, even in the dark ages of unreflecting ignorance, men and women experienced shame and confusion of spirit when they formed alliances on the purely animal plane. There was an inner consciousness that something sacred had been profaned. It was the voice of the Holy Ghost, or All-Mother, in the human soul, pleading for the diviner marriage, for the consecration of the passional nature by the higher sentiments and affections, that pure and noble offspring might be ultimated therefrom, in the image or form, and after the likeness or essential qualities of the Godhead.

The prostitution of the affectional nature of the sexes, by marriages of passional attraction, merely, which induced shame and confusion in the dark ages, manifested itself in the increasing light of the world, in decided unhappiness and loss of health and self-respect in women; and in satiety and cowardice in men. And these qualities exhibited themselves in the latter, during the absence of desire, in ill-nature and cruel injustice toward women, whom, even while they courted, they contemned. For, unregenerate men were too proud, and too selfish, to blame themselves for the sin in which they habitually indulged, and too weak to break its trammels, and resolve to strive for the freedom of a pure and elevated manhood; and so they followed the ignominious example of Father Adam, and cast upon women all the blame of their weakness and demoralization. And, consequently, women have been denounced, all through the ages, as guileful, beautiful, and, yet, *weak creatures, the tempters of the strong*, who are represented as being armed with superior knowledge and wisdom, and the finer powers of a cultivated and logical understanding. Certes, consistency was not a virtue of the Childhood and Youth of the World.

And, because of the gross abuse of the passional nature of the
Human Family, all through the ages of the past, the divine office of Maternity has been shamefutly degraded by both sexes;
but, more particularly by Man than Woman; for the reason that
he is not naturally as religious as she; his soul is not as responsive to the voice of the Spirit, because he does not approach as
near to the *heart* of Intelligent Nature, as Woman, Heaven's appointed Mother and re-creator of the human race after the Divine Order.

Christianity,—the sublime Philosophy of Intelligent Nature,
which reveals the *fullness of the Godhead*, and the consequent
broad and democratic level of Human beings, as children of the
Divine Father and Mother,—was Woman's earliest and truest
friend.   For eighteen centuries the Holy Ghost, Comforter, or
Divine Mother, has been silently, yet mightily at work, producing grand moral results in the realm of mind, even as the unseen but powerful influences of material nature, in bringing
forth, in its annual order, a new world of fruits and flowers.

Woman's capabilities and destiny were, of necessity, a SEALED
BOOK in the dark, physical ages; because sex was only recognized in its external manifestations; its high spiritual offices
were not perceived.   The pearls of Heavenly truth could not
be given to the ignorant, unreflecting millions; because they
would trample them under foot; and so the people were obliged
to be fed with crumbs from the Master's Table, accordingly as
they were able to receive and appropriate spiritual food.   It
does not appear that the prophets of Israel were illumined on
the profound truth of THE GOD Male and Female; and the consequent relative value of Woman in the scale of Intelligent Nature, as the representative of the Divine Mother of Humanity,
even as Man is the representative of the Divine Father.   And,
thus, their statements of human relations and obligations were,
ex necessitate, crude and partial.

Before the advent of the Mediative Son of God, Woman was
regarded, indeed, by the masses of Mankind, as the mere servant of the passions; while the Philosophers of those days believed and taught that she was destitute of a soul; and yet, not-

withstanding this deficiency in her organization, the special object of her existence was to propagate *men* with *immortal souls!* And the peculiar influence of these early and illogical teachings are still apparent, as we have already shown, even in the higher forms of Democratic Christian civilization. Ye ghostly Sages of the night of Time, were ye permitted to bar the pearly gates of Paradise against your Mothers, as punishment for enduring the fearful pangs of maternity, to give birth to such unnatural offspring?

But the indignant heart of the Christian is appeased by the written Word of Revelation: No man in Heaven, nor on Earth, was found *worthy to open the* DIVINE BOOK of INTELLIGENT NATURE, nor to loose the seals thereof, neither to look thereon. For only the pure in heart shall see God. But the Lamb that was slain, by the sin of the world that he came to redeem from error, was found pure and holy, and worthy to take the Book and to open the seals thereof. He was able, because of the profound depth of his human and divine love, the purity of his noble manhood, and the subtle power of his comprehensive reason, to perceive and to understand the divine marriage of the Heavens, and, hence, the relations of Man and Woman to the Divine All-Parent as children, and to the divine Humanity as brethren.

And, for the reason that the Mediative Son of God viewed all human relations from the lofty altitude of Cause, he understood Woman's nature, capabilities and destiny, as clearly as Man's; and, consequently, his statements of human relations and obligations were impartial and comprehensive. How holy and binding the marriage relation must have appeared to him, from his elevated plane of observation, and knowledge of the sacred marriage of the Heavens!—which was also the prescribed order of marriage for all the sons and daughters of earth, who were made in the image and after the likeness of the Divine Father and Mother God.

The Mediator's view of the sancity of the marriage sacrament is clearly and forcibly presented in the New Testament, in his reply to the Pharisees, who inquired—tempting him to say something contrary to the Law of Moses—Is it lawful for a man to put away his wife? Jesus answered and said unto them, What did Moses command you? And the Pharisees said, Moses suffered to write a bill of divorcement, and to put her away. The Christ replied: For the hardness of your heart he wrote you this precept. But from the beginning of the creation God made them male and female. For this cause shall a man leave his father and mother, and cleave to his wife; and they *twain* shall be one flesh. What therefore God hath joined together, let not man put asunder. Language could not express more clearly and strongly the Redeemer's understanding of the high moral obligations of those who accept the marriage relation.

An additional reason why the Divine Mother, Comforter, or Holy Ghost, has not yet been recognized in her own individual and independent existence, is because that the belief in a TRIUNE, instead of a DUAL Godhead, has obtained in the Church and World. The *Sacred Family Trinity*, revealed by Heaven to Mary, through the angel Gabriel, in order to show to the sons and daughters of God on earth their true relation to Deity, and the sacredness of parental obligations, was interpreted by the Fathers of the Church, of the partially developed ages, or Youth of the World, to signify TRIUNE GOD; and the minds of the millions were, and still are, limited by this erroneous view of the Godhead.

The Mediative Son of God did not so expound the Gospel of Intelligent Nature. He speaks of himself always as the Son, Mediator, or Representative of Heaven, exercising delegated authority. All power is *given* unto me in heaven and in earth. And, again: Thinkest thou that I cannot now pray to my Father, and he shall presently *give me* more than twelve legions of angels? And, again: My Father is greater than I. It is true that the Son frequently declares: I and my Father are ONE. But, in the context, he immediately exhorts his beloved disciples, in the most touching and impressive language: Be ye also one, *even as we are one*. And in our dear Redeemer's tender and beautiful prayer to the Father for his disciples, as he drew near to the close of his divine ministrations to humanity, he includes in loving remembrance all the family of Man: Neither pray I for these alone, but for them also who shall believe on me through their word; that they all may be one; as thou, Father, art in me, and I in thee, that they also may be one in us: that the world may believe that thou hast sent me. *And the glory which thou gavest me I have given them; that they may be one, even as we are one:* I in them, and thou in me, that they may be made perfect in one; and that the world may know that thou hast sent me, *and hast loved them, as thou hast loved me.* On one occasion, in order to illustrate the character of his Gospel and Mission, Jesus took a little child in his arms, and said unto the multitude: Whosoever shall receive one of such children in my name, receiveth me; and whosoever shall receive me, *receiveth not me, but* HIM *that sent me.* When the Jews accused Christ of blasphemy, because he claimed that God was his Father, he teaches the world, in his wise reply, the exalted nature of human beings, and the comprehensive significance of THE FATHER: Is it not written in your law, I said, Ye are Gods? If ye called them Gods, unto whom the word of God came, and the Scriptures cannot be broken; Say ye of him, whom THE FATHER hath sanctified, and sent into the World, Thou blasphemest; because I said, I am the Son of God?

Neither did the early Apostles and disciples of the Mediative Son understand and teach that Christ is God himself incarnate, accordingly as the Trinitarians of the Christian Church of to-day believe and teach the doctrine. It is written in Hebrews: God, who at sundry times and in divers manners, spake in times past unto the fathers by the prophets, hath in these last days spoken unto us by his Son, whom he hath *appointed* heir of all things. Again; the Spirit itself beareth witness with our spirit, that we are the children of God: And if Children, then heirs; heirs of God, and *joint heirs* with Christ. St. Paul, who was a profound logician and possessed a grand generalizing mind, renders a clear, concise and masterly statement of the Redeemer's Mission, as well as of his relations to the Divine and to the divine Humanity, in the following comprehensive language: As in Adam, the natural man—all die; even so in Christ, the spiritual man—shall all be made alive. Then cometh the end, when

51

he shall have delivered up the Kingdom to God, even the Father, when he shall have put down all rule, and all authority and power. For he must reign, till he hath put all enemies under his feet. The last enemy that shall be destroyed is death. For God hath put all things under his feet. But when He saith, All things are put under him, it is manifest that He is excepted, which did put all things under him. And when all things shall be subdued unto him, then shall the Son also himself be subject unto him that put all things under him, that God may be all in all.

This passage from the Scriptures is a fuller and grander presentation of Christ's mediatorial office, and of His relations to the Divine, and to the divine Humanity, than has ever yet been received and taught in the Christian Church. But, in her noble reasoning age, when she shall rise superior to the traditional religion of her Youth, and the scales of ignorance and prejudice shall fall from her eyes, and she shall be re-baptized with the Holy Ghost and with fire, and the Spirit itself shall witness with her spirit that she is walking in beauty, innocence and power, side by side with the Bridegroom; THEN she will see with joy and thanksgiving that the text above cited contains a glorious promise of universal redemption.

St. Peter, in the Acts of the Apostles, expresses his own views, clearly and forcibly, respecting the relations of Christ to the Divine, and to the Divine Humanity, and adds his testimony to that of St. Paul, in regard to the universality of the Mediator's Mission. He shall send Jesus Christ, which before was preached unto you: whom the heavens must receive until *the times of restitution of all things*, which God hath spoken by the mouth of all his holy prophets since the world began. For Moses truly said unto the fathers: A *Prophet* shall the Lord your God raise up unto you of your brethren, *like unto me;* him shall ye hear in all things whatsoever he shall say unto you.

And, in all that is written of the Prince of Peace, from Genesis to Revelation, we learn that he is missioned, by the King of Kings, to put all enemies of Deity under his feet,—to subdue them with the divine Gospel of Love The last enemy that shall be destroyed is Death. And the last enemy to be de-

stroyed for the individual, for the Church, and for the World of
Man is Death.   And, it is to be overcome by *virtue*, and by
knowledge of *eternal life* in ever-perfecting order, as the soul of
Man stretches grandly forward and upward toward the Infinite
Source of existence, forever and forever.

The sting of Death is *sin*, saith the Apostle Paul, and the
strength of sin is the law, (which law demands holiness of heart
and mind, and willing and loving obedience to the great principles of the Gospel of Intelligent Nature—justice and love.)   But,
thanks be to God, which giveth us the victory through our Lord
Jesus Christ. .For, by walking in his footprints, we become
children of Light, Law and Love, over whom Death hath no
power.

When the Human Family shall learn, through the Gospel of
Intelligent Nature, the sublime truth that what is termed death, is
not a going out of the vital spark of existence into darkness—nor
uncertainty—nor fearful annihilation; but a glorious change to
higher and higher spheres of life through God's eternal ages; then,
the last enemy of Man will be destroyed; death will be lost in
fullness of life, and the kingdoms of this world will become the
kingdoms of our Lord and Savior Jesus Christ.

He who illumined the dark valley of the *shadow* of death with
the glorious truth of immortality, he who himself led captivity
captive, and taught the World, by the elevated example of his
pure and holy life, as well as by the truth of Revelation, how to
obtain the victory over the last enemy of Man, is even now on
earth, is even now leading the noble army of the faithful Soldiers of the Cross forward in the van of truth, and going forth
from conquering and to conquer.   Our Lord is marching on !
And Death and Hell flee away before him.   But, Alas ! the
Church, the Bride, the well beloved, is seized with alarm at the approach of the Bridegroom, for her wedding garments are folded
in a napkin, and her lamps are not trimmed and burning.

It does not appear from the New Testament that the disciples
of Christ understood fully His divine Gospel, or Philosophy of
Intelligent Nature, and that they were able to see the Divine
Mother of Humanity, vailed in the Comforter and Holy Spirit.

For, at this period of human unfolding, the popular mind was too gross to perceive the subtle spiritual philosophy of the Gospel, and comprehend its deep, interior significance. The truths of the Spirit must be spiritually discerned. And the Church was influenced by the peculiar character and enlightenment of the outside world. A strong, twofold power, the extremes of mental action—*philosophy* and *prejudice*—acted also against the reception of this advanced truth. First, the *philosophy* of human conditions and requirements in the undeveloped ages (when masculine energy, rather than feminine, was demanded on the physical plane of action to control and develop material interests; and, on the moral plane, to govern, by constraint and restraint, the undisciplined and erratic Childhood of the human race,) was received by the ignorant millions and became their standard of truth and action: and, second, *prejudice* against new phases, or presentations of old, familiar forms of truth into which the people had been indoctrinated in their early years,— and which their Fathers had believed for many generations,—and which they had regarded as sacred and unalterable, because the highest that could be given to Man, acted as a strong barrier against the reception of fuller and broader principles in the progress of the Human Family toward maturity.

And, when we recollect that, prior to the advent of the Mediator, the finest and most comprehensive minds concluded, from their limited observation of the nature, conditions and requirements of mankind, that the principles which they discovered to be then in operation, presented the whole grand order and truth of Intelligent Nature, instead of its simple alphabet;—and when we recollect that these lights of the World concluded farther that, because of the dominance of the Masculine power *then* observable, it must always continue supreme in the Universe; and that, as a legitimate sequence, Woman was an inferior creation, and must always remain so, and could not, therefore, be admitted to the abodes of Male blessedness in the Paradise of the immortal Gods; when we remember this, we repeat, it is not amazing that the humble disciples of Christ were unable to recognize the Divine Mother of the Godhead. They had been carefully instructed in the solitary majesty and glory of the Almighty Father; and the doctrine carried with it the sanctity and power of accumulated ages of testimony.

This view of the subject enables us to better understand the wisdom of Christ's method of teaching, by vailing his profoundest truths in parables, and by presenting the *individuality* of the Divine Mother of the Godhead, in the sacred and endearing name of Comforter, or Holy Ghost. How tenderly and truly he represents the Divine Mother to his disciples in the following language: If I go and prepare a place for you, I will come again and receive you unto myself; that where I am there ye may be also. If ye love me, keep my commandments. And I will pray the Father, and he shall give you another COMFORTER, even the Spirit of Truth, to guide you into *all* truth—into the knowledge of the *fullness* of the Godhead Male and Female—and to abide with you forever. How comprehensive, in this connection, is the word *forever!* The Mediative Son clearly saw that the Comforter, or Divine Mother, once received into the heart and mind of the Human Family, could never again be rejected. Because, thenceforth, all Nature, animate and inanimate, which is full of the tender and profound lessons of her fostering care, would keep her in everlasting remembrance.

The Mosaic Dispensation of LAW and AUTHORITY, represents the Divine Father of the Godhead in the character of Administrative Justice; while the Christian Dispensation of LOVE and FREE-WILL represents the Divine Mother of the Godhead in the character of Reconciling Mercy. The two dispensations were clearly and finely prefigured to the World at Mount Horeb. And, behold the Lord passed by, and a great and a strong wind rent the mountains, and brake in pieces the rocks; but the Lord was not in the wind: and after the wind an earthquake, but the Lord was not in the earthquake: and after the earthquake a fire; but the Lord was not in the fire:—and after the fire *a still small voice*, that talked with the Prophet of Israel.

After the sublime display of Omnipotent Power on the material plane, which rent the mountains, shook the earth to its deep centre, and burst forth in flame; how impressively the *still small voice* of the Holy Spirit speaks to the human soul.   It is the voice of the Christian Dispensation of LOVE, the voice of the Comforter. of the Divine Mother of Humanity; yea, it is the voice of the Heart of Deity, gentle and low; and refreshing, As the dew of Hermon, and as the dew that descended upon the mountains of Zion; where the Lord commanded the blessing, even life forevermore.

CHAPTER XII.

Thou shalt love the Lord thy God, with all thy heart, and with all thy soul, and with all thy mind.

This is the first and great commandment.

And the second is like unto it, Thou shalt love thy neighbor as thyself.

On these two commandments hang all the law and the prophets.

The Church Universal of the advancing intellectual and moral ages will take her stand broadly and grandly on the sublime Philosophy of the Gospel of Intelligent Nature, taught by the Mediative Son of God, leaving her members free to believe as much of form, or of doctrine, contained in past interpretations of the Word, as they shall require for staves to aid them in ascending the heights of the mountain of Zion. And then she will be able to show clearly to the World the philosophy of the past conditions of her Infancy, Childhood and Youth, and Justify the ways of God to Man, from the accumulated experiences and teachings of all the Ages.

It has been said, in the First Part of the present work, that when the Mediator declared to the Jews, that LOVE TO GOD AND LOVE TO MAN IS THE FULFILLING OF THE LAW, he *then* announced the simple yet comprehensive CREED of the Christian Church Universal. And the great Democratic Philosopher of Nazareth was capable of this broad generalization of truth; because he looked forth upon life from the lofty altitude of Cause, and saw, with far-extending and all-embracing vision, the radii of Deity from the centre to the circumference of Nature. He beheld the fine spiritual emanations of the Godhead scintillating through space, and informing all human kind with intelligent spiritual life and uniting in a perfect, harmonious whole, the vast Universes of matter and of spirit. And thus all human beings were, to his comprehensive mind, sparks of Divine Creative Intelligence, thrown off upon physical nature for a limited season, to clothe themselves in material forms and learn the Alphabet of Creation. For, Man and Woman, being evolved from the Soul of Nature, embodied the constituent parts of all principles; and were therefore required to comprehend their relations to animate and inanimate existence. And it was essential for them to possess physical forms in order that they might commence with, and progress from, the first principles of knowledge in the realm of matter, up the ascending spiral of inductive philosophy, to the lofty sphere of CAUSE; individualizing themselves in truth, and perfecting themselves in virtue; and, thus, that they might be able at length to claim, from a *knowledge* of their own origin, nature, and destiny, their high alliance to the Cause of cause.

It was the exalted Mission of the Mediative Son of God to aid the wandering children of Paradise, who had become too deeply absorbed in the physical and sensual things of their *material* surroundings, to recognize their true and high relation to the Spiritual Source of existence, and to return to Deity with all their heart and mind and soul, rendering loving obedience to the Perfect Law of Love, and enjoying the true liberty of the universe as children of the Divine Father and Mother God. The dear Mediative Son would not that the least of all the sons and daughters of Deity should bury *the one talent* in the earth of the physical nature, but that its possessor should improve and double it by the acquisition of knowledge and the practice of virtue. He would that the at-one-ment should be perfect, and all-embracing. And, consequently, His mission was needfully twofold, as we have already shown, in order that it might be adapted to all the conditions and requirements of the Human Family, including two distinct periods of development, Youth and Maturity. And, thus, we find, that in the first Christian Era, his teachings were addressed more particularly to the heart, or the affections of Man; while, in the second Christian Era, upon which the Church and World have already entered, his Gospel will make a stronger appeal to the *reason*, or understanding of the Human Family. And, this double mission of Christ has always been recognized by the Church. But the character of the Second Advent, and its peculiar service to Humanity, has not been, thus far, clearly comprehended and taught by her various Denominations.

And, we find in confirmation of this view of the twofold mission of the Mediative Son of God, that Christ presented to the Church in her heroic and affectional Youth, the constant and loving care of the All-Parent for the sons and daughters of earth. Ay, he addressed the *heart* of the people, seeking to win them, through love, from error, sin, and consequent misery, back to the paths of virtue, peace and attending happiness.

How thrillingly the Mediator illustrates the ever-constant and watchful love of Heaven, in the touching parables of the Lost Sheep, and of the Prodigal Son. In the former, the Good Shepherd is represented as leaving his flock of ninety-nine in the wilderness, and going forth to seek the *one little one* that had gone astray; in the latter, the Father goes out from home to meet the returning wanderer, who had spent all his goods in riotous living. Whose heart has not been moved to its profoundest depth, in reading that ? When the repentant son was returning to his parents, While he was yet a great way off, his Father saw him, and had compassion, and ran and fell on his neck and kissed him. And the son said unto him, Father, I have sinned against heaven, and in thy sight, and am no more worthy to be called thy son. But the Father said to his servants: Bring forth the best robe, and put it on him, and put a ring on his hand, and shoes on his feet; And bring hither the fatted calf, and kill it, and let us eat and be merry: For this, my son, was dead, and is alive again; he was lost and is found.

And, by this method of appealing to the heart of Man,—at a period when the Human Family were more responsive to truth through the affections, because the reasoning powers were but partially developed,—the Mediator sought to energize the soul,

52

to kindle its aspirations, and awaken the desire to know more of the Munificent All-Father; and, thus, that the *mind* of the World might be prepared to receive, through love, the profound Philosophy of the Gospel of Intelligent Nature, in its farther advanced period of unfolding.   And, what an important lesson was conveyed to the Church, as well as to individuals and parents, in reference to their duty toward the erring, by the Parable of the Prodigal Son !   There is a deep philosophy inculcated in this peculiar treatment of the unfortunate members of the Human Family who go astray.   For nothing but the most considerate kindness and tenderest love can reclaim the wanderers.   The fatted calf must be served for them, and they must be robed in beautiful garments and adorned with jewels; then they will be drawn to goodness by its attractive exterior, and learn to love the practice of virtue.   Many men and women engaged in reforms are apt to think that their erring brothers and sisters ought to be thankful for and satisfied with the humblest lodgings and coarsest fare.   But, they are often repelled and disheartened under such meagre conditions, and their reformation becomes hopeless.

The Second Mission of the Mediator to the reason or mind of Man, was included in the First; but the people of the Youthful period of the Church and World were unprepared to worship God with understanding hearts.   And Christ's appeal to the Intellect of Man for the recognition of principles, awaited, of necessity, the World's riper age of Reason and Knowledge.   And we are forced to the conclusion that the Gospel of Intelligent Nature could not be fully understood by the early followers of Christ, and perfectly exemplified in their lives, because they were undeveloped Youth, and reason was but partially operative.

The Mother Tongue is acquired slowly by children and youth from the lips of loving parents and teachers.   And they must first be instructed to read before they are prepared to learn and understand the grammatical construction, or science of their native language.   It is even so with the comprehensive System of Natural Religion, taught by the Mediative Son of God.   It must be first received through the affections, with child-like faith, as the loving *words* of the Mother are treasured in the hearts of her little ones, before it can be fully scanned by the reasoning powers of the mind, and carefully studied in reference to principles. And, in taking a philosophic view of the action and progress of the human mind, we observe that the principles received by one age, with unquestioning faith, are critically reviewed by the reasoning mind of another.

It is, indeed, the character of the individual and of the national mind, to review the traditional, or inherited, opinions of youth, and submit them, in maturer years, to the test of riper judgment. And they who are fortunate enough to retain, through all the sifting experiences and the severe disciplines of later years, their early love for, and faith in, God and Man, will be able to discriminate clearly between the false and the true; and, in divesting themselves of youthful errors, they will preserve the pearls of truth, and treasure up immortal riches. For, *love* is keen-visioned, and far-sighted; they libel, who call her blind. While they who lose their love, lose also their better judgment; and, in seeking to cast off early errors of opinion, they fling away with them the precious gems of truth, and leave themselves rayless, barren and unprofitable. And they grow more and more, instead of less and less, prejudiced with years, because of their abnormal condition and relation to truth. And their views of civil, political and religious questions are only worth quoting for the purpose of showing how far human beings are capable of perverting their reason. And such sterile and un-beautiful persons will denounce men, *en masse*, as villains; woman, as vain, artful and heartless, and life as a miserable failure. And, wherever they go, they throw off a moral malaria, and receive back an exaggerated reflection of their own restless, dissatisfied and unhappy minds; and thus continue to cry, as they journey toward the grave, from which they recoil with apprehension and terror: All is vanity and vexation of spirit.

In the Mediative Son dwelt ALL THE FULLNESS OF THE GODHEAD. And the profound doctrines which he embodied in his teachings, were the hidden things of Deity, which were wisely concealed from the prophets and philosophers of the Childhood and early Youth of the World; because the millions were unprepared to be instructed in them. The people of those times of ignorance were too much absorbed in sensual appetites and passions, and too undeveloped, mentally, to perceive spiritual truths with the *reason*, and thus to recognize themselves intellectually, from the Philosophy of Intelligent Nature and from Revelation, children of the Divine Father and Mother God.

In verity, the world has always misinterpreted and desecrated the high principles which it was too undeveloped to comprehend. The elevating truths which exalt men and women of high degree, serve only to debase, more and more, those of low moral and intellectual stature. The glorious principles of *Liberty*, which ennoble enlightened Nations, are degraded into ruinous *license* by ignorant and barbarous Peoples.

But a period always arrives, in the history of individuals and of Nations, when it is needful that advanced truths should be taught, in order to meet the demands of progressed conditions among the members of the great Human Family. The intuitive minds of every age will be fed from the Master's table on the Heavenly manna of spiritual truth, which the sensual and undeveloped millions are prohibited from touching. For in God's righteously administered Government he does not permit the sons and daughters of genius to famish on the stinted and meagre fare that satisfies the cravings of less capacious souls. And those who are born out of due time, and fed on Angels' food, are Heaven's appointed standard-bearers of truth for the World:

> To rally all the sentiment for right,
> And give direction to its growing power.

And these inspired leaders have ever been, and still are, the representative persons of their time and age. They act in the moral world, as a crystalline lens in the natural; they attract many rays of truth and concentrate and focalize their light, and the hearts and minds of the people glow and burn in their presence. And persons of such comprehensive intellects are not only representatives of the knowledge and wisdom of the past and present; but they are the inspired prophets of the future. They are types of human capability and perfection. And they are accordant in their physical, intellectual and moral qualities, and, consequently, in harmonious relations to the truths of Nature, AT-ONE with God, and, intuitively receptive of Heavenly Wisdom, Light and Love, which they impart to Mankind.

Our Lord Jesus Christ stands pre-emineut in this class of intuitional minds. His advent marked the grandest Era in the history of Mankind. It had become needful, in the advancement of the Human Family from Childhood to Youth, that a higher Religious Dispensation than Judaism should be given to the World, in order to meet the wants of a farther progressed, and still progressing people. For the awakening reason of Man ever seeks to know more of God. It is everywhere radical and far-reaching in its tendency. It would glance backward to the source; and, forward to the ultimate of principles, to grasp the whole of truth, and rest its arguments upon indestructible foundations. The desire of all the Ages has been to reach *central truths*, to comprehend the great Creative Intelligence of the Universe, and the relations of the Human Family to Deity. The Mediative Son was sent on earth to answer the earnsst question of the Ages;—for the All-Father and All-Mother would satisfy the desire of their children to know more of THE GOD. He was commissioned from above to indoctrinate the Human Family in the profound Philosophy of Intelligent Nature, and baptize them Children of God.

In Christ dwelt all the FULLNESS of the Godhead, in order that he might the more perfectly represent both the Divine Father and Mother to their Human Offspring. But, as before stated, his teachings were adapted to two distinct periods of development in the Church and World—the affectional and heroic, or Youthful Period; and the farther advanced Reasoning Age— and, consequently, the FULLNESS *of the Godhead, Male and Female*, was needfully vailed for a season, until the *affectional nature* of Man, which was then in the ascendant, should be controlled by the higher faculties of the mind, by the reason and moral sentiments. And, not until the Christian Church shall become broadly enlightened, and able to look at principles, independently of the prejudices of education, or of the doctrines of a traditionary religion, will she be capable of comprehending the interior truth of the Gospel, contained in its profound Philosophy of Intelligent Nature; and, of receiving, into her regenerated heart and mind, the sacred Comforter, or Divine Mother of Humanity.

But, although the Church of the First Christian Era was unprepared to receive the baptism of the Holy Ghost, and to perceive and accept, in its true significance, the doctrine of the FULLNESS OF THE GODHEAD; yet, it was essential that it should be taught in the *letter of the Word;* because it is the pivotal truth of Nature, and the vital principle of the Christian Religion. It is, in verity, the germ of the Gospel of Intelligent Nature, on which depends the perfect Christian fruit of the intellectual and moral ages. And it is the character of all germs, natural and spiritual, to seek concealment for a season, and await some propitious period in the future for their unfolding. The germs of the physical world are enclosed within the seed, that they may be protected from severe conditions and sheltered from the chilling frosts of Winter. And, in a corresponding manner, this most precious germ of truth was needfully enveloped in the letter of THE BOOK, until the fitting time for its development, until the genial Spring-warmth of the Sun of Righteousness should enable it to expand in spiritual beauty, fullness and perfection.

But, notwithstanding the Mediative Son of God vailed this precious truth, and other high principles, in figures of speech and in parables, yet, he manifested an earnest desire that they should be recognized and accepted by all who were able to understand. His often repeated words, after addressing the multitudes which thronged him for instruction,—He that hath ears to hear, let him hear,—admit of no other interpretation. Although our dear Redeemer dared not lisp to an ignorant and prejudiced age the holy and cherished name of MOTHER GOD! Yet, his noble life of use and love was a perfect and beautiful representation of Divine Maternity to the Sons and Daughters of Earth.

The Atonement, or at-one-ment of Man with Deity, of the first Christian Era, was of necessity partial, as the candid inquirer after truth must admit; for the reason that the Gospel of Christ did not and could not, in the undeveloped Youth of the Human Family, reach and regenerate the whole nature of Man, the reasoning mind as well as sympathetic heart—as stated in the preceding argument.   For the human being can only be truly AT-ONE with the Divine. when all the varied powers of heart and mind are intelligently responsive to Heavenly truth and love. And, they who have seen only the *masculine phase* of Deity, have taken but a partial view of the Godhead, and, consequently, experienced but a partial at-one-ment with the All-Parent.   And because of the undeveloped condition of the people of that Era, and their consequent limited perception of truth, and inability to recognize the FULLNESS OF THE GODHEAD, the Second Advent of Christ becomes a logical as well as spiritual necessity for the perfection of his mission.

Again, we repeat, it is needful that the Gospel, or Philosophy of Intelligent Nature, should be received with the *mind*, as well as the heart of the World, in order that the at-one-ment be perfected, and the whole nature of Man become spiritually alive. The Reasoning Age of the Church and World requires a rebaptism of the Holy Ghost.   And the baptismal fire of Divine Maternity will, ere long, burn with quickening and purifying energy and power, until the old dead letter of doctrine shall be consumed.   And, when this shall be accomplished, the New, or renewed Christian Church Universal will be permeated with the living and elevating spirit of love; *then* the FULLNESS OF THE GODHEAD will shine forth upon her from the moral heavens in celestial ONENESS and glory.

But, the Second Advent of the Mediative Son of God, which was suggested to the Church of the first Era by his twofold mission, addressed to the *heart* and to the *mind* of Man, and including two periods of human unfolding, does not necessarily imply his second incarnation, as many Denominations of the Church believe and teach.   It does, however, imply a *full recognition* of the Gospel of Love, as the profound Philosophy of Intelligent Nature, with the *Reasoning Mind* of the Church and World, and a clearer spiritual perception of its sublime and comprehensive principles. Our beloved Redeemer, himself, hath said: Lo, I am with you alway, even unto the end of the world.   If he abide with the Bride forevermore, will he then appear again on earth incarnate ?   First in the Divine Order is the Natural, after, that which is Spiritual.   The first coming of Christ was in the natural form, and his first presentation of truth in the Letter of the Word; should we not then rationally look for his "second appearing " on earth in the Spirit of the Gospel which he taught ? —which truth was *then* addressed to the heart or affections of the Youth of the Human Family, but, *now*, to the understanding of their Reasoning Age ?

At the present Transitionary Period of the Church from the unquestioning faith of her Youth, forward to that of rational conviction, the Mediative Son of God is earnestly pleading with the understanding of his people, in the still small voice of love, for a review of his Gospel of Intelligent Nature, and a fuller and higher interpretation of its principles.   And he asks his beloved Church to remember what he once said to his disciples when he was on earth incarnate: God sent not his Son into the world to condemn the world, but that the world through him might be saved;—might be saved from its ignorance and consequent sin and thence, suffering, through knowledge of the true and better way.

Since the days of Swedenborg, the inspired Inaugurator of the Christian Era of Reason, the preparation of the Church and World for a re-baptism of the Holy Ghost, or an immersion of the Church into the Spirit of Truth, and a rational recognition of the Gospel of Intelligent Nature, has been rapidly advancing. The signs of the times already announce the *leading idea* of the Second Coming.   What means the Woman Question that is even now troubling the spirit of the age?   Society marvels to find Woman, who has quietly submitted to the injustice and oppression of centuries, seeking earnestly for the recognition of her Heaven-endowed individuality, for equal social, civil, and religious liberty with Man.   But it is not *she* who speaks; it is the Spirit of the Mediative Son of God speaking through her.   Equal Justice for all the sons and daughters of the Divine Father and Mother, is the soul of his Gospel of Intelligent Nature.

Ah! the Woman Question of to-day has a profounder significance than they who advocate it are aware. It is one form in
which *the central truth of Nature, and of the Christian Religion*, is
again presented to the heart and mind of the Human Family.
Not, now, as in the Youth of the Church, to become a dead letter, because the age was unprepared for the lesson; but to be
comprehended by pure and elevated minds, capable of understanding the Divine Marriage of the Heavens, and the equal representation of Man and Woman in the Godhead. And, through the
rational recognition of the Godhead, Male and Female, the at-one-
ment of the Human Family with Deity will be perfected in the
Maturity of the Church and World.

And the Mediative Son of God is not only speaking through
Woman, and calling upon her to be just to her own high nature;
but he is also pleading with the reason of Man, for the full recognition of Woman, in order that, through her, Man may also perceive and accept the Divine Mother of Humanity, and become
AT-ONE with God. And he pleads earnestly and tenderly with
the heart, as well as the mind of Man, that justice may be done
to the daughters of earth, for the sake of all high uses to be performed and for the sake of the regeneration of the World.

Earnest Reader, thou who art looking anxiously for the Second
Coming of thy Redeemer, knowest thou not that he is even now
seeking to become incarnate in *thee?* Knowest thou not that his
second incarnation will be in the Humanity that he loves? How
beautiful upon the mountains of Zion is the light of his coming!

Who of all the various Denominations of the Church of the
nineteenth century are now waiting to welcome the dear Mediative
Son of God? Who of all that professes to believe in him, and to
look for his second appearance on earth, have ears to attend to his
gentle voice of love? Who have hearts and minds and souls prepared to receive and entertain him, that he may enter in and finish
his work in them, and by them? Now is the appointed day and
hour. He stands at the door of every believer's soul, and knocks.
He asks of His Church, His Bride, His beloved, for a full recognition of the Comforter, the Holy Ghost, the Divine Mother of
Humanity. He asks for a full response of the *reason*, as well as

53

of the *affections* to His profound Gospel and Philosophy of Intelligent Nature.   He desires that the at-one-ment of the Human Family with Deity should be perfected.   He desires to complete His divine mission; to become, henceforth, incarnate in the Humanity that He loves.

When we pause to comprehend for a moment the sublime Gospel, or Philosophy of Intelligent Nature, extending from the centre to the circumference of the Universe, we are more forcibly than ever impressed with the profound import of the language of inspiration concerning the Second Coming of the Mediative Son of God: Whose voice *then* shook the earth; but now he hath promised, saying, Yet once more I shake not the earth only, but also heaven.   The prophetic hour is near, when Mankind will be indoctrinated in the great Central Truth of Nature—THE GOD, Male and Female—and all the powers of earth and heaven will be shaken.   For the Church and World are rapidly approaching maturity, and Reason is grandly active, preparing the way for its universal reception; and she will not rest from her labor, until the FULLNESS OF THE GODHEAD is clearly seen and acknowledged; and the social, civil and religious creeds of the Human Family are adjusted to this CENTRAL TRUTH.   Ay, Reason will not rest from her labor, until Man and Woman are alike recognized, in every part of the Globe, as beings of royal birth and princely heritage, as children of the Divine Father and Mother God.   She will not rest until the at-one-ment of Man with Deity is perfected, and the Redeemer of the World becomes incarnate in Humanity.

Oh! then, what fullness of praise and blessing will ascend to the dear All-Father and All-Mother from their loving and obedient sons and daughters.   The Church Militant and the Church triumphant, uniting on this profound Philosophy of Nature, will rejoice together; and Earth will re-echo the hallelujahs of the Heavens.

And, now, at parting, we appeal once more, with all our heart, and mind, and soul, to the Church of to-day, for a review of the Christian Religion with an enlightened understanding, and a higher and fuller interpretation of its comprehensive Philosophy. And we plead with the Church of the Reasoning Age, to accept for her creed, the comprehensive principles which the Mediative Son of God himself announced as containing the whole duty of Man; for all of her various Denominations would be able to unite on this broad platform of faith and practice. Ay, let her uplift the Standard of the Cross with the CREED OF THE CHRISTIAN CHURCH UNIVERSAL engraven upon it in letters of light: THOU SHALT LOVE THE LORD THY GOD WITH ALL THY HEART, AND WITH ALL THY MIND, AND WITH ALL THY SOUL. AND THOU SHALT LOVE THY NEIGHBOR AS THYSELF. ON THESE TWO COMMANDMENTS HANG ALL THE LAW AND THE PROPHETS. And we plead earnestly with the Church of the Reasoning Age to call upon her organizations of every name, throughout the United States and throughout the World, to awake and unite for co-operate action in the vineyard of the Lord.

Let the Church of the Reasoning Age of the World arise in her beauty, purity, and strength, even as she was seen in prophetic vision: Descending from God out of Heaven, adorned as a Bride for her Husband, with no spot, or blemish on her garments. Let her watchmen see, eye to eye. Let them Walk about Zion and go round about her: tell the towers thereof: mark well her bulwarks. And let them Lay judgment to the line, and righteousness to the plummet, that her foundations may rest securely, during the mighty upheavals which are, even now, shaking the moral world to its deep centre.

And let the motto of the Christian Church be—JUSTICE—for this is the essential spirit of LOVE—EQUAL JUSTICE for all the sons and daughters of the Divine Father and Mother God, of every nation and of every people of the whole earth—JUSTICE, although the Heavens should fall! For then they could only fall in benediction on a united brotherhood of Nations, on the CHRISTIAN CHURCH UNIVERSAL of the great Democratic Republic of the World.

SAN FRANCISCO :
PRINTED AT THE WOMEN'S CO-OPERATIVE PRINTING UNION,
424 MONTGOMERY STREET.